MARK

ABINGDON NEW TESTAMENT COMMENTARIES

MARK

C. CLIFTON BLACK

Abingdon Press
Nashville

ABINGDON NEW TESTAMENT COMMENTARIES
MARK

Copyright © 2011 by C. Clifton Black

All rights reserved.

This book is printed on acid-free paper.

Library of Congress Cataloging-in-Publication Data

Black, C. Clifton (Carl Clifton), 1955-
 Mark / C. Clifton Black.
  p. cm.—(Abingdon New Testament commentaries)
 Includes bibliographical references and index.
  ISBN 978-0-687-05841-9 (book - pbk./trade pbk. : alk. paper) 1. Bible. N.T. Mark—Commentaries. I. Title.
  BS2585.53.B53 2011
  226.3'07—dc23

                                                                           2011020544

11 12 13 14 15 16 17 18 19 20—10 9 8 7 6 5 4 3 2 1

MANUFACTURED IN THE UNITED STATES OF AMERICA

For

Victor Paul Furnish

CONTENTS

CONTENTS

CONTENTS

List of Tables

FOREWORD

The *Abingdon New Testament Commentaries* series provides compact, critical commentaries on the writings of the New Testament. These commentaries are written with special attention to the needs and interests of theological students, but they will also be useful for students in upper-level college or university settings, as well as for pastors and other church leaders. In addition to providing basic information about the New Testament texts and insights into their meanings, these commentaries are intended to exemplify the tasks and procedures of careful, critical biblical exegesis.

The authors who have contributed to this series come from a wide range of ecclesiastical affiliations and confessional stances. All are seasoned, respected scholars and experienced classroom teachers. They take full account of the most important current scholarship and secondary literature, but do not attempt to summarize that literature or engage in technical academic debate.

Their fundamental concern is to analyze the literary, sociohistorical, theological, and ethical dimensions of the biblical texts themselves. Although all of the commentaries in this series have been written on the basis of the Greek texts, the authors do not presuppose any knowledge of the biblical languages on the part of the reader. When some awareness of the grammatical, syntactical, or philological issue is necessary for an adequate understanding of a particular text, they explain the matter clearly and concisely.

The introduction of each volume ordinarily includes subdivisions dealing with the *key issues* addressed and/or raised by the New Testament writing under consideration; its *literary genre, structure, and character*; its *occasion and situational context,* including its wider social, historical, and religious contexts; and its *theological and ethical significance* within these several contexts. In each volume, the *commentary* is organized according to literary units rather than verse by verse. Generally, each of these units is the subject of three types of analysis. First, the *literary analysis* attends to the unit's genre, most important stylistic features, and overall structure. Second, the *exegetical analysis* considers the aim and leading ideas of the unit, deals with any especially important textual variants, and discusses the meanings of important words, phrases, and images. It also takes note of the particular historical and social situations of the writer and original readers, and of the wider cultural and religious contexts of the book as a whole. Finally, the *theological and ethical analysis* discusses the theological and ethical matters with which the unit deals or to which it points, focusing on the theological and ethical significance of the text within its original setting.

Each volume also includes a *select bibliography,* thereby providing guidance to other major commentaries and important scholarly works, and a brief *subject index*. The New Revised Standard Version of the Bible is the principal translation of reference for the series, but the authors draw on all of the major modern English versions, and when necessary provide their own original translations of difficult terms or phrases. The fundamental aim of this series will have been attained if readers are assisted, not only to understand more about the origins, character, and meaning of the New Testament writings, but also to enter into their own informed and critical engagement with the texts themselves.

Victor Paul Furnish
General Editor

PREFACE

My love for Mark can be traced as far back as 1982, to a seminar at Duke taught by Professor D. Moody Smith. It is one measure of his insight—many more are a matter of published record—that in the years since then I have returned to my notes from that class while teaching my own students and preparing this commentary. Thirty years ago there were not so many commentaries of high quality on this Gospel that students and pastors could consult. Since then Markan studies have exploded with dozens of commentaries, plus monographs by the bushel (see Telford 2009). As this book's bibliography verifies, I am a beneficiary of vast scholarly wealth. The nature of this series forbids my conversation with exegetical predecessors in a significant way. I can only direct readers to some of the works that have informed and challenged me, hopeful that others may also learn from them. If I have come to see Mark more clearly, it is because I stand on sturdy shoulders. The blame for remaining errors of fact and judgment rests on my shoulders alone.

This project's gestation has proved humiliatingly protracted. For their encouragement I must single out Harriet Black, Moody Smith, and Leander Keck. Kara Lyons-Pardue and Laura Sweat, candidates for the Ph.D. in New Testament at Princeton Theological Seminary, read earlier drafts, assisted me in editing, and offered useful criticism. Kathy Armistead and her compatriots at Abingdon Press fortified my resolve. Pheme Perkins, a member of this series' Editorial Board and herself the author of a fine commentary on Mark, read the entire manuscript, made sensible suggestions for its improvement, and rescued me from several blunders. By such colleagues and companions no author has been better supported than I.

My greatest thanks go to Victor P. Furnish, General Editor of the Abingdon New Testament Commentaries. Though the middle initial stands for Paul, it could as easily signify Patience. Across many years of waiting for this book's completion, not once did he express to me anything save sympathy and inspiration. Moreover, during a decade as my senior colleague in New Testament at Southern Methodist University, he modeled the highest standard of scholarship, integrity, and friendship. I owe him more than I can say. This commentary's dedication to him is a small token of my respect and affection.

C. C. B.
Princeton, New Jersey
September 2010

LIST OF ABBREVIATIONS

1 [2] *Apol.*	Justin Martyr, *First [Second]* Apology
1 *En.*	*1 Enoch (Ethiopic Apocalypse of Enoch)*
1–2 Macc	1–2 Maccabees
1QH	*Hodayot,* or *Thanksgiving Hymns*
1QM	*Milḥamah,* or *War Scroll*
1QpHab	*Pesher Habakkuk*
1QS	*Serek Hayaḥad,* or *Rule of the Community*
1QSa	*Rule of the Congregation* (Appendix a to 1QS)
1QSb	*Rule of the Blessings* (Appendix b to 1QS)
2 *Bar.*	*2 Baruch (Syriac Apocalypse)*
3 *En.*	*3 Enoch*
3–4 Macc	3–4 Maccabees
4QapocrDan ar	*Apocryphon of Daniel*
4QFlor	*Florilegium (= Midrash on Eschatology)*
11QMelch	*Melchizedek*
AB	Anchor Bible
ABD	1992. *The Anchor Bible Dictionary.* 5 vols. Edited by David Noel Freedman, et al. New York: Doubleday.
ABRL	Anchor Bible Reference Library
ACNT	Augsburg Commentaries on the New Testament
Acts Pil.	*Acts of Pilate*
ad loc.	*ad locum* (at the place)
Ag. Ap.	Josephus, *Against Apion*

Andr.	Terence, *Andria*
Ann.	Tacitus, *Annales* (*Annals*)
Ant.	Josephus, *Jewish Antiquities*
Ant. rom.	Dionysius of Halicarnassus, *Antiquitates romanae* (*Roman Antiquities*)
Apoc. Ab.	*Apocalypse of Abraham*
Apos. Con.	*Apostolic Constitutions and Canons*
Aram.	Aramaic
As. Mos.	*Assumption of Moses*
Ascen. Isa.	*Ascension of Isaiah* 6–11
AT	Author's translation
ATLAMS	American Theological Library Association Monograph Series
Aug.	Suetonius, *Divus Augustus* (*The Divine Augustus*)
AUSS	Andrews University Seminary Studies
b.	Babylonian Talmud (before the name of a tractate)
B.C.E.	Before the Common Era (= B.C.)
B. Qam.	*Bava Qamma* (rabbinic tractate)
BDAG	2000. *A Greek-English Lexicon of the New Testament and Other Early Christian Literature.* Revised and edited by Frederick William Danker. 3rd ed. Chicago and London: University of Chicago Press.
BDF	1961. *A Greek Grammar of the New Testament and Other Early Christian Literature.* Edited by F. Blass, A. Debrunner, and Robert W. Funk. Chicago and London: University of Chicago Press.
Ben.	Seneca, *De beneficiis* (*On Benefits*)
Ber.	*Berakhot* (rabbinic tractate)
BETL	Bibliotheca ephemeridum theologicarum lovaniensium
BibInt	*Biblical Interpretation*
BIS	Biblical Interpretation Supplements
BNTC	Black's New Testament Commentary

BZNW	Beihefte zur Zeitschrift für die neutestamentliche Wissenschaft
ca.	circa
C.E.	Common Era (= A.D.)
Cael.	Cicero, *Pro Caelio* (*For Caelius*)
Cassirer	1989. *God's New Covenant: A New Translation.* Translated by Heinz W. Cassirer. Grand Rapids: Eerdmans.
CBQ	*Catholic Biblical Quarterly*
CBQMS	Catholic Biblical Quarterly Monograph Series
CD	Cairo Genizah copy of the *Damascus Document*
Cels.	Origen, *Against Celsus*
CGNTC	Cambridge Greek New Testament Commentary
Claud.	Suetonius, *Divus Claudius* (*The Divine Claudius*)
Comm. Matt.	Origen, *Commentarium in evangelium Matthaei* (*Commentary on Matthew*)
Comm. Phlm.	Jerome, *Commentariorum in Epistulam ad Philemonem liber* (*Commentary on Philemon*)
ConBNT	Coniectanea biblica: New Testament Series
Cons.	Augustine, *De consensus evangelistarum* (*Harmony of the Gospels*)
Contempl. Life	Philo, *On the Contemplative Life*
Corp. herm.	*Corpus hermeticum*
CRINT	Compendia rerum iudaicarum ad Novum Testamentum
Danby	1933. *The Mishnah: Translated from the Hebrew with Introduction and Brief Explanatory Notes.* Edited by Herbert Danby. Oxford: Oxford University Press.
Decl.	Quintilian, *Declamationes* (*The Minor Declamations*)
Deut. Rab.	*Deuteronomy Rabbah*
Dial. Trypho	Justin Martyr, *Dialogue with Trypho*

Diatr.	Epictetus, *Diatribai* (*Dissertations*)
Did.	*Didache*
DSS	Dead Sea Scrolls
^c*Ed.*	*Eduyyot* (rabbinic tractate)
Embassy	Philo, *On the Embassy to Gaius*
Ep.	Seneca, *Epistulae morales* (*Moral Epistles to Lucilium*)
Epist.	Jerome, *Epistulae* (*Letters*)
^c*Erub.*	*Eruvin* (rabbinic tractate)
EUS	European University Studies
Exod. Rab.	*Exodus Rabbah*
Gen. Rab.	*Genesis Rabbah*
Geogr.	Strabo, *Geography*
Giṭ.	*Gittin* (rabbinic tractate)
Gk.	Greek
GNT	Good News Translation
Goodspeed	1939. *The Complete Bible: An American Translation.* Translated by Edgar J. Goodspeed. Chicago: University of Chicago Press.
Gos. Eb.	*Gospel of the Ebionites*
Gos. Thom.	*Gospel of Thomas*
Haer.	Irenaeus, *Adversus haereses* (*Against Heresies*)
Heb.	Hebrew
Herm. Sim.	Shepherd of Hermas, *Similtude*
Hist. eccl.	Eusebius, *Ecclesiastical History*
Hom. Act.	John Chrysostom, *Homiliae in Acta apostolorum* (*Sermons on Acts*)
IBT	Interpreting Biblical Texts
Ign. *Magn.*	Ignatius, *To the Magnesians*
Inst.	Quintilian, *Institutio Ortatoria* (*Education of the Orator*)
Int	*Interpretation*
IRT	Issues in Religion and Theology
j.	Jerusalem Talmud (before the name of a tractate)

JB	*The Jerusalem Bible* (1966)
JBL	*Journal of Biblical Literature*
JBLMS	Journal of Biblical Literature Monograph Series
Jdt	Judith
JJS	*Journal of Jewish Studies*
Jos. Asen.	*Joseph and Aseneth*
JR	*Journal of Religion*
JSNT	*Journal for the Study of the New Testament*
JSNTSup	Journal for the Study of the New Testament Supplement Series
JTS	*Journal of Theological Studies*
Jub.	*Jubilees*
J.W.	Josephus, *The Jewish War*
Ketub.	*Ketubbot* (rabbinic tractate)
KJV	King James Version (1611)
Lat.	Latin
Lattimore	1996. *The New Testament.* Translated by Richmond Lattimore. New York: North Point/Farrar, Straus, Giroux.
Let. Aris.	*Letter of Aristeas*
LNTS	Library of New Testament Studies
LSJ	1968. *A Greek-English Lexicon, with a Supplement.* Edited by Henry George Liddell, Robert Scott, and Henry Stuart Jones. 9th ed. Oxford: Clarendon Press.
Luc.	Plutarch, *Lucullus* (in *Parallel Lives*)
LXX	Septuagint
m.	Mishnah (before the name of a rabbinic tractate)
Mak.	*Makkot* (rabbinic tractate)
Marc.	Tertullian, *Against Marcion*
Meg.	*Megillah* (rabbinic tractate)
Mek.	*Mekilta* (before a biblical book)
Men.	Lucian, *Menippus (Descent into Hades)*
Metam.	Apuleius, *Metamorphoses* (*The Golden Ass*)
Miqw.	*Mikwa'ot* (rabbinic tractate)

Moffatt	1954. *A New Translation of the Bible Containing the Old and New Testaments.* Translated by James Moffatt. New York and London: Harper & Brothers.
Mos.	Philo, *On the Life of Moses*
MT	Masoretic Text
n.	footnote
N.B.	*nota bene* (note carefully)
NAB	The New American Bible (1990)
Nat.	Pliny the Elder, *Natural History*
NCB	New Century Bible
NEB	The New English Bible (1972)
Ned.	*Nedarim* (rabbinic tractate)
Neg.	*Nega'im* (rabbinic tractate)
NIB	*The New Interpreter's Bible*
NICNT	New International Commentary on the New Testament
NIV	The New International Version (1978)
NJPS	*Tanakh: The Holy Scriptures* (1999)
NovTSup	Novum Testamentum Supplements
NRSV	New Revised Standard Version (1989)
NT	New Testament
NTGJC	The New Testament Gospels in Their Judaic Contexts
NTL	New Testament Library
NTS	*New Testament Studies*
OT	Old Testament
Peregr.	Lucian, *The Passing of Peregrinus*
Pesaḥ	*Pesahim* (rabbinic tractate)
Phillips	1958. *The New Testament in Modern English.* Translated by J. B. Phillips. New York: Macmillan.
PNTC	Pillar New Testament Commentary
Pro Ecc	*Pro Ecclesia*
Pss. Sol.	*Psalms of Solomon*
QG	Philo, *Questions and Answers on Genesis*
Qoh	Qohelet (= Ecclesiastes)

Quaest. conv.	Plutarch, *Quaestionum convivialum libri IX* (*Table Talk,* Book 9)
Rab.	*Rabbah* (rabbinic midrash, preceded by biblical book)
Rab. Perd.	Cicero, *Pro Rabirio Perduellionis Reo* (*On Behalf of Gaius Rabirius on a Charge of Treason*)
REB	Revised English Bible (1989)
Rhet.	Aristotle, *Rhetoric*
RSV	Revised Standard Version (1952)
Šabb.	*Shabbat* (rabbinic tractate)
Sanh.	*Sanhedrin* (rabbinic tractate)
Sat.	Juvenal, *Satires*
SBLAB	Society of Biblical Literature Academia Biblica
SBLDS	Society of Biblical Literature Dissertation Series
SemeiaSt	Semeia Studies
SemeiaSup	Semeia Supplements
SHBC	Smyth & Helwys Bible Commentary
Sib. Or.	*Sibylline Oracles*
Sipra	*Sifra* (on Leviticus)
Sipre Deut.	*Sifre on Deuteronomy*
Sipre Num.	*Sifre on Numbers*
Sir	Sirach/Ecclesiasticus
SNTSMS	Society for New Testament Studies Monograph Series
SNTW	Studies of the New Testament and Its World
SP	Sacra Pagina
Spec. Laws	Philo, *On the Special Laws*
SPNT	Studies on Personalities of the New Testament
t.	Targum (Jewish commentary; before the name of a biblical book)
T. Ab.	*Testament of Abraham*
T. Benj.	*Testament of Benjamin*
T. Dan.	*Testament of Dan*
T. Iss.	*Testament of Issachar*

T. Jos.	*Testament of Joseph*
T. Levi	*Testament of Levi*
T. Naph.	*Testament of Naphtali*
T. Reu.	*Testament of Reuben*
Ta^{c}an	*Ta^{c}anit* (rabbinic tractate)
TDNT	1964—1976. *Theological Dictionary of the New Testament.* 10 vols. Edited by G. Kittel and G. Friedrich. Grand Rapids: Eerdmans.
Tob	Tobit
Trad. ap.	Hippolytus, *Traditio apostolica* (*Traditions of the Apostles*)
Verr.	Cicero, *In Verrem* (*Against Gaius Verres*)
WBC	Word Biblical Commentary
Wis	Wisdom of Solomon
WUNT	Wissenschaftliche Untersuchungen zum Neuen Testament
Yebam.	*Yevamot* (rabbinic tractate)
ZNW	*Zeitschrift für die neutestamentliche Wissenschaft und die Kunde der älteren Kirche*

INTRODUCTION

WHAT WE CANNOT KNOW

Authorship

> Now this is what the elder used to say: "Mark became Peter's interpreter and wrote accurately whatever he remembered, but not in order, of the things said and done by the Lord. For he had neither heard the Lord, nor had he followed him, but later on, as I said [followed] Peter, who used to offer the teachings in anecdotal form but not making, as it were, a systematic arrangement of the Lord's oracles."

That seems straightforward. It is the earliest known reference to "Mark" as a literary figure; the speaker is Papias, bishop of the Hierapolitan diocese of Phrygia (modern-day Turkey). Papias's comments are reported in Eusebius's fourth-century *Ecclesiastical History* (*Hist. eccl.* 3.39.14-16). "The elder" from whom Papias got his information is a certain "John," who may or may not have been the son of Zebedee. Neither John nor Papias bases an association of Mark with Peter on 1 Peter 5:13, which says nothing about the writing of a Gospel. On closer inspection we cannot be sure that Papias or John refers to the document we know as the Gospel of Mark, although later patristic writers veer in that direction (Black

2001a, 82-191). Early church tradition maintained the Second Gospel's association with a recognized apostle (usually Peter, sometimes Paul [see *Apos. Con.* 2.7.57; Jerome, *Comm. Phlm.* 24]) while preserving distance between that apostle and the Gospel's author (Black 1997). The patristic church usually situated the Second Gospel within a Petrine tradition without identifying it as the Gospel "according to Peter."

Like the other Gospels in the NT, the Second is anonymous. Within the book itself there is no claim of authorship. The traditional title, "According to Mark," was added to manuscripts during the second century C.E. or later, after a canon of four Gospels was emerging and it had become necessary to differentiate them (Hengel 1985, 64-84). The book's interpretation should not be governed by speculation either about an author who never identifies himself or about Peter's preaching, to which we have no firsthand access. If this Gospel's author, to whom we may conveniently refer as Mark or the Second Evangelist, was not preoccupied with his identity, then neither need we be.

Provenance

Many interpreters consider Mark's thirteenth chapter a pebbled-glass window, through which one may vaguely trace turbulent circumstances attending the Gospel's composition. Perhaps the Evangelist crafted this material in such a way that, when Jesus speaks of portents to four disciples on the Mount of Olives, he is alluding to circumstances with which the Markan church was engaged. Even so, there is no scholarly consensus on where Mark's Gospel was written and, correlatively, the precise matters to which the author was drawing his readers' attention. The current debate may be summarized as five alternatives.

Option #1: The earliest Christian traditions about Mark, especially Irenaeus of Lyons (ca. 130–200) and Clement of Alexandria (ca. 150–215), locate its composition in *Rome* (see *Hist. eccl.* 5.8.2-3; 6.14.5-7). This location appears dependent on Papias's report that "Mark became Peter's interpreter": Peter was long associated with Rome. While these ancient testimonies raise many questions for modern historians (Black 2001a), Rome is a plausible setting for a Gospel sensitive to Jewish and Gentile interests (10:2-12), mixed economic levels (10:17-27; 12:41-44), and political turmoil, especially Nero's persecution of Roman Christians (see below; also Hengel 1985, 14-58). Some scholars have made spirited arguments for Mark's Roman origin (Incigneri 2003; Winn 2008). Others think Rome too distant to account for some of the Gospel's features (Theissen 1991, 258-81) and wonder whether the tribulations suggested by Mark 13 tally with details of the Neronian persecution (Marcus 2000, 32-33).

Option #2: Galilee lies at the other end of the geographical spectrum. Identifying Mark's origin with Jesus' own has the advantage of greater transparency between the two: thus, when Jesus warns four of the Twelve that they "must flee to the mountains" after witnessing a particular catastrophe (13:14), Mark's own readers should do likewise. This interpretation, popular in the mid-twentieth century (Marxsen 1969, 151-206), has been revivified (Roskam 2004). A problem with this theory is that Mark and his readers do not appear well acquainted with ancient Palestine. The Evangelist repeatedly identifies Jewish customs and figures as though his readers do not know them (7:3-4; 12:18), translates Aramaic terms into Greek (5:41; 7:34; 15:22), and seems uncertain of Galilean geography (6:45, 53; 7:31).

Option #3: Syria mediates the first two possibilities: beyond Palestine, thus Gentile and near the Jewish war to the southwest, where "nation [rose] against nation" (13:8), but not so far away as Rome (Kee 1977, 100-105; Marcus 2000, 33-37). This, too, is plausible. There is no evidence, however, that Syrian Christians were persecuted in the mid-first century, whereas Tacitus recounts in gruesome detail assaults against Roman Christians of that era.

Option #4 posits that Mark was written to *no particular community at all,* but instead to the Christian world at large (Bauckham 1998). This proposal recognizes the likelihood that both Matthew and Luke used Mark as a source (see below); thus, it was already in general circulation. This theory rightly assumes that early Christian communities were in touch with one another, as Paul's letters confirm. Neither of these affirmations, however, requires the denial of Mark's origination in a particular city or region, to whose Christians the Evangelist first addressed his Gospel. Mark's emphasis on suffering, both Jesus' own (8:31; 9:31; 10:33-34) and that of his disciples, can be understood as directed to Christians experiencing trauma for the sake of Jesus and the good news (8:35; 10:29; 13:9-10).

Option #5 is a *reasoned agnosticism*. The evidence in Mark is so ambiguous that attempts to locate it are futile and exegetically unnecessary (Peterson 2000).

The Evangelist has done as good a job of cloaking his audience as of veiling himself. If the Gospel's details were more precise, if we knew conditions among first-century Christians around the Mediterranean basin with greater particularity, then portions of Mark (like its thirteenth chapter) would shimmer with special radiance. For its earliest readers they probably did. We are hobbled by an ignorance that is likely incorrigible. The circumstantial evidence for a Roman provenance seems stronger than that for others (Black 1993). However, if irrefutable proof emerged that Mark originated in Syria, Galilee, or somewhere else, it would not alter the interpretation that this commentary offers. To that degree I sympathize with the fourth and fifth options.

What We Can Infer

Literary Priority

A majority of NT scholars reckon Mark the earliest of the Gospels written: a position consolidated in the nineteenth century and upheld by ongoing research (Sanders and Davies 1989, 25-119). Intensive interest in Mark coincided with this judgment, which in turn spurred the original "quest for the historical Jesus." Mark remains among the basic sources used by investigators who attempt to reconstruct the historical Jesus and his

Jewish milieu (Meier 1991, 41-55), even though Mark's primary interests are religiously confessional, not those of a modern historian (Black 2009).

Markan priority among the Gospels is a working hypothesis, not a demonstrable fact. It seems more plausible than other possibilities, such as Mark's abridgment of Matthew (a position as old as Augustine, *Harmony of the Evangelists* [399], and still held by some). The logic of conventional scholarly assessment corresponds with what textual critics have learned by examining the NT's manuscript variants. Customarily, early Christian scribes (a) smoothed out rough wording, (b) introduced clarifications where meaning is obscure, and (c) elaborated texts instead of abbreviating them. Longer than Mark by a third, Matthew expands Mark's beginning (Matt 1:1–2:23), ending (28:8-20), and teachings of Jesus (5:1–7:29; 10:7-42; 13:24-30, 35-52; 18:10-35; 24:37–25:46). Matthew is a better Greek stylist than Mark; Luke is the most refined of all (Doudna 1961). To understand one Evangelist's trimming another's raggedness is easy; the reverse is harder to explain. As we shall see, Mark's narrative yawns with gaps, with which Matthew and Luke cope in different ways. The best example is Mark's ending, which quits at 16:8 in the oldest and best manuscripts. When Matthew and Luke no longer have Mark to control their narratives, they draw on different traditions to conclude their Gospels in ways less abrupt (see table 20). Accordingly, this commentary adopts the view that Mark was the earliest Gospel and a source for both Matthew and Luke. By scholarly convention "the Second Gospel" and its author, "the Second Evangelist," refer to canonical sequence.

Date

If Matthew and Luke used Mark as a source, then the latter must have been written some decades before the end of the first century C.E. Most scholars date Mark's Gospel shortly before or after 70, the year that Titus's Roman legions destroyed Jerusalem's temple (*J.W.* 6.7.2). Whether Mark knew that event as an accomplished fact is impossible to determine. Predictions of its toppling (13:1-2) and the reader's vision of the holy curtain's rending (15:38) suggest that Mark knows more than he actually says, but we cannot be as confident in this case as in that of Luke (13:34-35; 21:20-24; 23:27-31).

Traditional Sources

If, with few exceptions (e.g., 1 Cor 7:10-11; 11:24-25), Mark is our earliest recoverable source for material about Jesus, then it follows that we have no direct access to most traditions used in constructing this Gospel. There are thirty small overlaps of Mark's wording with that of Q: the hypothetical double tradition that most scholars of the Gospels accept as another source from which both Matthew and Luke drew (e.g., Mark 3:22-30 = Luke 11:14-22 = Matt 12:22-32). These intersections are few, substantively minor overall, and explicable as traditional variants between Q and Mark rather than as literary dependence of one on the other (*pace* Fleddermann 1995). Theories of a pre-Markan Passion Narrative or *Ur-Markus* (a primitive form of canonical Mark) have fallen on hard times: partly owing to the practical impossibility of their recovery (Black 1989), partly attributable to scholarly trends favoring the Gospels' interpretation in their final forms over conjectural reconstruction of anterior traditions (Anderson and Moore 1992). There are good reasons to suppose that Mark depended on earlier traditions about Jesus, even if their reclamation is beyond our capability. For example, if John was written independently of the Synoptic Gospels—a still unresolved question in NT research—then the general similarity of its Passion Narrative with Mark's suggests that each Evangelist was in touch with sequential, intersecting traditions about Jesus' last days (see table 16). Mark 9:42-50 (*ad loc.*) suggests that some sayings of Jesus became linked to others by catchwords. Mark's anecdotes about Jesus have formal parallels throughout the Hellenistic world (Moeser 2002). The Evangelist may have clustered some materials (see tables 1, 2, 3, 4, 8, and 9) or could have received them in prefabricated patterns; this commentary leaves those questions open for the reader to decide. Some material constellations are so sweeping or intricately plotted (see tables 10 and 19) that I join other interpreters in regarding them as probably Markan creations.

One source used by Mark is easily detected: the OT, usually in Greek translation (LXX). Although sophisticated arguments have been offered for Scripture's integration into his theological purposes (Marcus 1992; Watts 1997), the Evangelist's use of the OT is not as easy to characterize as Matthew's, whose "formula-quotations" are used as billboards in Israel's salvation history (e.g., Matt 1:22; 2:6, 18, 23). Sometimes Mark flags something "as it is written" (1:2-3; 7:6-7; 11:17; 12:10-11, 36), often referring to Isaiah or the Psalms (like much of the NT). For the most part, however, Mark's use of Jewish Scripture is allusive: if one knows the OT, one can catch its paraphrases (*ad loc.* 1:11; 4:10-12; 7:37; 10:2-9; 11:9) or images (1:6, 12-13; 4:35-41; 6:30-44; 9:2-8; 12:1-9; 13:24-28), but the Evangelist neither draws attention to them nor explains their significance. The same is true of the Passion Narrative, some of whose OT resonances were likely built into the tradition Mark inherited (14:27, 62; 15:24, 31, 33-34; N.B. 14:21a, 49b). The constant vagaries in Mark's use of Scripture are congruent with his theological attitude.

Genre

What kind of book is the Second Gospel? With what contemporary literature did ancient audiences associate Mark when they read it or heard it read? At present there is a core of interpretive agreement with vigorous debate around the edges. Bryan's proposal (1993) represents a rough consensus: viewed alongside Jewish and Greco-Roman writings 100 B.C.E.–200 C.E., Mark exhibits a cluster of traits found in Hellenistic biographies (*bioi*): a story centered on a subject, localized and narrated chronologically, that entertained and edified audiences inhabiting a predominantly oral culture. A caveat should be entered: ancient biographies operated with standards different from those of modern counterparts. In antiquity *bioi* were highly selective

and stylized, often idealized, presentations of subjects who typi-
fied characteristics that readers or listeners were invited to accept
or to reject. On its face that seems a reasonable, general description of what one finds in Mark's Gospel.

On further reflection at least three problems bedevil this clas-
sification. One says something about modern research; the other
two, some things about Mark. The more precisely a scholar tries
to frame the generic question, the faster a *bios* mutates into
something else. For this reason there are advocates for reading
Mark as Greek tragedy (Bilezikian 1977), novels either Greco-
Roman (Tolbert 1989) or Jewish (Vines 2002), "the cult narrative of the dead hero" (Wills 1997, 21), and "an eschatological
historical monograph" (A. Y. Collins 2007, 42). Like the blind
men with the elephant, each of these touches something resonant
with Mark, though none—perhaps not even *bios*—is an entirely
satisfactory identification. This leads to one of Mark's peculiari-
ties: as literature it is not purebred but a mongrel. The Second
Gospel incorporates many literary forms—parables, wondrous
deeds of the sages, the OT's prophetic legends (1 Kgs 17–2 Kgs
9) and apocalyptic elements (Dan 1–6)—that would have been
intelligible to first-century Christians. Another important trait of
Mark is its unabashed dedication to "the good news of Jesus
Christ" (1:1): not a dead hero, but the crucified Son of Man
raised from death by God (8:31; 9:31; 10:33-34). Forcing the
Second Gospel into a single pigeonhole is as unwise as dismissing
the generic question altogether. Comprising—occasionally twisting—many literary conventions, Mark is, at bottom, a religious
proclamation based on historical events. Experienced aurally, the
Gospel exerts extraordinary power, as its Tony-nominated recital
by Alec McCowen (1990) attests.

WHAT ONE MAY JUDGE

Mark's Influence in the Church

For the better part of two millennia the Second Gospel was
overshadowed by its neighbors in the canon. Except for ten hom-

ilies by Jerome (347–420), an important commentary by the Venerable Bede (673–735), and a *Paraphrase on Mark* by Erasmus (1466–1536), Mark was generally ignored or superficially glossed by patristic and medieval commentators (Kealy 2007). Some of this neglect lies at the doorstep of Augustine, who popularized a view of Mark as Matthew's lackey. Schildgen (1999, 35-62) has demonstrated that Mark's status as stepchild owed much to the church's perception that it was less useful than other Gospels in consolidating the church's life and doctrine, defending orthodoxy against heretical threats. Although its place in the NT canon was secure by the second century as a constituent of Tatian's Gospel harmony, the *Diatessaron* (ca. 170), Mark attracted comparatively little attention throughout the church's history. Though portions of it have always been read in Christian worship, the Second Gospel was not included in the Common Lectionary shared by Roman Catholics and Protestants until 1969.

That said, and with hindsight's benefit, one could argue that Mark's contribution to the church has been profound. Just as Paul inadvertently encouraged succeeding generations of Christian authors to formulate and transmit their thinking in letters (the NT's Deutero-Pauline tradition, the Catholic Epistles, Rev 2–3; the letters of Clement, Ignatius, and Barnabas among the Apostolic Fathers), so also Mark was evidently the first to compose a Gospel, paving the way for Matthew, Luke, John, and a host of noncanonical authors. We have no direct access to the earliest Christian oral preaching, whose presentation in Acts (e.g., 2:22-36) may owe as much to Luke's stylization as to historical reality. Beginning with Mark, however, we have in writing the basic format for the story of Jesus as the church, by its circulation and eventual canonization of that Gospel, chose to remember it: the template to which Matthew and Luke (perhaps also John) adhered while developing it. This was a momentous step in first-century Christian thought and practice. Augustine's assessment notwithstanding, Mark was the first Christian thinker to take that step.

Given its subsequent neglect, it is a good if unanswerable

question why Mark found its place, so fast and so firmly, among a quartet of Gospels whose later canonization merely ratified their popularity during Christianity's formative centuries. There is no evidence that Mark's canonical status was challenged. The obvious explanations—its association with a recognized apostle and an important church—do not entirely satisfy. As far as we know, the Second Gospel never circulated under Peter's name. The testimony of Papias may have forestalled that. Simply attributing a Gospel to the Twelve's acknowledged leader did not assure widespread acceptance, as the second-century *Gospel of Peter* proves. It is not until the second century that Mark's liturgical use in a Roman Easter vigil can be documented (Schildgen 1999, 50). The fourth-century liturgy linked most firmly with Mark stems from Alexandria, not Rome. Petrine and Roman prestige probably played a part in Mark's favorable reception. It is insufficient to account for it.

A Gospel for a Church in Travail

Could Mark have struck a chord among early Christians who knew, firsthand, betrayal by their own families for Jesus' sake— "hand[ed] over to councils, beaten in synagogues," standing before authorities for Jesus' sake to bear witness to the good news (*ad loc.* 13:9-13)? Whether Mark was composed for Roman Christians in the 60s, Tacitus (*Ann.* 15.44) corroborates that such terrors were not hypothetical but all too real:

> Therefore, to scotch the rumor [that a great fire in Rome was by imperial order], Nero substituted as culprits, and punished with the utmost exquisite cruelty, a class loathed for their abominations, whom the crowd styled "Christians." ... Accordingly, arrest was first made of those who confessed [to being Christians]; next, on their disclosures, vast numbers were convicted.... Every sort of derision was added to their deaths. They were wrapped in the skins of wild beasts and dismembered by dogs; others were nailed to crosses; others, when daylight failed, were set afire to serve as lamps by night.

"And you will be hated by all for my name's sake" (Mark 13:13a RSV). Because this Gospel is so riveted on human misery, especially that entailed by Christian confession, surely it was taken to heart by those forced to cope with the terrible implications of their allegiance to Jesus: a compassionate, healing Messiah who was spared none of faith's anguish (14:32-42; 15:16-37).

Related to this clear-eyed view of suffering is a deeper element of the Second Gospel: the subtle congruence of its narrative form with the substance of its message. Mark opens, "The beginning of the good news of Jesus Christ" (1:1). Its ending is left open, directing the story's characters to the place from which everything began (16:7-8). Between start and finish—which is no finish whatsoever—the narrative swings back and forth from confidence to perplexity. That ambivalence is captured even in single verses: "To you has been given the mystery of God's kingdom, but for those outside everything comes in riddles" (4:11 AT); "I believe; help my unbelief!" (9:24); and "There is nothing hidden, except to be disclosed; nor is anything secret, except to come to light" (4:22).

The unresolved tension that pulsates throughout Mark is announced near its beginning, in the first words uttered by Jesus (1:15 AT): "The time has been fulfilled, and God's dominion is near: turn your mind around, and trust the good news." How can the time *have been* fulfilled, yet God's sovereignty be only near, *not yet* arrived? That, in an elliptical nutshell, is "the mystery of God's kingdom." To begin living in that mystery requires a revolution of mind as hard as a camel's passage through a needle's eye (10:25), persistently trusting God's saving goodness in the face of catastrophe (5:35-36). Invading the present of Jesus and his contemporaries, of Mark and his audience in the first and twenty-first centuries, is God's true dominion, veiled in Jesus' ministry (3:21-25)—but this is only "the beginning of the birth pangs" (13:8b). The apocalyptic metaphor of God's new creation as a woman in labor (see also John 16:21; Rom 8:22-23) grasps the theological point: the water has broken, and *now*—a now that for the mother feels excruciatingly interminable—come the contractions until *finally* the child is born.

The pendular rhythm of fear and faith, faith and fear, is known by a synagogue administrator (Mark 5:21-23), a menorrhagic woman (5:24b-34), and even Jesus himself (14:34-36; 15:34). Nothing is hidden except to be disclosed. For now, however, the light comes only as flashes in the fog.

Living with Jesus in the Kingdom's Mystery

Mark's genius lies not in telling a story about Jesus, but in creating conditions under which the reader may *experience* the peculiar quality of God's good news (1:14). It is more than a matter of being led up to a mountain where Jesus is transfigured (9:2-8) before being steered to Golgotha where he is crucified (15:22-25), though these are crucial stops "on the way" (8:27; 9:33-34; 10:52). The Evangelist hurries one along breathlessly, "immediately" (1:10, 12, 18, 20, 21, 23, 29, 30, and so on; sometimes omitted from English translations), making sure that the reader lurches with the characters into one pothole after another. "What is this new teaching" (1:27a AT) that consorts with the flagrantly sinful (2:15), turning the pious homicidal (3:6), intimates into strangers (3:21; 6:1-6a), and mustard seeds into "the greatest of all shrubs" (4:32a)? What healer is moved by one supplicant (1:40-42) but offers another a cold shoulder (7:26-27)? What pilgrim saunters the temple one day (11:11) and unhinges its operations the next (11:15-16)? What teacher speaks well (12:28), impartially teaching "the way of God in accordance with truth" (12:14a), while spinning riddles intended to blind the sighted and to deafen the hearing, "so that they may not turn again and be forgiven" (4:11-12)?

Jesus' closest adherents, the Twelve, are among the most muddled. Who can blame them? They ask for an obscure parable's interpretation (4:10) and receive an answer even more confounding (4:11-32). They are told to feed thousands with next to nothing (6:37-38, 44). Their boat almost capsizes while their teacher sleeps (4:35-38). As they oar in rough waters, the teacher strides the waves, intending to bypass them (6:47-48). Putting the reader in the same boat, Mark structures conversations with Jesus that make little sense, if any (8:14-21; 9:9-13). The Twelve are craven, stupid, self-serving, and disobedient (4:40; 8:4; 9:34; 10:32, 35-37, 41; 14:37-40, 66-72): meet the average Christian. Besides, "their hearts were hardened" (6:52; 8:17). Who hardens hearts? God. Should not God's Messiah lift the burdens of those following him? What kind of Christ heads to a cross, handing his disciples another for themselves (8:31-35)? "Do you not yet understand?" (8:21).

From this cockeyed canvas issues "the messianic secret," a question posed more than a century ago (1901). William Wrede spotted passages in Mark that are intensely self-contradictory: demons (1:34; 3:11-12) and beneficiaries (1:44; 5:43; 7:36; 8:29-30; 9:9) who know Jesus' identity are silenced, "but the more he ordered them, the more zealously they proclaimed it" (7:36; see also 1:45). In the scholarly fashion of his day, Wrede explained this paradox by conjecturing the early church's need to reconcile its post-Easter faith with its inheritance of a nonmessianic tradition by projecting a Jesus who, though knowing he was the Christ, tried keeping it a secret (1971, 113-29, 227-28). The argument is as flawed as it is ironic. As far as we know, the allegedly inherited, nonmessianic tradition never existed. It was *Wrede* who projected onto Mark a reading tailored to fit his hypothetical reconstruction of early Christianity. Nevertheless, Wrede got some important things right. He recognized that the Second Evangelist was driven by theological principles greater than historical reportage (49-53, 130-31), and he identified secrecy as a major ingredient in Markan theology. That mystery keeps bumping into disclosure—especially by demoniacs, whose testimony would be incredible (1:23-24), and antagonists like the high priest (14:61) and Pilate (15:2), who do not believe the truth they unwittingly speak (see also 15:18, 26). "There is nothing hidden, except to be disclosed; nor is anything secret, except to come to light" (4:22). Even when dawn breaks and things come to light—God emptied Jesus' tomb, as promised (10:33-34; 16:4-6)—Mark leaves the tension unresolved to the very end: disciples flee the tomb, hiding faith's good news, "for they were *afraid*" (16:8, emphasis added). This Evangelist is more than "a master of surprise" (Juel 1994); he is the church's original master of suspense. Between the two lies a difference, as the twentieth century's best known "master of suspense" will be conscripted to explain (*ad loc.* 5:21-43).

It is to Mark's everlasting credit that he never "explains" the mystery of the kingdom of God. Soluble puzzles repay fleeting pleasure. Genuine mystery, which penetrates and upends this world, is given and withheld, concealed and revealed by God alone. Mark invites his listeners among the throngs, beside the Twelve, to catch from a baffling Nazarene traces of the kingdom "as they [are] able to hear it" (4:33). It is an amazing story, brilliantly told. Secular readers may judge it inspired. The church has believed that for a long time.

PALESTINE AT THE TIME OF JESUS

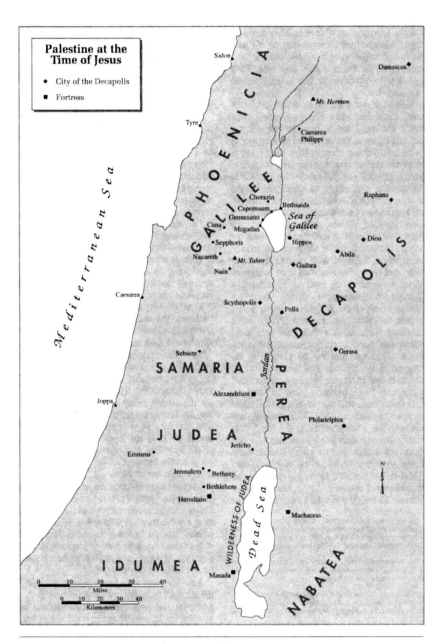

Palestine at the
Time of Jesus

♦ City of the Decapolis

■ Fortress

There are conflicts, the reconciliation of which lies beyond the powers not only of human effort but of human rational conception. One of them is the reconciliation of good and evil themselves in the scheme of nature.... To say that we know they will be reconciled is faith; to say that we see that they will be reconciled is blasphemy.

—G. K. Chesterton, *Charles Dickens* (1903)

Reverend J. C. Ramsey, a Southern man, comes from Wadesboro, North Carolina. Most Sundays, he and his wife take Sunday dinner with me, and I always try to have something nice for them. After dinner, we sit around the table and drink Postum and discuss the Bible, and that's something I do enjoy. We discuss the prophecies in the Bible, and the warnings, and the promises—the promises of eternal life. And we discuss what I call the mysterious verses, the ones that if you could just understand them they might explain everything—why we're put here, why we're taken away—but they go down too deep; you study them over and over, and you go down as deep as you can, and you still don't touch bottom.

—Joseph Mitchell, *Mr. Hunter's Grave* (1956)

COMMENTARY

THE PROLOGUE OF THE GOSPEL (1:1-15)

Mark opens with a simple statement (1:1) and a scriptural epigraph (1:2-3), followed by four elements: (a) a précis of John the baptizer's ministry (1:4-8), (b) Jesus' baptism by John (1:9-11), (c) Jesus' temptation (1:12-13), and (d) a transitional summary of the start of Jesus' own ministry in Galilee (1:14-15). In musical terms Mark 1:1-15 is a brisk overture, whose first notes announce a work that will unfold not as a Mozartian minuet but as a Beethovian blast.

The Gospel's Opening and Epigraph (1:1-3)

Titles for NT Gospels (such as "According to Mark") were added to the texts long after their composition, at a time when the early church recognized that the expression of its "gospel" in alternative literary forms required differentiation (Hengel 2000). The Second Gospel opens abruptly: literally translated, "Beginning of the good news of Jesus Christ [God's Son]." This comment raises important interpretive questions.

The Opening (1:1)

What is this clause "beginning" (*archē*, v. 1)? Is the author suggesting the beginning of the entire book? Not necessarily, unless we assume that "the good news" refers to a literary document (on which, see below). Does "beginning" refer only to the passages, immediately following, in verses 2-3 and 4-8? Possibly, though such an interpretation may be too limiting. Is the Evangelist thinking theologically (that the following narrative offers a summary of the gospel) or existentially (that the beginning of the good news occurs with the reader's encounter with Jesus, whose story Mark will now tell)? Perhaps so; yet these latter options may read more into the clause than it clearly connotes. We may consider the clause in 1:1 an abrupt technique to draw our attention to the upcoming scriptural quotations (vv. 2-3). To paraphrase: "Here's where the gospel originates—in Israel's prophetic Scripture."

Equally uncertain is the meaning of "the good news" or "the gospel" (*to euangelion*). Modern readers often assume reference to a literary document. Nevertheless, Paul's letters, written two decades before Mark, use the term *gospel* in reference to the Christian message of salvation accomplished by Jesus' crucifixion and resurrection (e.g., Rom 1:1; 1 Cor 15:1; 2 Cor 11:7; 1 Thess 2:2, 8-9). Although Mark tells us far more about Jesus' life than does Paul, the Evangelist concurs with the apostle in using the term *gospel* to refer to preaching, not to a literary composition (see Mark 1:14-15; 8:35; 13:10). (Not until Justin Martyr, around 150 C.E., is the term *gospel* clearly used for a book: *1 Apol.* 66.3; *Dial. Trypho* 10.2, 100.1.) Like Paul, Mark appears indebted to Isaiah's "proclamation of glad tidings" (LXX, *euangelizesthai*), the encouraging announcement of the Lord's promise to restore a shattered Israel (Isa 40:9; 52:7; 61:1). A cognate of the same Greek term—*euangelia* (glad tidings)—also occurs in imperial inscriptions of first-century Rome, with reference to the emperor's birthday and benefactions associated with his reign (Koester 1990, 3-4). For Mark's earliest readers, the term *gospel* likely activated reverberations both religious and political. Mark's presentation of Jesus' preaching resonates with the assurances of Second Isaiah: an *euangelion* now associated not with Caesar, but with Jesus, the new herald of a very different dominion (1:15).

The referent of this good news is Jesus "Christ": the "messiah" or "anointed one" (*ho christos*), a term that by Mark's time already enjoyed a rich history in Hebrew psalmody (45:7; 89:38, 51), prophecy (Isa 45:1; Hab 3:13), and Jewish apocalypticism (CD 7:18-21; 1QS 9:11; *Pss. Sol.* 17:32; 18:5, 7; see Neusner, Green, and Frerichs 1987). In Mark "Christ" usually appears as a title (8:29; 12:35; 13:21; 14:61; 15:32), though it can function as a proper name for Jesus (9:41) in the manner characteristic of Paul and other NT writers (Rom 5:6, 8; Col 1:24-28; 1 Pet 4:12-14). (For further consideration of "Christ," see the discussion of 8:27–9:1 *ad loc.*) "The good news of Jesus Christ" is grammatically ambiguous. Does Mark refer to the good news proclaimed *by* Jesus (a "subjective genitive"), the good news *about* Jesus (an "objective genitive"), or the good news whose substance *is* Jesus (a genitive of identification)? Later in Mark (8:35; 10:29; 13:9-10) the Evangelist differentiates, while correlating, what believers may do "for [Jesus'] sake and for the sake of the gospel." One may infer that a similarly "associative distinction" is present in 1:1.

Ancient manuscripts of Mark disagree on whether "Son of God" (*ho huios theou*) was included in the original text of Mark. Scribes tended to enlarge, rather than to abbreviate, the beginnings of books. The tendency to clarify through expansion inclines toward the shorter reading's originality, in which "God's Son" is absent from Mark 1:1. On the other hand, a strong combination of diverse witnesses favors the inclusion of a title that is undeniably important in Mark (3:11; 5:7; 12:6; 14:61), occurring at climactic points in this Gospel (1:11; 9:7; 15:39). The textual evidence is remarkably well balanced (see Swanson 1995, 7). If Mark had originally written the longer form, why would later scribes have truncated it?

What does "Son of God" signify about Jesus? In Greco-Roman antiquity that term carries many connotations, only one of which is "a divinized human being" (*Corp. herm.* 13.2). By virtue of their valor in combat or other exemplary conduct, heroes like Dionysius and Hercules were regarded as "children of Zeus" (*Diatr.* 3.26.31); an emperor like Octavius was acclaimed *divi filius,* "son of the deified" (i.e., "the previous emperor": *Aug.* 94.4). In the biblical tradition "son of God" referred especially to Israel's king (2 Sam 7:13-14; Pss 2:7; 110:3) or to the entire nation as beneficiary of God's solicitude (Exod 4:22-23; Jer 31:9, 20; Hos 11:1). As children mimic their parents, so too was a "son of God" expected to exemplify divine attributes, like righteousness (Wis 2:18). In later Jewish literature "son of God" is associated with the figure of the Messiah (*4 Ezra* 7:28-29; 13:32, 37, 52; 14:9; *1 En.* 105:2). Mark's earliest readers likely heard several nuances in its designation of Jesus as God's Son (see below, *ad loc.* 9:2-8).

◊ ◊ ◊ ◊

Mark's opening—crisp, forceful, compressed—anticipates the style of the scenes following it. This Evangelist does not ease his reader into the narrative; instead, one is hurled into a rapid-fire series of affirmations. Like the rest of this Gospel, those claims are ambiguous, patient of multiple interpretations that are not mutually exclusive. Here begins the good news, but that *euangelion* carries multiple connotations. Mark presupposes readers' knowledge of Jesus, identifying him as "Christ" and (perhaps) as "Son of God" without defining, much less defending, either ascription. Like the other Gospels, Mark offers a confession of Christian faith for those who have or aspire to such faith. *That* Jesus is the Messiah, whose advent spells glad tidings, is an assumption the Evangelist makes. *What it means* to believe that Jesus is God's anointed Son *and how* such faith discerns "good news" are complex issues that will haunt the reader throughout this Gospel.

The Epigraph (1:2-3)

Fond of asides (e.g., see also 2:10, 15; 7:3-4, 19b; 13:14; see C. H. Turner 1993, 23-35), Mark sets as his Gospel's epigraph a parenthetical reference to "the prophet Isaiah" (v. 2a). In fact, only verse 3 cites Isaiah (40:3), since the quotations in Mark 1:2b ("See, I am sending my messenger ahead of you") and 1:2c ("who will prepare your way") conflate material found in Exodus 23:20a and Malachi 3:1a, in a manner characteristic of later Jewish biblical interpretation (*Exod. Rab.* 32.9; *Deut. Rab.* 11.9; see Marcus 1992, 12-17). Mark's confusing attribution prompted some scribes to change the wording of 1:2 to "in the prophets," thus erasing doubts about the Evangelist's familiarity with Scripture. The quotations in verses 2b-3 are similar to, though not identical with, the LXX (the Greek translation of the Hebrew Bible).

Mark's adaptations of Scripture are noteworthy. The three quoted verses originate from works that refer to different phases of Israel's history. In its original context Exodus 23:20a promises that "an angel [or 'messenger'] of God" (see also Exod 14:19) would precede and protect Israel in its settlement of Canaan. Malachi 3:1a is part of a prophetic oracle to Israel (ca. 445 B.C.E.), promising that Yahweh's emissary, "my messenger" (Heb. *malachi*), would prepare the way for God's occupation of the temple and the nation's purification. In 4:5 Malachi identifies that messenger with Elijah: the prophet who, because he did not die but was taken up to heaven in a fiery chariot (2 Kgs 2:11), was expected someday to return to earth as herald of "the great and terrible day of the LORD." Isaiah 40:3 introduces Israel's great consolation. While in Babylonian exile (597–539 B.C.E.) an anonymous prophet encourages preparation of the highway that God would use to revisit his people and to lead them through the desert stretching from Babylon back to their Judean homeland. Members of the Qumran sect believed this passage in Isaiah referred to themselves: those who had renounced a society considered unrighteous and had exiled themselves to the Judean desert (1QS 8:12-16).

By selecting these texts to introduce his Gospel, Mark invites the reader to assemble and to tease out a number of important biblical themes. First, "a way" is once more being cleared for God's people: a divine intervention that will transport readers along "straight paths" (Mark 1:3c). Second, preparation of that way is again delegated to an envoy entrusted with God's message: an emissary who stands in line with Moses, Elijah, and

Deutero-Isaiah. Third, those led in that way are again called to abandon that to which they have become accustomed, for a life under radically changed circumstances: a shift no less extreme than that from the wilderness to Canaan, from foreign exile to a return home, from business as usual to "the Day of the LORD." Gentile readers of Mark, wobbly in their knowledge of Jewish Scripture, would have been acquainted with ceremonial processions, whose bystanders were encouraged to cheer a visiting senator or the emperor himself (Mamertinus, *Panegyric* 3.10.5). Those more familiar with Israel's history might have drawn subtler inferences from Mark's scriptural epigraph, since not everyone challenged by God to a radical change in life had proved able or willing to make it (see Exod 14:11-12; 16:2-3; Num 11:1-6; 14:1-3; Isa 57:1-13; Mal 3:2b-4; 4:1). Even those delighting in the Lord's unbroken covenant with Israel were asked, "[W]ho can endure the day of his coming, and who can stand when he appears?" (Mal 3:2a).

Mark's epigraph (1:2-3) is at once atypical of his Gospel, yet much in character. Unlike Matthew, whose "formula-quotations" of Scripture punctuate the First Gospel (e.g., 1:22-23; 2:5-6, 17, 23; 3:3; 4:14), the Second Evangelist does not obviously alert the reader to fulfillments of Scripture within his narrative (though see 7:6; 11:17; 12:10-11; 14:27). Most of Mark's nods toward Scripture are more allusive and depend on the capacity of readers with ears to hear (Mark 4:12/Isa 6:9-10; Mark 8:18/Jer 5:21; Mark 12:1/Isa 5:1-2; Mark 13:24-26/Ezek 32:7-8, Dan 7:13-14; Mark 15:34/Ps 22:1). Mark's reference to "Isaiah the prophet" conjures up for the biblically articulate reader a larger Isaianic chamber—replete with the images of wilderness (Isa 40:3; cf. Mark 1:4, 7-8, 12-13), rent heavens (Isa 64:1; cf. Mark 1:11), and tamed beasts (Isa 11:6-8; 65:25; cf. Mark 1:13b)—within which "the good news" (Isa 40:9; cf. Mark 1:1) again resonates. In any case Mark 1:1-3 weds the coming of Jesus Christ to a miniature panorama of Israel's history.

Yet, even as we observed in Mark 1:1, verses 2-3 leave as much unsaid as spoken. Isaiah explicitly bolsters Mark's point of view—but, by implication, so do the Scriptures from Exodus to Malachi. Exactly who, for Mark, is "my messenger," sent by the Lord? As yet we do not know. News that "the way of the Lord" (God? Jesus?) is again under construction is good indeed—unless the inadequacies of another, more popular, less newsworthy path are thus exposed, and their travelers along with it (see Watts 1997, 29-121).

The Ministry of the Forerunner (1:4-8)

Mark's thumbnail description of John seems to answer one question left dangling from verses 2-3: the identity of "my messenger" who prepares the Lord's way. The NRSV identification of John in verse 4 ("John the baptizer appeared") adheres to the wording of some ancient manuscripts—the majority of which, however, are best translated, "There was John, baptizing in the wilderness and proclaiming." The latter wording may have been the original: it is rougher, more abrupt, and diverges from Mark's tendency to describe John as "the baptizer" (*ho baptizōn*: 6:14, 24) or "the Baptist" (*ho baptistēs*: 6:25; 8:28; see also Matt 3:1; 11:11, 12; Luke 7:20, 33; 9:19). A scribe trying to clarify John's identity might have imitated the Evangelist's style more slavishly. It is worth contemplating that, given this Gospel's reports that some confused Jesus with John (6:14-16; 8:28), Mark may have left momentarily ambiguous exactly who in 1:2-3 is "preparing the way."

Beyond Christian sources, the Jewish historian Josephus corroborates much of Mark's report that John, "surnamed the Baptist," called the Jews to baptism and a life of righteousness, and was eventually arrested and executed by Herod Antipas out of "fear that John's powerful ability to persuade people might lead to some sort of revolt" against Rome (*Ant.* 18.5.2; cf. the different explanation for his death in Mark 6:14-19). Josephus tells us almost twice as much about John as about Jesus; of the two, John receives from Josephus greater praise (see Meier 1994, 19-99).

Mark's portrait of John highlights five features. (1) His appearance was in accordance with veiled scriptural precedents (vv. 3-4, 6). (2) The site of his activity was the wilderness, in the vicinity of the Jordan River (vv. 4-5). (3) Baptism, symbolizing "repentance for the forgiveness of sins" (v. 4), was the focus of John's ministry. (4) Popular Jewish response to that ministry was extraordinary (v. 5). (5) He acclaimed a successor, whose importance diminished John's own (vv. 7-8). Each of these aspects invites comment.

1. John's location in the wilderness or desert *(en tē erēmō,* v. 4) implies that his is the voice "crying out in the wilderness" (v. 3), in alignment with Isaiah. Like the Jewish sectarians at Qumran, Mark takes the prophet to mean that the desert is where the voice is crying out, not the place of preparation for the Lord's way, as the reading of Isaiah 40:3 in Hebrew suggests (see NRSV). Unlike Mark, however, the Qumranites suggest that *theirs* was the voice crying out in the desert (1QS 8:13-14; 9:19-20). Mark does not expressly forge an association of John with Exodus 23:20 and Malachi 3:1, as do Matthew (11:10) and Luke (1:76; 7:27). Most forthright of all in establishing a scriptural connection is the Fourth Gospel, wherein John expressly identifies himself as " 'the voice of one crying out in the wilderness,'...as the prophet Isaiah said" (John 1:23).

John's attire and diet—"dressed in camel's hair and a leather belt around his waist, and eating locusts and wild honey" (AT)—are frequently cited by commentators as echoes of OT characters: specifically, Elijah the Tishbite (2 Kgs 1:8) and the Nazirites, who abstained from wine (Num 6:3-4). The LXX and MT of 2 Kings 1:8 may be translated as referring either to a man in a hairy mantle (RSV) or to a hairy man (NRSV); however, neither 2 Kings 1:8 nor Zechariah 13:4 (which refers to a prophet's conventional garb) says anything about *camel's* hair. Mark's reference to a leather belt *(zōnēn dermatinēn)* more clearly alludes to the description of Elijah in 2 Kings 1:8 (LXX), even though leather belts were worn by many in the ancient world. More tenuous are connections between John and the Nazirites: their diet was not restricted to locusts and uncultivated honey; their abstention from wine is akin to Luke's portrait of John (1:15), not Mark's. Mark does not mention the most characteristic sign of the Nazirites' (temporary) vow: letting one's hair grow uncut (Num 6:5, 9, 19). To sum up: as Mark portrays them, John's dress and diet conform to those of poor desert nomads. Here an association with Elijah is at best whispered (a hairy mantle, a leather belt), not shouted—setting a pattern that will recur in this Gospel (6:15-16; 9:11-13).

2. Using other traditions, both Matthew (11:7) and Luke (1:80; 7:24) corroborate the locale of John's ministry as the wilderness. The references to Judea and the Jordan in Mark 1:5 appear to have led the other Synoptic Evangelists (Matt 3:1; Luke 3:3) to identify that desert more precisely: namely, the Wilderness of Judah, the southern portion of the Jordan Valley at the foot of the Judean hills. Such a location is plausible, since the region of the Lower Jordan is described as desert in the OT (Judg 1:16; Ps 63:1) and in Josephus (*J.W.* 3.10.7). Still, Mark's primary concern is to locate John "in the wilderness" (1:3-4), not to pinpoint that area itself (see also 1:12-13; Marxsen 1969, 36-38). Considered theologically, *the wilderness* is a multivalent term. In the OT the desert is where Israel's children rebelled against God (Pss 78:17-18; 106:13-33). It is also the archetypal locus of testing (1 Sam 22:4; 23:29; 24:1, 22) and of Israel's deliverance by God (Exod 19–24; Isa 41:18-20; 43:19-21; Hos 2:14-15). Similarly, the Jordan River had long been regarded as more than a body of water bisecting ancient Palestine's western and eastern sectors. As early as Psalm 42:7, the Jordan has figured as "a significant *metaphysical* reality within Judaism and Christianity" (Thompson 1992, 957), whose crossing symbolized transfer from one realm of life to another (cf. Heb 3:17-19).

3. As epitomized by Mark, the core of John's preaching is "a baptism of repentance for the forgiveness of sins" (v. 4). Later Christian explanations of baptism sometimes mask the fact that water rituals of various sorts were pervasive in Israel (e.g., Lev 14:5-6, 50-52; Num 19:13, 20-21). Associations of water with religious cleansing and bestowal of God's spirit are present in OT prophecy (Isa 1:16) and the DSS (1QS 3:6-12; 4:20-22;

5:13-14; 1QH 7:6-7; 17:26; see Chilton et al. 2010, 69-76).
Although not typically linked with baptism, repentance
(*metanoia*: "a turnaround of one's thought"; cf. Heb. *shub*) and
forgiveness (*aphesis*: literally, "release from one's indebtedness")
are fundamental metaphors in the message of the prophets (Isa
1:10-20; 55:7; Hos 6:1; Joel 2:12-13; Zech 1:4).

Mark 1:4 works out no precise relationship among baptism,
repentance, and forgiveness; apart from 3:29 this is Mark's only
mention of *aphesis*. One might compare Acts 2:38, which suggests that another baptism—"in the name of Jesus Christ"—was
preceded by repentance but eventuated in forgiveness and receipt
of the Holy Spirit. Even Luke, however, does not consistently
coordinate those concepts (cf. Acts 8:14-17, 36-39; 10:44-48).
The NT does not elaborate a standard procedure for baptism,
even less a systematic theology of it. Mark's primary concern is
to relate John's baptism and the summons to repentance and forgiveness. In this way are the Lord's paths straightened (v. 3; cf.
Isa 40:1-3).

4. The response to John's proclamation is staggering: "the
whole Judean countryside and all the people of Jerusalem"—
apparently the entire region of southern Palestine, in and around
Judea's capital—come out to the Jordan to confess their sins and
be baptized (v. 5). Mark is fond of hyperbole. That exaggeration
makes an important point here: a fervent, nationwide religious
revival is in progress, with John at its vanguard.

5. By comparison with the other Gospels, which elaborate
John's preaching in different ways (Matt 3:7-12; Luke 3:7-14, 17
[stringent eschatological teaching]; John 1:29-35; 3:27-30 [wit-
ness to Jesus]), in Mark the Baptist's proclamation is telescoped
and sharpened to a single point: the superiority—in power, wor-
thiness, and efficacy of baptism—of the (unnamed) one who will
come after John (vv. 7-8). In the Middle East to this day, submit-
ting oneself to another's feet is a menial, potentially offensive,
position. It was no less so in antiquity. To claim unworthiness to
stoop down and unlace another's sandal is, by its exaggeration, a
statement of utter self-abasement. John has baptized "with
water" (*hydati*, a more difficult formulation in Greek than the

phrase appearing in most manuscripts, "in water" [*en hydati*]). John's successor will baptize with holy Spirit, whose reinfusion of Israel was expected in the last days (Isa 11:1-2; Joel 2:28-32; Acts 2:17-22). A few scribal witnesses follow Matthew (3:12) and Luke's (3:16) lead by adding to that coming baptism "fire," the smelting furnace of destruction or purification. For Mark, as with John (1:33), baptism with the eschatological Spirit is promise enough.

At first Mark 1:4-8 seems a textual torso, without a clear point. Pondered more carefully, however, this passage reveals crucial information about the story to follow and this Evangelist's unique way of telling it.

To begin with, Mark's opening (v. 1) and scriptural epigraph (vv. 2-3) have primed the reader for a narrative to be launched by Jesus. Verse 4 catches one up short: "There was *John*" (AT). Part of Mark's narrative technique is to clarify for us that the Messiah's arrival was carefully prepared by God, for those who could discern clues in Scripture and in the activity of an eccentric desert preacher. Equally important, however, is the *surprising ambiguity* of Mark's presentation. Who is the messenger who has gone before the Lord's face, to prepare the way (v. 2)? Is it Jesus? Or is it John? Is John Elijah returned from heaven? According to Matthew, the answer is clearly "Yes" (Matt 11:13-14; 17:11-13). In the Fourth Gospel the answer is just as firmly "No" (John 1:19-21). For Mark, the answer is—"Maybe." If John were Elijah *redivivus,* and if the prophet Malachi be trusted, then the religious ante has been raised: like those throughout Judea and Jerusalem, the reader stands on the threshold of "the great and terrible day of the LORD" (Mal 4:5). Unlike both Matthew (3:7-12) and Luke (3:7-17), however, Mark does not nail down that hardly minor point. By the end of Mark 1:4-8, the reader is invited to ask of Jesus, as did the Baptist himself in Matthew (11:2-3) and Luke (7:19), "Are you the one who is to come, or are we to wait for another?" That strategy is typical of this Gospel: as often as it offers its readers answers, Mark leaves them grappling with deep questions about faith and its understanding.

A related aspect of this passage is noteworthy: the subtle but real similarities between the ministry of John and that of Jesus. As we shall witness below, with regard to 1:9-11, early Christians used different means to distinguish John and Jesus, and to confirm Jesus' greater authority. Mark 1:7-8 touches on that tactic: except for one sentence addressed to Herod in 6:18, the only preaching of John ever quoted by Mark is the Baptist's stress on the coming of an unnamed one, mightier than he. On the other hand, notice that, as John appears from out of nowhere; so too does Jesus (1:9). John attracts a stupendous audience; repeatedly, so also will Jesus (1:28, 37, 45; 2:2, 13; 3:7-10, 20; 4:1; 5:14, 21, 24b; 6:34, 56; 8:1; 9:14; 10:1, 46; 11:8; 12:12). John lived an impoverished, itinerant existence; so, it appears, did Jesus (6:4, 7-11). The preaching of John stresses repentance, forgiveness of sins, baptism, and greater things to come. Much the same will be true of Jesus' preaching (Mark 1:14-15; 2:5; 4:20, 25, 32; 8:31, 38–9:1; 9:31; 10:33-34, 38-39; 12:9; 13:5-37; 14:62). Throughout Mark's Gospel, people compare Jesus with John (2:18; 11:30-32), even confuse Jesus with John (6:14, 16; 8:27-28). Oddly, the eponymous practice for which John is best remembered—baptism—is something we never witness Jesus in Mark perform for others. Baptism in Mark carries, instead, a metaphorical weight, with reference to eschatological traumas, whose endurance is incumbent on the faithful (10:38-40).

Attend carefully to the Evangelist's technique: from the beginning of this Gospel, the identity of Jesus is, paradoxically, at once clear and obscure. Viewed *sub specie aeternitatis* (under the aspect of eternity), Jesus is God's Son (1:1); regarded within conventional frames of reference, however, his significance is easily confused. *That* Jesus is the Messiah, Mark has no doubt (1:1); *what* messiahship means or entails, as distinguished from those roles played by other figures like John, is subject for intense debate.

The Spirit and the Satan (1:9-13)

The last major section of Mark's prologue consists of two episodes, concisely narrated. By comparison with Matthew (3:13–4:11; cf. Luke 4:1-13), Mark's account of Jesus' baptism and temptation appears slight. While Luke's account of the baptism (3:21-22) is Mark's equal in economy, the Third Gospel uses this occasion to record a genealogy of Jesus (3:23-38; cf. Matt 1:1-17), which Mark lacks. The Fourth Evangelist may allude to Jesus' baptism (1:29-34) but never narrates it as such; nor does John intimate a narrative of Jesus' temptation. A vital task for the interpreter of Mark 1:9-13 is to restrain one's impressions based on familiarity with the other Gospels. Here as elsewhere, it is important that we allow Mark to speak with his distinctive voice.

Jesus' Baptism by John (1:9-11)

Alongside his crucifixion, **Jesus' baptism by John (Mark 1:9-11)** may be the most secure datum in the history of Jesus, and for the same reasons: in both cases the facts were indisputable, embarrassing for early Christians, and demanded theological interpretation. No doubt Jesus was baptized by John, since all of the Synoptic Gospels narrate it (Matt 3:13-17; Mark 1:9-11; Luke 3:21-22). If John baptized Jesus, then it would have been assumed that John was Jesus' mentor and Jesus, one of John's subordinates. Undercutting the force of that assumption is the most logical explanation for the Baptist's avowal of subservience before "the one who is more powerful than I" (Mark 1:7), which Matthew accents by describing John's reluctance to baptize Jesus (Matt 3:14) and Luke (3:21) finesses by implying, without describing, Jesus' baptism by John. Another embarrassment for the early church lurked in Mark's clear statement (1:4-5) that John's baptism symbolized forgiveness of sins, of which the Judean masses have repented. If Jesus himself was without sin, which Mark never claims but many Christian traditions upheld quite early (see John 7:18; 8:46; 2 Cor 5:21; Heb 4:15; 7:26; 1 Pet 1:19; 2:22; 3:18; 1 John 3:5), then of what did he have to repent and be forgiven? That very question is articulated in an account of Jesus' baptism in the fragmentary *Gospel according to the Nazarenes,* known to us through St. Jerome (ca. 342–420): "But [Jesus] said to [his mother and brothers]: Wherein have I sinned that I should go and be baptized by him? Unless what I have said is ignorance [a sin of ignorance]." By contrast, Mark appears unflustered by such christological consternation: of all the Gospels, his is the most straightforward statement of Jesus' baptism by John.

Mark is deeply interested, however, in theological dimensions of Jesus' baptism, intimated by this anecdote's three-part structure: (1) Jesus' transit from Galilee to Judea, summarized in "biblical" phraseology (v. 9); (2) extraordinary events attending his emergence from the Jordan's waters (v. 10); and (3) a formula of divine approbation and acclamation (v. 11). Verse 9 creates a portentous mood with wording redolent of Scripture: "And it came to pass in those days" (KJV, *kai egeneto en ekeinais tais hēmerais*; see Exod 2:11; Luke 2:1). Mark sketches Jesus' journey to be baptized by John in the Jordan. Nazareth was a small agricultural village in the lower portion of Israel's northernmost region, Galilee (from the Hebrew word *galîl,* meaning "circle"), which geographically was part of southern Syria. The distance from Nazareth to the Lower Jordan bordering Judah (see 1:5) was more than sixty miles (see the map, "Palestine at the Time of Jesus").

Things heat up with Jesus' emergence from the waters of his baptism (v. 10). Mark introduces these events with his first of forty-two uses of the adverb *euthys,* which may be translated "at once," "immediately," or simply "then." (Typically it is rendered "straightway" in the KJV, which led to Mark's characterization in later centuries as "the straightway Gospel.") Then follows a dramatically balanced set of clauses: Jesus' ascent and vision (v. 10ab), matched by the Spirit's descent (v. 10c). The heavens ripped apart is an apocalyptic image, signifying divine disclosure (see Isa 64:1; Ezek 1:1; John 1:51; Acts 7:56; Rev 4:1; 11:19; 19:11); not accidentally, Mark returns to this symbol near the end of his Gospel (15:38). The other aspect of Jesus' vision is equally apocalyptic: the descent of God's spirit upon (literally, "into," *eis*) him (see above, on Mark 1:8; see also 1 Sam 10:6, 10; Rev 1:10; 4:2). The adverbial phrase *hōs peristeran*, "as a dove," probably does not refer to the Spirit's physical appearance (*sōmatikos*), feathers and all, as we find in Luke (3:22). In Mark this phrase modifies not the noun ("the Spirit"), but the descriptive participle ("descending on him"). In other words, the Spirit's descent was "fluttering" or "hovering," perhaps "brooding"—as God's spirit, or wind, swept across the waters of primordial chaos before creation (Gen 1:2; cf. *b. Hag.* 15a; Keck 1971).

In verse 11 the vision is complemented by an audition: a divine proclamation of the sort that rabbis of later centuries would style as a *bat-qôl*, "daughter of [the heavenly] voice" (a rumbling reverberation; see John 12:28-29): "You are my Son, the Beloved; with you I am well pleased." This announcement is addressed uniquely to Jesus, and Mark's readers are permitted to overhear it. Unlike the wording in Matthew (3:17: "*This* is my Son, the Beloved," emphasis added) or in John (1:32-34, the Baptist's testimony to what he saw and heard at Jesus' baptism), there is no suggestion in Mark that anyone other than Jesus heard his heavenly acclamation.

Like the Gospel's epigraph (1:2-3), this pronouncement blends different portions of Scripture (most likely from the LXX). Clearest is the coronation announcement of Psalm 2:7. By the Lord's decree, Israel's king is acknowledged as metaphorically sired by God: "You are my son." For the characterization of Jesus the Son (see 1:1) as "Beloved," one must reach beyond Psalm 2 to, perhaps, Genesis 22:2: therein, God identifies Isaac as Abraham's son, "your favored one" (NJPS). "With you I am well pleased" may be a muffled echo of Isaiah 42:1: the introduction to the first of Deutero-Isaiah's Servant Songs—"This is My servant, whom I uphold, / My chosen one, in whom I delight" (NJPS; see also Matt 12:18; 2 Pet 1:17). There is some evidence to support the theory that, even before the Christian era, some Jews interpreted both Psalm 2 and 2 Samuel 7 (Nathan's oracle to David) as messianic (Juel 1988, 59-88). Although the Evangelist does not expressly tie that knot in 1:9-11, there is little doubt that whoever wrote Mark 1:1, with its confession of Jesus as Christ, recognized in his baptism an unusual coronation: a muted revelation.

◊ ◊ ◊ ◊

Already we have observed Mark's compression of much theological reflection within a tight compass. Another instance of the Evangelist's dexterity is discernible in the narration of Jesus' baptism, in which Mark coordinates God, Jesus, and the Spirit. Of these three, God's spirit, the spirit of holiness, appears the least developed throughout this Gospel: after 1:12 the Holy Spirit will be mentioned by name only at Mark 3:29; 12:36; and 13:11. That does not mean, however, that the donation of the Spirit at Jesus' baptism is a trivial element. Throughout this Gospel, Jesus will be depicted as battling unclean spirits of disease and the demonic (e.g., 1:23, 26-27; 5:2, 8, 13; 9:17, 20, 25). Jesus' triumph over these forces has its origin in his receipt of the Spirit at his baptism. Later Trinitarian theology develops the interconnections and their implications among the three figures in play at Mark 1:10-11—God, God's Christ, and God's spirit—by articulating what Mark only implies: that God is properly understood only in relationship with the Son baptized by the Father's spirit (cf. 1:1; see Black 2010).

The most salient thing we learn from this passage about God is that, in Mark's view, God acknowledges—with a dramatically apocalyptic demonstration—the most intimate, familial relationship with Jesus (a theme that resurfaces in the story of Jesus' transfiguration: 9:2-8). This aspect merges with Mark's Christology, whose presentation in 1:9-11 is as complex as it is subtle. By quoting a royal psalm, then collapsing it into clipped paraphrase of resonant passages from Genesis and Isaiah, Mark suggests an extraordinary amount about Jesus in a remarkably veiled manner. At his baptism, Jesus' true identity is disclosed—though only to himself and to the reader—as Israel's anointed king (Ps 2:7), God's elect, spiritually endowed servant (Isa 42:1), as beloved yet susceptible of suffering as that servant (Isa 53) and of sacrifice as Isaac was for Abraham (Gen 22:2). At the baptism Mark renders a cameo of his full portrait of Jesus, which will emerge throughout the rest of the Gospel (see Mansfield 1987, 15-44). That no one knows this but Jesus and the discerning reader is altogether consonant with a Messiah who will shroud his true identity in secrecy (3:11-12), whose mysterious kingdom is perceptible only to those given grace by God to recognize it (4:9-12).

Jesus' Temptation in the Wilderness (1:12-13)

Those who recall its counterparts in Matthew (4:1-11) and Luke (4:1-13), to say nothing of its romanticizing by such modern novelists as Nikos Kazantzakis (1960, 247-64), may feel let down by Mark's narration of **Jesus' temptation in the wilderness (1:12-13)**. Like much in the Second Gospel, the account could hardly be terser—all the more reason, therefore, to attend closely to those details that Mark does provide (see also Gibson 1994).

"Immediately" (*euthys*) the scene shifts from the Jordan's waters to a nameless wilderness. Mark allows neither Jesus nor the reader to bask in the warm assurance of the *bat-qôl* in 1:11. *At once* Jesus is forcefully pitched, thrown out (*ekballei*), into the desert, a symbolic site for arduous testing (1 Sam 22:4; 23:29; 24:1, 22; see above, on 1:4). The instigator for this trial is the same Spirit that has descended on Jesus in his baptismal waters. Unlike Matthew and Luke, Mark leaves unspecified the nature of Jesus' temptations. Their agent, however, is the Satan, a figure that by Mark's time had evolved from terrestrial adversaries (1 Sam 29:4; 1 Kgs 5:4; Ps 109:6), to a prosecutorial maligner on God's celestial cabinet (Job 1–2), to a malevolent seducer of Israel's royalty (1 Chr 21:1). In the OT apocrypha and pseudepigrapha, much of which was composed in the era between the biblical testaments, the figure of Satan (known also by other names, such as Asmodeus or Mastema) flourishes under Persian influence as personified wickedness, a ringleader of demons (*Jub.* 23:29; *As. Mos.* 10:1). Exactly how Mark understands Satan is hard to determine, since this Gospel says so little about him. Within the immediate context of 1:9-11, complemented by the presence of ministering angels in 1:13, it is likely that Mark intends this vignette as another shaft of apocalyptic light into Jesus' ministry. The curtain of everyday Judean life is again drawn aside, exposing the principalities and powers with which Jesus has been thrown into battle: a contest to which Mark will subsequently refer (3:23, 26; 4:15; 8:33). Both Moses and Elijah also endured a trial lasting "forty days" on Horeb, the Lord's mount (Exod 34:28; 1 Kgs 19:8; cf. Mark 9:2-4); Elijah, too, was attended by angels (1 Kgs 19:5, 7; see also Ps 91:11-13).

Most mystifying in Mark 1:12-13 is Jesus' being "with the wild beasts." Exactly what the Evangelist intends by this is any-one's guess. The most obvious supposition is to align the beasts with Satan, as threats to which Jesus was exposed (Cranfield 1959, 59; Taylor 1981, 164). Less obvious, though not for that reason farfetched, is the possibility that Mark here alludes to the restoration of conditions in paradise before the fall (see Gen 1:28; 2:19-20; Ps 91:9-14; Isa 11:6-9; 65:17-25; Perkins 1995, 535). The clearest expression of such hope, replete with much of the *dramatis personae* of Mark 1:12-13, can be found in the pseudepigraphical *Testament of Naphtali* (ca. 105 B.C.E.): "The devil will flee from you; wild animals will be afraid of you, and the angels will stand by you" (8.4; see also *T. Benj.* 5.2; *T. Iss.* 7.7). Later some rabbis favored an equation never made in the book of Genesis, by identifying Satan with the serpent in the garden (*b. Sotah* 9b; *b. Sanh.* 29a). If Mark is traveling along this track—sketching Jesus as New Adam in an Eden under reconstruction—then the Evangelist could be using different words to express something like Paul's depiction of Christ as Last Adam, through whom all humanity will be revivified (Rom 5:12-21; 1 Cor 15:20-28; Guelich 1989, 38-40). Mark, however, is nowhere so explicit about this as Paul; neither does the Evangelist develop an Adamic Christology. The overall sense of Mark 1:12-13 is clear enough, though we shall never be able to pinpoint the meaning of all its details (see Gundry 1993, 54-62).

◊ ◊ ◊ ◊

Spirituality is an ambiguous term, sometimes understood as self-improvement through religious or other cultural practices. With the Spirit as propulsive agent of Jesus' prolonged struggle with Satan, Mark's understanding of spirituality assumes an aspect rougher, darker, and closer to the experience of the fourth-century Desert Fathers: "a kind of death of our own being, our own self," entailing liberation from "a world that is plunging to disaster" (Merton 1960, 18, 23; see also Minor 1996). This Gospel will not be the tender account of a kindly teacher roaming the Galilean calm. Here is a story of apocalyptic warfare, with this world a theater for cosmic combat between demons and angels, between a seductive Satan and God's anointed (J. M. Robinson 1982, 69-80). Observe that Mark does not end this tale with Matthew's defiant "Begone, Satan!" (4:10 Goodspeed) or with any assurance that Jesus' trials are over (Best 1965, 10). Mark's version of the temptation is left open-ended. There are in this Gospel other tests to be faced, other deserts to traverse. We have not seen the last of Satan (Garrett 1998, 51-88).

The baptism and temptation of Jesus in Mark are a diptych of light and dark, dramatizing the context within which Jesus' ministry in this Gospel will be played out. Unlike Matthew, for whom all the circumstances of Jesus' birth, baptism, and temptation have didactic value (see Matt 1:23; 3:15; 4:4, 7, 10), and unlike Luke, who implies that Jesus' triumph over initial temptation was part of his ministry (see Luke 3:23; 4:1-13), Mark intimates that baptism and temptation constitute a preparation for Jesus' ministry. Yet Mark 1:9-13 presents Jesus as a remarkably passive figure. Though he comes out of Galilee to the Jordan, the recurring emphasis in these paired tableaux is not on what Jesus does but on what is done to him: baptism by John, receipt of the Spirit, acclamation by heavenly voice, propulsion by the Spirit, temptation by Satan, and ministry from angels. Along this way the reader is hurled into a maelstrom of eschatological conflict, following one who has come that is mightier than John. Metaphorically, Mark's readers are being "baptized with the Holy Spirit" (1:8; cf. 10:38-39) and are beginning to take the measure of what that means, for good and ill.

TRANSITION: THE BEGINNING OF JESUS' MINISTRY (1:14-15)

There is considerable disagreement whether Mark intends for 1:14-15 to conclude the material preceding or to introduce the next major section of his narrative (Keck 1966). Good arguments can be made for both interpretations. On the one hand, these verses refer to key figures (John, Jesus) or ideas ("the good news," repentance) that introduced 1:1-13. On the other, with 1:14-15 Jesus takes center stage, announcing a climactic fulfillment that projects the reader into representative aspects of his ministry, to which Mark will immediately turn. Since 1:14-15 so clearly functions in both respects, it is pedantic to separate them. This is a transitional passage, which pivots, Janus-like, both backward and forward (van Iersel 1998, 104-8). It is not, for that reason, to be tossed aside as mere narrative glue. Throughout his Gospel, Mark formulates such summary reports for three tightly interwoven reasons: to build bridges from one anecdote to another, to summarize the pith of Jesus' activity, and to point up important theological issues or topics (e.g., 1:21-22, 32-34; 3:11-12).

Mark 1:14-15 is an unusually fertile summary report, bearing multiple seeds that will flower in this Gospel. First to be noted is a designation of time: "after John was handed over" (AT). The passive infinitive *paradothēnai* is a word of many nuances, all of which become manifest as this Gospel unfolds. In 1:14 it is often rendered "arrested" (RSV, NRSV, REB), alluding to the gruesome tale of the Baptizer's arrest and execution to come (Mark 6:14-29). Idiomatically, the word can refer to the maturation or ripening of grain (4:29). The sense of legal disposition, from one authority to another, appears in Mark's account of Jesus' appearance before Pilate (15:1, 10, 15). Most often in Mark, the term connotes betrayal (3:19; 7:13; 9:31; 10:33; 13:9, 11, 12; 14:10, 11, 18, 21, 41, 42, 44). Mark 1:14 sounds a powerful, dissonant chord in this Gospel: the inevitable handing over of Jesus, of those who follow him, and—in this case—of the one who preceded him. As in modern English, there are many ways in Koine Greek to express this idea of arrest; it is no accident that in 1:14

Mark has opted for a locution emphasizing John's passivity at the hands of his captors, which chimes with the passivity of Jesus observed in 1:9-13. Mark continues to align Jesus with John even while he differentiates them, as well as to suggest that the hidden hand guiding human affairs actually belongs to God.

Next, a designation of place: "Jesus came to [the region of] Galilee." Unlike Matthew (4:12-17), Mark does not draw on Isaiah 9:1-2 to characterize "Galilee of the nations," thus foreshadowing the breakout of Jesus' ministry among Gentiles; nevertheless, Mark sets the stage for such international incursions to come (see, e.g., 3:7-12; 5:1-20; 7:1-31). Historically, these encounters were likely: Galilee was a crossroads for major trade routes linking Syria, Egypt, Jerusalem, and Palestinian ports. In Mark the Messiah begins his work not in Judea, even less in the Holy City, Jerusalem, but instead in Galilee: the area from which he came (1:9), the outlying territory where Jews and Gentiles were cheek by jowl and to which, at this Gospel's end (16:7), Jesus' followers are commanded to return (Freyne 1980, 257-343).

The term with which the Evangelist epitomizes Jesus' preaching is "the good news" or "the gospel" (v. 14), the same shorthand adopted in Mark's first verse. Here, as there, to euangelion carries both religious and political connotations of a sovereign reordering (Isa 40:9; 52:7; 61:1) in which Mark's readers are summoned to place their faith, or trust (pisteuein, v. 15). The good news Jesus preaches is that "of God" (v. 14), a significant reminder that, as focused on Jesus as Mark indisputably is, christology has an irreducibly theological basis (Boring 1999; Malbon 2009). In hindsight, the reader better understands the gospel that Mark claims is beginning (1:1): it is God's presence and restorative power, mediated by Jesus himself.

A thumbnail description of the gospel's content is offered in Mark 1:15, reasserting a pattern of time and place introduced in 1:14. This time, however, is apocalyptic; this place, eschatological. Unlike chronos, measured by calendar or clock, kairos in biblical literature refers to "critical time" or "opportune season": not the quotidian everyday, but D-Day; not just any hour, but the time come for a mother's deliverance (cf. Luke 1:57; 2:6; see also Mark

11:13; 12:2; Ezek 7:12; Dan 7:22; 12:4, 9; Gal 4:4; Eph 1:10; 1 Pet 1:11; Rev 1:3). Albeit a metaphor derived from the world of oriental potentates (see Duling 1992), "the kingdom of God" (*hē basileia tou theou*; or *tōn ouranōn*, "of heaven") does not intend any one-for-one correlation of God's will with earthly monarchies. Rooted in Jewish apocalypticism (e.g., *1 En.* 10:1–11:12; 25:3-5; 62–63; *As. Mos.* 10:1-10; esp. *Pss. Sol.* 17:3), "the kingdom of God" refers to God's universal dominion over mortal life and human monarchies. In God's reign, justice is and will be done; those now faithful to God while socially marginalized or persecuted will ultimately be vindicated. Central in Jesus' teaching, the phrase "the kingdom of God" appears in all of the earliest Gospel traditions: Mark, Q, sources unique to Matthew and Luke, and (briefly) John (see Chilton 1984). This image is critical in Mark's theology to describe an eschatological power, invading historical time and space, which is mysteriously active in Jesus himself (see also 4:10-12; 9:1; 10:14-15, 23-25; 14:25). Because humans do not naturally bend themselves to God's sovereignty (10:15, 23), entrusting oneself to the kingdom—better, "God's kingship"—requires repentance, the turning or revolution of one's thoughts and actions (1:14). Like the Synoptic tradition generally (Luke 7:18-23 = Matt 11:2-6; Luke 7:28 = Matt 11:11; Luke 11:20 = Matt 12:18; Mark 4:26-32; Luke 7:20-21; 16:16), Mark 1:15 suggests that the kingdom of God intersects with all times, yet in this life cannot be confined to any time (see Guelich 1989, 44). The first two verbs in verse 15 (*peplērōtai*, "is fulfilled"; *ēngiken*, "is at hand") are conjugated in the perfect tense, which in Greek suggests something that has happened in the past (4:11) with present or future consequences (9:1; 15:43). Even though the phrase "kingdom of God" never appears in the OT, God's transcendent sovereignty is an ancient Israelite conviction: because God *already* rules, God *will* rule (Hooker 1991, 55-58). The gospel of God is Jesus' summons—within Galilee and to Mark's readers—to repentance and faith, along the horizon of the kingdom's birth pangs and its heralds' afflictions (Schweizer 1970, 45-47).

Capped by the strategically placed narrative summary in 1:14-15, Mark's prologue interweaves this Gospel's many melodies with impressive economy and structural elegance (Boring 1990). Here is "the good news of God" (v. 14): the coming of God's Son (v. 1), the beloved one in whom God is well pleased (v. 11). The Spirit that hurls Jesus into the wilderness (v. 12), after descending on him at his baptism (v. 10), is the same with which, John claims, Jesus himself will baptize: God's holy spirit (v. 8). "The way of the Lord" to which the Gospel's epigraph testifies (v. 3), the highway prophesied by Isaiah (v. 2) and Elijah and recalled by John the Baptist (vv. 4, 6), is the same path on which the God of Jewish Scripture first set his chosen people Israel.

Equally clear to Mark's reader is the importance of Jesus of Nazareth, the figure on whom this Gospel will concentrate. Jesus and no other (vv. 7-8) is the Christ, God's anointed agent (v. 1) and cherished Son (v. 11), the herald par excellence of God's good news (vv. 14-15). The obscure wording in verse 1 is pregnant with theological significance: for Mark, the gospel is, simultaneously, what Jesus begins to preach (v. 14) and what readers begin to perceive in Jesus himself. "Jesus both announces the good news and is himself the good news" (Hoskyns and Davey 1981, 88). Thus, Christology and theology are inseparable and mutually interpreting: Mark's readers understand Jesus through his presentation of God; one understands God through his acclamation of Jesus.

The apocalyptic cast of Mark 1:1-15 foreshadows the rest of the Gospel. Though Mark's readers over nineteen centuries may forget the fact, "Christ" or "Messiah," a fundamental description of Jesus in the Second Gospel (1:1; 8:29; 9:41; 14:61; 15:32), is an important image in Jewish eschatological belief before and after the NT era (11QMelch 18; 2 Bar. 29:2–30:1; 39:7; 72:2; 4 Ezra 12:32; m. Ber. 1:5; m. Sotah 9:15; y. Ta^can 68d). The Spirit's advent (Mark 1:8) and the heaven's rending (1:10) are, as noted, venerable apocalyptic motifs in OT prophecy (e.g., Ezek 1:1; Joel 2:28-32). Equally apocalyptic in tenor are satanic trials and angelic ministrations (Mark 1:12-13; cf. Dan 3:25, 28; Jub. 10:22-23; 23:29; 1 En. 100:5; 1QM 13:10), the fulfillment of the *kairos,* and the in-breaking of God's kingdom (Mark 1:15; cf. Rev 1:3; *As. Mos.* 10:1, 3). In Mark repentance and faith (1:4, 15) are not commendations of generally religious behavior; they are situation-specific, apt responses in a time of crisis. If Mark's reader is better positioned than most of the Gospel's characters to hear and recognize the sounding of an alarm, that recognition is due to the fact that, by reading the Gospel's prologue, the reader has been made privy to an array of information and its proper interpretation unknown by the ensuing drama's figures, save Jesus himself.

JESUS' AUTHORITY, RESISTED BY AUTHORITIES (1:16–3:6)

Mark's first main section is anticipated in 1:14-15: the summary statement of Jesus' appearance in Galilee, announcing the good news of God's kingdom. That two-verse segment is a hinge on which a critical turn of the narrative swings. Whereas 1:1-13 (plus the overlapping vv. 14-15) sets the stage, introduces key figures, and focuses many of the Gospel's themes, the material in 1:16-45 offers the reader representative glimpses of Jesus' early ministry and initial reactions to it. Among those responses is demonic resistance (vv. 24, 39), foreshadowed by Satan in 1:13. In 2:1–3:6 that opposition intensifies and becomes evident even among recognizable members of Galilee's religious circle, the scribes (2:6, 16) and the Pharisees (2:16, 18, 24; 3:6).

Breakthrough in Galilee (1:16-45)

On a first reading the pericopae (passages) assembled in 1:16-45 may seem "a day in the life of the Messiah," haphazardly recounted: here a healing, there a teaching, punctuated by exchanges with disciples, demons, and sick people. Although Mark probably inherited these "specimen scenes" (Anderson 1976, 93) from oral traditions, their arrangement is not as higgledy-piggledy as may first appear. Mark 1:16-20 describes the summons of the first members of the Twelve, the inner circle of Jesus' disciples, thus aligning them with Jesus himself in 1:14-15. At the other end of this subsection, 1:40-45, motifs of tension (vv. 40, 41, 43) and conflict (vv. 42, 44-45) loom large, casting a shadow that will grow darker in the subsequent subsection, 2:1–3:6. Legends involving the earliest members of Jesus' entourage (vv. 16-20, 29-31, 35-39) are interspersed among dramatic tales of healing (vv. 21-28, 32-34, 40-45). At approximately the halfway point, we find a brief tale in which alternating themes of training the disciples and curing the sick converge (vv. 29-31). Throughout 1:16-45 the Evangelist delicately conflates or contrasts a broad range of issues: leading and following, healing and teaching, unclean spirits and restorative cleanliness, the sequestration and eruption of knowledge, proximity and distance. The fact that Mark so subtly juxtaposes these elements is a testimony to his skill as a narrative theologian.

Jesus' Calling of His Disciples (1:16-20)

All of the Gospels recount different, stylized stories of **Jesus' calling of his disciples** (cf. Luke 5:1-11; John 1:35-51). In substance and comparative brevity, Matthew's account (4:18-22) is most like Mark's (1:16-20), which is sparest of all.

The Sea of Galilee was also known by many other names in antiquity: "the sea of Chinnereth" (Num 34:11; Josh 12:3), "the lake of Genenesar[itis]" (*J.W.* 2.573; 3.515-16; *Ant.* 5.84; 18:28, 36), "the lake of Gennesar[et]" (*Nat.* 5.71; 1 Macc 11:67; Luke 5:1), and "the lake of Tiberias" (*J.W.* 3.57; 4.456; cf. John 6:1; 21:1). Although Mark and Matthew speak of it as a "sea" (*thalassa*), "lake" (*limnē*) is a more accurate description of the Galilee: a temperate, freshwater lake forming part of the Jordan Valley rift that separated Galilee from the non-Jewish regions of Gaulanitis and Decapolis. Plentifully stocked with scores of different species of fish, the Galilee was the center of a considerable fishing industry for such lakefront towns as Bethsaida (Mark 6:45; 8:22) and Tarichaeae (*Geogr.* 16.2; *Nat.* 5.15, 71; *J.W.* 3.506-8). It is within that commercial context that one should read Mark 1:16-20: the two pairs of brothers are professional fishers. This is especially obvious in the case of Zebedee's sons: their circular nets, boat, and hired men (vv. 19-20) denote a business concern within the managerial class.

There is no suggestion whatever that any of these fishermen have previously met or heard about Jesus. To assume such enervates the power of the story as Mark tells it: at Jesus' sheer command, "immediately" (*euthys: ad loc.* 1:12), the professionals drop everything and go. This is no skylarking, as Mark's language indicates: Simon and Andrew leave their nets behind and "follow" (*ēkolouthēsan*) him. This is Mark's first use of a term that becomes synonymous with being a disciple of Jesus (2:14, 15; 6:1; 8:34; 10:21, 28, 32, 52; 15:41), an allegiance that involves the missionary responsibility to "fish for people" (1:17). So, too, do James and John leave behind their father (1:20). Mark did not have to explain to his audience what that implied. In a setting where poverty was prevalent (Freyne 1988, 135-75), James and John's precipitate departure from their business would jeopardize their family's livelihood and risk dissolution of the household: the basic social institution in which ancient Mediterranean economy was embedded. By contrast, Shaphat and his wife at least received a good-bye kiss from Elisha when their son left the family farm to take up Elijah's mantle and answer his mentor's call (1 Kgs 19:19-21).

Mark's Gospel is a story not only about Jesus, but also about those who follow him (Best 1981). It is no wonder, therefore, that the first of Jesus' disciples should be introduced so early. The surprises arise in the Evangelist's manner of narration. Mark 1:16-20 quietly pivots around the related questions of authority and ultimate obedience. Unlike other rabbis, sought out by would-be adherents who became disciples only after a considerable period of training, Jesus here and there throughout this Gospel assumes complete initiative in summoning his disciples. As instantly as the call is issued, so also is it accepted. As God's kingdom breaks in (1:15), previous patterns of life are reconfigured; families are dissolved without warning. The pain of that rupture, muted in 1:16-20, becomes vivid later in Mark (10:28-31; 13:12). Jesus will promise Peter that things better and worse await (10:28-31; 13:9-11, 13). In 1:16-20 the reader begins to understand that repentance involves casting off conventional responsibilities, that trust in the gospel implies worldly insecurity, that discipleship to Jesus carries a price (Barton 1994, 23-67).

The Healing of a Man with an Unclean Spirit (1:21-28)

Capernaum is the site for **the healing of a man with an unclean spirit (1:21-28)**. Known today among Arabs of the region as Tell Hum, *Kephar Naḥûm* (Nahum's Village) was a town on the northwest shore of the Sea of Galilee (*J. W.* 3.10.8). Among the structures unearthed across a century of archaeological exploration are dwellings that include a house associated with Simon (see below, 1:29-31), an octagonal church dating to the mid-fifth century C.E., and two synagogues, variously dated. Like Mark, the other Gospels refer to Jesus' activity in a Capernaum synagogue (Matt 12:9-14; Luke 4:31-37). The synagogue was one of Judaism's most vital institutions (L. I. Levine 2000, 124-59), serving as a Jewish community center (*Ant.* 14.235, 259-61) and a place for judicial and penal proceedings (Mark 13:9; Acts 22:19). The synagogue's principal importance, however, was as a religious institution. After the fall of the second (Herodian) temple in 70 C.E., religious activities in the synagogue became more extensive. During the first century, synagogue worship was apparently limited to holidays (such as New Moon and Sukkoth) and the Sabbath (Mark 1:21). Such Sabbath worship in the synagogue included reading of the Torah (*Ag. Ap.* 2.175; Philo, *Hypothetica* 7.12; Acts 15:21) and from the Prophets (*Haftarah*: Luke 4:17-19; Acts 13:15; cf. *b. Meg.* 3.1-9), sermons (*Contempl. Life* 28; *Mos.* 2.215; *Hypothetica* 7.13; Luke 4:20-21; Acts 13:15), and instruction (*Mos.* 2.216; *Spec. Laws* 2.62-63; *Ant.* 16.43). As Mark 1:21-28 opens, it is the latter—serious study in the synagogue on the Sabbath—in which we find Jesus and his interlocutors engaged.

With the chosen four (1:16-20) implicitly in tow, "they enter into Capernaum." (The verb is conjugated in the "historical present," vividly describing a past action with the present tense: Mark's signature style [N. Turner 1993, 225-26]). "Right away" (*euthys*: omitted by the NRSV) in the synagogue he taught (perhaps "he began to teach": an inceptive connotation of the imperfect tense). Characteristically (2:13; 6:2, 6b, 30, 34; 10:1; 14:49), Mark portrays Jesus as teacher without describing the content of that teaching. The Evangelist is interested in the *effect* of Jesus' teaching on its auditors: here, for the first but hardly the last time in this Gospel, they are bowled over (see also 1:27; 2:12; 5:20, 42; 6:2; 7:37; 11:18; 12:17). The reason for their astonishment is the "authority" or "power" (*hē exousia*) implicit in Jesus' teaching, lacking in that of "the scribes." Here lies irony: "the scribes" (*hoi grammateis*) were recognized among the synagogue's leaders. To them were entrusted many responsibilities, including record keeping and handling of correspondence, maintenance of archives, and perhaps also scholarship (Levine 2000, 409). Jesus commands with consummate authority, as the end of this pericope will underline (1:27). It is the difference between charisma and custodianship.

A challenge to Jesus' authority erupts immediately (*euthys*) and terrifyingly: "in their synagogue, a man with an unclean spirit" (v. 23). In the parlance of that time, this person is a demoniac (see 3:22, 30; 5:2, 15-18); Mark's reference to his unclean spirit reminds us, by contrast, of descent of the Holy Spirit (v. 10), who has driven the Son of God into earlier battle with Satan (vv. 11-13). Thus, in Capernaum there is a renewed, apocalyptic skirmish with demonic forces, as suggested by the challenger's defensive shriek: "What have you to do with *us* [cf. 1 Kgs 17:18]? Have you come to destroy *us*?" (Mark 1:24, emphasis added; see also 5:9 *ad loc.*). Additional evidence of struggle lies in the challenger's manipulative knowledge of identity and deployment of names: "Jesus, Nazarene—I know who you are, the Holy One of God" (v. 24 AT). In antiquity knowledge of one's name or identity was thought to exert power over that one (Gen 2:19-20; 32:27-29; Exod 3:13-15; Judg 13:17-18; see

Burkill 1963, 72-80). By dressing him down (*epetimēsen*) and muzzling him (*phimōthēti*), Jesus exerts his superior power (Mark 1:25), in accordance with ancient methods of exorcism (see *Ant.* 8.46-48). Jesus' command that the demon leave its victim is fulfilled; the screams and convulsions attending this exorcism tint the spectacle with violence, reminding one of the awesome powers in combat (1:25-26; see also 9:25-26). At this point in ancient tales of healing, one expects to find acknowledgment of the therapy's effectiveness (Theissen 1983, 47-80). So it is in Mark, though the confirmation is of an unusual sort. The acknowledgment comes not from the one healed, but from flabbergasted spectators, who, like a Greek chorus, offer quarrelsome commentary on what has just happened: "What is this? A new teaching—with authority [*exousia*]—even the Unclean he commands—and they obey him" (v. 27 AT). (As the text and footnote of the NRSV indicate, it is impossible to know with certainty how to punctuate these clauses.) Interestingly, this tale ends on precisely the notes with which it opened: now, however, the Galilean world—and the world of Mark's readers—has a clearer view of that authority with which Jesus teaches (see v. 22). It is not that of the scribes; it is *kainē* (new): not merely novel, but different, fresh, and indeed superior (see 2:21-22). In hyperbolic fashion that by now appears typically Markan (see 1:5, 45; 3:7-10), Jesus' fame sweeps beyond a single synagogue, stretching the breadth of the Galilean countryside (v. 28).

Mark 1:21-28 is the first of this Gospel's four tales of exorcism (see also 5:1-20; 7:24-30; 9:14-29). Whatever else one may say of Mark's picture of Jesus, this Nazarene is an exorcist. Modern psychiatrists and social scientists have formulated intriguing theories about the political forces that bear on experiences of demon possession: especially among marginalized persons subjected to the terrors of colonial oppression, reported cases of schizophrenia and other mental illness occur more frequently than normal (Waetjen 1989). Mark's Gospel, like other

NT writings, offers the reader an alternative mythic structure: this world is an arena of cosmic contest, in which powers clean and unclean wage war (see Twelftree 2007). Having endured his own satanic trials (1:12-13), Jesus in Capernaum prevails over demons that very clearly recognize their enemy for who he is: the Holy One of God (1:23-24). It is not that Mark denies earthly powers in favor of some unreal world of dreams and nightmares. Rather, this Gospel invites its readers to acknowledge a hidden, insidious world of evil that can break out even within positive institutions like the synagogue. As we have seen in Mark's prologue (1:1-15), so also here: Jesus is a healer—and more. At the vanguard of God's in-breaking kingdom, he is routing demonic forces.

That apocalyptic role merges into Jesus' *teaching*, whose superior authority the Evangelist underlines at this pericope's beginning and end (1:21-22, 27; see Robbins 1984, 75-123). Others, like John the Baptist, preach (1:4); with the sole exception of 6:30, however, in Mark the only legitimate teacher is Jesus (1:21-22; 4:1-2, 38; 5:35; 6:34; 8:31; 9:17, 31, 38; 10:17, 20, 35; 11:17-18; 12:14, 19, 32; 13:1; 14:14, 49). The reason is clear: Jesus teaches with unique *authority*, or power, whose divine source the reader knows from the circumstances attending Jesus' baptism (1:9-11). By placing 1:21-28 beside 1:16-20, and by situating both after 1:14-15, Mark encourages readers to perceive the authority with which Jesus speaks and acts as one and the same, exuded by the one through whom God's kingdom has drawn near. "His word is action" (Schweizer 1970, 51).

The juxtaposition of these passages—Mark 1:14-15, 1:16-20, 21-28—demonstrates something else: forceful though he is, Jesus does not compel universal obedience. Commanded by Jesus, four fishermen drop their nets. Capernaum's unclean spirit meets its match. Nowhere, however, does Mark indicate that the witnesses to this exorcism trusted Jesus or his teaching. In fact, the Evangelist relates their dumbfounded disagreement (*suzētein*: "What is this?" v. 27). Amazement is no more tantamount to faith than celebrity is to obedience (v. 28). Only those who repent and trust can appropriate the gospel (v. 15).

The Healings at Simon's House (1:29-31)

The healings at Simon's house offer a glimpse into Jesus' itinerant ministry. Primarily on the basis of Greek and Roman graffiti on the walls of its largest room, a miserable dwelling excavated in Capernaum's Insula Sacra has been identified as the house of Simon Peter. While that cannot be proved beyond the shadow of doubt, the structure does show evidence of having later been renovated to serve as a meeting place for Christians, who from the first century onward associated it with Simon (Finegan 1992, 107-10). Paul corroborates Mark's assumption that Simon (or "Cephas," the Aramaic form of the nickname "Peter") was married (1 Cor 9:5).

In his essay *Concerning the Interrogation of the Sick*, Rufus of Ephesus, a Roman medical writer (ca. 110–180), assumes that high fever is not an indication of disease but an ailment itself, like epilepsy, of which memory loss and other diagnostic clues are symptomatic. Likewise, Mark 1:30 suggests that feverishness is an ailment that has driven Peter's mother-in-law to her bed. Most interesting in Mark's description of her healing is its simplicity: the fever departs after Jesus merely takes her by the hand and lifts her up (a technique of later rabbinic healing: *b. Ber.* 5b). This is a far cry from the magical remedy of quartan fever (feverish chills with paroxysms occurring every three or four days), described in Pliny's *Natural History* (28.11): wrapping a caterpillar in linen, tied down by a thrice-knotted thread. Jesus' gesture is repeated in other healings narrated by Mark (5:41; 9:27). In all these there may be the faintest whisper of Jesus' own "lifting up": the same verb, *egeirō*, appears in the announcement of his resurrection (16:6). As in 1:21-28, some confirmation of this woman's cure is expected; that which Mark supplies in 1:31 is suggestive: "She began to wait on [*diēkonei*] them" (AT). The basic meaning of this word and its cognates is menial service, often at table (see Matt 22:13; John 2:5, 9). Lest one jump to the conclusion that Mark has bought into conventional assumptions about "women's work," one should recall that the same verb is used to describe the angels' ministry to Jesus during his wilderness temptation (1:13). Later in Mark, true greatness will be ascribed to a servant (*diakonos*: 9:35; 10:43); many female disciples of Jesus, watching his death by crucifixion, are remembered for having ministered (*diēkonoun*) to him while in Galilee and Jerusalem (15:41). Attendance to the needs of Jesus and his followers—here, by implication (see 1:21), on the Sabbath—is no small thing (9:41). That partly explains why the metaphor of service, *diakonia*, so quickly slid into the early church's repertoire of descriptions of Christian ministry (Acts 21:19; Rom 11:13; 1 Cor 12:5; Eph 4:12; Col 4:17; Heb 1:14; Rev 2:19; see J. N. Collins 1990).

Another Summary Report (1:32-34)

Mark 1:32-34 is another summary report (see above, 1:14-15), providing transition to the next day of Jesus' ministry while at the same time recapitulating, with elaboration, his Capernaum ministry to this point. At sundown on Saturday evening, Sabbath restrictions would be lifted (cf. 1:21; *m. Šabb.* 7.2): the lid is off, and "the whole city" has now gathered at the door (presumably, of Simon's house). The word Mark uses for this assemblage, *episynagō* (v. 33), catches the eye: Is there a suggestion that Jesus' temporary residence is now competing with the *synagogē* in which yesterday he cast out an unclean spirit? At any rate, those gathering seek more of the same: they bear to him, literally, "all those who have it bad and are demonized" (v. 32). If anything, Jesus' power is magnified: "He cured many who had it bad with all kinds of diseases, and cast out many demons" (v. 34a AT). While the quest of "the whole city" for healing exemplifies Mark's tendency to exaggerate (1:5, 32, 37), it also intimates a universal yearning for restoration that characterizes Jesus' ministry (Marcus 2000, 200-201).

One might skate over 1:34b; it is reminiscent of Jesus' silencing of the unclean spirit in 1:25. What appeared there as an important demonstration of Jesus' superior power in a contest of will has a different resonance—at once more general and more mysterious—at this pericope's end. "And he would not permit the demons to speak, because they knew [or 'recognized'] him." This is Mark's first, clearest injunction of silence about Jesus' identity. Some scribal traditions, probably following the lead of Luke 4:41b (cf. Matt 12:16), add wording to Mark 1:34b in order to sharpen the point: "because they knew him to be [the] Christ." Although our earliest and best manuscripts do not contain these additional words, the scribes who added them are sniffing a trail that Mark will lay down in 3:11-12 and circuitously develop elsewhere (see 1:44; 5:43; 7:36; 8:30; 9:9, 30). Such prohibitions have been cumulatively assembled in support of an alleged Markan construct, the so-called messianic secret (following Wrede 1971, esp. 115-49). In our most reliable manuscripts of Mark 1:34, however, no reference is made to speaking of Jesus as Christ, much less of its suppression. "*Messianic se-crecy*" as such may be observable elsewhere in Mark, but interpretive caution is best served by careful examination of the Gospel's evidence on a case-by-case basis (W. C. Robinson 1973). There is no doubt that Jesus' struggle with the demons in Mark is waged, not only over their hostile occupation of poor unfortunates, but also over their (importunate?) recognition of *him*. On that muffled note this pericope ends. Why it does so is quite mysterious.

The anecdotes of Jesus' healings in 1:29-34 provide more than mere adhesion between the seams of Mark's narrative. The Evangelist uses such passages to disclose subtle but important details. For instance, Mark extends Jesus' power as an exorcist into other forms of healing: a matter of great interest in antiquity, as exemplified by the cult of Asclepius (Klauck 2000, 154-68). Another point: not until 1:29-30 do we learn two significant things about Simon. First, he is prosperous enough to own a house; second, if he has a mother-in-law, then he also has a wife. No less than the Zebedee brothers (1:19-20), Simon is a man of substance, perhaps with family obligations. One begins to infer some of the social consequences of his and brother Andrew's decision to leave their nets and follow Jesus in vagabond ministry.

We should recall this passage when, later in Mark (10:28), Peter cries to Jesus, "Look—we left behind everything and have followed you" (AT). Peter is not exaggerating. His discipleship, like others', carries considerable cost.

Peter's mother-in-law is the first woman to appear on the Markan stage. Her healing by Jesus inaugurates a long series of episodes in this Gospel, which reveals Jesus' sympathy for the needs and circumstances of women (5:21-43; 7:24-30; 10:2-12; 12:41-44; 13:17; 14:3-9). Simon's mother-in-law both receives and reciprocates Jesus' ministry (1:31), thus anticipating other women who will demonstrate persistence in faith (7:26-29), selfless piety (12:42-44), memorable devotion (14:6-9), and steadfast service to Jesus (15:40-41). Most of these women are nameless, save Mary Magdalene, Mary the mother of James and Joses, and Salome (15:40). All are noteworthy for the quality of their faith and integrity of their deeds, thus displaying authentic discipleship (cf. 9:42-50; Kinukawa 1994; Miller 2004, 17-30).

Mark ends this summary statement on the enigmatic note that Jesus silenced the demons "because they knew him" (1:34b). The unclean spirits persist in their supernatural recognition of their archenemy, a perception that Mark's readers share only because we who have read its prologue (1:1, 11) know what Jesus knows. Capernaum's question—"What is this?" (1:27)—will eventually yield to the disciples' more pointed query: "Who then is this?" (4:41). In this Gospel Jesus is in no hurry to answer that question and, indeed, proves insistent that his identity not be disclosed until the time is right. Why? What is the proper time? Such things remain temporarily hidden in Mark because concealment is the necessary correlate of that mysterious revelation to which apocalypticism (literally, "uncovering of the head") refers (Burkill 1963, 62-85).

Return to the Desert (1:35-39)

Mark 1:35-39 is concentrated on Jesus' return to the desert, in an attempt to withdraw from the rigors of his teaching and healing. The Evangelist's stage setting is characteristically verbose

(N. Turner 1993, 224-25): "In the morning, while it was still very dark" (v. 35). Mark emphasizes Jesus' retreat: "He went out and got away" (AT). His destination is important: "a deserted place." As in 1:3-4, 12-13, the desert conjures up many biblical images, most of them negative: that which is barren and waterless, therefore uninhabited (Mark 8:4), desolate (Acts 1:20; 8:26; Gal 4:27), perilous (2 Cor 11:26), and inhospitable (Heb 11:38), the abode of demons (Luke 8:29). Such a locale, this time selected by Jesus (Mark 1:35; cf. 1:12), stands over against Galilee's widespread gossip and madding crowds (1:28-33). Possibly Mark suggests another point of contrast by what Jesus chooses to do while in the wilderness: he prays, the first such characterization of Jesus in this Gospel (6:46; 14:32-39; see also 11:25; 13:18). As in English, many Greek verbs connote prayer. The one used here, *proseucheto*, suggests offering up prayers for something, the extension of oneself to God. What Jesus does not do is muster a revolutionary movement, which, according to Josephus, the leaders of some messianic movements did in the desert (*J.W.* 2.259, 261; 6.351; 7.438; see also Acts 21:38), probably in hope of fulfilling prophetic promises (Isa 40:3; Jer 31:2; Ezek 34:25; Hos 2:16).

With the appearance of "Simon and his companions" (v. 36), Mark whispers for the first time a theme that will grow louder and more insistent in this Gospel: the distance between Jesus and his closest followers. Jesus has opted for solitude; Simon and the others intrude. Mark says that they "relentlessly sought" or "hunted [him] down" (*katediōxen*). While the verb may suggest an innocent or positive nuance, usually it connotes hostile pursuit. (The root verb, *diōkō*, often suggests persecution or harassment; see, for instance, Matt 5:11-12, 44; 10:23; BDAG 254, 516). After finding him, Simon and the posse tell Jesus, "Everyone is searching for (*zētousin*) you" (v. 37). Though not so obviously here, this verb acquires sinister overtones as the Gospel unfolds: practically everyone in Mark who is "searching for" Jesus does so with misguided or malicious intent (3:32; 8:11-12; 11:18; 12:12; 14:1, 11, 55; cf. 16:6). Jesus' response to Simon seems distant: rather than accede to an implied request for immediate return to Capernaum, Jesus exhorts them to accompany him to neighboring hamlets, "For it is for that reason that I came out" (v. 38 AT). In spite of Simon's report, Jesus has his own mission to follow throughout the whole of Galilee, extending his exorcisms and preaching in others' synagogues (v. 39; cf. 1:14, 21-28).

◊ ◊ ◊ ◊

Mark is a Gospel of contradictions, some of which emerge from this passage. Clearly, Jesus is no hermit; rather than confine his ministry to a single area, he deliberately proceeds into the wider, multicultural world that was first-century Galilee. Yet, as portrayed by Mark, Jesus is a remote figure, who withdraws by night into barren places. He takes the initiative to select his missionary companions; however, when Simon and others search out their leader, Jesus moves in a different direction. Communion with his disciples ranks behind communion with God through prayer. For the first time in Mark one observes another tension that becomes more pronounced as the narrative unfolds: a peculiar push and pull between salutary distance and ominous proximity. As Jesus *withdraws*, others close in on him, occasionally with hostile intent or effect (see 1:45; 3:7-10, 19b-35). As Jesus *approaches*, others sometimes pull back or away from him (see 5:14-17; 6:1-6a). This odd dynamic is captured in 1:39: he came preaching in *their* synagogues, *driving out* demons that seem to infest every corner of Galilee.

Jesus and the Leper (1:40-45)

Throughout history, leprosy has been among the most feared and mysterious diseases. Stigma and quarantine for its sufferers remain within the living memory of some who may read this commentary. Most scholars concur that leprosy in the Bible (*tsara'at* in the OT; *lepra* in the NT) does not refer primarily to Hansen's disease: the bacterial infection of flesh, skin, and nerves that, left untreated, culminates in deformity, disfigurement, and (in extreme cases) blindness. In antiquity leprosy refers generically to a wide range of dermatological problems, scabrous "outbreak," as well as fungal discoloration of fabrics and houses (see Lev 13:1-59). Those suspected of having contracted leprosy were sometimes— though not always (Exod 4:6)—reckoned to be sinners (2 Kgs 5:1-27; 2 Chr 26:16-21). More consistently, *tsara'at* was feared for polluting not only holy items (Lev 22:4) but also the mundane sphere of persons, objects, and premises (Lev 14:36, 46-47). Since the disease was not in the main contagious, exactly why leprosy was regarded tantamount to defilement remains a matter of debate. Some think that aversion to what is obviously irregular lies deep-seated in many cultures (Douglas 1966); others point to a long-standing association of *tsara'at* with death (see Num 12:12; Milgrom 1991, 816-26). The ancients seem to have believed that serious dermatological irregularities could be healed only through divine intervention (Num 12:10-12; 2 Kgs 5:7; Matt 11:5; Luke 7:22); until then, the victim could be banished to safe-guard the community from presumed contamination (2 Kgs 7:3-10; 2 Chr 26:19-21). Leviticus 14 details ancient Israel's rites for purification of suspect persons (vv. 1-32), houses (vv. 48-53), and garments (13:58) that priests declared clean.

After Jesus' decision to push beyond Capernaum (Mark 1:38), a leper pleads with him, confident in Jesus' ability to cleanse him (v. 40). Whether in Mark the sufferer's appeal is piously accented by his kneeling, as diverse ancient manuscripts record (see Matt 8:2; Luke 5:12), is difficult to decide with certainty but does not significantly bear on the text's interpretation. A more difficult and important issue lies in the manuscript discrepancies for 1:41: Is Jesus' immediate response to the leper one of compassion (*splanchnistheis*: thus, KJV, Goodspeed, Moffatt, RSV, JB, NIV, NAB, NRSV) or of anger (*orgistheis*: thus, REB)? This is a diffi-cult puzzle to solve because it equally flouts two accepted text-critical principles for adjudication: the more difficult reading is surely that which attributes anger to Jesus, yet the more intelligi-ble characterization of Jesus' pity receives support, by a substan-tial margin, from the most varied and widespread ancient manuscripts. It is easy to imagine scribes changing "anger" to "compassion"; the reverse is hard to explain. Elsewhere in Mark the reasons for Jesus' aggravation (3:5) or indignation (10:14) are clear enough. Here, no explanation is offered. With that we must rest content, resisting the temptation to indulge in armchair psychology of Jesus' emotions (Juel 1990, 36-37). While assumptions about irrecoverable Aramaic traditions behind the Greek text of Mark are quite hazardous, 1:41 presents a case in which such an appeal may illuminate this mystery. Semitic terms for compassion and rage are more similar and more easily confused than their Greek counterparts: thus, in Syriac, *ethraham* (he took pity) and *ethracem* (he was infuriated; see Metzger 1994, 65).

Jesus touches his petitioner, expressing his will that the leper be cleansed (v. 41; see also v. 31). In this act there is unuttered poignance: Jesus dares to touch the untouchable (Edwards 2002, 69-70). Right away (*euthys*) the disease leaves the sufferer's body, and he is cleansed (v. 42). Notice that the restoration has two parts—medical and social—much as we would expect from the prescriptions in Leviticus 13–14. The social aspect requires the community's satisfaction, which only the priest can provide. That explains Jesus' direction that the one healed present himself for cultic examination and offer sacrifices, in thanks to God and as demonstrative grounds for reintegration into the community (1:44b; see Lev 14:1-32; Luke 17:12-14).

And there the matter should end—were this only a story of a leper's healing. At two points, however, Mark inserts a christological component. First, in 1:43, Jesus expels (*exebalen*; see also 1:12, 39) the one cleansed, "sternly warning" him. The latter phrase is a common though vapid translation of the Greek participle *embrimēsamenos,* whose root meaning is "to snort" as would an agitated horse (Thucydides, *Peloponnesian War* 461; see LSJ 540). Mark is no more forthcoming here than in verse 41 to give a reason for Jesus' strong reaction. In 1:44a Jesus invokes on someone for the first time a prohibition that nothing about what has happened be said to anyone (see also 5:43; 7:36; 8:26, 30; 9:9). As soon as that command is issued, it is flagrantly disobeyed, with two consequences (1:45). First, having gone out, the erstwhile leper "began to proclaim [or 'preach': *kēryssein*, 1:1:4, 14] it freely, and to spread the word [*ton logon*, 2:2; 4:14-20]." Again Jesus' fame spreads, even as it had after the exorcism in

Capernaum (1:28). This time Mark conveys that idea through the subtle use of Christian terminology—"the word"—for missionary discourse (see Acts 4:29, 31; 8:4; 13:5; 15:36; Rom 10:8, 15; Col 1:23; 2 Pet 1:19). Another result of that proclamation is, as before, to curtail Jesus' freedom of movement (see 1:33, 37). Now, barren places (*erēmoi topoi*, v. 45, translated by the NRSV as "the country") do not remain so for long (cf. 1:35). Even in the wilderness "people came to him from every quarter."

By definition, disease entails diminution. Still, it is noteworthy that the infirmities cured by Jesus in Mark tend to be those in which personal and social dissolution are at their worst: mental illness involving individual disintegration (1:23-24) and, in 1:40-45, scale disease that isolates its victims from the social network. The leper's tragedy lies not in his medical condition, about which the rituals in Leviticus are silent, but in the community's fearful response that his proximity will pollute them. It is not the leper's disease that is contagious but his *impurity* (an assumption that becomes explicit in rabbinic literature: *m. Kelim* 1.4; *m. Neg.* 13.7). If such fear seems remote to modern readers, we need only remind ourselves of comparable forms of social ostracism to which sufferers of cancer or AIDS can be subjected (Sontag 1989). Within that context it is critical to note that Jesus in Mark 1:40-45 does exactly what is asked of him: not merely to heal, but *to cleanse*. He removes the cause of pollution, connoted by leprosy, and by upholding "what Moses commanded" (v. 44)—priestly inspection and sacrificial offering—he ensures that the one healed can be reintegrated into society. Rather than being contaminated by the sufferer's condition, Jesus *de*contaminates not only the disease but its social stigma as well.

The price paid by Jesus for healing others is his own social disturbance. Throngs reappear, impeding his designs (1:33). Whereas in the previous pericope Jesus was unable to escape a search party in the desert (1:35-37), now he can no longer enter a city openly (1:45). It is ironic that by means of their transaction in 1:40-42, the leper and Jesus effectively change places: the former had been unable to enjoy social contact; the latter must now endure too much. The tension between distance and proximity, observed in 1:35-39 and elsewhere, reappears in Mark 1:45. The reason for that imbalance, according to the Evangelist, has to do with premature disclosure of information that should be kept confidential (1:44). Though this motif is often put under the umbrella of the messianic secret, here it is Jesus' popularity, not his messiahship, that the Evangelist underlines. On the other hand, *secrecy* is very much an issue for Mark in 1:43-44, a matter larger than that of Jesus' identity. "Untrammeled preaching and spreading of the word" (1:45 AT) also fall within strictures of concealment—while simultaneously violating those restrictions (see 4:26-32; see Räisänen 1990, 144-49, 245-47).

An Increasingly Controversial Ministry (2:1–3:6)

Mark 1:16-45 announces basic themes that will recur throughout the narrative. Jesus' power has come into focus. Charismatically claiming his first followers (vv. 16-20), he has demonstrated a qualitatively different authority from that of recognized "professionals" (vv. 22, 31, 40-41), which terrifies unclean spirits who recognize a superior force (vv. 23-26, 34a). While able to silence demons (v. 34b), Jesus has not evaded followers and admirers (vv. 33, 35-37, 45b) or constrained those most indebted to him (vv. 44-45a). Thus, the complex social dynamics of Jesus' ministry have become evident. While restoring those who live on society's margins (vv. 23-27, 30-31, 40-45), his ministry has dissolved families (vv. 16-20) and disrupted his own social interaction (vv. 35-38, 45). The apocalyptic character of God's kingdom, central to Jesus' preaching (1:14-15), is now obliquely manifest. The reader has entered a looking-glass world of demons and pollution (vv. 23-27, 32-34, 40-42), of cultic piety and tainted synagogues (vv. 23, 39, 44), where women exercise ministry (v. 31b) and preachers are hushed, only to preach more vigorously (vv. 43-45). The alienated recognize Jesus (vv. 24, 40); his companions are starting to miss the point

(vv. 35-37). That which must be secreted is exposed (vv. 44-45), what is open is becoming suppressed (v. 45), and for all of Jesus' triumphs, nothing is altogether what it seems or should be.

Mark 2:1–3:6 inverts the issues lying in the preceding section's foreground and background. If 1:16-45 highlights Jesus' power, with opposition stirring in the shadows, in 2:1–3:6 resistance to Jesus' authority occupies center stage. As in 1:16-45, the next section of the narrative exhibits careful construction, interweaving five anecdotes by the motif of controversy. Healings of a paralytic (2:1-12) and of a man with a shriveled hand (3:1-6) create bookends for three debates that concern *eating*: dubious table-fellows (2:13-17), the question of fasting (2:18-22), and the plucking of grain on the Sabbath (2:23-28). The two bookends, characterized by spiritual heart disease (2:6, 8; 3:5), are themselves conflations of material turned inside out: accusation of Jesus (2:5-10a) framed by his authoritative healing (2:1-4, 10b-12); the same healing (3:3-5) framed by murderous accusation (3:1-2, 6). The effect is a chiasm: an inverted ladder whose center is climactic (see Dewey 1980):

Table 1: *The Structure of Mark 2:1–3:6*

A. An encounter with a paralytic (2:1-5, 10b-12) and some scribes (2:6-10a)

    B. The scribes' challenge to the disciples about Jesus' eating (2:13-17)

        C. The disciples' feasting and the bridegroom's removal (2:18-22)

    B.' The Pharisees' challenge to Jesus about his disciples' eating (2:23-28)

A.' An encounter with the Pharisees (3:1-2, 6) and a man with a withered hand (3:3-5)

Other delicate threads cross-stitch this material. This much, however, indicates a literary strategy governed by theological reflection.

An Encounter with a Paralytic and Some Scribes (2:1-12)

The scene shifts back to Capernaum (v. 1), the village on the Sea of Galilee's northwest bank where Jesus' healing and teaching ministry commenced (1:21). "The house" to which he repairs is unspecified. While the NRSV and other versions imply that it was Jesus' own residence ("at home"), the Greek is vague (KJV: "in the house"; Lattimore: "in a house there"; JB: "he was back"). Traditions as early as the fourth century locate the paralytic's healing in Simon's house (1:29-33; Finegan 1992, 110). Mark's interest is simpler (v. 4): to move the action indoors, beneath a roof. As usual (see 1:33, 37, 45), many are gathered (*synēchthēsan*, a verbal cognate of "synagogue") to hear Jesus teach (2:2). Typically, Mark leaves unspecified the subject matter: "the word" (*ton logon*, v. 2) is indefinite (see 1:45) though may suggest "the good news" (*to euangelion*, 1:14-15). As in Capernaum's synagogue (1:21-23, 27), teaching gives way to healing with the approach of four bearing a paralytic (2:3). Entry through the doorway being impossible (v. 2), the carriers "unroofed the roof" (v. 4 AT), which, in Palestinian design, would have consisted of crossbeams covered with thatch and hardened mud. Through a makeshift opening, they lower the paralytic to Jesus.

At this point, one would expect the healing to occur, then be confirmed and acclaimed—all of which are postponed until verses 10b-12 (cf. 1:40-45; Bultmann 1963, 212-13). It is surprising to find, instead, Jesus' commendation of their faith (*pistis*) and announcement of forgiveness for the paralytic's sins (2:5 JB). "Child" (*teknon*) is a term of endearment, not age-specific (see also 10:24, 29-30); the passive construction "your sins are forgiven" (*aphientai sou hai hamartiai*) implies that God is the agent of release. Since forgiveness was not requested, this response twists the tale in a different direction, immediately pursued in verses 6-10a: Jesus' authority to release sins, challenged by scribes at the scene. There are two ways to account for what the Evangelist is doing here; both contain a measure of truth. One is that Mark has adapted a short, illustrative tale of Jesus' healing by sharpening its theological point, recasting his inherited material into a "paradigm" (Dibelius 1935, 37-69). Another possibility is to perceive in 2:1-12 two different pieces of material, one (vv. 5-10a) inserted into the middle of the other (vv. 1-4, 10b-12). The latter technique is known by many names: a Markan interpolation, intercalation, interlamination, or sandwich. This, a signature of the Evangelist's literary style, invites the reader to interpret one tradition about Jesus in the light of another that Mark has folded into it (von Dobschütz 1928; Shepherd 1993; see table 2). However one explains the narrative shift in 2:1-12, clearly Mark uses a healing story as a vehicle for examining the disputed authority by which Jesus speaks and acts. His word and deed were previously conflated, their power thus underlined, by an exorcism in Capernaum's synagogue (see 1:25-27), where his authority was contrasted with that of the scribes (1:22)—expressly those who challenge Jesus here (2:6, 8). As there, so also here: Mark portrays the scribes (hoi grammateis) as a unified group, which, though not historically accurate, reflects the Evangelist's view of them as trained leaders generally unified against Jesus (though cf. 12:28-34; see Saldarini 1988, 241-68). These scribes do not overtly confront Jesus; they are "reasoning in their hearts" (2:6 KJV). The bone of their unvoiced contention is that, since no one but God can forgive sins, by doing so Jesus has committed blasphemy (2:7). Strictly speaking, blasphemy is the invocation of a curse upon God or a slander of the holy Name, either punishable by death (Lev 24:15-16). The implication drawn—as Mark presents it—is that, by pronouncing forgiveness, Jesus has infringed on a prerogative that is exclusively God's (Exod 34:6-7; Isa 43:25; 44:22).

"Perceiv[ing] in his spirit" his adversaries' internal questions, Jesus challenges them (2:8) by posing a riddle: Which is easier to pronounce, forgiveness or healing (2:9)? That is a tricky question. Forgiveness, which is not obviously subject to confirmation as is the restoration of paralyzed limbs, appears easier *to say*. Forgiveness of sins fell within the purview of priests who offered temple sacrifices (Sanders 1992, 106-12): here there is no temple, Jesus is no priest, and the repair of breaches between humans and

Table 2: *Mark's Traditional Intercalations*

Framing Unit	*Interpolated Unit*
2:1-5a + 2:10b-12 Healing of the paralytic	2:5b-10a Jesus' authority to forgive
3:1-3 + 3:5b-6 Healing of the man with a withered hand	3:4-5a Healing on the Sabbath
3:19b-21 + 3:31-35 Jesus' friends and family in opposition	3:22-30 Dispute over Beelzebul and forgiveness
5:21-24a + 5:35-43 Healing of a synagogue leader's daughter	5:24b-34 Healing of a hemorrhaging woman
6:6b-13 + 6:30 Mission of the Twelve	6:14-29 Death of John
11:12-14 + 11:20-25 Cursing a fig tree, with interpretation	11:15-19 Clearing the temple
14:1-2 + 14:10-11 Judas's collusion with the chief priests	14:3-9 The woman's anointing of Jesus
14:53-54 + 14:66-72 Peter's denial	14:55-65 Sanhedrin hearing
15:6-15 + 15:21-32 The sentencing and execution of Jesus	15:16-20 The soldiers' mockery

God is an important matter. Without giving these scribes opportunity to debate *that* enigma in their hearts, Jesus claims to verify his authority (*exousia*) to forgive sins on earth (2:10) by issuing to the paralytic a pertinent word of healing: "To you I say: Get up, pick up your stretcher, and go home" (2:11 AT). Jesus' mysteriously indirect mode of self-reference, "the Son of Man" (*ho huios tou anthrōpou*, v. 10), will be considered in greater detail at 8:27–9:1. At this point it is sufficient to note that Jesus asserts his sovereignty over normal constraints, be it sin or disease or even the Sabbath's observance (see 2:28).

Verse 12 rounds off the healing story in predictable fashion (1:22, 27): the paralytic arises and leaves, just as Jesus commanded (2:11), in full view before an audience thoroughly astonished. The contentious scribes have faded away, as one would expect if this were the conclusion of a healing tale in which they did not originally appear (2:1-4 + 10b-12). The spectators' glorification of God reminds us, as have 1:14-15 and the oblique reference to "the Son of Man," that Jesus in Mark points not to himself but to God's good news. If a man's limbs are no longer disabled, has his soul been straightened out as well? That and the healer's bona fides are left for the reader to decide.

The relationship between healing and forgiveness runs deep in biblical thought (2 Sam 12:13; 2 Chr 7:14; Isa 19:22; 38:17; 57:17-19; Jer 3:22; Hos 14:4; see Kee 1986, 9-26). Although it occasionally took the harsh shape of moral cause and effect— "Who sinned, that this one was born blind?" (John 9:2 AT; cf. Exod 20:5; 34:7; Ps 109:13-15; Isa 65:6-7)—such a correlation is also denied (Ezek 18:20; Luke 13:2-4; John 9:3), inviting one to contemplate different forms of brokenness before God and humanity's concomitant need for restoration and wholeness. Mark 2:1-12 moves in that latter stream. In one sense the scribes correctly recognize what is at stake in Jesus' assumption of forgiveness: in some psalms it is assumed that healing and forgiveness are interchangeable, and both are of God's prerogative

(Pss 41:4; 103:2-3; 147:2-3). Far from accepting that God is present in Jesus to forgive and to heal, some scribes tacitly slander the one they believe is slandering God.

By contrast, those who approach Jesus with trust in his healing power—and Mark includes among them not only the paralytic but also his escort—exhibit what disputatious scribes lack: *faith* (2:5). Here is the first time that faith appears in a Markan miracle story (see also 5:34, 36; 9:23-24; 10:52). There, as here, faith seems less a matter of reflective belief, more an aggressive confidence that tears off a roof to secure what it needs. Elsewhere, as here, faith *precedes* Jesus' mighty act of restoration: faith is the stimulus for healing, not its consequence. In effect, the paralytic and his carriers demonstrate by their relentlessness (2:4) that they indeed believe the good news that Jesus proclaims (2:2; 1:14-15). The Evangelist's reference to Jesus' spirit (2:8) may also remind the reader of his superior ministry, or "baptism," promised by John (1:8).

The scribes in 2:6-10 will have none of that, and Mark is careful to conclude this tale by saying that the crowd is left wondering, not that people have been convinced of the source of Jesus' power. This story, like so many in this Gospel, uses the tension generated between authority and controversy to pose a fundamental decision between faith and distrust (Marshall 1989, 78-90). Those who, in spite of impediment, trust that Jesus exercises God's restorative power implicitly realize that he can say, "You are forgiven" and "You can get up now," possessing the authority to make both stick. Those who in spite of their learning or position regard Jesus as a presumptuous fraud can understand neither what he is doing nor what he is talking about.

◊ ◊ ◊ ◊

Jesus among Tax Collectors and Sinners (2:13-17)

Mark 2:13-17, which highlights Jesus' consorting with tax collectors and sinners, comprises three elements: (1) a transitional comment, moving Jesus from indoors (2:1-12) to the lakeside, where he continues to teach gathering multitudes (v. 13; see also

1:21-22, 45); (2) Levi's calling (2:14), whose imagery and wording (*paragrōn*, "walking along"; *akolouthei*, "follow") recall Jesus' summons of Andrew and Simon (1:16-17); and (3) Jesus' justification for fraternizing with undesirables (2:15-17), couched in a paradigmatic story "not more descriptive than is necessary to make the point for the sake of which it is introduced" (Dibelius 1935, vii). While the heart of this episode lies in a Pharisaic challenge to the disciples about Jesus' dining practices, verses 13-14 remind the reader of typical features in Mark's characterization of Jesus: he remains on the move, still teaching, magnetically attracting crowds and charismatically summoning disciples.

Levi, son of Alphaeus, does not appear among Mark's listing of the Twelve (3:16-19; cf. Matt 9:9; 10:3, which identify this figure as "Matthew" and place him among Jesus' inner circle). Mark seems more interested that "there were many [such] who followed him" (2:15). Levi's importance stems from his job, which creates the link with Jesus' dinner companions in verses 15-16: "tax collectors and sinners." Taxes and their collection formed a complex system in first-century Palestine (Donahue 1971). Levi's "sitting at the tax booth" (or "customs office," *to telōnion*, v. 14) is the clue to a particular kind of *telōnēs*: an employee, subcontracted by a supervisory official (cf. Luke 19:2), who collected indirect taxes or duties on the transport of goods at commercial centers like Capernaum. Just as abruptly as the fishermen abandoned their trade (Mark 1:16-20), Levi leaves behind lucrative employment. Not only in the NT, but also in Roman and later Jewish writings, tax collectors were despised, in general for their presumed extortion and, among Jews, for their contact with Gentiles and (at least in Judea) for their collaboration with the forces of Roman occupation (Michel 1972, 99-103). At least by the third century C.E., though probably earlier, the rabbis considered tax collection one of the "despised trades" that no observant Jew should adopt (*m. B. Qam.* 10.2; *m. Ned.* 3.4; *b. Sanh.* 25b).

Having entered a house (whose owner is as unspecified in 2:15 as in 2:1), Jesus reclines at supper with "many tax collectors and sinners." The word *sinners* (Gk. *hoi hamartōloi*; Heb. *resha'im*) refers to the notoriously wicked: those Jews unrepentantly engaged in business practices, like usury, that flagrantly flouted God's law (Sanders 1985, 174-211). Here and elsewhere (Matt 11:19-20 = Luke 7:34; 15:1-2), "sinners" were probably associated with "tax collectors" because both groups evoked among their fellow Jews the suspicion of "professional sinfulness," perhaps even political betrayal. The degree of Jesus' intimacy with social outcasts is suggested by his eating with them: then as now in the Middle East, to be invited to a meal is an honor; to dine with someone is to embrace the familiarity of kinship (2 Kgs 25:27-30; Sir 31:12–32:13; see Jeremias 1971, 115-16). The supper table has "friend-making character" (*Quaest. conv.* 614A-B).

That is the sticking point in the question put to Jesus' disciples by "the scribes of the Pharisees." We met "the scribes" in 1:22 and 2:6. Currently, great scholarly debate swirls around "the Pharisees"—their origins, beliefs, and degree of influence—because our sources of information about them (Josephus [*Ant.* 18.12-15; *J.W.* 2.162-63], the NT, rabbinic literature) are spotty, biased in different directions, or considerably later than the NT era (Neusner 1979). It may be that Mark himself knew little in depth about Pharisees or other Jewish leaders in the time of Jesus. By the first century C.E. the Pharisees in Palestine had emerged as an important religious and political interest group, substantial in numbers, nonaristocratic in composition, and small in actual power (Sanders 1992, 380-412). Their eminence derived from their piety, learning, and scrupulous regard for the law (Sanders 1992, 412-51; Meier 2001, 289-388). While Mark stereotypically presents the Pharisees as Jesus' chief antagonists in Galilee (see also 2:24; 3:2, 6; 7:1, 3, 5; 8:11, 15; 10:2; 12:13), the issue in Mark 2:15-17—table-fellowship with recognized sinners—was sufficiently contentious that one can imagine its exercising some strictly observant Jews (see Sanders 1992, 420-37).

In 2:8 Jesus responded to some scribes' internal quarrels; in 2:17 he answers a charge lodged by them with his disciples. His reply is couched as a double-edged similitude, whose emphasis falls on its second member: just as those who are well have no need of a physician but "those who have it bad" (*hoi kakōs echontes*), so too Jesus has come to call not righteous folk, but sinners. Such a calling necessitates not distance from, but intimacy with, the flagrantly unrighteous.

There are two easy ways to misconstrue this pericope. One is to force its punch line in 2:17 into unfounded equivalence with either the ministry of John the Baptist (1:4-8) or Jesus' summons in 1:15: thus, Jesus dined with sinners and tax collectors who— one presumes—had tacitly repented of their unrighteousness. Such a reading makes hash of the first half of Jesus' similitude: Jesus does *not* pay house calls on the healthy. That is just what "the scribes of the Pharisees" find so disturbing: not that Jesus would encourage righteousness, but that he would apparently sanction wickedness by profligate forgiveness of sins (see 2:5-7) or association with relentless sinners without first demanding their repentance (Sanders 1985, 200-211).

Related to that exegetical misstep is another: immediately siding with the Markan Jesus, who of course sees the world the way we do, against a caricatured Pharisaic position that naturally we would never hold. If, as there are good reasons to hold, the Pharisees dedicated themselves to the proposition that all of life should be consecrated in the light of a living scripture and tradition (Meier 2001, 311-32), then it is important to recognize therein a humane sentiment that many modern believers would share. The conflict in Mark 2:13-17 is not some flat, simplistic disagreement between religious or ethical wrong and right. This controversy is over competing visions of how a righteous society is properly formed. Does one uphold the highest standards of fidelity to God through dissociation from their dilution, or does one transform corruption through engagement with its practitioners?

The Bridegroom, the Patch, and the Wineskins (2:18-22)

The central segment in this series consists of sayings about the bridegroom, the patch, and the wineskins (2:18-22). In 2:16 adversaries attacked Jesus through his disciples; in 2:18 the challenge comes to him about them. Here the question centers on fasting. Proceeding from 2:13-17, the train of thought seems to be, If Jesus does not abstain from dining with society's pariahs, what does one make of his disciples' refusal of fasting? While that spontaneous practice was apparently common in Israel (Judg 20:26; 1 Sam 7:6; 31:13; Ezra 8:21-23; Ps 35:13; Dan 9:3, 20-22; Jonah 3:7-9), the only public fast prescribed in Scripture was on the Day of Atonement (Lev 16:29, 31; 23:27, 29, 32; Num 29:7). Jewish asceticism, including fasts for contrition's sake, may have waxed in the popular piety of Hellenistic Judaism (Tob 12:8; Jdt 4:9; Luke 18:12; *J.W.* 2.8.5; *T. Jos.* 3:4), which includes the era of John's disciples (Luke 7:18-23 = Matt 11:2-6; John 1:35; 3:25-30) and those of the Pharisees (Mark 2:18). For the Roman historian Suetonius, "fasting like a Jew" was a social commonplace (*Aug.* 76). Hence, the question for Jesus: Why does everyone else fast, but not your followers?

Jesus' reply to this straightforward question is elliptical, falling into three parts (Mark 2:19-20, 21, 22). Whether Jesus or the Evangelist is responsible for this odd conjunction of three riddles is a fine question, which need not be resolved before making sense of Mark's narrative. The first logion (vv. 19-20) draws an analogy between the time of Jesus' advent and a wedding celebration: in both cases deliberate abstention from food would be inappropriate. When the bridegroom is removed from the scene, fasting will take place. Some form critics perceive in these verses the church's justification for its own fasting, contrary to Jesus' practice (Bultmann 1963, 18-19). This view is debatable, since there is no evidence that the earliest Christians practiced fasting while mourning the dead Jesus. The point of Mark 2:19-20 depends on its context, particularly 2:21-23. Still, the image of Jesus as "the bridegroom" intersects with other Christian traditions that, drawing on OT imagery (Isa 54:4-8; 62:4-5; Jer 2:2;

Ezek 16:1-63; Hos 1:2-9), depict God's covenantal union with Israel as a marriage (John 3:29; 2 Cor 11:2). The bridegroom's discordant removal "on that day" rattles against a related tradition, which symbolizes the eschatological consummation as a wedding banquet (Matt 22:1-14; 25:1-13; John 2:1-12; Rev 19:9-10; 21:2).

Building on the image of bridegroom and wedding guests (literally, "the sons of the bride-chamber," v. 19), two homey illustrations follow: stitching an unshrunk patch on an old garment (v. 21) and the pouring of new wine into old skins (v. 22a). The latter image would have been familiar to a Palestinian audience, who enjoyed fine Galilean wines stored in whole goat hides. Neither case addresses the question of fasting; both posit endeavors to reconcile an old state of affairs with something fresh (*kainos*: vv. 21, 22b; see 1:27). Such attempts are not merely futile but disastrous: the tear in the fabric becomes worse (2:21); both the wine and the skins are lost (2:22b). The moral (v. 22c): "New skins for fresh wine!"

Mark 2:18-22 offers an excellent example of how the Evangelist invites his readers to piece together seemingly discrepant fragments into a coherent, multifaceted idea. Common to the bridegroom, the patch, and the wineskins is the notion that particular circumstances call for differences in approach. One size does not fit all. Whereas fasting, unshrunk patches, or reused wineskins are not bad as such, their use is wholly inappropriate for weddings, old clothes, or fresh wine. Lest we read such dicta as homespun wisdom from a farmer's almanac, we should attend closely to the eschatological, particularly christological, point sharpened in 2:20. Obliquely, the assertions in Mark 2:18-22 are about incompatibilities created by the new reality associated with "the bridegroom": Jesus, who bears glad tidings of God's irrupting sovereignty (1:14-15). If old forms of piety are no longer observed by Jesus and his disciples (2:5-10a, 16-17, 18), it is because he is rendering them obsolete in a

hidden yet energetic way—just like fresh wine, whose continuous fermentation bursts old skins without vent (Job 32:18-19). Such a claim threatens those who adopt unsuitable strategies that make only a bigger mess of what they try to fix. Things are mysterious; we cannot see the real activity inside until old skins begin to pop. The context is ominous because in an appointed day the bridegroom will not leave of his own accord but will be taken away—implicitly, by the same God who has anointed him as his beloved Son (1:9-11).

◊ ◊ ◊ ◊

Who Is Lord over the Sabbath? (2:23-28)

Again aimed at the conduct of Jesus' disciples (2:23), the fourth in this series of controversies touches a point of Sabbath observance. At issue is not the disciples' eating of produce from another's fields (Deut 23:25) but their plucking ears of corn on the Sabbath, which may have been considered tantamount to reaping (thus, a later Talmudic proscription in *b. Šabb.* 73b). Although Mark dramatizes the Pharisees as a united front against Jesus' followers (v. 24), Pharisees and other Jewish groups debated among themselves which activities were permissible on the Sabbath (*Jub.* 50:6-13; CD 10:14–12:5; Luke 14:1-6; *m. Šabb.* 7.2; *m. Betzah* 5.2; see Chilton et al. 2010, 116-32). The Sabbath was normative in establishing Jewish identity within and beyond Palestine. Theologically grounded in both the creation narrative (Gen 2:1-3) and the Decalogue (Exod 20:8-11; Deut 5:12-15), Jewish observance of the Sabbath is corroborated in canonical, extracanonical, and pagan literature throughout the NT era (Whittaker 1984, 63-73). From sundown on Friday until sundown on Saturday, Jews encouraged one another to enjoy a day of delight (Neh 8:9-12; Isa 58:13-14), laying aside ordinary work (Amos 8:5) and fighting only in self-defense (1 Macc 2:29-41). As Philo of Alexandria, a contemporary of Jesus and Paul, put it: "[The Sabbath's] object is rather to give men relaxation from continuous and unending toil and by refreshing their bodies with a regularly calculated system of remissions, to send them out renewed to their old activities" (*Spec.*

Laws 2.60). Qualms over plucking grain on the Sabbath (cf. Deut 23:25) exemplify a case of "attenuated casuistry": safeguarding the Sabbath from profanation by hedging it with multiplied restrictions (Moore 1958, 2:26-39). What might appear to modern readers as trivial should be regarded in its best light, which later rabbis would formulate into a pious principle: "Be as heedful of a light precept as of a weighty one" (*m. 'Abot* 2.1 [Danby]; 4.2), which resembles an early Christian axiom (Luke 16:10-12).

Jesus' reply to this Pharisaic critique (Mark 2:25-28) is interesting in several respects. In form it is a nice example of biblical counterquestion, citing scripture (1 Sam 21:1-6) against scripture (by implication, Exod 34:21, developed in *m. Šabb.* 7.2), as later rabbis would do. Jesus adopts a mode of Jewish argument, even when disagreeing with a particular outcome. A detail in Jesus' recital of David's story is incorrect: not Abiathar (1 Sam 22:20) but Ahimelech was the chief priest of Nob (1 Sam 21:1). This mistake discomfited Mark's copyists, most of whom modified the wording of verse 26 either by suggesting the event's occurrence during Abiathar's lifetime (if not his high priesthood) or by excising reference to the high priest altogether (following Matt 12:4 and Luke 6:4; see Swanson 1995, 34-35). The precedent cited by Jesus does not directly address the matter in dispute. On the one hand, David and his retinue did not violate the Sabbath; on the other, David was a historical figure, which would not carry the probative weight of clear scriptural precept (*halakah*, to use the later rabbinic term; Daube 1956, 67-71). (Matthew's modification of Mark, focusing on temple service [12:1-8], is a technically superior argument.) The capstone of Jesus' rebuttal is not the legality of David's consuming "the bread of the Presence," loaves presented on the holy table in the tent of meeting before "the LORD's face" (AT) but eaten by the priests (Exod 25:30; Lev 24:5-9). The refutation's nub lies in the twofold claim of Mark 2:27-28: (a) the satisfaction of human need (in this case, hunger) lies at the heart of genuine Sabbath observance (v. 27); and (b) in perceiving the law's intention, "the Son of Man" (Jesus) shows himself sovereign even over Sabbath (v. 28). The first of these claims is irreproachable on Jewish principle. Israel dedicated the

Sabbath as a day of rest and festive banqueting; Israel was not constrained by the Sabbath when a higher obligation, such as saving a human life, demanded fulfillment (cf. *Mek.* Exod. 31:13). The second claim—that "the Son of Man" (see Mark 2:10) is uniquely positioned to cut across all debate over what is permissible on the Sabbath—is controversial in the extreme.

Two basic principles—one ethical, the other theological—are operative in Mark 2:23-28. The former is that the Sabbath, while belonging to God (Ezek 20:12, 16, 20), was created to satisfy human need; human beings have not been created for the sake of Sabbath observance. Satisfaction of human need takes precedence over fulfillment of religious obligations (2:27), a topic to which Mark will immediately return (3:1-6; see also 7:1-23). As far as we know, Israel never regarded the Sabbath as a fast day; meal preparations were completed before the Sabbath commenced (*m. Šabb.* 2–4). Jesus and his disciples have been presented as roaming itinerants unable to complete mealtime preparations in advance of the Sabbath. They, like David and his company, "were hungry and in need" (2:25). In those circumstances strict observance of Torah yields for the sake of the needy.

The theological issue raised by this pronouncement story is at once more central and more oblique: Who is Jesus that he can authoritatively make such determinations about a holy day definitive for Jewish identity? The centrality of that question is suggested not only by the larger context of 2:1–3:6 and its concentration on Jesus, but also by this passage's punch line (2:28), which refocuses this story christologically. While the tale of David and his hungry companions does not directly touch the dispute over Sabbath observance, that precedent hints at matters latent elsewhere in this Gospel. If David and his compatriots could eat food set aside for religious observance (1 Sam 21:1-6), then how much more— at least by implication—can the disciples of Jesus, David's son who is yet greater than David (Mark 10:47-48; 12:36-37), do the same? If David ate the bread of the Presence, which none but priests could legally consume (2:26), is Jesus justified in exercising priestly prerogatives of forgiveness (2:5) and arbitration of what transpires in the courts of "the house of God" (2:26; cf. 11:15-19)? On what basis may one conclude that "the Son of Man"—referring to Jesus (2:10)—exercises lordship even over the Sabbath? What authority, therefore, does "the Son of Man" hold (cf. 1:27; 2:10)? While readers of Mark to this point know more about Jesus' identity than any of its characters, even they may leave this passage with more questions than answers.

Jesus Returns to the Synagogue (3:1-6)

In the last of five controversial tableaux, the site of his pious instruction (1:21-22) amid demon exorcisms (1:23-27, 39), Mark sets the scene: among those present are a man whose hand is shriveled (3:1) and an unspecified "they" (3:2), whom we assume (from 2:24), correctly (3:6), are the Pharisees. As in the previous episode (2:23-28), the disputed point is the legality of activity on the Sabbath (3:2): a leniency by Jesus so memorable that one detects its traces in various Gospel traditions (Luke 13:10-17; 14:1-6; John 5:1-18; *Infancy Gospel of Thomas* 2.2-3). The structure of Mark 3:1-6 neatly inverts that of 2:1-12. In that passage the healing of a paralytic (2:1-4 + 10b-12) framed a controversy over Jesus' authority to forgive sins (2:5-10a). Here the controversy (over Jesus' healing on the Sabbath: 3:2-5b + 6) frames the cure, which receives slight attention (3:1, 5cd).

As Mark dramatizes it, Jesus himself forces the issue: "Rise up and come out into the middle" (3:3 Cassirer). Herein lies another echo of the story that opened this series: Jesus' command to the man with the withered hand is expressed with the same Greek verb (*egeirō*) used in healing the paralytic (2:11). Jesus' question in 3:4a is as elliptical as his other questions to challengers in this section (2:9, 19, 25-26). No observant Jew would endorse killing or doing harm on the Sabbath; none would dispute the legality of doing good and saving life on that day. Though codified much later, such mishnaic precepts were recognized during the time of Jesus: "Every case where life is in danger supersedes the Sabbath" (*m. Yoma* 8.6). Such a question, however, does not appear relevant to the facts of this case. While afflicted, the man in Mark 3:1 does not require immediate treatment to live; because his life is not at risk, his cure could wait until the following day (Lachs 1987, 199-200). Silence can betoken confusion as well as consent; in this case (3:4b), angry and mortified (1:41, 43), Jesus interprets silence as symptomatic of "cardioporosis" (*hē pōrōsis tēs kardias*), "hardness of heart" (3:5b). That metaphor, a biblical commonplace for stubborn obtuseness (see Exod 9:34-35; 1 Sam 6:6; 2 Chr 36:13; Ps 95:8; Eph 4:18), is pertinent here: it was "in their hearts" that a group of scribes questioned Jesus' impious audacity to release the paralytic's sins (2:6-8; cf. 2:16). So simply does Mark describe Jesus' restoration of the man's deformed hand (3:5cd) that it seems almost a throwaway conclusion. In itself that healing is not this story's focus. Instead, the cure triggers a plot against the physician (2:17), a conspiracy among those scheming on the Sabbath to kill (3:4).

That scheme is described laconically (3:6), every word of this conclusion fraught with significance. Immediately (*euthys*: see 1:10; also 2:8, 12), the Pharisees—by now, Jesus' recognized adversaries (2:16, 18, 24)—"went out" (*exelthontes*). In Mark the Pharisees, among others, will prove themselves on the outs with Jesus (see 4:11b). With the Herodians the Pharisees seek a "council" or "plot" (*symboulion*); the only other occurrence of this word in Mark is near its end, at 15:1, where another coterie of Jewish leaders hands Jesus over to the Roman prefect. Just who "the Herodians" were remains conjectural (Richardson 1996, 259-60); Mark may have inherited traditions referring to a group whose members were not altogether clear to him (Cook 1978, 29-51). The Herodian dynasty, extending from Antipater I (ca. 100 B.C.E.) to Agrippa II (28–93 C.E.), was notable for its cooperation with Roman rule (Schürer 1973, 1:219-513). Mark suggests some kind of intrigue between Pharisees and the Roman forces of occupation (see also 6:14-29; 8:15; 12:13; Matt 22:15-

16). However shadowy the conspirators, their object is clear: the destruction of Jesus (Malbon 2000, 131-65).

If Mark 1:16-45 consists of type-scenes exhibiting Jesus' "fresh teaching with authority" (1:27a AT), 2:1–3:6 exhibits an escalation of bitter conflict stimulated by his activity among the religious establishment and devout laity. In this section's opening act, some scribes debate against Jesus in their hearts (2:6-8); by its end, some hard-hearted Pharisees are hatching a plot with partisans of Herod (Antipas, 4 B.C.E.–39 C.E.) to do away with Jesus. Secrecy evokes secrecy on planes both horizontal and vertical: the shadow of John's arrest, under which Jesus inaugurated his announcement of God's in-breaking kingdom (1:14-15), meets its dark mirror image in the *symboulion* formed against Jesus (3:6). From now on there can be no doubt, not only of the authority by which Jesus speaks and acts (1:1, 8, 9-11, 24), but also of its outcome: his destruction by those who, for religious or political reasons, are as threatened by Jesus as those afflicted by disease or demonism or sin are attracted to him (1:23, 28, 32-34, 37, 40, 45; 2:1-5, 13, 15; 3:3). By his own prediction, "The days will come when the bridegroom is taken away from them" (2:20a).

In Mark's view the bases for these controversies between Jesus and his antagonists are not his mighty works as such, even less some presumed envy for his "doing good." Jesus in this Gospel is a radical figure, whose actions and pronouncements strike at the root of what it means to be faithfully Jewish. Prompted only by an expression of trust in him, he releases sins (2:5, 10a). If not technically blasphemous, this seems an outrageous declaration from a layman (2:7), which effectively preempts the need for cultic offerings (Lev 4:1–6:7). He enjoys fraternity of the dinner table with notorious quislings and the flagrantly wicked, without demanding that they first put their houses in order (Mark 2:15-16). His disciples feast while others think it better to fast (2:18). Worst of all, he runs roughshod over accepted standards of

Sabbath observance (2:23–3:6): alongside circumcision, the defining feature of first-century Judaism. When the Son of Man comes wielding authority on earth (2:10a) and lordship even over the Sabbath (2:28), preexisting assumptions and conditions cannot remain the same—and their advocates, understandably, neither appreciate nor approve.

Those defenders of the status quo are neither frivolous, nor impious, nor stupid (Perkins 1995, 559-60). To the best of our ability to discern, both the scribes and the Pharisees were groups generally respected for their learning and religious devotion. So claimed Josephus, around 105 C.E.: "This is the great tribute that the inhabitants of the cities, by practicing the highest ideals both in their way of living and in their discourse, have paid to the excellence of the Pharisees" (*Ant.* 12.15; see also Nickelsburg and Stone 1983, 24-30). Under what kind of stress are a community's pillars—those who uphold its highest ideals—motivated to plot the death of a Galilean teacher and healer (Mark 3:6)? To this question, Mark will have more to say. For now, it is clear that "the good news of God" (1:14) does not appear as such to all those one might expect to embrace it. The gospel ferments anew; some old skins cannot grasp it (2:22).

The Evangelist does not psychoanalyze his characters. His focus remains on Jesus and on the mysterious, threatening, and threatened figure that he cuts. Jesus submits no credentials for his deeds and words; he simply speaks and acts, then allows his witnesses to draw their own conclusions (2:4-5, 10-12, 13-14, 27-28; 3:1-6). His claims for himself are circumlocutory: a physician (2:17), a bridegroom (2:19-20), the Son of Man (2:10, 28). His power (*exousia*) is undeniable (2:10-12; 3:5), but its source and interpretation are obscure almost to the point of inscrutability (2:9, 17b, 19-22, 25-26, 28; 3:4). Clearly, he is no hooligan: at his command withered limbs become whole (2:11-12; 3:5); by his actions the Sabbath is renewed (2:27-28) and society's outcasts enjoy a place at the table (2:15). Feasting, not fasting, is the order of his day (2:19); it is time to glorify God (2:12). Why, then, is Jesus so troubling? What is it about the new that rips it from the old (2:21)? Why must the bridegroom be taken away (2:20)?

TRANSITION: THE EXPANSION OF JESUS' MINISTRY (3:7-12)

Bookending 1:14-15, Mark 3:7-12 is another strategically positioned summary report, which recapitulates Jesus' activity while laying a foundation for the next phase of his ministry among "insiders" and "outsiders" (3:13–6:6a).

After a long series of sharp encounters (1:35–3:6), Mark pulls back for a wide-angle view of Jesus' escalating popularity within and beyond Galilee (a motif introduced in 1:28). The tension between distance and proximity, established in 1:32-39, 45, returns in 3:7-8: although Jesus and his disciples have withdrawn to the sea ("of Galilee": 1:16), a great multitude (*poly plēthos*) follow (*ēkolouthēsan*) them. This description is double-edged. The throngs' attraction to Jesus inverts the response of Pharisees and Herodians so repulsed by him that they plot his elimination (3:6). Yet, by nearly crushing him, the multitudes also threaten Jesus' well-being. His disciples prepare a small boat for emergency escape (3:9).

In a single sentence (vv. 7-8), Mark captures the viral spread of Jesus' popularity, beginning with regions south of Galilee. Judea was the venue for John's ministry (1:5). Its capital during the rule of Herod the Great (37–4 B.C.E.) was Jerusalem, Israel's "holy city" (Isa 52:1) and, in the view of Pliny the Elder (*Nat.* 5.14), the most celebrated among ancient Eastern cities. It will be Jesus' climactic destination in the Gospel's second half. South of Jerusalem, in Judea's hill country, lay the territory of Idumea, Herod's homeland and a juncture for important trade routes. Moving northeasterly, Mark takes the reader beyond the Jordan River, which empties into the Dead Sea (Lake Asphaltitis). Including Idumea and allusion to Perea, the Transjordan territory west of the Decapolis, Jesus' fame far exceeds the baptizer's (1:5). Mark leaps to the Phoenician coastal cities of Tyre and Sidon, both in the Roman province of Syria, northwest of Galilee. While Mark's knowledge of Palestinian geography can be unreliable (e.g., 7:31), mention of these regions and cities indicates that news of Jesus' activity is attracting crowds from all

quarters. (See the map, "Palestine at the Time of Jesus.")
Idumea, the Transjordan, Tyre, and Sidon also foreshadow Jesus'
later ministry among Gentiles on Israel's fringes (5:20; 7:24, 31;
8:22, 27).

Another motif in this summary is Jesus' interaction with sufferers and the unclean spirits (3:10-12). Mark presents each
group in subtle correspondence and contrast with the other.
Because Jesus has cured so many, those afflicted with various diseases "pressed upon him [*epipiptein autō*] to touch him" (3:10).
Previously, Jesus has initiated therapeutic touch (1:31, 41); later,
as here, the sick touch their healer (5:27-28; 6:56; 8:22). No
action beyond his harsh rebuke is needed to quell unclean spirits,
who, conceding the Son of God's superior force, cry out and
"[fall] down before him" (*prosepipton autō*, 3:11). Mark does
not report Jesus' response to the sick. As in 1:34 Jesus hushes the
demons: they know his identity (so also 1:24; 5:7) and, if not
silenced, would make it known to others (3:12). Jesus' reaction is
more than an instance of what some imprecisely designate as
"the messianic secret" (Wrede 1971, 24-34): Mark 3:12 does not
refer to messiahship. The salient aspect is Jesus' refusal of a
philosopher-healer's godlike self-presentation, epitomized in
Empedocles's *Purifications*:

> But I go about [among] you as an immortal God, no longer as
> a mortal. When I come...into the busy towns, to men and
> women, I am honored by [all]; however they follow after me in
> their thousands, to learn where the path [leads] to gain, some
> requiring sayings from the oracle, others seeking to experience
> a word that brings healing in their manifold sickness, having
> already long been riddled by severe pain. (Boring, Berger, and
> Colpe 1995, 121)

With noteworthy economy Mark 3:7-12 gathers the
Evangelist's thematic threads to this point, preparing the reader
for the narrative's next stage. Mark continues to keep a tight
focus on Jesus' healing power and authoritative command (cf.,

e.g., 1:14-15, 17-18, 21-28; 2:5, 10-12; 3:3-5). Spirits holy and profane remind readers that Mark's story adopts an apocalyptic perspective. Israel and the nations form the terrestrial theater for a cosmic battle between God's envoy and the forces of disease and demonism. In 1:14-15, the first of Mark's transitional passages, Jesus proclaimed the irruption of God's kingdom on this world's stage; 3:7-12 summarizes what the shifting sovereignty from Satan (1:13) to God entails. Exactly where those whom Jesus calls (1:16-20; 2:14) and heals (1:34, 38, 40-42; 3:3-5) stand in this struggle remains moot. These figures are obviously needy, obedient, and serving (Williams 1994, 89-104). Even they, however, are cast in shadow: Simon Peter leads a posse in search of Jesus at prayer (1:35-37), a leper disregards an injunction of silence (1:43-45), and the multitudes press upon Jesus, impeding his movements (1:45) and jeopardizing his life (3:9). In Mark's next main section, Jesus continues to offer "new wine." Fresh skins can accept it; older skins are ruptured under its pressure (2:22).

JESUS' PARABOLIC MINISTRY AMONG INSIDERS AND OUTSIDERS (3:13–6:6A)

Mark 1:16–3:6 has highlighted primary aspects of Jesus' ministry: exorcism, healing, and teaching. In 3:13–6:6a a heretofore minor motif assumes prominence: disparate reactions to Jesus' activity. A snippet of Jesus' instruction within this segment offers the reader a key for construing varied responses: "for you [inside]"/"for those outside" (*hymin* [*esō*]/*de tois exō*, 4:11). Those who intuit Jesus' true significance welcome his teaching and conduct; outsiders misinterpret him, sometimes radically so. The identity of those "inside" and "outside"—that is, where Jesus' members of the audience stand with respect to God's kingdom—is surprising; its reasons, mysterious (4:11). That air of mystery pervades Mark 3:13–6:6a.

Who Are Closest to Jesus? (3:13-35)

Mark 3:13-35 is an overture for the whole of 3:13–6:6a. Binding 3:13-35 is Mark's answer to the question, "Who is 'with' Jesus?" That preposition is both spatial and figurative. Who are Jesus' closest associates: his friends and family? And who is in closest alignment with Jesus' purposes? In 3:13-35 the reader learns that these two groups overlap, but only partially.

Jesus' Selection of the Twelve (3:13-19a)

Jesus' selection of the Twelve as his personal entourage (3:13-19a) happens when "he goes up into the hills" (AT), which, unlike the areas in 3:7-8, are unspecified. Throughout this Gospel, as in the OT (Exod 3:1, 12; 19:1-25; Deut 5:1-27; 10:1-11; 1 Kgs 19:8), "the hill country" or "the mountain" (to horos) typically designates a place of divine disclosure (Mark 6:46; 9:2-13; 13:3, 14; 14:26). From out of the hordes in 3:7-8, or perhaps from among the unnamed disciples in 3:9, Jesus calls to himself, simply, "those he wanted." With equal simplicity they come to him. Verse 14 includes the first of Mark's ten references to an inner circle of twelve disciples (see also 4:10; 6:7; 9:35; 10:32; 11:11; 14:10, 17, 20, 43). No explanation is given for this number. Probably, it symbolizes Israel's twelve tribes (Num 1:4-16; 13:1-16; Acts 7:8), as Q suggests (Luke 22:30 = Matt 19:28). Mark says that Jesus "made" (epoiēsen) twelve, a verb whose nuances range from simple formation to authoritative appointment (LXX 1 Kgs 13:33; 2 Chr 2:18; Heb 3:2).

That Jesus "named [them] apostles [apostolous]" (see NRSV footnote) is attested in several ancient Greek witnesses. Many other manuscripts delete this wording, which could have been added under the influence of Luke 6:13. There is no reason to assume that Mark regards "the apostles" as a group with special status, a judgment toward which Paul (1 Cor 9:1; 15:3-11; Gal 1:1) and Luke incline (24:10; Acts 1:15-26). As clarified by a cognate verb in Mark 3:14 and confirmed in 6:7-13, 30, apostoloi in this Gospel connotes the term's basic meaning of Jesus' "emissaries," "those dispatched" to represent him. In the first instance, Jesus calls twelve to be with him (v. 14). On that basis he delegates to them two responsibilities that he himself has executed (vv. 14b-15a): preaching (1:14, 38-39) and authority (or "power," *exousia*) to cast out demons (1:34, 39). The Twelve are not the only ones in Mark's Gospel who "proclaim freely" and "spread the word" (1:45) or cast out demons in Jesus' name (9:38). This fact suggests that, while the Twelve are especially close to Jesus, they are not Jesus' only disciples in Mark. Already Peter's mother-in-law has ministered to Jesus (1:31). Nor is Levi, called by Jesus to follow him (2:14), identified as one of the Twelve.

The names of the Twelve and their ordering (3:16-19) vary in the New Testament (John 1:40-41; 21:2; Acts 1:13). The lists in Matthew (10:1-4) and Luke (6:14-16) most closely resemble Mark's, probably because the Second Gospel was their source. First Corinthians (15:5) and Acts (6:2) mention "the twelve" without identifying all its members. In Mark, as elsewhere, Simon receives priority (see also 1:16, 29-30, 36). To him Jesus gave the name "Peter" or "Stone" (*petros*, here for the first time in Mark): a symbol of imperturbability as far back as the Greek tragedians Sophocles (*Oedipus Rex* 334) and Euripides (*Medea* 28; see BDAG 809b). Paul (1 Cor 1:12; 3:22; Gal 1:18; 2:9-14) and John (1:42) remember "Peter" by its Aramaic equivalent, "Cephas" (in colloquial English, "Rocky"). Less certain is Mark's etymology of "Boanerges," the name given the sons of Zebedee (Mark 3:17; cf. 1:19-20). One cannot convert this term's consonants and vowels into any Semitic construction that would suggest "Sons of Thunder" (*huioi brontēs*). The closest equivalent in antiquity—*onomazetai embrontaion*, "house of thunder"—refers to a domicile struck by lightning (Diodorus of Sicily, *Historical Library* 8.11.2; BDAG 179b-180a). Andrew, remembered as Simon Peter's brother (Mark 1:16, 29; John 1:40-42), follows fourth in Mark's list of the Twelve. Another Simon is surnamed "the Cananaean" (3:18), perhaps deriving from an Aramaic term for "fanaticism" or "zeal" (cf. "Simon the Zealot" in Luke 6:15; Acts 1:13). In the mid-first century C.E. the Zealots were a Jewish party in hostile revolt against the Roman Empire

(Hengel 1989). The sense of Judas's surname, "Iscariot" (3:19a), is obscure. It could refer to "a man from Kerioth [-hezron]" (Josh 15:25; Jer 48:24), alternatively to an Aramaic word *sakar* ("fraud" or "one choked"; cf. Matt 27:5) or to a term (*sicarios* [Gk.]; *sicarius* [Lat.]) for an "assassin" or "murderous bandit" (BDAG 480b). There is no mistaking Mark's note about Judas as "the one who also handed [Jesus] over" (AT): the same verb, *paradidōmi,* appears in 1:14 to describe John the baptizer's arrest. Not only do Mark's readers know of the plot to destroy Jesus (3:6); now they know of the informer who, from among Jesus' own followers, will assist in its execution.

Identifying Jesus' Family (3:19b-35)

The setting and structure of Mark 3:19b-35, identifying Jesus' family, resemble those of Mark 2:1-12. In both cases a controversy between Jesus and scribes over the origin of his power lies at the heart of each pericope (2:6-7; 3:22), situated amid a large crowd "at home" (2:1; 3:19b). In both, Jesus' response to his accusers is elliptical (2:8-9; 3:23-27), turning the bone of contention in unexpected directions. In 2:7 the scribes accuse Jesus of blasphemy (*blasphēmei*); Jesus replies by asserting the authority of "the Son of Man" (*ho huios tou anthrōpou*) to forgive sins (*aphienai hamartias*) on earth (2:10). In 3:22 the scribes assail Jesus as trafficking with demons; Jesus speaks of blasphemies (*hai blasphemiai*) and sin (*hamartēmatos*) of which "the sons of men" (*hoi huioi tōn anthrōpōn*) may or may not be forgiven (*aphethēsetai,* 3:28-29). Mark 2:1-12 and 3:19b-35 employ interpolated traditions: in both pericopae one segment of material is sandwiched within another (see table 2). In the present case—the insertion of the scribes and Jesus' dispute (3:22-30) between the responses of those associated with Jesus (3:19b-21 + 3:31-35)— the materials are welded with repeated words ("and there came" [*kai erchetai*] those "who were saying" [*elegon,* vv. 19b, 21] or "called" [*kalountes,* v. 31]; "home" [*eis oikon,* v. 19b], "house" [*hē oikia,* vv. 25, 27]; five iterations of "mother and brothers" [vv. 31-35]). Mark invites the reader to interpret each of these entwined pericopae in the light of its mate and, perhaps, to consider them also in the light of 2:1-12.

The Evangelist sets the stage simply: "And he goes home" (3:19b AT). (Most ancient manuscripts change the singular subject to a plural—"And they go home"—to include the companions called in 3:16-19a.) To ask "*whose* home" will only mislead: "home" is a typical site for much of Jesus' teaching in Mark (see, e.g., 1:29, 32-33; 7:17, 24; 9:28, 33; 14:3, 12-16) but is hardly a throwaway location. Households constituted the fundamental social units in antiquity (Safrai and Stern 1976, 728-92). This venue assumes special significance in 3:19b-30, where crucial domestic matters—where one eats (v. 20), with whom one is close (v. 21), divisions of a house (v. 25), despoiling a house (v. 27), who is Jesus' family (vv. 31-35)—tumble upon one another. The crowd is so large that it prevented them from eating (3:20; cf. the burdens created by crowds in 1:37; 2:2). Meals are a time not merely for nourishment, but for intimate association (Gen 18:1-8; Ps 41:9). By its sheer size, the multitude threatens Jesus on both counts.

Most of the oldest manuscripts convey the subject of 3:21 vaguely: "when those around him heard [about this]." The later, Western tradition, which tends to take interpretive liberties, reads, "when the scribes and the rest heard about him." That change smooths out the *dramatis personae* in verses 21-22 and erases any suspicion that those close to Jesus thought him crazy and wanted to haul him away. That scandalous assertion is exactly what Mark intends, as exegetes since Jerome have acknowledged (*Letter* [108] to *Eustochium*). (Matthew [12:24-32, 46-50] and Luke [8:19-21; 11:17-21; 12:10] avoid this suggestion by doctoring Mark's obscure comment in 3:21 and by eliminating his intercalation of the scribes' accusation into a family disturbance; see Best 1986, 49-63.) The NRSV translation, "his family" (v. 21), renders a Greek idiom (*hoi par' autou*) with a Semitic basis that usually refers to one's relatives (Moule 1959, 52). Mark makes clear their motive for attempting to seize Jesus: "He has gone out of his mind."

Description of this familial conflict is temporarily suspended in order to bring onstage "the scribes who came down from Jerusalem" (3:22 RSV, JB, NRSV). In Mark the scribes are those scholars—"the duly accredited theological teachers of God's people" (Cranfield 1959, 143)—whose teaching has been unfavorably compared with Jesus' own (1:22), who have expressed both tacit and blatant hostility to Jesus (2:6, 16). Not for the last time (see 7:1) the Evangelist identifies scribes as having come down to Galilee from Jerusalem, reminding the reader of rumors about Jesus that have extended to that Judean city (3:8) and anticipating the site of Jesus' arrest and death (10:32-34). (Though Jerusalem is south of Galilee, the city rests on an elevation. Thus, it is customary to speak of "coming down" from or "going up" to it [see 10:33].) The charge registered against Jesus is the gravest yet: trafficking with demonic powers. The etymology of the name "Beelzebul" (which Syriac translators and Jerome's Vulgate rendered "Beelzebub") is uncertain, with suggested derivations ranging from "lord of the flies" to "lord of the heaven," "the master of the house" (cf. Matt 10:25b), "lord of the dung," "the adversary," and "Baal, the flame." Mark and the other Synoptic Gospels regard "Beelzebul" as synonymous with Satan (3:23, 26; Matt 12:24-27; Luke 11:15-19), the agent of Jesus' wilderness temptations in Mark 1:12-13. The further identification of this figure with "the ruler of demons" reminds one of the demons (1:32, 34) or "unclean spirits" (1:23) that Jesus has cast out (1:23-26; 3:11-12). Alignment of evil spirits with satanic ringleaders like Asmodeus, Mastema, or Belial reaches deeply into intertestamental Jewish literature (Tob 3:8, 17; 1QS 1:18, 24; 2:5, 19; 1QM 13:12; 14:9; *Jub.* 10:1-14; 11:1-5; 23:29; *As. Mos.* 10:1; *T. Levi* 19:1; cf. 2 Cor 6:15). A correlation of the claims in Mark 3:21-22—demonic possession, madness, social estrangement—is drawn both by Jesus' critics in John 8:48-49 and by critics of Hellenistic philosophers like Alciphron (*Letters of Courtesans* and *Letters of Farmers*; see Boring, Berger, and Colpe 1995, 174-75). Later rabbinic traditions revile "Yeshu [of Nazareth, who] practiced sorcery and led Israel astray" (*b. Sanh.* 107b; *b. Sotah* 47a). The implied logic of the scribes' accusation in Mark 3:22 is that only one in league with the demonic hierarchy could so readily dispose of its forces.

Jesus' response to this charge is mysterious. He neither rebuffs nor distances himself from his accusers; instead, "he called them to him" (3:23). Rather than offer a straightforward answer, he speaks to them "in parables": Mark's first reference to what the reader will learn is Jesus' customary mode of teaching (4:2, 33-34). In the biblical tradition, parables (Gk. *hai parabolai*; Heb. *meshalîm*) were originally not illustrations used to clarify, but proverbs or narrative riddles that provoked questions without resolving them (Ps 78:2; Prov 1:6; Ezek 17:2; Hab 2:6; Sir 47:17). Mark 3:23 presents the first of Jesus' riddling replies, which approximates the form of a rhetorical question: "How can Satan cast out Satan?" The next three verses elaborate that teasing proposition with a trio of general conditions, almost identically formulated:

A. If a kingdom is divided against itself, that kingdom cannot stand (v. 24).
B. If a house is divided against itself, that house cannot stand (v. 25).
C. If Satan rises up against himself and is divided, he cannot stand (v. 26a).

Following from A and B—observations of everyday organizations—the implication is that the same must hold true for C, concerning a supernatural commonwealth. The last portion of verse 26b educes a further implication: "[Satan's] end has come." That, however, is not the capper of Jesus' response, which continues with three more observations, all seemingly irrelevant and unsolicited:

D. To plunder a strong man's house requires first tying up the strong man (v. 27).
E. People will be forgiven their sins and whatever blasphemies they utter (v. 28).
F. Blasphemies against the Holy Spirit constitute an eternal sin and are, therefore, unforgivable (v. 29).

Statements A, B, and C appear straightforward: Satan's commonwealth is every bit as susceptible to internal division and instability as this world's kingdoms and families. There is, however, a disturbing aspect embedded in Jesus' three claims: each shares with those of his antagonists the assumption that a diabolical realm bears on this world's social institutions. By adopting the scribes' premise, Jesus leads them to an awkward, indeed paradoxical position. If they *deny* what Jesus asserts is generally the case, then they are thrown at odds with the basis of their own accusation. If they *accept* Jesus' assertion as just so, then they end up agreeing with Jesus and thereby contradict their own accusation (Tannehill 1975, 177-85). Even if one accepts Jesus' premise (as would his antagonists) as well as his conclusion (as only his supporters would), all is not thereby resolved. There is an inherent tension between the reasoning of verses 24-26a, which assumes that Satan's kingdom has not fallen, and the point of verse 26b, the claim that it has (Marcus 1999). Statement D, the aphorism about trussing up the strong man in order to burgle his house, suggests a partial reconciliation: one activity has been accomplished (binding a bruiser) so that another may proceed without having been completed (pilfering his goods). Thus it seems to follow: Jesus can continue to thwart demonic powers not because he is in cahoots with them, but because he has bound Satan. Such a claim (v. 27) is the clearest refutation of the scribes' original allegation (v. 22): Jesus indeed "has Beelzebul"—but not as a collaborator. Jesus has Beelzebul at his mercy—though not utterly so, since some portion of the strong man's house remains inviolate, some aspect of Satan's enterprise still stands (Riches 2000, 145-79).

Underlined by the firm pronouncement "Truly I tell you" (a recurrent formula in Mark [8:12; 9:1, 41; 10:15, 29; 11:23; 13:30; 14:18, 25, 30]), statements E and F shift Jesus' response to his challengers in a more aggressive direction. The narrator's comment in verse 30 specifies the point of linkage: "for they had said, 'He has an unclean spirit'" (cf. v. 22 and John 7:20; 8:48). Aligning Jesus with demonic forces is tantamount to committing a sin that cannot be released (v. 29), unlike all other sins, which are forgivable (v. 28). Ascribing demonism to Jesus is a deadly form of abuse: it is blasphemy, which, in Hellenistic Greek as in modern English, connotes the desecration of God. In both the LXX and the NT blasphemy is ultimately violation of God's majesty (2 Kgs 19:4, 6, 22; Isa 52:5; Rev 13:6; 16:11, 21), though penultimately it comprises derision of godly persons or things (Isa 66:3; Ezek 35:12; 2 Macc 8:4; 12:14; 15:24; Acts 6:11; Titus 2:5). So also in Mark 3:28: identifying as diabolical the one who conveys God's holy spirit (1:8, 10) is a peculiar blasphemy, beyond the pale of normal remission.

Mark closes his interpolative circle by returning to Jesus' family, now specified as his mother and his brothers (v. 31). Here, as in 6:3 and, indeed, throughout the NT (John 2:12; 7:3, 5, 10; Acts 1:14; 1 Cor 9:5; Gal 1:19; see also *Gos. Thom.* 99; *Gos. Eb.* 5), Jesus' identification with respect to mother and brothers, in the absence of his father, is odd, given the assumption of patrilineal descent in Jewish antiquity. Although calling to him, significantly they are "standing outside": as outsiders, they are implicitly identified with those who have judged Jesus mad (v. 21) and associated with others who have gotten him flagrantly wrong (v. 30). The crowd's report to Jesus that his family members are outside, asking for *(zēteō)* him, reminds the reader of Simon Peter, who invaded Jesus' privacy with the report, "Everyone is searching for you" (1:37). There, as here, the verb has a misguided, ominous connotation that becomes evident as this Gospel unfolds (8:11-12; 11:18; 12:12; 14:1, 11, 55). More immediately, Mark implies that the scribes' belief that Jesus travels with unclean spirits (3:22, 30) corresponds to his family's belief that he is unhinged. The briefer wording of 3:32, which appears in the oldest manuscripts of Mark and is reflected in the NRSV footnote, is more likely to have been what the Evangelist originally wrote, later expanded to conform with the aphorism's wording in 3:35. The redefinition of Jesus' family in verses 34-35 is multidimensional. Spatially, it comprises not outsiders, but those "on the inside" who encircle Jesus (a distinction to be highlighted in 4:10-12). Fraternally, its kinship is based not on blood, but on obedience to God's will—with which, by implication,

Jesus is aligned. The phrase "the will of God" appears only here in Mark (v. 35; cf. 14:36). Religiously speaking, Jesus' real family is the faithful church, surrounding him and obedient to their common Father (see 8:38; 13:32; 14:36; cf. Matt 23:9). To the family members identified by the crowd—"your mother and your brothers" (Mark 3:32)—Jesus conspicuously adds "my sisters" (v. 35), which females in Mark's own community would surely have heard as a reference to them. Precisely because the family was the primary social unit in antiquity, Jesus' redefinition of kinship in 3:34-35 concludes the entire passage on a note as scandalous as his suggestion, in 3:29-30, that Jerusalem's scribes have just committed unpardonable blasphemy.

Families actual and figurative play a significant role in Mark 3:13-35. Verse 31 has proved problematic in the history of Roman Catholic exegesis: Jesus' *adelphoi* (brothers) has sometimes been translated very loosely as "cousins" in order to reconcile Mark with the later doctrine of Mary's perpetual virginity. Moreover, verse 21 throws an embarrassing shadow across Jesus' mother. The Second Evangelist was ignorant of subsequent piety focused on Mary (Meier 1992). Mark is interested in contrasting responses to Jesus by different "families," real and surrogate. His kinfolk consider him deranged (vv. 21, 30). In their place Jesus forms a group of twelve intimates (vv. 13-19) and reformulates family ties in terms of those doing God's will (vv. 34-35). The identification of "family" with "church," though by no means unique to Mark (see also Acts 1:12-14; 2:43-47; Rom 8:22-23; Eph 2:19-22; 1 Pet 3:1-12), would have been important to early Christians whose confession had ripped apart their own families (see Mark 13:12-13; John 9:1-41; Barton 1994, 220-25). That said, this segment of Mark evinces sensitivity to the fact that any household—including the church—can become so riven that it collapses (3:25), that Jesus' own circle harbored his betrayal from the beginning (3:19).

In Mark the presence of Judas among those whom Jesus

wanted to call (*proskaleita*, 3:13) parallels the hostile scribes whom Jesus also calls (*proskalesamenos*, v. 23) to hear his parables. Both times Jesus does not turn his back on active or potential adversaries; it is they who reject him. In its most extreme expression, that repudiation takes the form of "blasphemy against the Holy Spirit," "an eternal sin" (v. 29). Previously, scribes attributed blasphemy to Jesus for releasing a paralytic's sins, on the ground that only God may remit them (2:5-10). In that case Jesus challenged "such questions in [their] hearts" but did not reproach them as unpardonable. Though bewildered, the scribes were attempting to protect God's sovereignty. By placing Jesus among Beelzebul's ranks, however, scribal misapprehension has now devolved into blasphemy: derision of the Holy Spirit by which Jesus expels unclean spirits and enunciates God's will (see also 1:21-28). Why is this sin unforgivable? Mark does not elaborate, leaving such riddles (3:23) for Jesus' audience to unravel. Throughout its subsequent history, the church has worried over this question (Donahue and Harrington 2002, 134-35). Regarding Jesus as diabolical may put one beyond the pale because one thereby drives oneself away from the true agent of forgiveness (see "the deathward sin" in 1 John 5:16-17). To extend the metaphor in Mark 2:17: one will never surrender to therapeutic surgery if one is so deluded that she thinks her physician is a homicidal monster. To place Jesus in league with Satan may be so utterly perverse that its proponents place themselves under conditions in which forgiveness is a practical impossibility.

Nevertheless, the mystery of God's will, at work in Jesus, remains pervasive and insoluble in Mark 3:13-35. Satan's sovereignty has not yet imploded, though an end has been made of him (3:26). What the reader of Mark has witnessed to this point is "the raiding of the strong man's house" (3:27)—begun though not yet completed, "an eschatology that is in process of realization" (Jeremias 1972, 230). With Jesus' advent, Israel has begun to be reconstituted (3:13-19); this world swings on its hinges, away from demonic captivity toward the kingdom of God (1:14-15; 3:7-12). During the interval before its consummation, God's sovereignty remains concealed (3:12), subject to betrayal (3:19) and rank blasphemy (3:29-30). Its character can be expressed only obliquely, in riddles (3:23-29, 33-35; so also 2:9-28). And so Mark 4 delves more deeply into the parabolic aspects of "the secret of the kingdom of God" (4:11).

Jesus' Parabolic Teaching (4:1-34)

Mark 4:1-34 comprises one of this Gospel's two largest blocks of essentially uninterrupted teaching. (The other is 13:1-37.) This section's recurring motif is "the kingdom of God" (4:11, 26, 30), the keynote of Jesus' preaching (1:15). Its form of expression is in parables (v. 2; cf. 3:23).

By the first century C.E. the term "parable" (Heb. *mashal*; Gk. *hē parabolē*) had enjoyed a long history of use in Semitic and Greek culture (Boucher 1977, 86-89). In the OT *meshalîm* can refer to proverbs (Prov 1:1; 10:1; 25:1), bywords (Deut 28:37; 1 Kgs 9:7), blessings and curses (Num 23:7, 18; 24:3, 15, 20-23), and taunts (Mic 2:4; Hab 2:6). In Ezekiel (17:1-21; 24:3-14) *meshalîm* are allegories with or without explanations. Such oracles shade into riddles: fables (Judg 9:7-20; 2 Sam 12:1-7) or brainteasers (1 Kgs 10:1-5; Sir 22:14-25). After the NT era, Jewish *meshalîm* can refer to apocalyptic visions (*4 Ezra* 4:44-50; *1 En.* 37:1; 38:1; 45:1) or homespun analogies (*Sipra Num.* 86; *Sipra Deut.* 356). Aristotle attributes to Socrates a parable arguing against selection of public officials by lottery, which would be like randomly picking representative athletes regardless of their athleticism (*Rhet.* 2.20.1-8). The Latin rhetorician Quintilian considers the parable a comparison of things whose resemblance is unclear (*Inst.* 5.11.22-23). Something like that understanding, blended with prophetic and apocalyptic riddles, underlies C. H. Dodd's now classic definition: "At its simplest the parable is a metaphor or simile drawn from nature or common life, arresting the hearer by its vividness or strangeness, and leaving the mind in sufficient doubt about its precise application to tease it into active thought" (1961, 5).

Mark 4:1-34 is elegantly organized (see also Marcus 1986, 221-23; Moloney 2002, 85-86):

Table 3: *The Structure of Mark 4:1-34*

A. Introducing the parables (4:1-2)
   B. A sower's seeds (4:3-9)
      C. Parables and perception (4:10-12)
         D. The seeds' reception (4:13-20)
      C.' Disclosure and reception (4:21-23 + 4:24-25)
   B.' Other sowers' seeds (4:26-29 + 4:30-32)
A.' Concluding the parables (4:33-34)

As in 2:1-36 the structure 4:1-34 is chiastic: an inverted staircase whose central landing sums up the steps leading to and from it.

Introducing the Parables (4:1-2)

The Evangelist introduces the parables (4:1-2) with characteristic vocabulary and syntax. "Again" is one of Mark's favorite adverbs (occurring twenty-seven times); "began to," one of his preferred locutions (twenty-six instances); "the crowd," a customary noun (thirty-seven times). Verse 1 is awkwardly formulated. Like most translations, the NRSV smooths over some roughness: "he got into a boat on the sea and sat there" felicitously renders Mark's odd comment that Jesus "sat in the sea after he had gotten into a boat."

Jesus teaches from a boat after the crowd has become too large for him to continue on the lakeshore (4:1; cf. 3:9-10). This description picks up a theme developed early in Mark: the teacher's attraction of multitudes (1:28, 33, 36-37, 45; 2:2, 13; 3:7-8, 20), requiring that he distance himself from them (1:35; 3:21, 31-32). Jesus continues his ministry in public places, often off the beaten track of conventional institutions. Of this there is a faint suggestion in the verb used in verse 1 for the crowd's gathering: *synagō* (see also 2:2; 5:21; 6:30; 7:1), the verbal cognate for the noun "synagogue" (1:21, 23, 29, 39; 3:1). One may translate the first half of this verse either "he began to teach them many things in parables" (NRSV) or "he taught them a great deal in parables" (Lattimore). Pedagogy matches topography: creating space between himself and his listeners by moving into the lake, Jesus' mode of teaching also generates distance between them. The crowd is located "on the ground" (a superfluous note, reworded by Matthew [13:2]), just as seed is sown "on the ground" in the riddles Jesus now spins (4:5, 8, 20, 26, 28, 31).

A Sower's Seeds (4:3-9)

The parable of a sower's seeds (4:3-9) is well attested in the Gospels, appearing also in Matthew (13:3-9), Luke (8:4-8), and the *Gospel of Thomas* (9). Jesus' opening address is arresting (cf. Deut 6:4; Judg 9:7; Isa 28:23; Ezek 20:47), with a double emphasis elided in most English translations: "Listen—Look" (Mark 4:3 AT). The figure of the sower is colorless, and his procedure seems indiscriminate (Chrysostom, *On Matthew* 4.4–5.1). Jeremias (1972, 11-12) opined that in ancient Palestine sowing would precede tilling, but the evidence for that is thin and may miss Mark's point: the land is not carefully prepared (Drury 1985, 56-58). The stress in this parable lies on the interval between sowing and plowing, when the seed is subject to conditions preventing germination (*Jub.* 11:11). Contrary to the NRSV, *para tēn hodon* should probably not be rendered "on the path" (v. 3); the preposition *para* suggests that the seed is sown beside the path (Moule 1959, 50-51). That translation better fits the parable's details: one would not expect a traveled path to be rocky, thorny, or rich (Mark 4:5, 7, 8), but the soil adjacent to a walkway could be all those things. The planting is indiscriminate; the seed falls where it will (vv. 4, 5, 7, 8).

The seeds are susceptible to disparate circumstances, which go from bad to worse. The birds gobble up (*katephagen*) one seed soon after it falls (v. 4). Another, landing in pebbly soil, springs up right away but, scorched by the sun, soon withers and is rootless (vv. 5-6). Still another seems on the verge of fruition, only to be throttled by thorns. If the listener has expected this parable's adherence to folklore's "rule of three," she is disappointed: each outcome is worse than its predecessor. Verse 8 shatters the now established pattern in every respect: not only do these seeds "take"; they do so under inauspicious conditions. The soil into which they fall is not just "good" (thus, NRSV); it is *kalēn*— "superb" or "rich" (JB). These do not merely yield fruit; they grow up (*anabainonta,* also used of choking thorns in v. 7), explode (*auxanomena*), and bear in orders of ascending magnitude: thirty-, sixty-, hundredfold. There is no consensus on these percentages: some think such fecundity would have been extraordinary (Schweizer 1970, 90-91; Marcus 2000, 292-93); others regard them as unexceptional (France 2002, 192-93). In Mark's context, however, the results are surely staggering. Seventy-five percent of the sowing ended in abject failure; twenty-five percent has blossomed exponentially (Donahue 1988, 34; cf. Gen 26:12, where a hundredfold yield is a great blessing). Unlike a kindred similitude in *4 Ezra,* which concludes that "those who have been sown in the world will not all be saved" (8:41), Mark 4:3-8 ends on an exhilarating note that forces reconsideration of the entire parable. Without evident reason the contrast between cause and effect is vast: between careless, failure-ridden sowing and bountiful produce. Prophetic admonition to Israel underlies Jesus' exhortation for listeners to pay attention (Mark 4:9; cf. Ezek 3:27; see also Mark 4:23; 8:18; Matt 11:15; Luke 14:35; Rev 2:7, 11).

Parables and Perception (4:10-12)

The scene shifts. Jesus is by himself, save for "those around him with the twelve" (4:10 AT). Curious wording: Jesus is hardly alone if surrounded by these others, but a contrast is suggested between the multitude in 4:2 and a smaller gathering. Private explanation often follows public instruction in Mark (4:34; 7:17; 9:28; 10:10; 13:3). That they ask about "the parables" (plural) is odd: only one has just been told. Still, 4:3-8 contains several obscurities. Jesus' comments on parables and perception (4:10-12) constitute one of this Gospel's notorious knots (4:11-12).

According to Mark, the parables create a scripturally warranted division among Jesus' audience (vv. 11-12). "You"—implicitly, those around him along with the Twelve—are contrasted with "those outside" (*tois exō*), reflecting the change of scene between 4:1-9 and 4:10. Each group receives something different. To the disciples "has been given the secret [or "mystery," *to mystērion*] of the kingdom of God." The implied agent of the gift is God. Unlike Matthew (13:11) and Luke (8:10), Mark speaks of a singular "secret" given to Jesus' disciples, without any confirmation that they "know" what that secret is or how it might be unraveled. This *mystērion* is associated with God's sovereign rule (*tēs basileias tou theou*), the epitome of Jesus' Galilean preaching. Though the Evangelist has not referred to "the kingdom of God" since 1:15, it may have been implicit by contrast in Jesus' parabolic reference to Satan's kingdom in 3:24. Beyond association with God's kingdom, this secret's content is not defined. In a general way it probably refers to the "mystery" surrounding God's cosmic purposes, withheld from most but graciously revealed to a select few in apocalyptic literature like Daniel (2:18-19, 27-30, 47), *1 Enoch* (68:1), the DSS (CD 3:18; 1QH 5:36), Paul's letters (Rom 11:25; 1 Cor 2:1, 7; 4:1), the Deutero-Pauline tradition (Eph 1:9-10; Col 1:26-27; 2 Thess 2:7; 1 Tim 3:9), and the Revelation to John (1:20; 10:7; 17:5, 7; see Marcus 1984). To those outside—who expose themselves as such, as did his mother and brothers (3:21-32), by their inappropriate response to Jesus—"everything comes in parables."

The justification for God's offer of mystery and parables to, respectively, insiders and outsiders is drawn (without attribution) from Isaiah 6:9-10: the Lord's commission that the prophet address Israel in a way that hardens its obstinacy and hinders its restoration. The history of this passage's transmission—from the LXX's Greek translation of an irrecoverable Hebrew text, to a later Aramaic rendering in a rabbinic interpretation of Isaiah, to the sixth-century Hebrew of the MT—is complicated (M. Black 1967, 153-58), indeed confounding. Mark's wording appears to blend extant Greek and Aramaic versions of Isaiah 6:9-10, with a peculiar emphasis on divine confusion. Isaiah 6:9-10 is adopted throughout the NT (Acts 28:26-27; Rom 11:1-10; John 12:40) as a way of interpreting rejection of the gospel. Mark's use of Isaiah's oracle looks backward, to those like Jerusalem's scribes who accused Jesus of demonism (3:22), as well as forward, to family members who deliver up to death those who follow Jesus (13:12-13).

The sharpest nettles in Mark 4, however, are two simple words in verse 12: *hina*, "in order that," and *mēpote*, "lest." Despite heroic efforts to soften its blow (Moule 1959, 142-43; Guelich 1989, 211-12), the plainest meaning of verse 12 is that Jesus' parables *intend* to blind and to deafen, without which those so stymied might turn back and be forgiven (BDF 187b; Marcus 2000, 298-307; Edwards 2002, 133-35). Indirect confirmation that Mark intends a "hardening theory" just that hard is supplied by Matthew (13:13) and Luke (8:10), who, while following Mark, relax the severity of 4:12 in different ways. Mark's view of Jesus' parables inclines toward an epistemological predestination: those who do not understand Jesus and his ministry *cannot* understand, by God's design (Donahue 1988, 40-42). As baffling as that seems, such a claim has a conceptual affinity with Exodus (9:12; 10:20; 11:10), in which the Lord hardens Pharaoh's heart against Moses' demands (Drury 1985, 41-42), and 1 Corinthians (1:20-24; 2:12-14), in which God's gospel of the crucified Messiah withholds understanding from those who have not received God's spirit (Räisänen 1990, 123-37). Likewise, the use of parables to convey divine secrets is a familiar theme in such apocalyptic writings as *4 Ezra* (4:26-43), *1 Enoch* (38:1–69:29), and *2 Baruch* (22:3-8; see Patten 1983).

The Seeds' Reception (4:13-20)

Jülicher's classic investigation (1899) attacked the notion that Jesus' parables are allegories, whose details should be allegorized. In antiquity, however, the membrane between parable and allegory was porous (see Mark 12:1-12), and Jesus' audiences have long been inclined to attach allegorical equivalents to his parables' details (Kissinger 1979, 1-43). Evidence of that tendency is found in Mark 4:13-20, whose allegorization of the seeds' reception is an early Christian interpretation of 4:3-9, dramatizing missionary hardships and the difficulty of discipleship. Such themes recur, sans parabolic attire, in Paul's letters (Rom 8:35; 2 Cor 4:8-9; 2 Thess 1:4).

Mark 4:13 opens with two pointed questions: "Do you not understand this parable? How then will you understand all the parables?" (RSV). Elsewhere in Mark, Jesus chastises his disciples for their lack of understanding (6:52; 8:17, 21). The second question in verse 13 is the more intriguing. To what does it refer: the mysterious explanation of the parables' purpose in 4:11-12 or to the parable in 4:3-8? Since both are parabolic, either is possible. The second is more likely, given the ensuing explanation. Discernment of the seeds is somehow critical for interpreting all of Jesus' parables, especially those in Mark 4:21, 24, 26-29.

The interpretation in verses 14-20 is hard to follow because the meaning of "the seed" (in vv. 4-8) fluctuates (cf. also *4 Ezra* 8:41–9:37). In verses 14 and 15b, it stands for "the word" (*ho logos*), which at its simplest could refer to a speaker's subject (see Mark 1:45; 2:2), though here may connote "the gospel" about Jesus Christ (thus, e.g., 16:20; Luke 1:2; Acts 1:1 and throughout; Eph 1:13; 1 Thess 1:5, 6, 8; Jas 1:18; 1 Pet 1:23; 1 John 1:1; Rev 1:2, 9). That is likely the primary nuance in Mark 4:14-15b, which then would suggest various outcomes of Christian preaching (the main reason for inferring that vv. 14-20 stem not from Jesus but from later Christian reflection). At verse 15a there is a shift: the seed is now identified as "those who are beside the path" (AT). That may refer to early audiences of Christian preaching. "Beside the path" (*para tēn hodon*) acquires new significance: farming experience (v. 4) has become a metaphor for those *beside* "the way"—discipleship of Jesus (e.g., Acts 2:28; 9:2; 16:17; 19:23; 24:14)—who do not follow it. Demonic deprivation is the cause of such rejection of the gospel: Satan comes and removes "the word implanted" in its recipients (Mark 4:15). While Satan is not identified with the ravenous birds (4:4), there remains a hint of the diabolical as a devouring power, always on the prowl (1 Pet 5:8).

The parallelism between Mark 4:5-6 and its interpretation in 4:16-17 is more explicitly developed than that between verses 4 and 14-16. "And these are the ones" (v. 16) refers, in context, to another group of recipients of "the word." Seed sown on rocky ground is comparable to those quick to accept the word with joy but who are not firmly rooted. The point of comparison is shallowness, "no depth of soil" (v. 5 AT). Superficiality and meager rootage (Wis 4:3-5; Sir 40:15) cannot withstand the scorching heat (v. 6) of tribulation and persecution "on account of the word" (v. 17). Later in Mark (10:30; 13:19, 24) Jesus promises his followers "tribulation" and "persecution"; such suffering is the peculiar outcome of Christian discipleship. Characteristic of shallowness is a lack of persistence (v. 17); such plants, or people, wither away (4:6) or—mixing the metaphor—get tripped up (*skandalizontai*). Again Mark introduces a metaphor that recurs later in his Gospel, that of stumbling over Jesus (6:3; 9:42, 43, 45, 47; 14:27, 29). It is a fine question whether the mention of stony turf (*to petrōdes*, 4:5) subtly alludes to Simon, whom Jesus nicknamed "Rocky" (3:16; Tolbert 1989, 145-46). Because a plural form of the Greek noun occurs in 4:16 (*ta petrōdē*), the Evangelist's concern is for more than a single disciple. By the time he exits this narrative, nevertheless, Simon is a startling example of short-lived faith, which cannot take the heat and apostatizes (14:29-31, 54, 66-72). "The others [plural] that are sown" (v. 18 AT) refers not to the word but to those auditors consumed by "thorns": the worries of this age (*hai merimnai tou aiōnos*) and the allure of wealth (v. 19). Unlike Q (Luke 12:22-31 = Matt 6:25-34), which develops Jesus' teaching on anxiety about survival, in Mark's Gospel pitfalls surrounding wealth, notably its deterrence of unstinting discipleship, receive greater attention (10:23-25). Shifting the terms of comparison, worldly desires choke (*sympnigousin*, v. 19) the word and render it sterile, much as thorns choked (*synepnixan*, v. 7) the seed's capacity to bear fruit.

The interpretation's climax (v. 20) mirrors and elaborates,

using many of the same terms, the climax of the parable itself (v. 8). The seeds (plural in v. 20, as in v. 8) are correlative to recipients; the singular fruit, to the word received. The receptive listener does not "fall into fine loam" but, in a sense, *is* that fertile soil. Fruit that grows abundantly is like someone who obeys the word and welcomes it. Whether one speaks of seed in superb soil or appreciative listeners of the word, there are comparable measures of fruitfulness. Some are thirty times more productive than usual; others, sixty times; still others, a hundred times. In every case, however, some seeds scattered—some proclamations of the word—take root and surpass conventional expectations of productivity. Why some so welcome the word is left unexplained, even though reasons for a seventy-five percent failure rate have been offered. The predestinarian comments in 4:11-12 may assist interpretation: if one deeply receives and embraces the word so promiscuously disseminated, its fruitful exploitation remains entirely in God's hands.

Disclosure and Reception (4:21-23 + 4:24-25)

Two parabolic remarks follow, concerning disclosure and reception (4:21-23, 24-25). Neither extends the metaphor explored in 4:3-8 and 4:13-20, though both adopt commonplace domestic images as theological points of comparison. One thread connects verses 4:21-25 with all that has preceded: the mysterious dynamics of divine gift and human accountability.

The mystery of God's gift is underscored in 4:21-23. To this point Mark 4 has emphasized hearing (vv. 9, 12b, 15, 16, 18, 20); the parable in 4:21 recollects this chapter's comparable interest in seeing (vv. 3, 12a). The usual translation of Jesus' question in 4:21 is represented in the NRSV: "Is a lamp brought in to be put under the bushel basket, or under the bed, and not on the lampstand?" Though a reasonable paraphrase in modern English, such a rendering obscures two important features of the question's construction in Greek. First, verse 21 is introduced with the particle *mēti*, which in Greek is a way of introducing a rhetorical question that invites a negative reply. A way of conveying that sense in colloquial English is like this: "A lamp doesn't come...—does it?" Implied in that rendering is a second, interesting aspect in 4:21. Literally (in Greek), the hypothetical lamp is not "brought" or "carried"; rather, it does or does not "come" (*erchetai*). The Aramaic of the biblical period tends to avoid the passive voice. There is, however, another possibility: namely, that "the gospel" or even Jesus himself is here personified as a lamp, a source of illumination (Anderson 1976, 136)—an implication drawn out elsewhere in the NT (John 1:4-5; 9:5; Rev 21:23). There is kindred OT imagery: a lamp can refer to Israel's illumination by the Lord (2 Sam 21:17; 22:29; Zech 4:2), usually through his law (Ps 119:105; Wis 18:4).

The sense of Mark 4:21 is clear enough: a lamp's purpose can be realized only if suspended from a lampstand. Put it under a "bushel basket" (Lat. *modius,* a bucket able to contain a little over two gallons), and its light is extinguished. The same is true of placing a lamp beneath a bed, with the added risk of combustion for the blissfully ignorant sleeper. Verse 22 is an unusually clear interpretation of the preceding: conceding that indeed there are things secret (*krypton*) or hidden away (*apokryphon*), *such things are not meant to remain so.* Instead—in divine perspective—the *purpose* of secreting things *is ultimately to make them manifest* (another divine passive construction). Here is a miniature paraphrase of the parables' purpose in 4:11-12. God is the author of darkness and light, the agent of secrecy and disclosure (similarly, Job 36:30, 32; Isa 45:7). Jesus' parables adhere to that venerable, perplexing, scriptural precedent. Perhaps that is among the things that anyone with hearing ears should attend to (Mark 4:23): the prophetic caution in 4:9 ("[She] who has ears to hear"), reiterated here more vaguely ("[If] anyone has ears to hear").

The transitional exhortation in 4:24a conflates the metaphors of vision and audition in 4:21-22. Unfortunately, that blending is obscured in most English translations: "Take heed" (RSV); "Consider carefully" (NIV); "Pay attention" (NRSV). All these attempts to smooth out the rough Greek—*blepete ti akouete*: two curt, oxymoronic imperatives—mask Mark's sly conjunction of human senses, previously summoned in 4:3 ("Listen; look") and developed in 4:12. Verse 24a invites a literal, delightfully offbeat translation: "Look what you hear." "Measuring" in 4:24b has already been implied in verse 21 (the *modius*). Adapted to different purpose in Q (Luke 6:38b = Matt 7:2), the metaphor's development in Mark 4:24c ("and still more will be given you") creates a link for the kindred yet harsher comment in 4:25c: "For to those who have, more will be given; and from those who have nothing, even what they have will be taken away." Verse 25 does not say that *exceedingly* more will be given to one who has (cf. Matt 13:12; *Gos. Thom.* 41). Mark 4:24-25 returns us to 4:11-12: the enigmatic interplay between human receptivity to the mystery of God's dominion and God's sovereign authority to dispense, or to remove, that capacity for reception. As in 4:11-12, so here: both the gift and the aptitude for its receipt lie within divine, not human, purview. That interpretation is reinforced by a mélange of verbs conjugated in the divine passive: "it will be measured"; "it will be amplified"; "it will be given"; "it will be deprived."

To summarize this segment: Mark 4:21-25 responds to a question embedded in 4:13-20: Why do comparatively few accept God's gospel? Mark's response is consistent with the "hardening theory" in 4:10-12. The parables and their interpretation are intrinsically baffling, befitting "the mystery of the kingdom of God" (4:11), and yet that mystery is intended for disclosure in God's good time. Because God is now sovereign, notwithstanding appearances to the contrary (1:14-15), God alone confers and withholds all gifts of hearing and of sight, all shafts of light and of darkness. One will be measured by the yardstick one uses, not because God is constrained by a principle of tit for tat, but because the only reliable yardstick one has is that which God has given. What recipients of God's mysterious revelation have is irreducibly a gift, not the product of self-engendered insight.

Other Sowers' Seeds (4:26-29 + 4:30-32)

Framing 4:3-9, Mark considers God's kingdom (*hē basileia tou theou*) with parables about other sowers' seeds (4:26-29, 30-

32). The first of these (4:26-29) is without parallel in the other Synoptic Gospels: the only Markan parable of which that may be said. For Dodd (1961, 140-44), Mark 4:26-29 exemplifies Jesus' "parables of growth": "the crisis [of God's kingdom] which has now arrived is the climax of a long process which prepared the way for it" (144). Provided that one does not exaggerate the kingdom's present realization, which this parable does not stress, there is truth in Dodd's claim about a "process." More pointedly, the details of the seed's maturation—from initial germination (v. 27, *blasta* [blast off!]), first a blade, then an ear, then full grain in the ear (v. 28)—suggest inevitability in the kingdom's coming, even as a plant's flowering follows a steady course of development. Other aspects of this parable are equally noteworthy. While the hypothetical sower has a hand in the proceedings by throwing the seed onto the ground, afterward there is no question of human involvement in agricultural success. To the contrary: "The earth bears fruit automatically" (*automatatē*), apart from human effort. Underscoring that point is a description of the planter, who sleeps and arises, "night and day," again and again, while the spore sprouts and grows, "he knows not how" (v. 27, RSV). Thus Mark returns to a critical point in the preceding segment: the unmitigated gift of God's kingdom (see also Luke 12:32; 22:29). Mark 4:21-25 (and vv. 11-12) underlines the revelatory character of God's activity in this world through Jesus. So, too, does 4:26-29 end on an apocalyptic chord: sending in the sickle for the fruit's harvest is a durable image for the final judgment (Joel 3:13; Rev 14:14-20), which moderns still recognize in the Grim Reaper.

In the final parable of Mark 4 (vv. 30-32), the listener is invited to consider a mustard seed. As a matter of botanical fact, the *brassica nigra* is not the smallest of all that is sown; however, a number of ancient Greek and Jewish proverbs regard it as such, as do other aphorisms of Jesus (Matt 12:20; Luke 17:6; *Gos. Thom.* 20). Mark 4:30-32 sharpens the striking contrast between the seed's insignificance and the capacious plant emerging from it. In the shade of its great branches the birds of heaven can roost: an OT image that suggests God's protection through an appointed monarch, such as restoration of the Davidic house (Ezek 17:22-24; 31:1-9; cf. Dan 4:1-27). Later Jewish texts refer to Gentile converts to Judaism who roost "under the wings" of God's effulgence in the eschatological age (Moore 1958, 1:330; cf. LXX Zech 2:11). Mark, however, injects a neat fillip into this venerable trope: unlike Matthew (13:32) and Luke (13:19), which offer the clichéd antithesis between "smallest of seeds" and (magnificent) tree, Mark subverts the listener's expectations by comparing the tiniest of seeds with "the greatest of all the vegetables" (*meizon pantōn tōn lachanōn*, v. 32). The effect is hilariously ludicrous: God's kingdom begins as the smallest of seeds but grows up to become the greatest of—zucchini. Though this be only a blue-ribbon squash, its branches are lush enough to shelter the vulnerable.

Concluding the Parables (4:33-34)

Mark leaves some threads dangling. First, according to verse 33 Jesus spoke "the word" (*ton logon*) in many such parables as those recounted in 4:3-32, which may be regarded as representative, not exhaustive. Second, those to whom he told such parables remain as curiously indeterminate as their ability to comprehend is uncertain. Even though Mark 4:12 indicates that everything is in parables for those *beyond* the Twelve and other intimates, there is no indication in the rest of Mark 4 that the audience of Jesus' parables is anyone *other than his disciples. To them* he explains the sower's seeds (vv. 13-20); *to them* he speaks cryptically of divine gifts and human receptivity (vv. 21-25). While the precise audience of verses 26-29 and verses 30-32 is unidentified, there is no reason to suppose it has ceased to be the disciples. Either Mark is not utterly consistent in his point of view, or he is inviting readers to consider that "insiders" like the Twelve often stand alongside "outsiders," much as Jesus' family and Jerusalem's scribes are both literally and figuratively outsiders to Jesus' teaching in 3:19b-35—and, for that reason, elicited parables (3:23). There is merit in this second possibility, because Jesus' questions of "those who were around him along with the twelve" (4:10) assume that they do *not* understand the parables (4:13; cf. Matt 13:51). Speaking in parables "as they were able to hear" (Mark 4:33) resolves nothing about the degree of their understanding: one could interpret that comment as suggesting that the parables were told to relieve or to heighten the incomprehension of Jesus' listeners. Verse 34 compounds the mystery: privately, Jesus "settled" everything with his disciples, though Mark never indicates they were the better for it.

The peril besetting any interpreter of Mark 4:1-34 is trying to explain too much. The chapter's parables seem so simple that they can be forced into a Procrustean bed, justifying all sorts of religious ideas alien to Mark. Given the disciples' imperceptiveness (4:13), the first step in an attempt to make sense of the parables should be a humble silence, a refusal to rush toward exegetical judgment, and a persistent willingness to listen and to observe (4:3, 24), revising one's impressions in the light of further consideration.

While drawing on everyday objects and episodes familiar in an agrarian culture—seeds and sowing, harvest and reaping, lamps and measures and vegetables—it is clear that these "dark sayings" do not intend to promote desirable religious or moral conduct. Over and again, the persons in the parables are colorless, noticeably passive, hardly agents at all. Sow they may, and reap; the vital activity, however, remains beyond their ken and control, subject to plentiful hazards (ravenous birds, scorching sun, this world's worries), their own rootlessness, and surprises, both predictable and unexpected, as they sleep and arise and sleep again. The Evangelist's conjugation of verbs in the divine passive offers an important clue to the meaning of the whole. Mark 4 is not interested in religious or political projects, dependent on human initiative and measured by mortal standards. Instead, this chapter offers glimpses of the kingdom of God, God's sovereign authority, which through Jesus' words and deeds is irrupting into the everyday world (Ambrozic 1972, 46-135). If some among

Jesus' audience enjoy even a shred of insight into his teaching, it is clear that such comprehension is God's gift and not the product of his listeners' education, industry, or cleverness (4:11-12, 24-25; Juel 1994, 45-63; Black 2008).

What do these parables teach about God's kingdom? Neither here nor anywhere in Mark does Jesus talk directly, in analytical terms, about the kingdom's character. His descriptions are invariably allusive, "truth told on the slant" (Emily Dickinson): "With what can we compare the kingdom of God?" (4:30); "[it] is as if..." (4:26). The medium is the message: a parable—literally (in Greek), something thrown beside another—is irreducibly mysterious (4:11), "a certain shock to the imagination" (Wilder 1964, 72), at once concealing as much as it reveals (4:33-34). Perhaps this, for Mark, is as reliable as any indicator that Jesus truly operated in God's sphere of authority, not one with which this world is familiar: a fundamental human inability to grasp its dimensions, even less to manipulate its power (Kermode 1979, 23-47). The parables cannot be evaded: they put their listeners on the spot and force decisions.

For all their mystery, some consistent strands are discernible in Mark 4. Most obvious is the claim that God's sovereignty subverts in the most preposterous manner all human expectations (Dahl 1976, 141-55). Seventy-five percent of a planter's effort is seemingly wasted; the remaining twenty-five percent takes root, for no apparent reason, and thrives with remarkable prolificacy. Things are hidden for the purpose of exposure. A seed explodes, its fruit matures, without the slightest cultivation. The smallest of seeds becomes the biggest of vegetables—not sequoia, but leafy enough for nesting. Such images are intended not to clarify but to stupefy—which is, in itself, an absurd clarification. Those receiving such instruction remain comically stumped. The kingdom of God does not operate in accordance with received opinion and the violence of this world's principalities. At every point it upsets conventional wisdom, turns, and defies it again.

From that claim it follows that God's kingdom is radically apocalyptic, in that term's precise sense: its character can be revealed, the veil lifted, only by God to those whom he chooses (Donahue

and Harrington 2002, 152-56). The astringency of Mark's epistemology, his view of the conditions under which understanding is
possible, is at once a balm to the vulnerable, frail as seeds, and an
indictment of those who presume some inside track onto the
workings of the Almighty. The apocalypticism of Mark's parables—bristling with Satan (4:15), tribulation and persecution
(4:17), this age's anxieties (4:19), sickle and harvest (4:29), unresolved mystery and dark disclosure and intensified obfuscation
(4:11-12, 24-25)—reminds the reader of the eschatological spirit
suffusing the Gospel to this point (1:9-11, 13-14, 21-28; 2:18-22;
3:11-12, 22-26, 28-30), thus raising the stakes of this word's sowing (4:14). While the parables in Mark 4 have a deceptive charm,
there is nothing cute about them. Their accessibility lulls readers
into dropping their guard just long enough to realize that "the
gospel of God" (1:14) has invaded their world to convict them of
their own blindness, deafness, and spiritual sclerosis (4:12)—much
as an adulterous, murderous king was once hoisted on his own
petard by the simple story of a pet lamb's slaying (2 Sam 12:1-15).

Worth pondering is the christological import of these parables
(Beavis 1989). Jesus is the only source in Mark for parables of
the kingdom and their interpretation (3:23-30; 4:10-12, 33-34;
12:1-12). Early readers of this Gospel who confessed Jesus as the
Messiah (1:1) knew very well how his story ended. As this narrative unfolds, the Evangelist withholds nothing of its climax and
denouement (8:31; 9:31; 10:33-34). It is, therefore, a fair question to ask whether the Evangelist implicitly invites the reader to
regard Jesus *himself* parabolically (Donahue 1979). To consider
such a possibility does not constrain one to flat-footed interpretation (Jesus = "the sower [who] went out to sow"), though
Mark's parables are capable of conveying multiple meanings,
both superficial and profound. The point is a risk presented by
the Evangelist to his readers: Is one willing to allow this Gospel's
presentation of Jesus, as paradoxical as this world's unsettling by
God's kingdom, to reconstruct one's apprehension of the Christ?
Like a sower's seeds, a muffled lamp, a secret seed, the smallest
seed—like the divine kingdom to which all these are patently or

latently compared—Jesus in Mark is never exactly what he appears. Like his parables, he flouts expectations, wrenching assessments of achievement and failure inside out. In this Gospel "there is nothing hidden, except to be disclosed; nor is anything secret, except to come to light" (4:22)—including, and especially, the crucified Messiah.

Who Does These Mighty Works? (4:35–6:6a)

In this segment Mark returns to Jesus' wondrous deeds, accented in the Gospel's earliest chapters (1:16–2:12; 3:1-6). An interest in Jesus' identity, previously adumbrated (1:1, 11, 24; 2:7c; 3:11-12, 22), is now developed more explicitly.

Table 4: *The Structure of Mark 4:35–6:6a*

A. "Who then is this?" (4:35-41)
      B. "What have you to do with me?" (5:1-20)
            C. "Come and lay your hands on her"
               (5:21-24a)
                  D. "If I but touch his clothes"
                    (5:24b-34)
               C.' "Why trouble the teacher any
                  further?" (5:35-43)
A.' "Is not this the carpenter?" (6:1-6a)

The parallelism is not exact. Although one may divide 5:1-20 into two scenes (vv. 1-14a, Jesus' confrontation with unclean spirits; its aftermath in vv. 14b-20), this pericope has no exact analogue in the rest of the section. One step of the staircase is missing. The rest of this chiasm, or crisscrossed arrangement of material, is obvious.

"Who Then Is This?" (4:35-41)

Though brief, Mark's account of a tempest's stilling is salted with details omitted by Matthew (8:23-27) and Luke (8:22-25).

For example, Mark's account sets this episode at evening, which makes the lake crossing more dangerous (v. 35). Because Jesus' activity has been in Galilee (3:6, 19b), "go[ing] across to the other side" suggests crossing the lake from west to east (cf. Luke 8:22), headed toward the Roman province of Gaulinitis. "Leaving the crowd" (v. 36a) suggests another of Jesus' private colloquies with the Twelve after public teaching (see also 1:29, 35; 3:7a; 4:10). That pattern's disturbance, also witnessed elsewhere (1:36; 3:7b-8), recurs here with the mention of "other boats...with him" (4:36c). That some disciples took him with them in a boat "just as he was" (v. 36b) is as cryptic in Greek as in English translation. Perhaps Mark is suggesting that no special precaution was taken for a crossing fraught with peril.

The flotilla's escort immediately disappears; attention is narrowed to the ship carrying Jesus. Even today, sudden squalls on the Sea of Galilee can be terrifying (Taylor 1981, 274). In vivid detail Mark depicts "a mighty blast of wind, and waves cascading into the boat, such that already the boat was filling" (v. 37 AT). Tightening the narrative focus, Mark leads the reader into the ship's stern, where Jesus is "asleep on the cushion" (v. 38). Throughout the biblical tradition, the sea is associated with chaos that only the Lord can master (Gen 8:1; Exod 14:21-22, 26; Pss 74:13-14; 89:8-9; 104:4-9; Jonah 1:4-5; *T. Naph.* 6:29). Sleep is a typical posture of trust in God (Job 11:18-19; Pss 3:5; 4:8). By contrast, the disciples' strident appeal to Jesus— "Teacher, don't you care that we are dying?" (Mark 4:38b AT)— recalls the wording of several psalms (35:23; 44:23-24; 59:4b). The correspondences with Psalm 107:23-39 are so striking that Mark 4:35-41 seems almost a theological interpretation of that psalm.

Mark's modifications of that scriptural template are noteworthy. Two harsh verbs express the sea's stilling (4:39a). The first, "Be quiet!" (*siōpa*), was used to dramatize the silencing of Jesus' antagonists (3:4b); later it will return in describing his quieting of the disciples (9:34) and his own silence before the high priest (14:61). The second, "Shut up!" (*pephimōso*), is the same verb Jesus used to rebuke an unclean spirit (1:25). Thus, in Mark

4:39b, diabolical forces that threaten human life again meet their match in Jesus.

Jesus' riposte to his disciples is no less harsh: "Why are you such cowards? Do you still have no faith?" (4:40 AT). Matthew (8:25-26) and Luke (8:24a, 25a) use different words to soften both the disciples' cry to the sleeping Jesus and his rejoinder. In Psalm 107:23a those who "went down to the sea in ships" have ample justification for terror in a tempest; Mark uses this occasion to point up a lack of faith, or trust (*pistis*), among Jesus' followers. To this point in the Gospel, Jesus has called upon his listeners to entrust themselves (*pisteuete*) to the good news of the kingdom's encroachment (1:15) and, in acknowledgment of companions' faith (*pistis*), has released a paralytic from his sins (2:5). Faith or trust (*pistis*) and its lack (*apistian*) recur at critical points in this segment of Mark (5:34, 36; 6:6a). As in 4:40, so also in 5:15, 33, and 36: *pistis* is contrasted with *phobos* (fear)—not the fear of the Lord that is the beginning of wisdom (Pss 111:10; 112:1; Prov 9:10; 15:33), but the fear that manifests itself in cowardice (*ti deiloi*).

Sailors for whom the Lord calms the tempest respond with gladness at being safely delivered (Ps 107:30). By contrast, this group of seamen (Mark 4:41) "feared a great fear," the awe with which mortals react to divine manifestations (Exod 3:1-6; Isa 6:1-5; Jonah 1:10, 16; Luke 2:9; see Dwyer 1996). They ask one another who this Jesus is. As this pericope concludes, their question dangles, like that of the scribes' about Jesus' authority to forgive sins (Mark 2:7). Anyone familiar with Scripture knows that only divine power can quell chaotic waters (Gen 1:2, 6-9; Job 38:8-11; Pss 65:5-8; 93:3-4; 107:28b-30; Isa 51:10; Jer 5:22). Doubtless Mark would concur (see 1:11). His primary interest, however, is to leave the reader with the disciples at sea, wondering just who Jesus really is and the bases on which a valid conclusion may be drawn.

"What Have You to Do with Me?" (5:1-20)

Mark 5:1-20 is the second and longest of this Gospel's four presentations of Jesus as exorcist (see also 1:21-28; 7:24-30;

9:14-29). As in other cases, Mark seems as interested in conclusions drawn from the exorcism as in the mighty work itself. For that reason, this "playlet" may be divided into two acts: the contest itself (vv. 1-13) and its consequences (vv. 14-20). Both subsections have been abbreviated in Luke (8:26-39) and radically truncated by Matthew (8:28-34).

Act One: The Exorcism (5:1-13). The boat's portage on "the other side of the sea" refers to the Galilee's east bank: "the country of the Gerasenes" (5:1), modern Jerash. In his commentary on John, Origen rejected both Gerasa (Mark 5:1; Luke 8:26) and Gadara (Matt 8:28) as too distant for the actions described in Mark 5:1-2, 6, 13 (*Commentary on John* 6.24). Scribes who copied these Gospels were equally perplexed by Mark's geography, whose accuracy is still challenged (Meier 1994, 650-52). Some, like Origen, repositioned this miracle's setting in Gergesa (probably modern Kursi or Kersa) because that location comports with the story's details: Gergesa was an ancient village on the Lake of Tiberias (= Sea of Galilee) with a promontory. (Modern Kursi contains remnants of a memorial to the miracle of the swine; see Finegan 1992, 115-16.) The best manuscript evidence for Mark 5:1 locates the story in Gerasa, about fifteen miles southeast from likely portage on Tiberias (Metzger 1994, 72). The Second Evangelist's grasp of Palestinian geography seems shaky at best (see Mark 7:31).

Mark's description of this man with an unclean spirit (5:2-5) surpasses both Matthew and Luke for its frightening, piteous detail. The encounter between Jesus and the afflicted is immediate, with the latter emerging from his abode among the tombs (vv. 2-3a). For modern readers the latter description is creepy enough, though deeper, religious points are embedded here. Contact with corpses is defiling in the Levitical tradition (Lev 11:7-8; 22:4b, 6a; Num 5:2; 6:6; 9:6). Even more pointedly, "[those] who sit inside tombs / And pass the night in secret places" (Isa 65:4-5a NJPS) among swine (Mark 5:11-13) typify a stubborn nation that rebels against the Lord's holiness (see Watts 1997, 157-60). In Mark 5 Isaiah's oracle is inverted in two important ways. First, unlike disobedient Israel, insisting that the

Lord keep his distance from them, the man with the unclean spirit approaches and kneels before Jesus (v. 6). Second, while the Lord promises to punish an idolatrous Israel (Isa 65:5a-10), Jesus receives this tormented figure (Mark 5:2, 8-13a). That for which the prophet had prayed—"If You would but tear open the heavens and come down" (Isa 64:1a NJPS)—has already occurred at Jesus' baptism (Mark 1:10-11). Beyond these features the Evangelist emphasizes that this demoniac is a terror to his neighbors (v. 5a), a danger to himself, owing to a demon that stirs its host to self-injury (v. 5b), and impossible to restrain (vv. 3b-4). A menace to himself and others, the victim possesses the terrifying strength of the darkest supernatural forces. The chance of a cure seems hopeless.

The demoniac's response to Jesus is confused, befitting someone suffering severe mental illness. Seeing Jesus, the man runs and kneels before, or worships (*prosekynēsen*), him (v. 6), prostrating himself before a superior authority—as have the unclean spirits generally, with respect to Jesus (3:11). Yet there is resistance comparable to that in 1:23-24, shouted in similar words: "What have you to do with me, Jesus, Son of the Most High God? I adjure you by God, do not torment me" (5:7). As in 1:34, so also here: with supernatural perception, unclean spirits immediately recognize Jesus and the threat he poses for them. Appropriate to this tale's setting in the region of the Decapolis (5:20), "the Most High God" was a title that Gentiles applied to Israel's God (Gen 14:18-20; Num 24:16; Isa 14:14; Dan 3:26). Like the naming of Jesus, the quasi-magical adjuration against him is the unclean spirit's ploy to repel the exorcist (*ad loc.* Mark 1:24), who has made the first move to expel the demon (5:8). Jesus' counteroffensive continues with a demand for the spirit's name: to know him intimately enough that he may be overcome (again, see 1:24). *Legion* (5:9) was a Roman regiment of six thousand soldiers. In the apocalyptic theater of Mark's narrative, colonial oppression converges with personal possession (Myers 1988, 190-92).

With the spirit's plea that it not be driven from the country

(5:10), the tide turns. Acknowledging that Jesus cannot be out-conjured and exorcism is inevitable, the demon begs for its place of expulsion. (Twitching the geopolitical thread, there may be a further suggestion that occupying forces resist ceding conquered territory.) "Send us into the swine," feeding on a nearby hillside (vv. 11-12). (In both 1:24 and 5:9 the subject swings from singular to plural, suggesting a form of what later psychiatry styles as multiple personality disorder.) By Levitical precept (Lev 11:7-8) pigs are as unclean as tombs, unclean spirits, and Gentile legionnaires. Jesus gives the demons permission to inhabit the swine, setting the stage for a climax at once fitting, frightening, and repulsive. The herd, numbered at two thousand—another instance of Mark's delight in hyperbole (see 1:33)—throw themselves down the steep bank and drown in a watery chaos (5:13; cf. 4:35-41). Jesus has proved himself an exorcist par excellence and a clever trickster in binding Satan's minions (3:27). Defilement has been implicitly purified, *kashrut* vindicated with a horrific vengeance. The swine, however, were a source of some Gentile's agricultural livelihood—a point that may partially account for the citizenry's ambivalent response to Jesus in the next scene.

Act Two (5:14-20). Since Mark could have ended this tale at verse 13 (as Matthew nearly does [8:33-34]), its second act repays careful attention. Having witnessed the swine's destruction, the herdsmen flee and spread the news (*apēngeilan*) in the city and neighboring hamlets (Mark 5:14a). Typically for this Gospel (e.g., 1:32-33; 2:13, 15; 3:7-10, 20), a crowd gathers (5:14b). What they take in is more placid than what Jesus witnessed on arrival (5:2-8): they see him and the erstwhile demoniac, now seated, dressed, and of sound mind (*sōphronounta*). Their immediate reaction: fear (5:15). Exactly what they fear is unexpressed, though by now the reader knows that, for Mark, fear is the opposite of faith (4:40-41). The witnesses tell their story of what happened (5:16). The auditors' immediate response: begging (*parakalein*) Jesus to leave their territory (v. 17). Thus recurs, in a different form, the oscillation of attraction and repulsion that has attended Jesus from Mark's earliest chapters (e.g., 1:35-39; 2:15-17; 3:9-12, 31-35). Once again Jesus' demonstrations of healing do not of themselves commend faith in him to those not already so disposed (see also 3:21-22). In a sense the villagers' petition plays out Jesus' aphorism in 4:24: "Watch what you hear; by the measure you measure it will be measured out to you" (AT). Those, like these country folk, who refuse Jesus do more than find themselves faithless (4:25); they drive away from themselves faith's proper object. This episode displays anti-evangelism: messengers report what they have seen Jesus do (5:16), and the message's recipients do not repent but turn him down cold (cf. 1:15). As requested, Jesus leaves. The gospel does not coerce acceptance.

The exception to this rebuff is the man who was healed, who keeps begging (*parekalei*) "that he might be with [Jesus]" (5:18)—the language Mark has previously used in describing the first responsibility of a member of the Twelve (3:14-15a). Now it is Jesus' turn to refuse (5:19a), but not without giving the man a mandate: to return home, to his own, and tell them how much the Lord (*ho kyrios*) has mercifully done for him (5:19b). This commission seems to fly in the face of Jesus' previous injunctions *not* to tell of what has happened (1:44; 3:12), though in this case there are some unusual factors: Jesus is *leaving* a region that has *rejected* him. The man obeys (5:20; cf. 1:45), though with some final twists. He preaches (*kēryssein*: see also 1:4, 14, 38, 39, 45; 3:13) not merely at home but throughout the Decapolis, a federation of ten Gentile cities among which Pliny's *Natural History* (5.16, 74; first century C.E.) includes Gadara and Galasa (the latter, probably the same as Gerasa; Finegan 1992, 117). He proclaims what *Jesus* did for him. Whether this constitutes adherence to or deviation from Jesus' command is debatable: in Mark, "the Lord" can refer either to God (12:11, 29-30, 36; 13:20) or to Jesus (1:3; 2:28; 7:28; 11:3, 9; 12:37; 13:35). All were amazed at this proclamation, reprising a theme first announced in 1:22. Astonishment may be more positive than repudiation (5:17); it is not, however, the same as faith.

The stories of Jairus's daughter (5:21-24a + 35-43) and the woman with chronic hemorrhaging (5:24b-34) may have originally been independent of each other (Bultmann 1963, 214-25). (The first tale recalls Elijah's resuscitation of a widow's son [1 Kgs 17:17-24] and Elisha's restoration of the Shunammite's son [2 Kgs 4:18-37].) If Mark himself combined these tales, then we have another of this Gospel's narrative intercalations (see table 2). Much of the Evangelist's artistry lies in the subliminal level at which these interwoven stories operate (see Shepherd 1993, 139-72).

"Come and Lay Your Hands on Her" (5:21-24a)

Jesus returns to the lake's west bank (v. 21). Again (cf. 4:1-2) a great crowd gathers around him beside the Galilean water. The narrator's "camera" zooms in to frame a single figure among the throng: Jairus (only one of two named interlocutors in a miracle story; cf. 10:46). Though the office of a synagogue leader (*archisynagōgos*) is well attested in epigraphical and literary evidence of the first and second centuries C.E. (see Luke 13:14; Acts 13:15; 18:8, 17), that figure's precise duties are uncertain. An archisynagogue likely assumed general responsibilities for a synagogue, an important place of Jewish study and prayer (*ad loc.* Mark 1:21-28). Such a figure could have been the institution's primary financial benefactor (L. I. Levine 2000, 390-402). Although Jewish leaders have resisted Jesus' ministry in this Gospel (2:6-9, 16, 24; 3:1-5), to the point of plotting his destruction (3:6), here (and later: 12:28-34; 14:42-57) Mark makes clear that not all Jewish authorities were hostile to Jesus. By prostrating himself before Jesus (5:22), this VIP is unashamed to submit himself to Jesus' healing power. He begs Jesus on behalf of his young daughter (*thugatrion*, an affectionate diminutive of the sort Mark favors [C. H. Turner 1993, 123-26]), which in colloquial English could be translated as "little girl." She is at death's door (v. 23). In contrast with Matthew's parallel narrative (9:18), Jairus's daughter has not yet died. In Mark she is at the very point of death (*eschatōs echei*), though her father clings to the hope that she may yet be saved (or "made well," *sōthē*: see also 3:4; 6:56; 10:52) if only Jesus will come and lay his hands on her (5:23). Therapeutic laying on of hands, though rare in contemporary Jewish stories of healing, appears in some Greek and Roman stories (Theissen 1983, 62-63, 92-93) and is frequent in Mark (3:10; 5:28; 6:5, 56; 7:32; 8:22, 25). Jesus complies (5:24a), setting the stage not just for healing but also for a crucial lesson in the dynamics of faith.

"If I But Touch His Clothes" (5:24b-34)

At this point the Evangelist deftly creates a tale of two pities. The second begins with slight stage business: the press of a following crowd. Time is of the essence—the child is on the verge of death—yet the healer's progress is already delayed (5:24b). Again the narrator's camera focuses on another face in the crowd: a woman who, unlike mighty Jairus, is one of the nameless "little people" who populate the Second Gospel (Rhoads and Michie 1982, 129-36). She has suffered chronic discharge—in effect, perpetual menstruation—for a dozen years. Among ancient Jews such a condition was multiply miserable. By implication, she has been unable to bear children, both a cultural expectation (Gen 16:1-6; 30:1-8) and an incomparable source of joy (Ps 113:9). She is as much defiled and defiling as the demoniac among Gentile tombs (Mark 5:2-3). For twelve years she has been ritually unclean, without possibility of purification (Lev 15:19-30; Chilton et al. 2010, 195-200, though some question its pertinence here: A. Y. Collins 2007, 283-84). Physicians have proved incompetent to treat her: a typical complaint in antiquity (Tob 2:10; Sir 38:1-15), though, as Dowd points out (2000, 57-58), intelligible in a world where Soranus (*Gynecology* 3.10) knew of physicians who prescribed bloodletting (!) for women's hemorrhaging. This woman has wasted her resources on failed cures (Mark 5:26). An infertile female, ritually impure and a source of others' defilement, poor, and desperate: Mark goes to great length to help the reader sympathize with her predicament. In the time it takes to absorb these details, the reader thinks again of Jairus, for whose daughter precious minutes are dwindling.

The woman takes a bold, if stealthy, step forward: she moves into the crowd—transgressing society's invisible boundary against the impure—and touches Jesus' cloak from behind (5:27). Believing in the magical power of holy people—as does Jairus (5:23)—she thinks that if she but touches even his garments, she will be healed (or "saved," *sōthēsomai*: 5:28; see also 3:10). As she believed, so it happens: "immediately her bloody flow dried up, and she knew in her body that she was cured of her affliction" (5:29 AT). Were this merely the story of an unfortunate's healing, there it could end (and does, in Matt 9:22). Mark has still other issues to pursue.

"Immediately" (Mark 5:30; also 5:29) Jesus is inwardly conscious (*epignous en heautō*) that power (*dynamis*) has seeped out of him: precisely mirroring the woman's bodily awareness that she has been cured (5:29). The reader is privy to Jesus' self-awareness, and hers, in a way that none of the other characters are. Thus, Jesus' reaction—asking who touched his clothes—makes sense to the reader, though not to Jairus and the crowd. This prompts his disciples to express what by now is a recurrent Markan theme: their misunderstanding of the master (v. 31; 1:35-37; 3:19a; 4:13, 38, 41; typically downplayed in Matt 9:20-22 and Luke 8:45-46). Brushing them off, Jesus inaugurates a search to determine the one responsible for that power-draining touch (5:32).

The clock is still ticking...

Fearful and trembling, whether for having been caught out (see Luke 8:47) or from the shock of realizing that she has indeed been cured (thus, Mark 4:41; 5:15), the woman confesses "the whole truth"—including, presumably, her case history and the reasons for her action (vv. 25-28)—throwing herself at Jesus' knees (v. 33), as Jairus had done (v. 22). Jesus replies with comfort and hope: "Daughter, your faith [or 'trust': *pistis*; see also 2:5] has saved [or 'healed,' *sesōken*; see also 5:23, 28] you: Go in peace, and continue being healed from your affliction" (5:34 AT). The first half of Jesus' command is a customary Jewish blessing for wholeness (*shālōm*: Judg 18:6; 1 Sam 1:17; Acts 16:36; Jas 2:16); the latter, a present imperative (suggesting durability) that assures her healing is permanent. In an instant Jesus is able, without even trying, to do for this daughter of Abraham what the professionals have been unable to accomplish across a dozen futile years.

"Why Trouble the Teacher Any Further?" (5:35-43)

Jesus has gone out of his way to attend to a nameless suppliant, has healed her, and has sent her away in peace. What about Jairus? Amid the hubbub, the search, and the pedestrian conversations, the sands of his daughter's hourglass have been running out. It is critical that we have known, since 5:23-24a, that the mission to Jairus's house is an emergency. Who better to underline the brilliance of Mark's technique than the popularly acknowledged "master of suspense," Alfred Hitchcock (Truffaut 1984, 73)?

> There is a distinct difference between "suspense" and "surprise," and yet many...continually confuse the two. I'll explain what I mean. We are now having a very innocent little chat. Let us suppose that there is a bomb underneath this table between us. Nothing happens, and then all of a sudden, "Boom!" There is an explosion. The public is *surprised,* but prior to this surprise, it has seen an absolutely ordinary scene, of no special consequence. Now let us take a *suspense* situation. The bomb is underneath the table and the public *knows* it, probably because they have seen the anarchist place it there. The public is *aware* that the bomb is going to explode at one o'clock and there is a clock in the décor. The public can see that it is a quarter to one. In these conditions this same innocuous conversation becomes fascinating because the public is participating in the scene. The audience is longing to warn the characters on the [movie] screen: "You shouldn't be talking about such trivial matters. There's a bomb beneath you and it's about to explode!"

At Mark 5:35 the bomb goes off. "*While* they were talking" (AT)—reminding the reader that the delay in 5:24b-34 need not have happened—unnamed messengers arrive from Jairus's house to say, "Your daughter's dead. Why are you still bothering the teacher?" For a report so heartrending, the language is callous and utterly witless: Jesus is more than a teacher, as both the reader and Jairus understand, and the archisynagogue has hardly been troubling him. To the contrary: for readers sympathetic to this father's misery, the long episode with the woman has surely troubled *them,* even as they have been whipsawed by her plight. In typically biblical fashion (Auerbach 1953, 3-23) the narrator supplies no words to express the father's devastation; all is left to the reader's imagination. "Overhearing what they said," Jesus interposes a shaft of hope into Jairus's despair: "Don't be afraid; just keep trusting" (5:36 AT). (The verb *parakousas* may be also be rendered "ignoring [the report]"; in that case the sense would be that Jesus "disregarded it," urging Jairus to do likewise [thus, Goodspeed, NIV, Lattimore]). By now Mark's reader knows that Jesus is not whistling in the dark. Between fear (*phobos*) and faith (*pistis*) so many characters have swung: the disciples and their teacher in the tempest-tossed boat (4:40-41), the Gerasene and his audience (5:15, 17-20), and the frightened woman whose trust proved sufficient (5:33-34). Jesus permits only Peter, James, and John (see 1:16-20; 3:16-17; 9:2; 14:33) to accompany him to Jairus's house (5:37), in seclusion typical of Markan and other biblical stories of healing (5:40; 7:33; 8:23; also 1 Kgs 17:19; 2 Kgs 4:4, 33).

At last the scene shifts to the archisynagogue's house. As in 5:24b-34 Mark does not hurry things to conclusion but allows the rest of the story to unfold in painful detail. The reader encounters not physicians (5:26) but another group of "professionals": mourners for hire (5:38; see, e.g., Jer 9:18-20; *b. Ketub.* 4.4). Beyond their scorn of Jesus (5:40a), their very presence explains his expulsion of them: their grief is possibly remunerated, certainly faithless and premature, as pointless as the woman's medical expenses (5:26). Jesus' reply to the sobbing is cryptic: "Why your racket and crying? The little child isn't dead but only sleeping" (5:39 AT). If that is literally true, the messengers' report in 5:35 was erroneous, and the little girl's revival will be of qualified magnitude. On the other hand, then as now, "sleeping" is a euphemism for death (Eph 5:14; 1 Thess 5:10). In any event Jesus' observation raises a derisory laugh (see also the skepticism in 5:31, 35), prompting him to bounce the mourners from the death chamber (Mark 5:40ab).

Joining with the father and mother, with Jesus and his associates, crossing the threshold where the child lay (5:40c), the reader reaches the end of this emotionally complex tale. By implication, Jesus has just been defiled by the touch of a woman with a bloody discharge (5:27); now, in 5:41, Jesus is defiled by touching a presumed corpse (Num 19:11-13). " '*Talitha koum*,' which means, 'Little girl [literally, 'little lamb'], get up!'" (5:41) is one of several Semitic expressions that Mark translates, presumably because they would otherwise not be understood (7:11, 34; 11:9-10; 14:36; 15:22, 34, 42). In Greek-speaking ears the sound of Aramaic might remind Mark's readers of incantations in other miracle stories of that era. One might compare a story about Apollonius of Tyana (ca. 4–96 C.E.), who "touched [a] dead woman, spoke a few incomprehensible words, and thus awoke the girl from apparent death" (*Life of Apollonius* 4.45). Early Christians could have heard in Mark's terms for the child's rising, *egeirō* (5:41) and *anistēmi* (5:42) the language of resurrection (see Mark 6:14; 12:23-26; 16:6, 9, 14). At Jesus' command the little girl arises and, perhaps to verify permanence of her vitality (cf. 5:34b), walks about (5:42a). That "she was twelve years of age" curiously entwines with the other woman whose health Jesus has just restored. That "daughter" (5:34) suffered a pathological flow for twelve years (5:25); aged twelve, Jairus's young daughter (5:23) is on puberty's cusp, roughly when female menses begin— which the woman's body was unable to stop. Like other audiences (see 5:20), Jairus's household is thunderstruck (5:42b). Once more (1:34, 44) Jesus enjoins strict confidentiality (5:43a). That the recovered child be given something to eat (5:43b) may touch on the folk wisdom that revenants cannot eat (see Luke 24:29-42). Since mealtimes in the Bible are occasions for social reintegration (*ad loc.* Mark 2:16), Jesus is also doing for the child the same as for her elder "sister." Far from being defiled himself (see Douglas 1966, 1-57), Jesus has reversed the polarity of contamination, fully restoring two of Israel's daughters to their proper homes, from which they have been horribly estranged.

"Is Not This the Carpenter?" (6:1-6a)

A story about Jesus' rejection at home (paralleled in Matt 13:53-58 and Luke 4:16-30) offers Mark a poignant, edgy, and whimsical commentary on Jesus' parables (4:1-34) and the astonishing works he has performed in 4:35–5:43. Fittingly, if oddly, it rings down the curtain on what may be regarded as the Second Gospel's second act.

As the geography has not shifted since 5:21, Jesus remains in Galilee, returning to his hometown (*hē patris*). Reminding the reader that Jesus' story is also the story of his disciples (see also 1:16-20; 3:13-19a), Mark reports that they continue to follow him (6:1). For the second time (1:21) Jesus visits and teaches in a synagogue on the Sabbath (6:2a). Many are astounded (*ekplēsso*, 6:2b) by him, as were others in Capernaum's synagogue (1:22, using the same Greek verb). Like his earlier listeners (1:22b, 27), these ask the source of Jesus' authority (6:2c). So far, so predictable.

The questioning turns darker in Mark 6:3a. Jesus' mother and brothers have appeared in a futile attempt to whisk him away (3:21, 31-32). Among the women who will watch his crucifixion (15:40) is Mary the mother of James and Joses, who may or may not be a different woman from Jesus' mother. The identification of Jesus in 6:3a is quirky. Customarily, a Jewish child was identified patrilineally; yet neither here nor anywhere in Mark is Jesus "son of Joseph," as in Matthew (1:16-24; 2:13, 19), Luke (1:27; 2:4, 16; 3:23-24, 30; 4:22), and John (1:45; 6:42). One explanation is that by this time Joseph had died; another, that there was doubt about Jesus' paternity (note John 8:41b; Meier 1991, 222-29). The former seems more likely, but thereby hangs a hook: if Jesus, an itinerant minister, was the eldest son of a widowed mother, then abdication of her support would have indeed been scandalous (Perkins 1995, 593) though not inconsistent with his teaching elsewhere (10:29-30). Another disconcerting point is his identification as "the carpenter," by far the best-attested wording of Mark 6:3a. In antiquity there was nothing inherently offensive about carpentry (see 2 Kgs 12:11; Sir 38:27; *Ant.* 15.390), though Sirach 38:24–39:11 snubs "blue-collar" occupations in comparison with study of Torah (Camery-Hoggatt 1992, 141). Celsus, Christianity's second-century critic, mocked the religion's founding by an artisan. Origen's rebuttal—"In none of the Gospels current in the churches is Jesus himself ever described as a carpenter" (*Cels.* 6.34)—suggests either that he forgot Mark's wording or (more likely) that he knew Mark in a form already modified in accordance with Matthew's identification of Jesus as "the carpenter's son" (13:55; Metzger 1994, 75-76). The Greek noun *ho tektōn* is a general term for a builder; it could refer to a carpenter, a woodworker, a stonemason, or a craftsman in metal (Batey 1984). Mark 6:3c clarifies the upshot of the synagogue's response to Jesus: "And they took offense at him," or more literally, "they stumbled over him" (*eskandalizonto en autō*). This verb is the same as that in 4:17, characterizing "the rocky ones" who, though receiving the word temporarily, are rootless and fall by the wayside.

At Mark 6:4 this legend mutates into a "paradigm" (Dibelius 1935, 37-69): an anecdote capped by a memorable aphorism. This saying—the prophet bereft of honor at home—is well attested in the Gospel tradition, with variants in Matthew (13:57b), Luke (4:24), John (4:44), the *Gospel of Thomas* (31), and *Oxyrynchus Papyrus* 1.6. Mark's version is among the most developed, detailing a prophet's dishonor in his homeland (*hē patris*), among kin (*hoi suyngeneusin*), and in his own house (*hē oikia autou*). The last item is an explicit link with 3:25-27: the divided house, exemplified by Jesus' own family, who think him mad (3:21, 31-32). The logion about the prophet honored everywhere but at home also recalls the wisdom saying in Mark 2:17b: Jesus' calling is not to the familiar righteous but to alien sinners. Reiterating that rueful testimony, 6:1-6a concludes with Jesus' inability to do any mighty work at home (6:5a; cf. his *refusal* to do so in Matt 13:58 and Luke 4:25-27). The exception: a few sick folk, whom he heals by applying his hands (6:5a; 5:23, 27-

28, 41). Those healings, which some would consider impressive, Mark throws away as an aside—like a tossed seed blooming into a mighty vegetable, leafy enough for a bird sanctuary (4:32). Throughout 6:1-6a Mark keeps twisting his tale. After days at sea and on the road Jesus astonishes his hometown (vv. 1-2). Familiarity breeds contempt (v. 3). Jesus expects that (v. 4) but cannot do a thing for them (v. 5a) except, incidentally, heal a few sick folk (v. 5b). The last reversal is vintage Mark: after many tales culminating in the audience's astonishment (1:27; 2:12; 4:41; 5:20b, 42), now Jesus is the one flabbergasted (*ethaumazein*)—not by a mighty work, but by such an impenetrable unfaith (*apistia*; 6:6a). "[T]hose expecting nothing from God will not be disappointed" (Hare 1990, 70).

Mark 4:35–6:6a is a reprise of 1:21–2:12: a series of wondrous works, executed by Jesus as harbinger of God's kingdom, punctuated by comments—alternately clear and cryptic—that point up theological issues fundamental for this Evangelist. Equipped with mysterious revelation afforded by Jesus' teaching (3:19b–4:34), the reader is reenlisted with the Twelve (3:13-19a) onto a spiritual battlefield—of chaos (4:35-41), demonism (5:1-20), sickness, and death (5:21-43)—being reclaimed through God's power. What does the reader learn from this latest foray?

First, attention remains riveted on Jesus: who he is, what he represents (Gundry 1993, 237-300). This segment opens with the disciples' astounded question, "Who then is this?" (4:41), and closes with the Galilean townspeople's doubting identification, "Isn't this the carpenter, Mary's son?" (6:3 AT). In between, his enemies the unclean spirits know their deadly adversary on sight—Jesus, "Son of the Most High God" (5:7)—while his disciples and some equally benighted see in Jesus little but a teacher (4:38; 5:35). Still others, like Jairus (5:23) and the hemorrhaging woman (5:28), intuitively perceive him as one who can help those at the end of their rope. Finally, what is important about Jesus is not a particular title or claim for him. It is, instead, recognizing in him God's appointed instrument (1:9-11) of a power sovereign over evil, illness, and death.

Jesus' mighty works are never ascribed to any dominion other than God's (1:15; 3:35; 5:19). In his ability to tap God's healing power, Jesus recalls the similar capability among Israel's prophets and holy men, such as Elisha (2 Kgs 4:32-37) or Hanina ben Dosa (first century C.E.; *b. Yebam.* 121b; *b. Ta'an.* 24b; *b. Yoma* 53b; Vermes 1973, 72-80). Mark distinguishes Jesus from the Almighty as God's "Son" (1:11; 3:11; 5:7a) or "the Holy One of God" (1:24); God is glorified for the gifts that Jesus bestows (2:12b; 10:18; Boring 1984). Yet Jesus crosses the line into a purview typically reserved for God alone (2:7; 4:41). That recognition gives Jesus' spiritual anointing at his baptism its distinctive character, by God's own accreditation (1:9-11), lends to his authority its peculiar punch (1:27; 2:10a; 2:12c; 2:27-28; 4:41), suggests his unusual affinity with and intuition of God's will and earthly activity (3:35; 4:13-20, 26-32), and opens the possibility of confusing the Lord God with the Lord Jesus (1:3; 2:28; 5:19-20). Jesus wields an unprecedented power for good that must be temporarily cloaked, to be unveiled when God's time is ripe (4:21-22, 29).

To know Jesus in Mark 4:34–6:6a is to penetrate beneath the Galilean prophet, acknowledging that only one so attuned to "the mystery of the kingdom of God" (4:11), parabolically cloaked (4:3-34), can properly deploy its power for the reclamation of God's creation from chaos and disease. Jesus is God's eschatological agent, retaking the field of a damaged creation from the diabolical forces of its occupation and restoring the ecology of God's sovereignty on earth (1:32-34; 3:11-12; J. M. Robinson 1982). When Jesus is so viewed, his teaching in 2:15-28 and 3:23–4:34 becomes intelligible, important, and trustworthy (Broadhead 1992). That is why those whose vision of Jesus is constricted or warped (3:21-23; 5:17; 6:3) are unable to receive his help. They do not want it. If they did, they would have to admit their own sickness rather than try to convince the physician that he is as sick as they are (see 2:17; 3:22). Those who sincerely (2:5, 11-12; 3:1-5; 5:23)—even dementedly (1:23-24;

5:6-7) or pusillanimously (4:38) or surreptitiously (5:27-28)—seek God's healing from Jesus are never refused or disappointed.

Thus one arrives at the matter of faith (*pistis*), which in Mark 4:35–6:6a acquires finer definition and deeper coloration. Faith, or trust, is a human response to calamity. All the occasions for faith in 4:35–6:6a are manifestly hopeless situations: peril at sea, possession by a legion of demons, chronic and incurable illness, sickness tipping over into death. (The demoniac is unable to express appreciation of Jesus until after his cleansing [5:18]; its unlikely, surrogate expression issues from the unclean spirit itself [5:6-7].) The one occasion on which Jesus' healing power is compromised is in his home synagogue, characterized by skepticism and offense (6:2-3).

Unlike those described in John's Gospel (2:11; 4:46-54), Jesus' mighty works in Mark do not stimulate faith. The sequence flows in reverse: first comes faith, fostering conditions in which God's power to restore, executed by Jesus, can be realized (Mark 5:23, 34a). Even in 4:35-41, faith is at work to quell a deadly tempest: not faith among the disciples (4:40), but the trust of Jesus himself, peacefully asleep (4:38). Only in 6:1-6a is Jesus largely, though not completely, hindered because of unbelief (6:6a). Jesus' mighty works in 4:35–6:6 are noteworthy not for their happy endings—which Apollonius and Hanina also enjoyed—but for what they disclose about observers' faith.

In these stories *pistis* and *apistia* are not presented as static qualities. Faith waxes and wanes. Were that not so, there would be little reason to contrast the demoniac's long-distance run to Jesus (5:6) with a detailed account of how unavailing all previous treatments have been (5:3-5). Though her situation is hopeless, the woman bulls her way through the crowd to touch Jesus (5:24b-28). No matter how fatal the news, Jesus tells Jairus, "Keep trusting" (5:36 AT). Despite the Galileans' faithlessness, Jesus remains able to heal a few (6:5b-6a). Faith in Mark is neither a block of unassailable belief nor an arrow released irrevocably toward its target. Faith is an oscillating fan: veering from one extreme or another, caught for a time by weak mortals before slipping from their grasp, in need of Jesus' encouragement.

Because faith has more to do with human volition than with cognition, its opposite in Mark 4:35–6:6a is cowardice (4:40) or fear (5:15, 33, 36): a lack of conviction in, or repudiation (6:3c-4) of, Jesus' ability to wield God's healing potency. Ultimately that power is unvanquished, even if temporarily stayed by death (5:39, 41-42a).

Strangely—and for that reason predictably (4:1-34)—shadowy figures on the margins exhibit trust in God (4:34–6:6a). Those thinking themselves close to Jesus, friends of the family (6:1-6a) and even the Twelve (4:40; 5:31), are at best imperceptive (5:31), at worst craven (4:40). Mark keeps turning the screw that holds in place "insiders" and "outsiders" (4:10-12, 33-34); "being an insider is only a more elaborate way of being kept outside" (Kermode 1979, 27). The powerless can tap reservoirs of restorative faith that elude those with conventional authority (Marshall 1989, 75-133).

REVELATION AT MEALTIME (6:6b–8:21)

Jesus' ministry has already pushed against Galilee's northern edges (3:7-8; 5:1-20); in Mark's third segment its orbit is expanded. The Twelve are dispatched on mission (6:6b-13). Three times they and their teacher cross the Sea of Galilee (6:32, 45; 8:13). Jesus ventures into Gentile territory: Tyre, Sidon, and the Decapolis (7:24a, 31). Jesus continues to teach (6:6b, 30; 7:6-23), cast out demons (6:7b, 13a; 7:24-30), and cure the sick (6:13b, 53-56; 7:31-37). The disciples are privy to striking expressions of Jesus' authority (6:45-52), now disclosed to bigger audiences (6:30-44; 8:1-10). Tensions are ratcheted up (6:14-29; 7:1-15; 8:11-13); increasingly, Jesus baffles those closest to him (6:37-38, 48-52; 7:17-18; 8:14-21). Secret things remain impossible to hide (6:31-33; 7:24, 36; cf. 4:22). Hearts grow mysteriously harder (6:52; 7:6, 19, 21; 8:17).

In this section the kingdom's "insiders" and "outsiders" (4:11-12) continue to be revealed in surprising ways. Most of these episodes involve food: a state dinner (6:14-29), two wilderness feedings (6:30-44; 8:1-10), and a debate over kosher practice

(7:1-23). A woman pleads for crumbs from Israel's loaf (7:24-30); the disciples bumble over bread (6:52; 8:14-21).

◊ ◊ ◊ ◊

Astonishing Ministry, Ambivalent Consequences (6:6b-56)

Mark 6:6b-56 consists of five episodes, hanging from a discernible narrative line:

Table 5: *The Structure of Mark 6:6b-56*

A. The mission of the Twelve (the story fans out) (6:6b-13)
    B. A royal feast (6:14-29)
    B.' A desert feast (6:30-44)
        C. A maritime epiphany (6:45-52)
A.' Jesus at the center in Gennesaret (the story folds in) (6:53-56)

Among these episodes familiar themes recur:

- Tension pulsates between privacy and expansiveness (vv. 6a/6b, 21/34, 45a/45b-46, 54/55), between attraction and resistance (vv. 31-32/33-34, 35-36/37a, 46-47/48).
- Jesus is an instrument of restoration and life (vv. 7, 41-42, 51a, 56b), standing at the center of others' bafflement (vv. 14-16, 37b, 49-50, 51b).
- The disciples' true character becomes clearer (vv. 8-13, 20, 29, 34, 37a, 43, 46, 52).

In a word: Jesus' uncanny power answers human need while provoking fresh questions.

The Mission of the Twelve (6:6b-13)

Rejected in his homeland (6:1-6a), Jesus turns to people in surrounding villages (v. 6b: a concise summary report, of which longer versions appear in 1:14-15 and 3:7-12). In 3:13-15 he has assembled the Twelve to extend his ministry of preaching and exorcism, which happens here. Nowhere in Mark are they entrusted with teaching, though they will claim to have done so (6:30). The line between teaching and preaching (v. 12) may not be firm (4:1-2); teaching and exorcism have been wedded early in this Gospel (1:25-27). At 6:7a Jesus takes the initiative: "*He* called the twelve and began to send them out" (emphasis added). Commensurately, the disciples' authority derives from Jesus' power (*exousia*) over unclean spirits (v. 7b; cf. 1:21-28; 3:11). Sending in pairs (v. 7a) reflects biblical custom, to assure safety and corroboration (Deut 17:6; 19:15; cf. Matt 18:16; Acts 13:2-3; 1 Tim 5:19).

Unusually meager equipment is ordered: only a staff, sandals, and a single tunic (vv. 8a, 9). (In Matt 10:10 even the sandals and staff are forbidden; cf. Luke 9:3; 10:4.) Bread, bag, money belt, and another tunic (or overshirt) are left behind (Mark 6:8b-9). For shelter Jesus' deputies must depend on the kindness of strangers. The Twelve should stay in one house until they leave for another (v. 10; cf. *Did.* 11.3-6). (On the importance of house churches in early Christianity, see Malherbe 1983, 6-12.) Disciples should expect rejection (v. 11a). When it happens, they should shake the dust from their feet "as a testimony against them" (v. 11b). This obscure action is reminiscent of a practice by Jews who, upon returning home, guarded against contaminating Israel with pagan dust (Neh 5:13; *b. Sanh.* 12a; *Tosefta Miqw.* 6.1; cf. Acts 10:28; 13:51; 18:5-6). Shaking off the dust appears to have been a prophetic demonstration: from those who repudiate the kingdom's heralds, nothing should be received, not even their dirt.

One may compare the attire and conduct of Jesus' "wandering charismatics" (Theissen 1978) with those of the era's philosophical street preachers (Hock 1992). Cynics were praised for guarding virtue (Diogenes Laertius, *Eminent Philosophers* 6.8, 35, 104) but vilified for disregarding conventional decency (*Peregr.* 17). An itinerant Cynic typically carried two shirts, a staff, and a beggar's bag (*Eminent Philosophers* 6.13; *Men.* 20.2). In Mark, the Twelve are forbidden the bag (6:8) and change of tunic (v. 9). Like Cynics (*Eminent Philosophers* 6.6, 38-67), Jesus' disciples lived hand-to-mouth while on the road; unlike them, the Twelve sought shelter in homes instead of on the streets (*Diatr.* 3.22). The Twelve were not philosophical gadflies, needling public commonplaces (cf. Hengel 1981, 5-6, 32). Moreover, the Twelve formed a community around Jesus; Cynic individualism militated against organization in societies (Malherbe 1983, 15-16).

Given the Twelve's less than stellar achievements in the story to this point (4:13, 35-41; 5:31), this pericope's conclusion is noteworthy (Henderson 2006). The Twelve depart, preach as Jesus commands, cast out many demons, and heal many who are sick (6:12-13). In the NT anointing with oil (v. 13b) is a gracious act (14:8; 16:1; Luke 7:38, 46; John 11:2), often with therapeutic associations (Matt 6:17; Jas 5:14; Rev 3:18). The proclamation "that all should repent" (*hina metanoōsin,* v. 12) is straight in line with Jesus' own (1:15) and, before him, with that of John the Baptist (1:4)—whose immediate reappearance (6:14-29) casts a long shadow over the sunshine of the Twelve's mission.

A Royal Feast (6:14-29)

This tale is one of Mark's fascinating anomalies. At sixteen verses it is the longest of the Gospel's discrete anecdotes. It offers the narrative's only flashback. Except for the plot to kill Jesus (Mark 14:1-2 + 10-11) and the discovery of the empty tomb (16:1-8), this is the only story in which Jesus never appears. Its primary character is a villain who never reappears.

◊ ◊ ◊ ◊

The scoundrel is Herod Antipas (ca. 21 B.C.E–post-39 C.E.), who, upon the death in 4 B.C.E. of his father, Herod the Great, was named tetrarch of Galilee and Perea, provinces bounded on the northwest by the Jordan River and on the southwest by the Dead Sea. Though Mark 6:14-29 presents our only encounter with this member of the Herodian dynasty, his partisans, "the Herodians," appeared in 3:6 and will return in 12:13 as Jesus' antagonists. As Mark suggests (6:14), Antipas may have been popularly regarded as "king," though he was a client of his patron, Emperor Tiberius

(*Ant.* 18.36, 101-5). The portraits of Antipas in Josephus and the NT do not exactly mesh, though there are areas of overlap that help us better understand Mark. (1) Antipas's decision to take as his (second) wife Herodias, the ambitious wife of one of his half-brothers and the daughter of another (*Ant.* 18.109-11, 136; cf. Mark 6:17), churned up political turmoil for him. Mark identifies Herodias as the wife of Herod's brother Philip (v. 17b). In spite of attempts to reconstruct a "Herod Philip" based on Mark (Hoehner 1972, 131-36), the most we learn from Josephus is that Philip was Herodias's son-in-law (*Ant.* 18.137); the identity of Herodias's first husband remains uncertain. (2) The Evangelist depicts Antipas as John's protector (6:20), maneuvered into authorizing his death (6:26a). For Josephus, the Baptist, "a good man" (*Ant.* 18.117), was so genuine a threat to Antipas that the tetrarch put him to death; unlike Mark, Josephus attributes John's death to Antipas's fear of a political revolt among the populace (*Ant.* 18.113-19). For that execution, Josephus believed, Herod suffered divine retribution through military defeat (*Ant.* 18.113-19). After John's death, Antipas and Herodias, ensnarled in imperial politics, were deposed and exiled (*Ant.* 18.252-55; *J. W.* 2.183). One historian assesses Antipas as "a minor ruler with a moderate impact" (Jensen 2006, 254); another, as "passive, indecisive, and weak" (Richardson 1996, 313). That composite tallies with Mark 6:14-29.

Through his disciples' missionary accomplishments (6:12-13), "Jesus' name had become known" (v. 14a), even to Herod. The rumor that Jesus' powers were attributable to "John the baptizer [who] has been raised from the dead" (v. 14b) is blunt and startling: the last the reader heard of John, he had been arrested (1:14a). Speculation about Jesus' identity, suggested by his works (1:27-28; 3:22; 4:41; 6:2-3), now acquires sharper, albeit misleading, detail: "Others said, 'It is Elijah.' ... others said, 'It is a prophet, like one of the prophets of old'" (6:15). Elijah, who had been whisked to heaven in a chariot of fire (2 Kgs 2:1-12), was considered by the prophet Malachi (mid-fifth century B.C.E.) as a harbinger of the Day of the LORD (3:1-2; 4:5-6). "One of the prophets of old" may allude, among other possibilities, to a prophet like Moses (Deut 18:15-22). Similar public theorizing about Jesus recurs in Mark (8:28; 12:35-37; 14:61; 15:2). Antipas has drawn his own conclusion: "John, whom I beheaded, has been raised" (6:16). The stage is thus set for the flashback (vv. 17-29).

That story is simple, if grisly. As Mark tells it, John, Herod, and Herod's wife were three sides in a political triangle. Defying Torah (Lev 18:13, 16; 20:21), Antipas had married his sister-in-law, for which John had challenged them (Mark 6:18). Herod admired his accuser, knowing him to be righteous and holy (v. 20). Herod's wife bore John a grudge and wanted him dead (v. 19a). Herod compromised: bowing to his wife, he had John arrested and jailed (v. 17); blocking her, Antipas protected John because he feared him (vv. 19b-20a). Unlike Matthew (14:5), Mark presents Herod as ambivalent toward his captive: John's teachings perplexed the governor, who nevertheless "liked to listen to him" (6:20b). "A happy day" (*hēmeras eukairou*!) for Herod's wife to have her way arose at a state dinner (v. 21). Enter Herodias's daughter (6:22), who "danced" and "pleased" everyone. (In Mark she shares her mother's name [v. 22a]; Josephus reports that the daughter's name was Salome [*Ant.* 18.136].) Fatuously, Herod vowed to give the girl whatever she asked (vv. 22b-23). After consulting her mother, the backstage maestra (v. 24), the child sprang the trap (v. 25). Herod was caught (v. 26). Saving face was an issue, though impious perjury may also have entered into the picture: one defaulting on an oath is guilty of taking God's name in vain (*Spec. Laws* 2.9-10). Antipas commanded the executioner to bring him the prisoner's head (v. 27a). The order was obeyed (v. 27b); the head, served on a platter, was delivered to the girl, who delivered it to her mother (v. 28). This gruesome tale ends on a poignant note: hearing of their teacher's death, John's disciples claimed the body and laid it in a tomb (v. 29).

Mark's reference to Elijah (v. 15a) reminds one of that prophet's confrontation with Ahab (1 Kgs 18:17-19), another weak ruler manipulated by his murderous wife, Jezebel (19:1-3; 21:1-26). "Righteous and holy" (Mark 6:20a), resolute before political oppressors (vv. 18-19), John recalls Eleazar, an elderly Jew who refused to compromise religious principles in the face of state-sanctioned death (2 Macc 6:18-31; 4 Macc 5:1–7:23). Herod's inflated vows (Mark 6:22b-23) echo those of smitten King Ahasuerus to Queen Esther: "What is your request? It shall be given you, even to the half of my kingdom" (Esth 5:2-3; 7:1-2). Embedded in Israel's story, Mark 6:14-29 acquires texture by evoking other sovereigns, feckless and ruthless, and the righteous folk ground up in their machinations.

Literarily, Mark 6:14-29 is a gem. Mark relaxes and unfolds the tale, suggesting time absorbed by the mission of the Twelve (6:12-13). The points at which the Evangelist repeats himself are justified by their stress: John's righteousness (vv. 18, 20) and unjust imprisonment (v. 17), Herod's riven conscience and conduct (vv. 17, 20, 26a), his foolishness (vv. 22-23, 26b), the girl's reiterated requests (the first [v. 24a], innocent; the second [v. 25b], ghastly), the ghoulish bucket brigade for a prophet's head (vv. 27-28), and the eerie prospect of John's having been raised from the dead (vv. 14b, 16b). Yet Mark compresses other details, springing them on the reader for maximum impact: the abrupt preface that the incarcerated John is already beheaded by Herod (v. 14b); the economy in sketching the dynamics among Herodias, John, and Herod (vv. 19-20a); the naïve mundanity of the girl's question (v. 24a), answered by her mother's simple brutality (v. 24b); and the terse report of the victim's burial (v. 29). Small items are "fraught with unexpressed background" (Auerbach 1953, 3-23), undetonated, and planted by the narrator to explode in the listener's mind. Was Herod haunted by reports of a prophet, Jesus, to consider him a revenant of another whom he had destroyed (v. 16; cf. vv. 20b, 27)? "[The dancing daughter] pleased Herod and his guests" (v. 22a): Lasciviously? Incestuously? Is she aware that she's only a pawn in a power play? In some perverse way does she enjoy her role? (Notice that it is *the girl* who insists that John's head be delivered on a salver.) Why does the executioner, ordered to bring the victim's head to his sovereign (v. 27a), deliver it instead *to the girl* (v. 28a)? Are we intended to detect, on a single occasion, the ironic coincidence of one leader's birth with another's death (vv. 21, 27b)?

Mark harnesses all of these elements to *theological* effect. Since Herod does not return in the Passion Narrative (cf. Luke 23:6-12), one might ask, "Why does Mark introduce Antipas at all?" The likeliest answer is that Herod Antipas foreshadows Pontius Pilate in the same way that John presages Jesus (cf. 1:1-15; 9:9-13; 11:27-33). Like Herod, Pilate, though nominally in charge, is amazed (15:5; cf. 6:20b) by circumstances surrounding an innocent prisoner (15:1b, 14a; cf. 6:17, 20a). Pilate, too, is swept up by events spinning out of his control (15:6-13; cf. 6:21-25) and unable to back down after being publicly outmaneuvered (15:15; cf. 6:26-27a). Figures like John and Jesus—both noticeably passive in their last hours (6:14-29 and 15:1-39)—face their respective moments of truth (the "opportunity," *hēmeras eukairou* [6:21]; "the season," *tō kairō* [12:2]), maintain their integrity, and die to placate those they offend (6:19a, 25b; 15:10-14). Because discipleship is so important in Mark, the end of 6:14-29 is surely significant: John's disciples display the courage and compassion to give their teacher a decent burial (v. 29). What will become of the Twelve after Jesus' crucifixion and death (cf. 14:27, 50-52; 15:40-47)? In all these ways this Markan flashback is at the same time a flash-forward.

A Desert Feast (6:30-44)

In 6:30 the disciples return from their mission (6:6b-13) and report to Jesus their activities. (The meantime is suggested by the long narrative in 6:14-29.) Except for a textual variant of 3:14 (*ad loc.*), only here in Mark are the Twelve referred to as *apostoloi*. Its use in 6:30 implies the term's original sense of "emissaries," though in Christian tradition it quickly assumes the special connotation of "a uniquely selected ambassador of Christ" (e.g., Acts 1:2, 26; Rom 1:1; 1 Cor 15:7; Gal 1:1). The disciples' declaration of "all that they had done and taught" is deceptively simple. While reminding the reader of the exorcisms and healings noted in 6:13, it jars against the report in 6:29 of other disciples' burial of their teacher's remains.

Though Matthew (14:13-14) and Luke (9:10-11) sharply abbreviate Mark 6:31-34, the Second Evangelist's details are not superfluous. Mark presents Jesus as consistently sensitive to human need, be it his disciples' fatigue (6:31a) or a crowd's confusion (v. 34b). The importance of temporary refreshment in a remote or "deserted place" (vv. 31, 32) picks up the thread of Jesus' earlier retreats (1:35, 45). Here as before (1:29-34, 35-39; 3:19b-20), private refuge provides counterpoint to a bustle around Jesus from "all the towns" (v. 33; 1:32-33): "goings" (vv. 31b, 33a) and "comings" (v. 31b) prompt a leave-taking by boat (v. 32; see also 3:9; 4:1, 36; 5:18; 6:45; 8:10). Another motif recurs in 6:31b, 33: the threat to Jesus' welfare posed by needy, irresistible multitudes (1:37; 3:7-10). As in 3:20b external pressure is so relentless that the teacher and his disciples cannot eat (6:31). (The term [oude] eukairoun, translated in the NRSV as "had no leisure," is a cognate of eukairou, which in 6:21 refers to Herodias's fine opportunity to destroy John the Baptist.) The more Jesus and his retinue attempt to get away, the faster everyone recognizes them, beating them to their destination (6:33; cf. 5:21, 24b). Instead of expressing irritation, Jesus has compassion on the crowds awaiting his arrival (6:34; see also 1:41; 8:2; 9:22). In them he perceives "sheep without a shepherd": an OT metaphor for the mass of Israel needing sustenance by God's deputy, who provides help for the helpless (Num 27:15-17; 1 Kgs 22:17; 2 Chr 18:16; Ps 95:7; Ezek 34:1-31; Jdt 11:19). The frenzy of Mark 6:31-34a is stilled in verse 34b by the image of Jesus' beginning, once more, "to teach them many things" (1:21-22; 2:13; 4:1-2; 6:2, 6b).

The substance of Jesus' teaching—for his disciples as well—will be a "gift miracle" (Theissen 1983, 103-6), the feeding of the multitude (6:35-44). Its immediate occasion is the lateness of the hour, the desolate setting, and the amplitude of need (vv. 35, 37b). The disciples' suggestion that the crowd be dispersed, to fend for themselves (6:36), does not alleviate their dearth of insight (4:13ab, 35-41; 5:31). Still, given the circumstances, their suggestion is not unreasonable. Jesus' reply—"You give them something to eat" (6:37a); "How many loaves have you? Go and see" (v. 38ab)—seems to toy with them (cf. John 11:9-13). A rag-tag dozen, lately dispatched without any resources (6:7-9), have not the two hundred denarii (about two-thirds of a day laborer's annual income: Matt 20:2, 9, 13) needed to feed this horde (Mark 6:37b). The report of their reconnaissance is equally ludi-crous: they have scrounged five loaves and two fish (v. 38c). This meticulous setup accomplishes at least two narrative objectives. It establishes the impossibility of the situation while ironically winking at the outcome: Jesus will salvage the unsalvageable.

In sharp contrast with its rambunctious beginnings (vv. 31b-34b) the rest of this tale unfolds in orderly fashion, with Jesus indisputably in charge.

(a) **The careful arrangement of the multitude (vv. 39-40).** Unlike Matthew (14:19a) and more so than Luke (9:14b-15), Mark draws order out of this hungry herd's chaos. Jesus "orders" (6:39; see also 1:27; 9:25) his disciples to arrange and seat the huge crowd "in groups [*symposia*] on the green grass" (6:39). "Symposia" suggests a formal banquet's conviviality (Plato's *Symposium* [ca. 380 B.C.E.]). "Green" implies lush verdancy (Deut 12:2; Song 1:16; Ezek 6:13): memorably, the pastures in which the shepherd Lord makes his sheep lie down (Ps 23:2; cf. Mark 6:34b). Row upon row (*prasiai prasiai*: literally, "by garden plots" [BDAG 860a] "of hundreds and of fifties" [Mark 6:40]) may echo Moses' ordering of Israel's ranks in Exodus 18:21, 25. Similar organizations were prescribed for occasions in the life of the Qumran community (1QS 2.21; CD 13.1; 1QSa 1.14-15).

(b) **The pious, orderly distribution of available resources (v. 41).** The guests properly ordered, Jesus acts as the meal's host (6:41). In the OT "looking up to heaven" is a reverential attitude (Deut 4:19; Job 22:26; Ps 123:1). It recurs in the Gospels' depic-tions of Jesus at prayer (Mark 7:34; John 11:41; 17:1) and in Mark 6:41 reciprocates the voice addressed *to* Jesus *from* heaven in Mark 1:11. "Taking" and "bless[ing]," "broke" and "gave" (6:41), summarize the essence of what later rabbis would pre-scribe as proper procedure at table, especially at Passover (*m. Ber.* 8.7; *b. Ber.* 35a, 46a; cf. Mark 14:22).

(c) **The astonishingly happy outcome (vv. 42-43).** The wording of 6:42a abbreviates the first half of Deuteronomy 8:10 ("You shall eat your fill"). Neither Mark nor the other Evangelists (Matt 14:20a; Luke 9:17a; John 6:12a) paraphrase the second half of Deuteronomy ("and bless the LORD your God for the good land that he has given you"), probably because the responsive blessing was tied with the gift of the land (see *b. Yoma* 39b; *b. Šabb.* 21b). Mark and the other Gospels emphasize the remarkably abundant leftovers: "twelve baskets full of broken pieces and of the fish" (6:43; Matt 14:20b; Luke 9:17b; John 6:13—one, perhaps, for each collecting disciple). Oddly, the Greek of Mark 6:43 reads, "they took up twelve full fragments of baskets." Some scribes straighten out the wording—"baskets of fragments" (Swanson 1995, 97)— even as do Matthew (14:20b), Luke (9:17b), and John (6:13).

(d) An understated exclamation of how remarkable the proceedings proved (v. 44). Mark reserves to the end the punch line: "Those who had eaten the loaves numbered five thousand men [*andres*, 'males']." Uncontrolled speculation about a particular significance for the number five thousand (for that matter, five [Mark 6:38c, 41], two [vv. 38c, 41], or twelve [v. 43a]) leads nowhere fast. Mark's point is the staggering number of those so incredibly fed.

Many of Mark's pericopae are densely stereophonic, impossible—or at least unwise—to reduce to a single track. Hearing this text properly requires listening in multiple channels.

First, the OT analogues for Mark 6:30-44 are unmistakable. Some verbal resonances have been noted (see above on vv. 34, 40, 41, 42), but the correspondences go deeper. Locating this gift-miracle in a "deserted place" recalls Israel's wondrous sustenance by God in the wilderness (Exod 16:13-35; Num 11:1-25). An even closer approximation of Jesus' feeding of the five thousand is the tale of Elisha's feeding of a prophetic guild with meager resources (2 Kgs 4:42-44; see *Marc.* 4.21, and Brown 1971). Little wonder that some identify Jesus as Elijah or his successors (6:15; 8:28). In 6:30-44, however, Jesus trumps Elisha's miracle at every point. With fewer provisions (five loaves and two fish [Mark 6:38] versus twenty barley loaves and fresh ears of grain

[2 Kgs 4:42a]), Jesus feeds a crowd fifty times larger (Mark 6:44/2 Kgs 4:43a) with more leftovers (Mark 6:43/2 Kgs 4:44).

Second, Mark 6:30-44 also chimes with Jewish expectations of an eschatological feast for God's elect: a hope at least as old as Isaiah (25:6-8), which acquired sharper definition in Jewish apocalypticism (2 *Bar* 29:3-8; 4 *Ezra* 6:52; 1QSa) and early Christian texts (Matt 22:1-10; Luke 14:15-24; John 6:1-15). Like 6:14-29, Mark 6:30-44 is a simultaneous flashback/flash-forward.

Third, and related to the second, Mark 6:30-44 anticipates Jesus' Last Supper with his disciples (14:17-31), whose narration in turn became the basis for the primitive church's celebration of the Eucharist. The verbal congruence is unmistakable:

Table 6: *Jesus as Host at Supper*

Mark 6:35, 40, 41	*Mark 14:17, 18, 22*	*1 Cor 11:23-24, 26*
When it grew late	When it was evening	
So they sat down	And when they had taken their places	
Taking the five loaves	He took a loaf of bread	The Lord Jesus... took a loaf of bread
Blessed and broke the loaves	And after blessing it he broke it	And when he had given thanks, he broke it
And gave them to his disciples	Gave it to them	
		For as often as you eat this bread... you proclaim the Lord's death until he comes.

Beyond the verbatim agreements Mark weaves other motifs from the Lord's Supper into the feeding of the multitude: the disciples' confusion (6:37bc; 14:19) and the image of Jesus as faithful shepherd (6:34a; 14:27b).

Fourth, by elegantly collocating and balancing two very different stories about banquets, Mark invites the reader to contrast the inner workings of a kingdom of this age with those of the kingdom of God, a matter that will be explicitly addressed in 10:42-44.

Table 7: *Herod's Feast / Jesus' Feast*

Mark 6:14-29: Herod's Feast	*Mark 6:30-44: Jesus' Feast*
Jesus' name had become known (v. 14a)	Now many recognized them (v. 33a)
"[T]hese powers are at work in him" (v. 14b)	The apostles told him all that they had done (v. 30)
Herodias wanted to kill John the Baptist (v. 19a)	Jesus had compassion on a great crowd (v. 34)
Perplexed, Herod fears others (vv. 20, 26)	The Twelve, confounded; Jesus, confident (vv. 37-38)
A state dinner for Galilee's upper classes (v. 21b)	A supper for the masses in a deserted place (v. 39)
A royal birthday banquet (v. 21a)	Five loaves and two fish (v. 38)
Braggadocio in a boisterous setting (vv. 22-23)	Simple prayer amid an ordered throng (vv. 39, 41a)
Intermediaries scheme backstage (v. 24)	Intermediaries serve in the open (vv. 41b, 43)
A righteous man suffers hideous death (vv. 25, 27-28)	Sheeplike thousands enjoy a full meal (vv. 34b, 42, 44)

Whether one construes Mark 6:14-29 as sandwiched between 6:6b-13 and 6:30-44 or regards 6:14-29 and 6:30-44 as a narrative diptych, the result is the same: a comparison of two lavish yet diametrically opposed meals that spell either death or life for the helpless. Malicious Herodias and face-saving Herod murder a righteous prophet. Compassionate Jesus, begrudging no one, draws on heavenly resources to satisfy human hunger.

A Maritime Epiphany (6:45-52)

Introduced by Mark's favorite adverb, "immediately" (*euthys*: 6:45, 50; e.g., 6:25, 27, 54 ["at once"]), the next episode's setting is murky. Bethsaida (v. 45) is on the Sea of Galilee's north-northeastern shore. If in 6:35 "it grew late," presumably evening had already come (see 6:47). Maybe 6:45-52 was originally independent of the preceding pericope. Moreover, this tale chimes with another, previously recounted in Mark.

Mark 4:35-41 and 6:45-52 may be considered "doublets": narrative variations on a single tradition (Bultmann 1963, 216). Even so, surely at 6:45-52 the Evangelist would expect listeners to recognize the earlier story. With the disciples, figuratively and narratively, Mark's readers are "in the same boat": after a temporary remove from his followers, Jesus mysteriously prevails over chaotic wind and waters, leaving his terrified disciples even more disturbed. In both tales four motifs intersect: (1) obliquely reminiscent of OT imagery, (2) Jesus' stupendous power is revealed, (3) not for its own sake but to serve needy, fearful disciples (4) who remain baffled by their teacher.Confidence and cowardice (6:50b; see also 4:40) define the poles between which Jesus' followers swing (5:33-34, 36; 9:24; 10:32; 11:22-23; 13:11-13; 14:29, 31, 66-72).

Table 8: *Two Wondrous Sea-Crossings*

Mark 4:35-41: *Jesus' Stilling of the Storm*	Mark 6:45-52: *Jesus' Walking on the Waters*
When evening had come (v. 35a)	When evening came (v. 47a)
Jesus directs his disciples to embark "to the other side" (v. 35b)	Jesus directs his disciples to embark "to the other side" (v. 45a)
Leaving the crowd behind (v. 36a)	Jesus dismissed the crowd (v. 45b)
Into the boat (v. 36b)	Into the boat (v. 45a)
A great windstorm arose (v. 37a)	An adverse wind (v. 48a)
Jesus, removed from his disciples, asleep (v. 38a)	Jesus, removed from his disciples, at prayer (vv. 45-46)
The disciples are distressed (v. 38b)	The disciples strain at the oars (v. 48a)
Awaking, Jesus rebukes the sea (v. 39)	Coming toward them, Jesus bestrides the sea (v. 49a)
The wind ceases; "a dead calm" (v. 39b)	Jesus gets into the boat; "the wind ceased" (v. 51a)
Jesus challenges their fear and faithlessness (v. 40)	Jesus bolsters courage: "Do not be afraid" (v. 50b)
The disciples "feared a great fear" (v. 41a AT)	The disciples are terrified at the sight of Jesus (v. 50a)
They wonder who Jesus could be (v. 41b)	The disciples are "utterly astounded" (vv. 51b-52)

Mark 6:45-52 is, however, no mere rehash of 4:35-41. The differences are noteworthy. In this account Jesus is in control from start to finish. He directs his disciples' activity (6:45a; cf.

4:36, suggesting their greater degree of agency). He dismisses the crowds (6:45b). He goes his own way (6:46-47, 48b). He sees and responds to the boatmen's torment (6:48-49; cf. 4:38, in which they rouse him to action). In 6:48a, 49a his command over natural elements is even more stupefying than in 4:39. His sheer self-identification intends consolation (6:50b), in contrast with his chastisement in 4:40. His mere reunion with his disciples calms a storm (6:51), which previously required direct rebuke (4:39).

In 6:45-52 Mark points up significant character traits that are softened or missing in 4:35-41. There is, for example, mention of Jesus' going up to the mountain to pray (6:46). Throughout this Gospel, Jesus prays (1:35; 14:32, 35, 39) and teaches about prayer (11:25; 13:18; 14:38). He also repairs to mountains or hill country (3:13; 9:2, 9), a familiar location for divine revelation in the OT (e.g., Exod 24:12-18). Indeed, in 6:45-52 Jesus emanates a weird, quasi-divine aura (Geyer 2002, 241-67). It is pretwilight: "early in the morning" (v. 48b), literally, "around the fourth watch of the night" (the darkest period, between 3:00 and 6:00 a.m.; *Ant.* 18.356). Jesus treads the waves (vv. 48a, 49a), as does the Lord God in Psalm 77:14-19 (cf. Ps 93:3-4; Job 9:8; Hab 3:15); "It is I" (*ego eimi*, Mark 6:50b) is the classic OT expression of self-revelation by Israel's God (Exod 3:13-15; Isa 41:4; 43:10-11; much developed in John [e.g., 4:26; 6:20, 35; 18:5-8]). Divine calming of human terror and natural tumult (Mark 6:50-51) is yet another scriptural motif (Ps 107:28-29). Perhaps to the OT we should also repair for help in interpreting the baffling comment, "[Jesus] intended to pass them by" (Mark 6:48b; absent from Matt 14:25-26; John 6:19). Divine self-disclosure to mortals never occurs head-on: when appearing to Moses (Exod 33:17-23) or to Elijah (1 Kgs 19:11-12), the Lord God "passes by" them. It is no less true that, throughout this Gospel, Jesus is typically way ahead of his disciples (1:16, 19; 2:14; 10:32; 14:28; 16:7); both metaphorically and spatially they are "followers" (1:18; 2:14-15; 6:1; 8:34; 10:28, 32, 52; 14:54; 15:41) who find it hard to keep up with their teacher (Burdon 1990, 45-52). More so than in 4:41, Mark emphasizes in 6:52

the Twelve's obtuseness. To be sure, Jesus has already accused them of not understanding the parables (4:13); still, 6:52b marks the first time in this Gospel that his own followers' "hearts" are said to have been "hardened" (Exod 9:34-35; 1 Sam 6:6; 2 Chr 36:13; Ps 95:6-8). The disciples are thus aligned with the Pharisees in obduracy (Mark 3:5) and the imperception of "those outside" (4:11-12). Like others in this Gospel, the Twelve *did not* comprehend Jesus because they *could not* comprehend him.

That "they did not understand about the loaves" is the only reason the Evangelist offers for their doltishness (6:52a). This makes a kind of sense if Mark intends that the reader recall the disciples' incredulity at Jesus' exhortation that they feed the multitude with their available resources (6:37-38). In effect, at the conclusion of this Gospel's most magnificent demonstration of Jesus' power (6:41-44, 48-51a), his disciples still cannot properly assess their teacher (cf. Matt 14:33). On the other hand, "not understand[ing] about the loaves" is hardly the most lucid explanation. Perhaps this choice of words is intended to generate in readers something of the mystification experienced by the Twelve (6:51b; see Young 1999). Mark has been described as "a book of secret epiphanies" (Dibelius 1935, 230). Nowhere is that characterization more apt than at 6:45-52: Jesus reveals himself as an epiphany of God, in a manner beyond its recipients' capacity to grasp.

Many details in Mark 6:45-52 recall the disciples' encounters with the risen Jesus in the other Gospels' Easter narratives (cf. Matt 28:1-10, 16-20; Luke 24:1-4, 13-39; John 20:1-31; 21:1-14). Especially noteworthy are their setting at daybreak (Mark 6:48b; Matt 28:1a; Luke 24:1; John 20:1; 21:4a), boats (Mark 6:45a, 47a, 51a; John 21:3c) or mountains (Mark 6:46b; Matt 28:16), the disciples' mistaking of Jesus as a ghost (Mark 6:49b; Luke 24:37b), and their perplexity (Mark 6:51-52; Matt 28:17; Luke 24:3-4, 41a; John 20:9a, 27). Some believe that Mark 6:45-52 originated as a tale of an appearance of the risen Jesus, later retrojected into the story of his ministry (Madden 1997). Others disagree (Boring 2006, 190-91). Stories of Jesus' resurrection appearances to his disciples may have influenced the manner in which Mark, perhaps also his antecedent traditions, recounted the story of Jesus' walking on the water. Possibly, the influence moved in the opposite direction. Weirdly, Mark 6:45-52 functions somewhat as the Easter epiphany absent from the end of this Gospel's best manuscripts (*ad loc.* 16:1-8). As in 6:49-52, stories of the risen Jesus present his disciples as wrestling with its truth and meaning (e.g., Matt 28:17; Luke 24:13-28, 36-43; John 20:1-10, 24-29). Following Peter's equivocation (14:28-32), Matthew's version of Jesus' walk on the waves strikes a vibrant Easter note: the disciples' worship of their Lord as the Son of God (14:33). John's version also ends happily (6:21); Luke does not recount this story. Only Mark leaves the theological chord unresolved, with the Twelve still stumbling over Jesus' God-given mastery of chaotic forces (6:51b-52; Dwyer 1996, 128-34).

Jesus at the Center in Gennesaret (6:53-56)

The subsection of Mark, begun with the Twelve's mission (6:6b-13), comes to an end with a crisp transition that in form and substance is like the summing up in 3:7-12 and especially 1:32-34. Common to all of these passages are (1) a terse scene-setting (1:32a; 3:7a; 6:53), (2) a depiction of widespread attraction to Jesus (1:33; 3:7b-8; 6:54-55), (3) the emphasis on human infirmity and need for relief (1:32b; 3:10b; 6:55b-56a), and (4) Jesus' ability to heal (1:34; 3:10a; 6:56b). Some things distinguish Mark 6:53-56 from comparable pericopae.

(a) **Confused geography.** Already we have seen (5:1) that the Second Evangelist is wobbly in Palestinian geography. That impression is confirmed in 6:53. Eight verses previously (6:45) Jesus has dispatched his disciples "to the other side, to Bethsaida." The implication is that Jesus is somewhere west of the Sea of Galilee and is headed northeast. It is bizarre that they drop anchor at Gennesaret, probably south of Capernaum on the Galilee's *northwest* shore.

(b) **The pattern of attraction.** At Capernaum (1:21) the town's

COMMENTARY

sick "gathered around the door" (1:33). In 3:7-12 Jesus withdraws to the sea but is pressed by hordes from a wide geographical compass (3:7-8). In 6:55-56 Jesus itinerates within "that whole region" (v. 55: presumably, eastern Galilee) and is followed from village to city to farm by the sick—literally, "those who have it bad" (*kakōs echontas,* v. 55; thus also 1:32)—who hear of his whereabouts (vv. 55-56a). Sometimes the sick are brought to Jesus on mats *(tois krabattois,* v. 55), as was a paralytic in Capernaum (2:1-4). Unlike 1:32-24 and 3:11-12, this summary says nothing of Jesus' exorcisms, though that form of healing opened this section (6:7, 13) and recurs in Mark (7:24-30; 9:14-29, 38-41). In 6:54 a subtle contrast is suggested between those who gladly and "at once [*euthys*] recognized" Jesus after his disembarkation and the inability of his terrified disciples, while in the boat, to recognize their own teacher (6:49-50a).

(c) **The mode of healing.** Reminiscent of the hemorrhaging woman in 5:28-30, many of the sick are healed merely by touching Jesus' garments. "The fringe of his cloak" (6:56) likely refers to the tassel (Num 15:37-41; Deut 22:12), which to this day adorns the prayer shawls of Orthodox Jewish males. Some evidence suggests that the tassel (Gk. *kraspedon;* Heb. *tzitzit*), worn by a holy man, was believed to convey therapeutic properties (Lachs 1987, 172). Unlike 5:34, which underlines the faith of the anonymous woman, the stress in 6:56 falls on the restoration (*esōzonto:* "were healed/saved") accomplished, in passing, by merely touching Jesus. This echoes the uncanny image of Jesus striding the waters, passing by the boatmen (6:48). In both cases Jesus is portrayed as sensitive to human need, one from whom divine power virtually seeps out: a fitting image on which to conclude a portion of Mark filled with marvels real or imagined (6:13, 14, 16, 41-44, 48-51).

Outside Insiders and Inside Outsiders (7:1–8:21)

The foundation of this subsection is 7:1-23, which demolishes the kosher separation of Jews from Gentiles (N.B. 7:14-15, 19b). So many boundaries are effaced in this portion of Mark that obscurity itself is a leitmotif:

- A strange pair of healings (7:24-37): (i) a Syrophoenician "dog" claims her share from a Jewish exorcist (vv. 24-30), after which (ii) an impediment to speech gives way to zealous proclamation, strenuously forbidden (vv. 31-37).
- A reprise (8:1-10)—evidently among Gentiles—of a feast in the desert.
- A strange pair of debates (8:11-21), in which (i) faithless Pharisees (vv. 11-13) and (ii) hard-hearted disciples (vv. 14-21) reveal their incomprehension of Jesus.

As in 6:6b-56 most of the pericopae in this section involve food: eating with defiled hands (7:2, 5), cleansing unclean food (7:19b), dogs that eat table scraps while the children are first fed (7:27-28), four thousand fed with a few loaves and fish (8:1-10), dangerous yeast (8:15), no loaves (8:14a, 16, 17a), and nineteen baskets of leftovers that have been overlooked (8:19-21).

What Defiles? (7:1-23)

Why has the Evangelist placed this controversy with the Pharisees (vv. 1-13) and its implications for discipleship (vv. 14-23) at this narrative juncture? There are conceptual and verbal links between this pericope and those preceding it, some obscured in translation. We have noted the peculiar oscillation from the disciples' obduracy about their teacher (6:52) to the multitude's enthusiastic receipt of his healing power (6:54-55). At 7:1, 3 the pendulum swings again, away from the crowd's attraction to the Pharisees' critical distance (cf. 7:14a). The swing from public ministry (7:1-15) to private instruction (7:17-23) repeats a pattern established in 6:34, 40-44 and 6:35-39. (Similarly, the disciples in the boat [6:45-52] may be contrasted with the multitudes after mooring [6:53-56].) Gennesaret is in northern Galilee (6:53). As 7:24 will clarify, Jesus is heading more deeply into Gentile territory—and Jewish separation from the nations is one of the points implicitly raised by 7:2-4, 15, 23b.

Verbal threads join 7:1-23 with 6:30-56. "Eating" is the most obvious (7:2-3; cf. 6:36-37, 42), though the Greek text is more pointed: the disciples "eat bread" (KJV; alternatively, "the loaves" [7:2]), recalling loaves distributed among the five thousand (6:38, 41, 44). In 6:52a the disciples cannot understand the loaves; in 7:18a their misunderstanding persists. "Their hearts were hardened" (6:52b); a diseased heart is the source of religious corruption (7:6, 19, 21). Other verbal reverberations are softer. "Marketplaces" (*tais agorais*) are among the venues Jesus has visited in 6:56a; "the market" (*agoras*) is where "all the Jews" get things to eat (7:3-4). Mark 6:56b emphasizes the attempt of the infirm to touch Jesus; in 7:3b, 4, 8 the Evangelist repeatedly uses the Jewish metaphor of "holding" (*krateō*) religious tradition (so translated by the NRSV in v. 8, though rendered as "observe" in vv. 3b-4). (The same verb recurs in 6:17, with reference to John's being "held," or "arrested.") A majority of textual witnesses oddly include "beds" (*klinōn*) among those things the Pharisees ritually wash (7:4; see NRSV footnote), reminiscent of the mats (*tois krabattois*) on which some of the sick were carried to Jesus (6:55). Whether Mark inherited traditions already so joined or the seams were created by the Evangelist is immaterial. Whatever their origin, they exist in the text.

The structure of Mark 7:1-23 is puzzling (see Marcus 1997). The subject shifts and the argument loses focus. If all but four verses were stripped away, a clear pronouncement story would remain, not unlike 2:23-28, complete with setup and punch line:

- 7:1-2: Some Pharisees and scribes observe that Jesus' disciples eat with unwashed hands.
- 7:5: They ask Jesus why this is so.
- 7:15: Jesus responds to the accusation with a general precept: defilement comes not from without but from within.

That line of thought is reasonably clear. Confounding Mark's reader are the various asides, tangents, and elaborations.

- 7:3-4: An explanation of strict Pharisaic practice (set off parenthetically in the NRSV).

- 7:6-13: A dense response by Jesus, which includes his critique of five things:
  (a) The tradition of the elders, as such (vv. 8, 9, with v. 9 essentially reiterating v. 8);
  (b) Vacuous worship of God, drawing upon OT prophetic indictment (vv. 6-7);
  (c) Egregious abuse of Corban (vv. 11-12);
  (d) Invalid interpretation of "the word of God" (vv. 10, 13a);
  (e) General castigation of "many things like this" (v. 13b), left unspecified.
  (The first four of these items seem subtly interrelated: [b] Empty worship of God and [c] abuse of Corban are particular instances of [d] transgression of Scripture, owing to [a] a supervening esteem for tradition that "God's word" neither substantiates nor ever intended.)
- 7:14: An expansion of the audience, from the Pharisees (and scribes: 7:1) to the crowds at large.
- [7:16: "Let anyone with ears to hear listen" (cf. 4:9): absent from some of the earliest manuscripts, though attested in a majority of texts of mixed quality; set as a footnote in the NRSV.]
- 7:17-23: Jesus' teaching on that which truly defiles (vv. 18b-23), prefaced by the disciples' inquiry "about the parable" (v. 17) and his chastisement for their failure to understand (v. 18a).

Teasing out the logic in all of this is a challenge, but here is an attempt. (1) Measured by its incisive statement, its subsequent development (vv. 17-23), and its widespread address (to "the crowd" [v. 14]), the cardinal issue lies in verse 15: the redefinition of Jewish defilement as what proceeds out of a person (see Svartvik 2007). This flies in the face of the OT's Holiness Code (Lev 17–26), the detailed regulations by which Israel was expected to separate (and thereby "purify") itself from other nations. (2) In response, Jesus in Mark contends that there are precepts (like Corban: v. 11), whose observance has been distorted, even flouted, by their traditional practice (vv. 12-13). Grant that, and several consequences follow. (3) Pharisaic interpretation and practice of Scripture are deemed pedantic (vv. 3-4), hypocritical (v. 6), in default of first principles (vv. 10-12), and more defensive of "human tradition" than of "the commandment of God" (vv. 7-9, 13). None of these conclusions is unexpected, given Mark's earlier presentation of Pharisees and scribes (2:1-12, 15-17; 2:23–3:6, 3:22-30). (4) By contrast, Jesus' different interpretive criteria emerge as normative for Scripture's proper understanding (7:6-15). As it was in the beginning, so in Mark it continues: "He taught them as one having authority, and not as the scribes" (1:22b).

Regarded historically, Mark 7:1-23 seems at points anachronistic in the time of Jesus. The earliest Mishnaic prescription for scrupulous washing *by priests* is about 100 C.E. (*m. Ber.* 8.2-4). The laity were not obligated to wash their hands before eating, though by Mark's day it is possible that some had piously adopted this practice (see Neusner 1973). If so, the Pharisees would have been natural candidates: in the matter of hand washing, the rabbinic houses of Shammai and Hillel aspired to a level of purity on holy days like the Sabbath (Sanders 1992, 431-40). Parenthetical explanation of Pharisaic practice (Mark 7:3-4) assumes an audience unfamiliar with Jewish customs in the late first century. In its present formulation the rejection of food laws (7:15) likely bespeaks a time in ancient Christianity after Jesus, when a Gentile majority did not observe *kashrut* (see Acts 10:14; 11:8). On the other hand, "there is clear evidence that [Jesus] did not regard the Mosaic dispensation to be final or absolutely binding" (Sanders 1985, 267; see also Booth 1986, 117-223).

We now turn to the structural components of Mark 7:1-23.

(a) **The presenting problem and Jesus' response (Mark 7:1-5, 14-15).** The basic issue raised by some Pharisees and scribes from Jerusalem—figures who usually spell trouble in Mark (see 2:6, 16, 24; 3:6, 22; 10:2)—is why Jesus' disciples eat with unwashed (and, therefore, defiled) hands (see Lev 15:11; 22:1-16). Underlying their query is a dedication to "walk" (see NRSV footnote; cf. Deut 5:33; Prov 8:20; 1QS 3:13–4:26; Acts 21:21; Heb 13:9) in accordance with "the tradition of the elders" (vv. 3, 5), which may refer to the oral law of customary practice that, according to later talmudic literature, was built as a protective fence around the written Torah (*b. ᶜErub.* 13a, 21b; *j. Ber.* 1, 3b; cf. Gal 1:14). That "all the Jews" washed their hands, their food, and their eating utensils (7:3-4) is likely another example of Markan exaggeration (see 1:32; 6:54). Some manuscripts of 7:3b emphasize personal bathing, which gives rise to the JB version: "They never eat without first sprinkling themselves." The adverb translated in the NRSV as "thoroughly [wash]" (7:3a) is only one of many attempts to make sense of the Greek word *pygmē*, which literally means "with [the] fist": "oft" (KJV); "ceremonial[ly]" (Goodspeed, NIV); "up to/as far as the elbow" (Moffatt, JB); and "hand against fist" (Lattimore). Whatever *pygmē* means, the context suggests deep religious devotion (BDAG 896b). It takes a while for Jesus to address the point of debate, but eventually his answer rebuts Leviticus (11:1-47) with universal application (7:15): nothing from outside a person is, upon entry, capable of defilement; the things coming out of a person defile. The Greek verb translated as "defile" is *koinoō*: literally, to make common; by extension, to render unclean or impure by common association (4 Macc 7:6; Acts 10:15; Heb 9:13; Rev 21:27).

(b) An elaboration of Jesus' answer (Mark 7:17-23). In 7:17-18a Mark reverts to typical narrative form: a shift from "the crowd" to the disciples in a "house," where their request for more information is met by Jesus' reproof of their misunderstanding (see 4:10-13; also 1:28-29; 3:19b-23; 4:33-34). The fact that Jesus is asked about "the parable" (*tēn parabolēn,* 7:17) indicates that, while his instruction in 7:15 may have been sharp, it is anything but clear for his followers. No wonder: given the OT's forthright differentiation of clean and unclean foods (Lev 11:1-23), Jesus' teaching is characteristically stark. (The reference to "parable" in 7:17 probably accounts for the additional wording in 7:16, imitating 4:9: see the NRSV footnote.) Again Jesus slams his disciples' failure to understand (7:18a; see 4:13, 30; 6:52); here, as elsewhere, the Twelve may serve as surrogates for those in the Evangelist's audience finding it hard to grasp the nettle. Jesus' defense of his bold statement in 7:13 is two-pronged.

First (vv. 18b-19a), he trivializes the ingestion of unclean foods by a gauche *reductio ad absurdum*: How can a person be tainted by something that so quickly passes into the belly and from there goes straight into the latrine (*ho aphedrōn*)? If anyone has missed the implication for kosher observance, Mark spells it out: literally, "[thus Jesus was] cleansing all foods" (v. 19b, absent from Matt 15:17). Second (vv. 20-23), Jesus details instruments of human defilement emerging from within the heart (*kardia*), the seat of religious conduct and moral sensibility (Ps 24:4-5; Jer 32:39-40; see Mark 3:5; 6:52; 8:17; 11:23; 12:30, 33).

Jesus identifies as "bad" (7:21a AT) or "wicked" (7:23 AT) twelve "dissensions" (*hoi dialogismoi* AT, v. 21a: a cognate for a verb used in 2:6, 8 to describe "questions" in the scribes' hearts). Cumulatively, these machinations constitute a vice list like those appropriated by other NT authors from the moral philosophers of their day (Rom 1:29-31; Gal 5:19-23; 1 Tim 1:9-10; 2 Tim 3:2-4; Titus 3:3; cf. *J.W.* 2.581; *T. Reu.* 3.6; *Ascen. Isa.* 2.5). (1) In this context (cf. Matt 5:32; 19:9; Acts 21:25) "fornication" is too particular as a good translation of *porneia* (Mark 7:21), which refers to all illicit forms of sexual intercourse (Rom 1:29; 1 Cor 5:1; 2 Cor 12:21). (2) Theft (*klopē*), (3) murder (*phonos*, Mark 7:21), and (4) adultery (*moicheia*, v. 22) are proscribed by the eighth, sixth, and seventh commandments (Exod 20:13-15; Deut 5:17-19; cf. Mark 7:10a; Exod 20:12; Deut 5:16). (5) Avarice (*pleonexia*, Mark 7:22) is like covetousness (against which, the tenth commandment: Exod 20:17; Deut 5:21); some Hellenistic moralists considered greed as one of the most disgraceful vices (BDAG 834b). (6) Wickedness (*ponēria*, Mark 7:22) refers to baseness, a lack of moral values (cf. Luke 11:39; 1 Cor 5:8). (7) *Dolos* (Mark 7:22), deceit, could also be translated as "cunning treachery" (AT; Rom 1:29). (8) *Aselgeia* (Mark 7:22) is licentiousness: transgressing social norms by letting oneself go (Eph 4:19; 1 Pet 4:2). (9) "An evil eye" (*ophthalmos ponēros*, Mark 7:22) is a metonym for malicious envy (Deut 15:9; Tob 4:7; Sir 14:10). (10) In Mark (2:1; 3:28-29; 15:29) God's true agents are objects of defamation (literally, "blasphemies," *blasphēmia*, 7:22). (11) Pride (*hyperēphania*, v. 22) refers to an inflated sense of self-importance (cf. Luke 1:51; Rom 1:30; 2 Tim 3:2; Jas 4:6; 1 Pet 5:5); (12) foolishness (*aphrosynē*, Mark 7:22), to lack of good sense or prudent judgment (cf. 2 Cor 11:1, 17, 21). All these vices refer to self-absorbed conduct that violates the social contract. Collectively, they are aligned with a corrupted religiosity that so abhors the common, the *koinos* (7:2, 5, 15), that community, *koinōnia* (cf. 1 Cor 1:9; Phil 2:1; 1 John 1:3b, 6), is perversely ruptured.

(c) **Divine commandment versus human tradition (Mark 7:6-13).** "Declar[ing] all foods clean" (v. 19b) and relocating defilement as evil that arises from within persons (vv. 20-23), Jesus has dismissed the transgression of "eating with defiled hands" (v. 2) by undercutting the religious assumption on which it is based: namely, that "whatever goes into a person from outside [can] defile" (v. 18b). On what basis, however, can Jesus invalidate that conventional presupposition? That is the argumentative burden shouldered by Mark 7:6-13.

Jesus' rejoinder is triply barbed. First (v. 6a), he cites prophetic scripture: Isaiah 29:13 (LXX, whose Greek form accounts for differences of wording in the NRSV, which more closely adheres to the MT). That citation, second, is turned in judgment against Jesus' questioners: they are "hypocrites" (*tōn hypokritōn*, v. 6a; see also 12:15). This is not simple slander. In Greek "hypocrisy" refers to a disjunction between public pretense and genuine intent (BDAG 1038a), which is precisely the indictment against Judah in Isaiah 29:13abc (Mark 7:6b): lip service to God despite a distant heart. "Eat[ing] with defiled hands" (7:5) is thus associated with a common prophetic condemnation: empty worship of God (Isa 1:10-20; 58:1-14; Amos 5:21-24). The distinction between outward (honor) and inward (distance) introduces, in turn, the fundamental contrast amplified in Mark 7:18b-23. The rest of the quotation from Isaiah (29:13d; Mark 7:7) sets up Jesus' third point of attack: abandonment of God's command in preference for human tradition (7:8). This reference to tradition (*hē paradosis*), literally, "that which is handed over," creates a link with "the tradition of the elders" (*tēn paradosin tōn presbyterōn*) in 7:3, 5. Although the Pharisees and their rabbinic successors highly esteemed *paradosis,* the term carries a sinister connotation in the Second Gospel: it is cognate to the verb *paradidōmi,* whose twenty occurrences in Mark almost always refer to unjust arrest or betrayal (e.g., 1:14; 3:19a; 9:31; 10:33; 13:9; 15:10).

The need to distinguish between "standing tradition" and "annulled [scriptural] command" (7:9) is exemplified by a shady practice of Corban (vv. 10-13a). According to Leviticus (1:2), a *qorban* (sacrifice) was an offering of something to God (cf. Mark 7:11c), which, when dedicated by oath, withdrew that religious gift (Gk. *dōron* [Mark 7:11b]) from secular use. Once such a vow was taken, it could not be legally broken (Num 30:3; Deut 23:24). Mark presents a case in which someone could escape responsibility of support by saying to one's parent, "Whatever support you might have had from me is Corban" (7:11)—and by that declaration violating the fifth commandment to honor one's father and mother (7:10a; 10:19; see Exod 20:12; Deut 5:16). For Mark, such an abrogation is tantamount to cursing a parent (7:10b), a capital offense (Exod 21:17; Lev 20:9). To commit the crime of parental neglect, under a religious pretense with traditional justification (Mark 7:12, 13b), nullifies God's word (7:13a). By the late second century rabbis contemplated legal fictions to absolve responsibility for the breaking of oaths, necessitated by misuse or abuse of *qorban* vows (*m. Ned.* 4.7-8; 5.6; 9.1; cf. *Spec. Laws* 2.16-17).

An abuse of *qorban,* real or potential, may seem irrelevant to hand-washing and other ablutions (Mark 7:1-5). Some analogies are detectable. In both cases Mark considers rituals with scriptural grounding, whose practice could distort Scripture's intent while acquiring a religious cachet as "traditional" (7:3-5, 11-13). "Honor" (*tima*) of God merely by one's lips (7:6b) was never intended to compromise genuine "honor" (*tima*) of one's parents (7:10a). Perhaps the deepest undercurrent permeating ritual purity (7:1-5, 15), *qorban* (7:10-13a), and sources of defilement (7:17-23) is the idea of "setting something apart" for pious practice: the removal of dirt by religious washing, the removal of resources by a religious vow, the removal of foods by kosher law, the removal of a people for preservation of its religious sanctity. Like his teaching in 7:6-23, Jesus' ministry in Mark describes an arc that transgresses accepted religious boundaries hedged around forgiving sins (2:1-12), dining with sinners (2:15-17), bending the Sabbath to human need (2:23-28), fraternizing with the unclean (5:1-43), and disrupting temple worship (11:15-19). By the time that the temple's curtain is torn down by divine intervention (15:38), God himself will obliterate traditional boundaries, reconfiguring what is clean and unclean, opening wide "a house of prayer for all the nations" (11:17b; cf. Isa 56:7). With exclamation points at verses 15 and 19b, Mark 7:1-23 serves as a manifesto for Gentile inclusion, cutting across the grain of pious Jewish separatism (cf. Acts 10:1–11:18; Gal 2:11-21; Col 2:20-23).

A Strange Pair of Healings (7:24-37)

Although they could have circulated independently of each other, the tales in 7:24-30 and 7:31-37 neatly fit at this point in Mark's narrative. Both are set in the region of Tyre, northwest of Galilee, from which Jesus has attracted many (3:8) and to which he himself now draws near (7:24a). Sidon (v. 31, and in many manuscripts of v. 24), was twenty miles north of Tyre. The region of the Decapolis (literally, "the Ten Towns"; see 5:20) spread east and southeast of the Sea of Galilee. The route taken by Jesus in 7:31 is ridiculously roundabout: as one commentator notes (Achtemeier 1978, 27), it is like traveling from Philadelphia to Washington, D.C., by way of New York City and central Pennsylvania. However weak the Evangelist's knowledge of geography (see also 5:1; 6:53), clearly this is Gentile territory, despised by Jews (Ezek 26:1–28:19; Joel 3:4-8). Jesus has just been teaching about religious conduct that breaks down Jewish separatism (Mark 7:15, 19b). Mention of an unclean (*akatharton*) spirit (v.

25a) recalls Jesus' cleansing (*katharizōn*) of all foods (v. 19b). The image of children who have been fed (*chortasthēnai*, v. 27) echoes the multitude that has been fed and filled (*echortasthēsan*, 6:42); the "bread" (*ton arton*) of 6:38, 41, 52 returns in "the children's bread" of 7:27 (obscured by the NRSV rendering, "food"). The masses seeking Jesus in 6:33, 55 return in 7:33; at Gennesaret they bring (*peripherein*) to him their sick (6:55), and in the Decapolis they bring (*pherousin*) to him a deaf man (7:32).

The stories in 7:24-30 and 7:31-37 are nearly mirror images of each other. Both focus on unfortunate people who suffer conditions that isolate them from society (vv. 25a, 32a). (In that regard we may recall "evil intentions" that tear the social fabric in 7:20-23.) Something "from within" the daughter and the deaf man incapacitates them: a demon (v. 30), stoppage in the ears (v. 33b), blockage of speech (v. 35). Proxies intercede on the sufferers' behalf, bowing before (v. 25) or begging (v. 32) Jesus (cf. 5:6, 12, 22-23, 33). The story of the Syrophoenician woman begins with Jesus' failed attempt to escape notice (7:24b); the story of the deaf man ends with Jesus' defeated order to tell no one (7:36a). The harder secrecy is pressed, the more widely the news is broadcast (v. 36b)—a contradiction pervading Mark (1:44-45; 2:1-2; 3:19b-20; 6:31-33) and multiply ironic for a story that ends with disobedience of a gag order against reporting Jesus' removal of a speech impediment (7:35b-36).

The differences between these tales are also interesting. Mark 7:33-34 renders with great detail Jesus' technique for healing the man (for some ancient parallels see Klauck 2000, 153-77): privacy of treatment (cf. 5:37), application of fingers on the sufferer's ears and tongue, use of spittle (cf. John 9:6), looking to heaven (cf. Mark 6:41b), sighing, and pronouncement of the cure. ("*Ephphatha*" [in Aramaic, 7:34] assumes, as in 5:41 and 7:11, that Mark's audience needs the Semitic term translated.) The cure's confirmation is also specific: literally, "his hearing was opened up, and his tongue's fetter was released, and he spoke straight" (7:35), all of which astounds beyond measure (v. 37a). Beyond Jesus' simple declaration of the child's healing (v. 29b) and its confirmation by her mother (v. 30), no details are recounted of the exorcism in 7:24-30 (cf. the more graphic presentations in 1:21-28 and 5:1-20). The little girl's healing takes place at home, removed from Jesus (7:30a; cf. 7:33). The punch line in 7:31-37 probably lies in the last verse, which—ironically, coming from Gentiles—acclaims Jesus with an OT paraphrase (Isa 35:5-6; Wis 10:21). By contrast, verse 30 is an anticlimax for Mark 7:24-30, whose manifest interest lies in the conversational thrust and parry between Jesus and the woman in 7:27-29a.

She is "a Gentile": literally, "a Greek" (cf. Rom 1:16; 1 Cor 1:24; 10:32; Gal 3:28; Col 3:11); her precise nationality is Syrophoenician (Mark 7:26a). Unconventionally for a woman in antiquity, she approaches Jesus for her daughter's exorcism (v. 26b). Nowhere in Mark has Jesus refused such assistance, and exorcisms have characterized the overthrow of Satan's kingdom by God's Son (3:11-12, 23-27) and his disciples (6:7, 13a). In 7:14-23 Jesus' teaching has dealt with the abolition of traditional distinctions between clean (Jews) and unclean (Gentiles). Thus, Jesus' reply to the mother's request is startling. By contrast with Matthew's version of the story (15:23-25), Jesus in Mark neither ignores her before relenting nor keeps her begging. At 7:27 he does, however, suggest a delay in her petition's fulfillment on grounds of priority ("let the children be fed first"), commenting on the ignobility (*ou . . . kalon*) of "taking the children's bread and pitching it to the dogs" (AT). For one who has just spoken of defilement that proceeds from within (v. 23), it is Jesus who appears ignoble, or at least woodenly conservative. There's no escaping the ethnic slur built into "dogs" (*tois kynariois*; see 1 Sam 17:43; 24:14; Prov 26:11; Phil 3:2; Rev 22:15; see Michel 1965). Would Mark have fabricated this detail and attached it to the figure who, nine verses later, will be cheered by Gentiles for "[having] done everything well" (7:37b)? Although there is little evidence on which to base firm conclusions (Jeremias 1958, 29-36), it is not impossible that the Jesus of history interacted little with Gentiles for the reason that Matthew (15:24) puts on his lips: "I was sent only to the lost sheep of the house of Israel." Both Matthew (Matt 5:47; 6:7; 18:17) and Paul (Gal 2:15) take a dim view of Gentile conduct, even though they, like Mark and other NT authors, are dedicated to Gentile evangelization (Matt 28:19; Acts 13:46; Rom 11:11; Gal 1:16; Col 1:27; 1 Pet 2:12). The question stands: Whatever Jesus himself may have believed, how does the reader interpret Mark 7:27-29a?

The persistent temptation is to get Jesus off the hook, somehow, usually by imputing to Mark 7:27-29 a "sweetener" without textual basis ("little puppies" are not offensive [van Iersel 1998, 250]). This not only strains credulity; it undermines the Evangelist, who, had he been as embarrassed as some of his interpreters, could easily have left out the pericope entirely. (Luke did just that.) Others suggest that Jesus was testing the woman's faith (Iverson 2007, 48-54). Although that is not out of character for the Markan Jesus (see 6:37a, 38a), other possibilities are suggested by 7:27. Jesus does not flatly refuse the woman's request; he does, however, prioritize "children" (*ta tekna* = Israel [?]) as preeminent beneficiaries (7:27a). In itself that is odd, since in antiquity a child occupied a station of claimless vulnerability (Oepke 1967, 636-48). Even children, however, are fed before lapdogs are (7:27a). While the reader reels from this affront, the Syrophoenician woman twists Jesus' maxim to deliver the riposte best suiting her situation: "Sir ['Lord': *Kyrie* (11:3; 12:37)], even the house-dogs under the table eat from the children's ['servants': *tōn paidiōn*] bitty scraps" (7:28 AT; see BDAG 575a). The acknowledgement of Jesus' superiority, the implied acceptance of his insult, the lowering of self *beneath* (*hypokatō*) the table, the subtle shift in Greek from one term for "children" to another that plays on both immaturity and servanthood (BDAG 750ab), the acceptance of crumbs: all these elements anticipate Jesus' definitions of discipleship (9:33-37; 10:13-16), congruent with the Son of Man's self-condescension (8:31; 10:41-45). *That* is what makes "this word" (*touton ton logon*) so apt and so convincing (7:29). Though listeners of the story may have been entertained by it, Jesus is more than conceding the witty moxie of a female outsider; he ratifies her claim to the gospel on the very grounds that he himself will explain in 10:28-31. She is not disappointed (7:30).

◊ ◊ ◊ ◊

Twentieth-century study of Mark's Gospel was preoccupied with its presentation of Jesus. More than that: christological scholarship has been fairly obsessed with titles like "Christ," "Son of God," and "Son of Man." Some investigators have asked whether such an approach to the question is adequate (Trocmé 1975; Keck 1986). The Second Gospel suggests that it is not. Mark's depiction of Jesus is complex; all of its elements cannot be analyzed and coordinated here. However, if one takes but a segment of Mark—7:1-30, for example—one may see that *Jesus' offensiveness* is an aspect of this Gospel's Christology irreducible to a title yet critical for the interpreter to wrestle with. A conservative reader will almost certainly be affronted by Jesus' claim that defilement comes from within, not from without (7:15, 23), and by the narrator's passing (!) comment, "Thus he made all food clean" (Lattimore). This, like Jesus' laxity in the matter of Sabbath observance (2:23-28), arouses the parishioner's suspicion: "I have always been troubled, Pastor, by...the feeling that our Lord Jesus was just a bit of a liberal" (Käsemann 1969, 16). Yet this Gospel offers no comfort to those of liberal sympathies who resist the notion that a socially progressive Jesus would ever say such a thing ascribed to him in Mark 7:27 or, worse, that the Gentile so insulted would countenance the slur (7:28; see Ringe 2001, 79-100). The deeper question with which Mark's reader must come to terms is whether she or he can follow a Christ so offensive as to die by crucifixion (15:22-41). An inescapable dimension of this Evangelist's Christology is the Messiah's repulsiveness. Jesus flummoxes everyone who boxes him into conventional expectations: the pious (2:1–3:6; 7:1-23), his family (3:19b-21), his disciples (8:33), and even some petitioners (7:24-30). If Mark's reader is not also abashed, it is a safe bet that its Jesus has been domesticated and his gospel has been neutered.

Another Desert Feast (8:1-10)

Even as Mark 6:45-52 appears a doublet of the tale recounted in 4:35-41, there is no reasonable doubt that 8:1-10 is a twin of

6:31-45 (For a more developed theory of traditional developments, see Achtemeier 2008, 55-116.)

The *similarities* between these two feeding miracles are numerous and obvious. The spine of both tales is the same, as are many of the details and, in some instances, the Greek wording.

Table 9: *Two Wondrous Feedings*

Narrative Element	Mark 6:31-45	Mark 8:1-10
1. Setting	The wilderness (*erēmon topon,* vv. 31-32, 35)	The wilderness (*erēmias,* v. 4)
2. Those in need	Famished hordes (vv. 34-36)	Famished hordes (vv. 1-2)
3. Jesus' response	Compassion (*esplanchnisthē,* v. 34)	Compassion (*splanchnizomai,* v. 2)
4. Jesus' intent	Feed the crowd (*ochlon,* vv. 34a, 37a)	Feed the crowd (*ochlon,* vv. 2, 6c)
5. Disciples' response	Dismissed for practical reasons (v. 37b)	Dismissed for practical reasons (v. 4)
6. The meager resources	Five loaves, two fish (vv. 38 41)	Seven loaves, small fish (vv. 5, 7)
7. Jesus hosts the meal	(a) Takes what is available (v. 41a)	(a) Takes what is available (v. 6b)
	(b) Offers to God: "blessed" (*eulogēsen,* v. 41)	(b) Offers to God: "giving thanks," "blessing" (*eulogeēsas,* vv. 6-7)
	(c) Disciples' distribution (vv. 39-40)	(c) Disciples' distribution (vv. 6-7)

8. The crowd's response	All eat and are satisfied (*esphagon... kai echortasth-ēsan*, v. 42)	All eat and are satisfied (*esphagon kai echortasthēsan*, v. 8a)
9. Plentiful leftovers	Twelve baskets full (v. 43)	Seven baskets full (v. 8b)
10. The size of the crowd	Five thousand (v. 44)	Four thousand (v. 9a)
11. Aftermath	(a) Jesus disperses (*apoluei*) the crowd (v. 45b)	(a) Jesus disperses (*apelusen*) the crowd (v. 9b)
	(b) Immediately (*euthys*) ministers;	(b) Immediately (*euthys*) ministers;
	(c) get into a boat (*embēnai eis to ploion*, v. 45a)	(c) get into a boat (*embas eis to ploion*, v. 10)

What of the differences between Mark's feeding miracles? (1) Overall 8:1-10 lacks many details of its sister story: Jesus' attempted retreat and its defeat by the multitudes (6:31-34a), the OT image of "sheep without a shepherd" and Jesus' teaching many things (v. 34b), the disciples' cajoling to dismiss the multitude (vv. 35-36), their protestation about the cost of provisions (v. 37b), and the organization of the crowd "in groups on the green grass" (v. 39). Mark seems to assume that by repeating only the most important items—Jesus and his disciples among a great crowd with nothing to eat—the reader will again (*palin*) catch their significance (8:1). (2) The numbers shift: loaves and fish (five/two [6:38, 41] or seven/"a few" [8:5-7]), baskets (twelve [6:43] or seven [8:8]), people fed (five thousand [6:44] or four thousand [8:9]). (3) The second time around Mark not only subtracts but also adds details.

- In 8:2-3 the welfare of the hungry throngs is more thoroughly developed.
- The language of thanksgiving, *eucharistēsas* (8:6), more clearly chimes with the words of institution of the Lord's Supper in the tradition recalled by Paul (see table 6).
- The "few small fish" (*ichthydia oliga*) are virtually an after-thought (8:7).
- The tangled Greek construction in 6:43 is straightened out in 8:8. Instead of "twelve full fragments of baskets" (silently amended in the NRSV), the leftovers are now "seven baskets of fragments" (AT).
- This story concludes with Jesus' departure for Dalmanutha (8:10), whose location is unknown (cf. Mark 5:1; 6:53; 7:31). Matthew (15:39) changes the destination to "Magadan": a Latin spelling for Magdala, a town on the Sea of Galilee's northwest corner, best known as the home of Jesus' disciple Mary (Mark 15:40, 47; 16:1). Following Matthew's lead, some late manuscripts of Mark 8:10 are changed to read "Magadan" or "Magdala" (Swanson 1995, 121). "Dalmanutha" may have been an alternative name for Magadan/Magdala (Finegan 1992, 81), but we cannot be certain.

Why does the Second Evangelist repeat a story that was recounted only forty-nine verses before? Commentators since Hilary and Augustine have considered this the feeding of a Gentile multitude, complementing that for thousands of Jews in 6:30-44 (more recently, see Wefald 1995). Although Mark does not say that—unless his listeners knew better the location of Dalmanutha than we—such an interpretation is reasonable. The immediate context is Gentile (7:24-31). Maybe after "the children [of Israel] have first been fed" (7:27), it is proper for "the dogs" in their own wilderness to eat the leftover scraps (7:28; cf. 1:4, 12-13, 35). (Crumbs, indeed: seven basketfuls, after four thousand have had their fill.) There are other possibilities, coherent with Mark's text. Given the eucharistic whispers in 6:41 and especially 8:6, perhaps the reader is being prepared by these two feedings to receive a third: Jesus' last supper with his disciples (14:17-25), which will appear, in contrast with 6:30-44 and 8:1-10, at once more modest and more consequential. Neither should we ignore the obvious: in the desert, history repeats itself (8:1-3; cf. 6:30-37a), yet the disciples' question (8:4) and their actions (8:5-10) imply total cluelessness amid an unmistakable déjà vu. In 6:52 the Evangelist informed the reader that the Twelve "did not understand about the loaves." In 8:1-10 it is painfully obvious that they still do not.

A Strange Pair of Controversies (8:11-21)

The Pharisees' return (8:11) after the feeding of the four thousand mirrors their previous appearance (7:1-2) after the feeding of the five thousand. They are here to argue (*suzētein*), a verb that characterizes the questioning that Jesus elicits in Mark (1:27; 9:10, 14, 16; 12:28). As usual (10:2; 12:15) they aim to test (*peirazontes*) Jesus, which aligns them with the ultimate tempter, Satan (1:13; cf. 3:22-30). The expression of their testing is "asking him for a sign from heaven." Repeatedly in this Gospel, Jesus is "asked for" or "sought" (*zētountes*), always with misguided (1:37; 16:6) or sinister motives (3:32; 11:18; 12:12; 14:1, 11, 55). Unlike John's Gospel (2:11; 3:2; 20:30; though cf. 4:48; 6:30), "signs" (*sēmeia*) carry a negative or at best ambiguous connotation here and elsewhere in Mark (13:4, 22; cf. 16:17, 20). To seek a sign from heaven is to demand verification of one's divine credentials (Exod 4:28, 30; Num 14:11; Deut 13:1-5; Isa 7:10-17). In Mark's context the Pharisees' demand appears not only hostile but also ridiculous: If "look[ing] up to heaven" (6:41) and, with next to nothing, feeding a total of nine thousand people were not adequate proof of Jesus' bona fides, what could be? But for Mark that way of reasoning is backward: Jesus' mighty works alleviate human suffering; they are not proofs of his identity. Seeking signs that corroborate Jesus' authority is relentless and leads nowhere: the faithless never get a heavenly sign that can change their minds

(15:29-32, 36-37) because their minds are made up in defiance of Jesus (3:21-22). In 8:12 Jesus responds accordingly, with a prophetic tinge: literally, "Certainly I tell you, if a sign be given this generation"—then the consequences are literally unmentionable (a Semitic circumlocution: 1 Sam 3:17; Ps 130:2 [LXX]; see M. Black 1967, 121-24). "Truly" (*amēn*) suggests firm insistence (3:28; 9:1, 41; see Jeremias 1971, 35-36). Evoking an OT expression of human faithlessness (Gen 7:1; Deut 32:5, 20; Ps 95:10), "this generation" recurs in Mark as Jesus' expression of judgment (8:38; 9:19; 13:30; cf. Matt 12:38-42; Luke 11:29-32). Jesus' "sigh[ing] deeply" (*anastenaxas*) recalls his sighing (*estenaxen*) while looking up to heaven, before healing the deaf man with impeded speech (7:34). Those ears Jesus could open because his help had been sought (7:32). For the determinedly deaf and forked-tongued who seek only his entrapment, Jesus can do nothing whatever (6:6a).

For the last time in Mark, Jesus gets into a boat and crosses the Sea of Galilee (8:13). Though his disciples are terrorized at sea (4:35-41; 6:47-52), the lake affords Jesus respite (4:1-2; 5:21a); it is when the boat docks that troubles emerge (5:1-2, 21bc-24; 6:53–7:2). Trouble for the Twelve is already brewing: they have forgotten (or "neglected," *epelathonto*; BDAG 374b) to bring bread, and they have only a loaf in the boat (8:14). Jesus says nothing of that; instead, he cautions them to beware the yeast of the Pharisees, with whom he has just tangled in 8:11-12, and the yeast of Herod, whom the reader met in 6:14-29. ("The Herodians," elsewhere paired with the Pharisees [3:6; 12:13], appears in some manuscripts, though "Herod" has better attestation.) "Yeast," fermented dough (*tēs zymēs*), often symbolizes a pervasive corruption hidden in humans (1 Cor 5:6; Gal 5:9; Ign. *Magn.* 10.2), akin to humanity's evil inclination, *yetzer hara*, in rabbinic literature (*b. Ber.* 17a; *Gen. Rab.* 34). Characteristically, Jesus' speech is riddled (3:23a; 4:1-32); the implication may be that his disciples should guard against insidious conduct, whether religiously or politically bent.

The ensuing conversation (8:16-21) between Jesus and his disciples is weirdly comedic: they talk past each other, and their few points of contact are fruitless. Literally translated, verse 16 reads: "And they debated [*dielogizonto*] to one another, 'We don't have loaves.'" *Dialogizomai* is the same verb used in Mark for others' bickering (2:6, 8; 9:33; 11:31), a cognate of the evil "intentions" (*hoi dialogismoi*) in 7:21. "We don't have loaves" is a non sequitur from 8:15, which does not logically follow from 8:14. The disciples' comment in 8:16 suggests concern for the circumstances in 8:14. Mysteriously "knowing" their argument (see also 4:13; 5:29; 13:28-29), Jesus replies, "Why are you arguing that you don't have loaves?" (8:17a AT). Then Jesus levels his harshest reproach of the disciples (cf. 4:13, 40), who still do not perceive or understand (8:17b; see also Jer 5:21; Ezek 12:2). "Are your hearts hardened?" (Mark 8:17c; cf. 3:5), he asks. From 6:52b the reader knows the answer is affirmative. Failure of eyes to see and ears to hear (8:18ab) recalls "those outside," for whom everything is in parables (4:11-12). "Do you not remember?" (8:18c) is a choice question to ask those who have just forgotten (8:14). The pop quiz in 8:19a, 20a recaps the events in 6:30-44 and 8:1-10, but the implications of the disciples' correct answers (8:19b, 20b) are left unexplained. Jesus' final, hanging question (v. 21)—"Do you not yet understand?"— recalls Mark's odd observation that the disciples' cardiac hardening is expressed by their not understanding about the loaves (6:52). Jesus appears frustrated. So do his disciples. So, too, may be Mark's readers.

Mark's earliest commentators attempt to soften the ambiguity of 8:14-21. Matthew (16:5-12) sands away the rough edges, clarifying what Jesus' disciples "of little faith" (v. 8) ought to know: a warning against Pharisaic (and Sadducean) leaven is metaphorical; the real concern is with their teaching (v. 12b) and has nothing to do with actual bread (v. 11). In Matthew the disciples ultimately get it (v. 12a; cf. 13:51; 14:33). Luke simply deletes the conversation in Mark 8:14-21: Jesus cautions his disciples against "the yeast of the Pharisees, that is, their hypocrisy" (12:1). Great is the temptation for any commentator to explain Mark when the Evangelist seems determined to keep things murky. If 8:19-20 has a recoverable point, it seems to be that preoccupation with a single loaf (v. 14), even no bread at all (vv. 16-17a), is misplaced when traveling with one whose leftovers are more than enough to sustain. Nevertheless, Mark does not *say* that, instead preferring to leave the interpretation open and to challenge his listeners' understanding (v. 21). In a section that opened with the disciples' ministry (6:6b-13) and is dominated by tableaux of eating (6:14-44; 7:1-2, 14-19, 27-28; 8:1-10), Jesus and the disciples' crosstalk about yeast and bread is an aptly maddening way to draw things to a close: an off-key demonstration of the Twelve's persistent resistance (see Bassler 1986). Whence comes that obstinacy? Is it a blindness that results from staring into divine revelation or, perhaps, from a diabolical power that undermines human will? By this point in Mark's narrative, have Jesus' demands upon the Twelve begun to weigh so heavily that their—and by implication the reader's—ability to shoulder them is more than they can manage (Tannehill 1979, 70)? Whatever its origin, the Twelve's continued incomprehension points the way into this Gospel's next major section, where the discord between Jesus and his followers becomes even more strident.

THE SON OF MAN AND HIS DISCIPLES (8:22–10:52)

Most commentators agree that Mark 8:22–10:52 is the pivot around which this Gospel's narrative turns. Up to now Jesus' identity and activity have been correlated with those of his followers (1:16-20; 3:7-19a; 6:1-13). In this section, lying near the Gospel's center, two of the Evangelist's primary themes—the character of Jesus' authority and the duties incumbent on his disciples—converge and are elaborated. Mark lays the foundation for his Passion Narrative, which immediately follows (11:1–15:47).

The structure of 8:22–10:52 is tripartite (Perrin 1971, 7-13). The hinges are three predictions of the Son of Man's destiny, which invariably elicit the Twelve's misapprehension of the teacher and of their own responsibilities. Their confusion prompts Jesus' teaching on the nature of his work and its implications for his followers (see Shiner, 1995).

Table 10: *The Tripartite Structure of Mark 8:22–10:52*

Prelude: A Two-Stage Healing: Mark 8:22-26		
A Prediction of the Son of Man's Destiny	*The Disciples' Misunderstanding*	*Teaching about Discipleship*
Mark 8:31	8:32-33	8:34–9:1
Mark 9:31b	9:32-34	9:35-37
Mark 10:33-34	10:35-41	10:42-45
		Postlude: The Calling of Bartimaeus: Mark 10:46-52

The first (8:31–9:1) and third (10:33-45) cycles of prediction/misunderstanding/instruction fall at this section's beginning and end. Almost equidistant between them is the second cycle (9:31-37). The intervening material (9:2-29; 9:38–10:31) spells out implications for Christology and discipleship while driving the narrative forward:

Table 11: *Two Interludes in Mark 9:2–10:31*

Interlude I (Mark 9:2-29)	*Interlude II (Mark 9:38–10:31)*
Jesus' transfiguration (9:2-8)	Defining the circle of discipleship (9:38-41)
What happened to Elijah (9:9-13)	Temptations to stumble (9:42-50)
The last exorcism (9:14-29)	Teaching about divorce and remarriage (10:1-12)
	Blessing little children (10:13-16)
	Possessions and God's kingdom (10:17-31)

Bookending this section are two stories of Jesus' healing of blind men, the only such tales in Mark. Spiritual blindness has already figured in the effect of Jesus' parables (4:12) and the condition of his closest followers (8:18). That, coordinated with the seamlessness of Jesus' healing and teaching (1:27), suggests that the placement of 8:22-26 and 10:46-52 is no accident. Mark 8:27–10:45 has been sandwiched between two tales of blind men to whom, with Jesus' aid, sight is restored. The theological implication is that the spiritual blindness of Jesus' followers may also be cured, though only with difficulty.

◊ ◊ ◊ ◊

To Take Up One's Cross (8:22–9:1)

Prelude: A Blind Man at Bethsaida (8:22-26)

Set in Bethsaida (see 6:45), this story resembles that of a deaf man's cure in 7:31-37. (Both tales appear only in Mark.) In both, (1) after the setting is established (7:31; 8:22a), (2) an unspecified "they" bring one suffering a physical disability to Jesus (7:32a; 8:22b), (3) whom they beg to touch the infirm (7:32b; 8:22b; see also 5:23). (4) Jesus takes the sufferer to a private place (7:33ab; 8:23a; cf. 5:37), where (5) he touches the afflicted part of the body, applying saliva (7:32cb; 8:23bc). (6) Both stories conclude with Jesus' admonition for secrecy (7:36a [forcefully]; 8:26 [obliquely]; see also 1:44-45; 5:43; 7:24). (Some scribes teased out the parallelism with 7:36 even more explicitly, adding to 8:26 a prohibition not to "tell anyone in the village" [see NRSV footnote].) Such healing stories are common in antiquity, involving royal personages or Asclepius, the god of healing (Boring, Berger, Colpe 1995, 175-76).

By now the reader recognizes the basic pattern; the deviations catch one's eye. In 7:34-35 one learns more of the healer's protocol, and the healing itself is dramatically instantaneous. In 8:23d-25a, by contrast, Jesus' procedure is more tentative ("Can you see anything?"), the result is temporarily inconclusive ("I can see people, but they look like trees, walking"), and Jesus must repeat the therapy described in 8:23. In contrast to the deaf man, a more passive figure whose body readily responds to Jesus' command (7:34-35), after Jesus' second touch Bethsaida's blind man "looked intently and his sight was restored, and he saw everything clearly" (8:25). In contrast with 7:36-37, which stresses defiance of Jesus' gag order, Mark's manifest emphasis in 8:25 lies in the reiterations of full restoration of sight after progressive therapy. After the labored catechism of 8:18-21, the attentive reader is primed for the section unfolding from this tale: Jesus' need to repeat instruction for myopic disciples (8:34–9:1; 9:35-50; 10:23, 24b-25, 42-45); their need to pay attention (9:7, 29); and the possibility of clear discipleship, ironically expressed in another blind man's healing (10:46-52). Perspicacity is no mandate for witness, however: Bethsaida's erstwhile blind man is told to go home (8:26).

The First Cycle: Declaration and Temptation at Caesarea Philippi (8:27–9:1)

Caesarea Philippi (v. 27a) is a border region between Syria and Palestine, located about twenty-four miles north of the Sea of Galilee, at Mount Hermon's southwest slope. Jesus and his disciples are "on the way" (*en tē hodō*), which can be read as both simple transit and religious adherence (see 1:2-3; 4:4, 15; 11:8; 12:14). Being "on the way" recurs in this section's second and third cycles (9:33-34; 10:32) and puts a period at the end of the entire section (10:46, 52).

En route he asks his disciples, "Who do people say that I am?" (8:27b). In Greek, as in English, this is clearly a question. Usually, when Jesus asks a question, its substance penetrates deeply into his interlocutor's (or the reader's) point of view and the answer is rarely obvious: "Why do you raise such questions in your hearts?" (2:8). "Who are my mother and my brothers?" (3:33). "Can you see anything?" (8:23d). "Why are you afraid? Have you still no faith?" (4:41). In 8:27b, 29a—for the first time in this Gospel—Jesus twice asks others their estimate of himself. The first inquiry probes *vox populi*; the second, what his disciples themselves think of him. Both answers are at once revealing and fuzzy.

According to the Twelve (8:28), the public's view of Jesus

scatters, yet tallies precisely with the possibilities proposed in 6:14-15: Jesus is believed to be John the Baptist, Elijah, or "one of the prophets" (perhaps like Moses, the law's great interpreter: Deut 18:15-22). All these figures were oracular prophets, remembered for speaking the Lord's word against unrighteousness and abuse of power (Moses: Exod 5:1–15:21; Elijah: 1 Kgs 17:1–19:21; 21:1-9; 2 Kgs 1:1–2:12; John: Mark 1:4-5; 6:18; Matt 3:7-10). Elijah was reckoned a divine messenger whose coming would precede "the great and terrible day of the LORD" (Mal 3:1-2; 4:5-6). Evidently some in first-century C.E. Palestine regarded John as Elijah *redivivus*, the climactic harbinger (Mark 1:7-10; Matt 11:7-19 = Luke 7:24-35). At least some of Jesus' mighty works have been reminiscent of Elijah's (*ad loc.* 5:35-43; 6:30-44).

Jesus intensifies the same question for his disciples (Mark 8:29a): "And you...who do you say I am?" (NEB, REB). Though Simon Peter was the first of the Twelve to be called (1:16; 3:16), to this point he has not been a featured player in the narrative (1:36; 5:37). Certainly neither he nor any of the Twelve has demonstrated insight into their teacher's identity (4:41; 6:49-50a, 51b-52; 8:18). At Caesarea Philippi he steps into the spotlight and speaks for them all: "You are the Messiah" (8:29b). Peter gives no basis for his statement; neither does Mark (cf. Matt 16:17). Peter's "confession" is in Mark 8:29b a blurting out (cf. Matt 16:16). Mark has opened, "The beginning of the good news of Jesus Christ" (1:1); this is only the second time that term has been applied to Jesus. In fact, only at 8:29 in Mark does a follower of Jesus ever claim that he is the Christ (cf. 9:41; 12:35; 13:21; 14:61; 15:32). Jesus' stern command (*epetimēsen*) that his disciples say nothing about him to anyone (8:30) is in character (cf. 1:34; 3:12; 5:43a; 7:36a). Mark 8:29-30 is the parade example of what has come to be known as "the messianic secret" (Wrede 1971), though "messianic silence" or "tacit messianism" might be a more precise characterization. Mark affirms Jesus' messiahship, but he never exclaims it or explains what he means by it.

The meaning of messiahship during the era of Mark's composition, and for this Gospel in particular, is at once complicated and quite simple.

In the past century some reputable scholars assumed a fairly uniform pattern of messianic expectation in Hellenistic Judaism (e.g., Moore 1958, 2:323-76; Schürer 1979, 514-47). These scholars constructed that pattern from later rabbinic sources, which now appear less reliable as an index for first-century Jewish thought (Sanders 1977, 59-84). The Hebrew term *meshiach*, "anointed," refers in the OT to Israel's prophets (Isa 61:1), high priests (Dan 9:25-26), kings real (Ps 2:2) or idealized (Isa 11:1-9; Jer 23:5-6), and even the Persian potentate Cyrus, who allowed exiled Israelites to return home (Isa 45:1). In itself there is nothing eschatological about the term, although the first-century B.C.E. *Psalms of Solomon* bends OT materials in that direction (see 17:1–18:13). The first-century C.E. *4 Ezra* (11–12) and *2 Baruch* (40, 72) envision an ideal, Davidic king who will judge the wicked and restore Israel's righteous remnant. Perhaps riffing "the Ancient of Days" in Daniel 7:9-10, *1 Enoch* imagines a heavenly "Elect One" (48:10; 62:5; 69:27). Often in fragments, the DSS (1QS 9:11; 1QSa 2:11-23) present a very complicated picture: ascetic Jews expecting Messiahs of both Aaron (a priest) and of Israel (a king) as well as a righteous teacher "at the end of days" (CD 6.7-11). Other apocalyptic literature, like Daniel, expresses a hope for Israel's restoration without express mention of a messiah (Dan 10:20-21). While we know of Jewish insurrectionists against Rome, like Theudas (*Ant.* 20.97-98; Acts 5:36) and "the Egyptian" (*Ant.* 20.169-71; *J.W.* 2.262-63), it is hard to ascertain to what degree "messianism" figured ideologically in their movements. Whatever their eschatological aspirations, if any, Second Temple Jews differed among themselves whether Israel's restoration would depend on a messiah. Those who believed such did not concur on what that messiah would look like (Neusner, Green, Frerichs 1987, 49-185).

It is anyone's guess what messianic connotations colored the traditions that Mark inherited. Far more speculative is what purchase such concepts might have had in the religious imaginations of Gentiles, if they dominated Mark's original audience. We simply do not know the answers—and to understand this Gospel, we do not have to. Mark demonstrates no interest in refuting received opinions about a messiah (contra Weeden 1971). The Evangelist shows every indication of doing the very thing observed in the literature we have surveyed: supplying his own distinctive meaning to the title "Christ." In this Gospel, especially in 8:22–10:52, Mark's presentation of Jesus orients the reader to how so ambiguous a term as *Christos* should be understood. In 8:30 the first things one learns are (1) that Peter made a valid claim, which (2) is hushed until a proper context has been constructed for its understanding. In the Second Gospel "Messiah" does not define Jesus; to the contrary, Jesus redefines the term "Messiah."

The prediction: At Mark 8:31 Jesus resumes his stance as teacher (see 1:21-22; 2:13; 4:1-2). The subject of this teaching, entrusted to the Twelve, is quite grim. Shifting *away from* messianism, Jesus turns instead to what the Son of Man must endure. As in 2:10, 28 the implication is that in referring to "the Son of Man," he speaks of himself. The predicate "must undergo" (NRSV) is a way of rendering the passive verb *dei*, first appearing here in Mark (later: 9:11; 13:7, 10, 14; 14:31). Occurring more than a hundred times in the NT, *dei* implies divine necessity: if the Son of Man must undergo what follows, that is because God, the unseen agent behind everything, wills it to be so. The Son of Man must suffer greatly, or suffer many things (*polla pathein*). The rest of 8:31 elaborates that suffering: rejection "by the elders, the chief priests, and the scribes." "Elders" (*tōn presbyterōn*) refers to senior lay leaders (Luke 7:3; Acts 4:8); in Mark 7:1-8 Jesus distanced himself from "the tradition of the elders" (vv. 2, 5). The "scribes" (*tōn grammateōn*), synagogue authorities upholding the elders' tradition, have been Jesus' principal antagonists in Mark (1:22; 2:6, 16; 3:22; 7:1, 5). Contemporary "chief priests" (*tōn archiereōn*), the temple's cultic administrators, appear here for the first time (cf. 2:26, referring to Abiathar during David's day). In 14:1–15:31 the chief priests will emerge as primary instigators of Jesus' arrest and execution, in cooperation with scribes and elders (14:43, 53; also 11:27). These three groups constitute the Sanhedrin, or supreme Jewish council, which will seek Jesus' conviction in Mark (15:1; cf. 13:9; 14:55). (Notice the absence of Pharisees, who are largely absent from Mark's Passion Narrative [only at 12:13].) That the Son of Man must be killed and after three days be raised are also of divine necessity. "And he said this plainly" (RSV 8:32a). This is no riddle (cf. 4:34). Jesus' affirmation in 8:31 is candid and clear.

Repudiation: Taking his teacher aside, Peter reacts by rebuking him (**8:32b**). Unlike Matthew (16:22), Mark does not soften Peter's response; there is only the harsh verb *epitimaō*, just used in verse 30 to describe Jesus' rebuke (*epetimēsen*) of his disciples against broadcasting his messiahship. Jesus used the same verb to stifle unclean spirits and a furious gale (1:25; 3:12; 4:39; 9:25). Instantly this verb recurs in 8:33: Jesus rebukes (*epetimēsen*) Peter, calling him Satan, the tempter (1:13). (Peter is the only figure in Mark whom Jesus addresses in this way.) The impression is unmistakable: by pulling Jesus aside, attempting to divert him from the ordained path that must be traveled, Peter is arrogating to himself an authority he does not hold and aligning himself with satanic forces by "setting [his] mind not on divine things but on human things" (8:33; cf. Rom 8:1-8; Gal 5:16-26). Mark 8:33 is no gentlemanly disagreement: here we have a life-and-death struggle between the divine and the diabolical. Peter's only recourse is to "get behind" the teacher, not ahead of him. The same applies to all the disciples, whom Jesus has not failed to notice (8:33a).

The subsequent instruction (8:34–9:1) crystallizes Mark's definition of discipleship. The audience includes the Twelve but is broadened to encompass a crowd (8:34a). This teaching is for anyone who would "come after [or behind] me" (AT): precisely the attitude of *following* that Peter temporarily refused (8:33). Such followers are admonished (a) to deny themselves, (b) to take up their cross, and (c) to follow Jesus (v. 34b). Self-denial implies the rejection of "setting your mind on human things": the very thing of which Peter proved incapable, and will again fail to do on the night of Jesus' betrayal (14:30, 31, 72). Because Jesus himself is headed to a cross (*ton stauron*; see 15:21, 30, 32), so must his followers. The subject of crucifixion will be addressed more fully at Mark 15:21-41. For now it is enough to note that in antiquity the cross was a political instrument of utterly humiliating, torturous execution: "To bind a Roman citizen is a crime; to flog him, an abomination. To slay him is virtually an act of murder. To crucify him is—what? There is no fitting word that can possibly describe a deed so horrible" (Cicero, *Against Verres* 2.66.170).

The paradox of cross-bearing discipleship is heightened in Mark 8:35. To produce a gender-inclusive translation, the NRSV generalizes ("those who want"/"those who lose") what in the Greek are pointed assertions about individual decision: "For if anyone might wish to save his life [*tēn psychēn*, 'inmost being'; see BDAG 1099ab], he will lose it; and if anyone will lose his life for the sake [of me and] of the gospel [*tou euangeliou*], he will save it." (A minority of ancient manuscripts omits "for my sake.") "For the sake of the gospel" is an important qualification: one may give one's life for no good purpose; to give one's life for the sake of the good news that Jesus instantiates is the only valid reason for self-sacrifice. Still, the paradox is unrelieved: in the economy controlled by the gospel, the only way to receive wholeness is to relinquish everything. The question posed in 8:36 is rhetorical. To paraphrase: there is no benefit in gaining the whole world—"human things" (v. 33), values and aspirations as this world defines them—if in so doing one forfeits one's deepest soul. Ultimately nothing in this world is worth exchanging for one's very center, the self that is claimed by the gospel (v. 37). Though evocative of Psalm 47:7-9, this viewpoint flies headlong in the face of prestige and reputation, "[the] love of honor...rooted in every human being" (Xenophon, *Hiero* 7.3); it dances with public disgrace and contempt, "shame [that] is in the eyes" (*Rhet.* 2.6.18). Hence the caution in verse 38, closely paralleled in Q (Luke 12:8-9 = Matt 10:32-33): the only shame that concerns a true disciple should be that expressed by the Son of Man for having abandoned him and his words "in this adulterous and sinful generation," which is no arbiter of honor and shame as the gospel redefines those qualities.

Mark 8:38–9:1 offers both warning and hope. It is an awesome prospect to appear with accountability before the Son of Man "when he comes in the glory of his Father with the holy angels" (cf. Matt 13:41; 25:31; John 1:51). In such a prospect, however, lies assurance that self-renunciation for the gospel's sake is neither futile nor masochistic. The faithful disciple who transcends this generation's wickedness will be vindicated, even as the slain Son of Man will be raised after three days (Mark 8:31).

Jesus' last word (9:1) is a bold, elliptical, and potentially embarrassing prophecy. What does it mean that God's kingdom will have come "in" or "with power" before some standing there "tasted death" (John 8:52; Heb 2:9; *4 Ezra* 6:26)? That kingdom has been "at hand" since the start of Jesus' ministry (Mark 1:15) and has since assailed Satan's house (3:23-27). Writing decades after Jesus' promise, Mark knew full well that history's final curtain had not yet come down (13:30-31). If 9:1 refers to the cataclysmic coming of the Son of Man, why does the Evangelist use an intensive double negative in 9:1 (*ou mē,* "by no means"), needlessly inviting instantaneous disproof? Moreover, how does one reconcile 9:1 with Mark's later insistence (13:32) that the timing of historical catastrophe is unknown to all—including the Son—but only to the Father? The Evangelist leaves the intent of the prophecy in 9:1 unresolved—unless the reader concludes that its resolution lies elsewhere in Mark's narrative (*ad loc.* 9:2-8).

◊ ◊ ◊ ◊

The origins and interpretations of "the Son of Man" (Gk. *ho huios tou anthrōpou*) are among the most vexing problems in the Gospels' interpretation. Here we may consider only some issues that bear on understanding Mark.

Most scholars agree that the earliest recorded reference to the term occurs in Daniel 7:13-14. Composed during the mid-second-century B.C.E. Jewish persecution by the Seleucid ruler Antiochus IV, this oracle offers hope for God's deliverance of Israel through the agency of "one like a son of man" (7:1-12). This "son of man" (Aram., *bar 'enash*[*a*]) has the appearance of a human being, a mere mortal, which is the term's basic meaning (see *ben 'adam* [Heb.] in Job 16:21; Pss 8:4b; 80:17; 146:3; Isa 51:12; 56:2; and "the sons of men" in Mark 3:28 KJV). The Danielic figure, however, is heavenly; while not called a "king" or "messiah," "the one like a son of man" is bestowed royal prerogatives by the white-haired Deity, "the Ancient of Days" (Dan 7:9-10). (In a different use of the term, devoid of heavenly sovereignty, God addresses the prophet Ezekiel ninety-three times as "son of man," suggesting both his humility and his separation from other humans for the prophetic task.) From Daniel 7:13-14 "one like a son of man" evolves during the late first century C.E. into a titular "Son of Man" with various connotations: a messianic "Righteous One" who executes judgment from a heavenly throne (*1 En.* 38:2; 46:1; 47:3; 48:10; 52:4; 69:27-29); an anointed, Davidic king who, though never called the "Son of Man," judges Roman rulers and vindicates righteous Israel (*4 Ezra* 7:28-29; 11:1–12:32); "the one whom the Most High has kept for many ages" (*4 Ezra* 13:26; cf. 13:28); "a blessed man from heaven's expanses, with a scepter in his hands, which God gave him" (*Sib. Or.* 5.414-33 [early second century C.E.]). In these traditions there is no unilinear development. They seem quite fluid, drawing from sources besides Daniel 7: among others, Isaiah 11:1-16; Psalm 2; the Servant Songs in Isaiah 42, 49, 50, 52–53; and Wisdom of Solomon 1–6 (whose righteous judge is killed by powerful opponents but vindicated in a heavenly court with an angelic retinue). Like Daniel, most of these books evidently emerged from circumstances of persecution, which comport with the typically heavenly, or transcendent, quality of their hoped-for vindicators (Nickelsburg 1992, 137-41; J. J. Collins 1995, 173-94).

Jesus' own references to the Son of Man remain intensely

debated. Did he use the term only as an oblique form of self-reference (Lindars 1983) or a general statement of the human condition (Casey 2007), which his disciples "eschatologized" (Vermes 1973, 160-91)? Did Palestinian Christians uniformly place the term as a title on his lips (Burkett 1999)? Did Jesus reckon himself the Son of Man, rejected and slain (Manson 1959, 211-36)? Did he think he would be exalted as the Son of Man (Jeremias 1971, 257-76)? Did he apply the term to himself in both mundane and transcendent senses (Theissen and Merz 1998, 541-53)? Did he refer to a heavenly Son of Man other than himself (Higgins 1964; Tödt 1965)? Did he employ it sometimes in reference to himself, sometimes in reference to another (Sanders 1985)? The evidence is so confounding that agreement on its interpretation may never be reached. Nevertheless, different traditions, all old and some independent of one another, preserve sayings of Jesus about the Son of Man (e.g., Luke 17:22-37 = Matt 24:26-27 [Q]; Mark 14:62; Matt 25:31-46 [M]; Luke 18:8 [L]; John 1:43-51; Acts 7:56), even though that term did not prove as popular for identifying Jesus as "Christ," "Lord," or "Son of God" (cf. Rev 1:13; 14:14). In the Gospels Jesus alone uses the term; no one ever addresses him as "[the] Son of Man."

Except for its aphoristic reference to "people" in 3:28, "the Son of Man" appears in Mark thirteen times. It has become commonplace to group those sayings into three categories.

Table 12: *The "Son of Man" in Mark*		
The Authoritative Son of Man on Earth	*The Suffering and Vindicated Son of Man*	*The Apocalyptic Son of Man to Come*
The one who forgives sins (2:10)	Rejected, killed; will rise again (8:31)	Of whom will he be ashamed;
Lord even of the Sabbath (2:28)	Not until after he is risen (9:9)	Father's glory with holy angels

	(8:38)
Must suffer and be treated with contempt (9:12)	In clouds, with power, glory; angels; will gather the elect (13:26-27)
Betrayed, killed; will rise again (9:31b)	Seated at right hand of power, coming with clouds of heaven (14:62)
Handed over, condemned, handed back over, mocked, spat upon, flogged, killed; will rise again (10:33-34)	
Has come to serve and to give his life as a ransom (10:45) Goes as written of him; woe to his betrayer (14:21) Betrayed into sinners' hands (14:41)	

1. In none of these sayings does Jesus bluntly assert, "I am the Son of Man." For that matter, nowhere in Mark does he flatly claim, "I am the Son of God," or "I am the Christ." (*Peter's* statement is muted [8:29-30]; Jesus accepts *the high priest's* claim [14:61-62].) Even though Mark refers to Jesus Christ (1:1), Mark's Jesus abjures those claiming messiahship (13:21-23). In

this Gospel, Jesus is noticeably reticent to identify himself and oblique when he does so.

2. When Jesus *does* refer to himself, usually it is to his identity as "the Son of Man." Sometimes he alludes to himself as "the Son" (13:32; cf. 12:6); only once as "Christ" (9:41). Jesus' preferred self-designation in Mark is cryptically roundabout.

3. The suffering and vindicated Son of Man (above) can only refer to Jesus. Contextually, the same is true of the pair of comments about the earthly, authoritative Son of Man. The three sayings about the apocalyptic Son of Man are most intriguing: they could be interpreted as Jesus' reference to a figure other than himself. In context, however, Mark probably intends for the reader to identify Jesus with this glorious Son of Man to come. For instance, since Jesus has just alluded to himself as "the Son of Man" in 8:31, would Mark expect the reader to apply that name to someone other than Jesus only seven verses later (8:38)? Whatever Jesus may have thought of himself, this Evangelist consistently believes that Jesus, and no one else, is the Son of Man (Hare 1990, 207-11).

4. Of these assertions Mark weights those referring to the suffering and vindicated Son of Man. Such sayings outnumber those in the other categories by a ratio of three or four to one.

5. Though we have sorted these sayings into groups for conceptual clarity, Mark gives the reader no reason to suppose that the three types are either distinct from or antagonistic to one another. Indeed, they are mutually interpretive (Hooker 1967, 178-82). The Son of Man exercises hidden authority "on earth" (2:10a) that will be manifest when he comes from heaven (13:26-27; 14:62). His apocalyptic vindication comports with his rising from the dead (8:31; 9:9, 31; 10:34b). His authority is constrained by scripturally mandated submission into sinful hands that reject, abuse, and kill him (8:31; 9:12, 31; 10:33-34a; 14:21, 41). He can restore life (2:10; 13:27) only because he gives up his own (10:45).

6. Mark does not expect a single title, even one with multiple connotations, to carry all of this Gospel's christological freight (Perrin 1995). Jesus "the Son of Man" begs to be interpreted in coordination with other designations (like "Son of God") as well as within the narrative framework that presents him as the

teacher whose insight is uniquely authoritative (2:23-28; 7:6-15) and the healer whose power over hostile forces will be consummated (1:21-28; 13:26-27; 14:62)—but only after he has relinquished his life to redeem others (10:45).

7. Between Mark's presentation of the Son of Man and that in Jewish literature there are intersections and divergences. Like *1 Enoch* and *4 Ezra,* Mark has apparently drawn not only from Daniel 7:13-14 but also from an eclectic array of OT scripture in fleshing out his portrait of Jesus as the Son of Man, including Deutero-Isaiah's Servant Songs (e.g., Isa 49:6bc/Mark 13:10; Isa 50:6/Mark 10:34; Isa 53:5-6, 10ab/Mark 10:45). (Despite Hooker's spirited attempt to overturn this interpretation [1959], some similarities are hard to deny; see Page 1985.) The Son of Man's suffering and the martyrdom of Jesus' disciples (8:34-37; 10:29-30, 39; 13:5-23) square with persecutions that preoccupy books like Daniel and *1 Enoch.* Jesus' derivative authority from God (1:9-11; 9:2-8; 12:1-12) matches "the Ancient One['s]" conferral of sovereignty on the Danielic Son of Man (7:13-14; also *Sib. Or.* 5.414-33). Like Ezekiel, Jesus acts with prophetic power and suffers others' bereavement (cf. Mark 6:30-44; 8:1-10; Ezek 4:1–5:17; 12:1-28; 24:15-27; see Schweizer 1970, 166-71). Like *1 Enoch* and *4 Ezra,* Mark associates the Son of Man with the Messiah (8:29; 14:61), trailing clouds of glory, attended by angels in a heavenly court; unlike them, the Evangelist stresses vindication of the faithful, not punishment of the wicked (8:38; 13:26-27; 14:62). In Mark the Son of Man's redemption is not limited to Israel, as it tends to be in Jewish apocalypticism. What sets apart the Markan Son of Man is the emphasis on his suffering, especially a death with redemptive consequence (10:45; 14:24). There is nothing comparable to this, for instance, in the DSS (J. J. Collins 1995, 123-26). Here the Second Evangelist goes his own way, stamping the Son of Man traditions with an indelible impression of the early Christian Passion Narrative.

A Christological Interlude (9:2-29)

Following the first cycle of prediction/misunderstanding/teaching (8:27–9:1), Mark presents three pericopae concentrating on

Jesus. The first is a mysterious epiphany (9:2-8); the second, a quizzical conversation between the teacher and his disciples (9:9-13); the third, the Gospel's final exorcism (9:14-29).

Jesus Transfigured (9:2-8)

"After six days" (v. 2 RSV; cf. Moses' ascent of Sinai in Exod 24:16), Jesus leads Peter, James, and John (5:37) up a high mountain for a private colloquy. What these three disciples witness—a supernatural transformation of Jesus—qualifies as one of this mysterious Gospel's most enigmatic events. Nothing else in Mark is quite like it, though the baptism of Jesus (1:9-11) and his appearance on the waves (6:45-52) also present divine revelations of Jesus' identity. Some commentators consider 9:2-8, like 6:45-52 (*ad loc.*), a "misplaced" or relocated post-resurrection appearance. Bultmann (1963, 260), for instance, believes this story to have originated in a resurrection appearance of Jesus, retrojected here in Mark "to serve as a heavenly ratification of Peter's confession [in 8:29] and as a prophecy of the resurrection in pictorial form." Another suggestion: this story depicts Jesus' permanent entrance into the heavenly world (Theissen 1983, 96-97). Such explanations stimulate more questions than they answer. If the Evangelist did not consider heavenly confirmation of Jesus' resurrection needful in chapter 16, why would he think it appropriate in chapter 9? Mark 9:2-8 addresses neither Peter's confession of Jesus nor the promise of Jesus' resurrection (8:31). Nor does it describe Jesus' permanent entry into glory: he never leaves the mountain for heaven, and at the end all things have returned to normal (9:8).

What Mark 9:2-8 offers the reader is a special kind of epiphany: an intersection of the glorious with the mundane, at which Jesus undergoes momentary metamorphosis. Its placement just here in the Gospel may be an odd fulfillment of Mark 8:38: Jesus' assurance that "the Son of Man [would come] in the glory of his Father with the holy angels [or messengers (*tōn angelōn*)]." Mark 9:2-8 immediately fulfills two aspects of that promise. On a high mountain, the biblical locus of divine revelation (Exod

19:3-25; 24:12-18; 1 Kgs 19:8), Jesus is transformed (vv. 2-3) in a manner reminiscent of the *kabod* or *shekinah,* God's essential splendor (Exod 16:10; Num 14:10; Ps 57:5, 11), as well as the dazzling imagery of apocalypticism (Dan 7:19; 12:3; *4 Ezra* 7:97; Matt 13:43; 2 Cor 3:18; Phil 3:21; Rev 3:5; 4:4; 7:9). Attending Jesus are figures reckoned in ancient Judaism as "holy messengers," Elijah with Moses (v. 4; cf. Mal 4:5-6; Sir 45:1-22; 48:1-16; *Mos.* 2.2.3.187). The glimpse of glory given Jesus' intimates in 9:2-8 satisfies the promise made in 9:1. Given the Evangelist's repeated references to God's in-breaking kingdom (1:15; 3:24; 4:11, 26, 30; 9:47; 10:14-25) and the Son of Man's present activity (2:10, 28; 8:31; 9:31; 10:33), there is no reason to suppose that Mark *must* refer in 9:1 to the kingdom's final consummation. More likely, 9:2-8 invites interpretation within Mark's proximate context.

The narrative of Jesus' transfiguration recalls several motifs announced in Mark 1:1-11: a temporal indication, a significant action of which Jesus is the recipient, a revelation attended by Elijah (or his surrogate, John the Baptist), a divine declaration, and scriptural coloring. Instead of Jesus' vision of the Spirit's descent from the split heavens (1:10), on the mountain the disciples behold a vision of Jesus' radiance and his conversation with Elijah and Moses (9:2-4). The key verbs in Mark's narration—literally, "was metamorphosed" (v. 2) and "there appeared" (v. 4)—are conjugated as divine passives, indicative of God's agency (see also 8:31). Likewise 1:9-10: Jesus *was baptized,* and the heavens *were torn* apart. All of these details prepare the reader for a final acclamation in Mark of Jesus as God's Son at 15:39 (see table 19).

◊ ◊ ◊ ◊

Considering 1:1, 9, we noted the ambiguity of the term *Son of God* in antiquity. Within and beyond Israel the king or emperor could be called "Son of God" (2 Sam 7:14-17; Pss 2:7; 89:26-27; Dio Cassius, *Roman History* 44.6; 53.27), as could be God's people (Exod 4:22-23; Jer 31:9, 20; Hos 11:1), the wise or righteous person (*Spec. Laws* 1.318; *QG* 1.92), charismatic figures (*b. Ber.* 7a; *Jos. Asen.* 6:3, 5; 13:13), angels and the heavenly host (Ps 89:6-7; *3 En.* 10:2; 48:8), and the Messiah (*4 Ezra* 7:28-29; 14:9; 4QapocrDan ar; see Hengel 1976, A. Y. Collins 1999). Given such a broad pattern of usage and the veneration of Jesus by early Christians, it would have been remarkable had he *not* been regarded as Son of God.

Only Mark, however, can tell us why he thinks Jesus should be so designated. At least some recurring elements can be teased from the Gospel.

1. Jesus, and nobody else, is "the Son of God." This is important to note because, for Mark, "Son of God" does not define Jesus. It is Jesus who defines "Son of God."

2. In this Gospel, Jesus rarely speaks of himself as "the Son [of God]." It is claimed of him by the heavenly voice (*bat-qôl*: 1:11; 9:7), by demons recognizing in Jesus the status of their enemy (1:24; 3:11; 5:7), by the high priest (using the pious circumlocution, "Son of the Blessed One": 14:61), and by the centurion at the cross (15:39). The exceptions to the rule are two abbreviated allusions to Jesus in a parable (12:6) and at 13:32 ("nor the Son, but only the Father"), where use of the term subordinates rather than exalts his position.

3. Mark's description of Jesus as Son of God is (a) couched in scriptural allusion, (b) tinted by apocalyptic motifs, and (c) unveiled at climactic moments. There is no evidence to suggest that the Evangelist went scrounging in Scripture to prove something about Jesus or discovered anything about him by studying eschatological tea leaves. Mark *assumes* that Jesus is the Christ and Son of God (1:1). From that revelation God's will (3:35), articulated in Scripture and expressed in apocalyptic event, comes into focus for the eyes of faith.

4. While some have argued that "Son of God" is Mark's primary designation for Jesus (Kingsbury 1983), the evidence of the Gospel is more complicated. Certainly it is an important acclamation, since only in this way does God address Jesus. Still, it is more accurate to say that "Son of God" counterbalances other modes of reference to Jesus, especially that which he himself

employs: "Son of Man," with its many connotations (see table 12). Likewise "the Christ" seems in itself an inadequate identification of Jesus in Mark (8:29); it must be juxtaposed with "Son of Man" and "Son of God"—all located within the context of Jesus' healing and teaching, life and death—in order to be rightly understood. The single best indication of this complexity awaits the reader in 14:61-64, where all the major titles collide, governed by the belief that Jesus' power is inseparable from his death.

◊ ◊ ◊ ◊

Mark 9:2-8 coordinates at least three concerns: (a) Jesus' relationship with his Israelite predecessors, (b) his distinctive identity vis-à-vis God, and (c) the proper response to such information. Like Mark 1:2-11, 9:2-8 demonstrates the continuity of Jesus' messiahship with scriptural precedent while showing how Jesus outruns all precedent (Thrall 1970). Whereas popular opinion mistakenly equates Jesus with Elijah or one of the prophets (8:27-28), Peter correctly identifies him as the Christ (8:29) but is hushed (8:30) and instructed about the Son of Man's God-given destiny (8:31). A comparable pattern unfolds in 9:9-13. The critical difference between the heavenly announcements in Mark 1:11 and 9:7c is the command that Jesus' audience listen to him. This is a direct order to pay attention *to Jesus*: a quotation from Deuteronomy, in which Moses enjoins Israel's obedience to a prophet, like him, whom the Lord God would raise up (18:15). By emphasizing Jesus among Elijah and Moses—only Jesus is transfigured; only he is singled out by the heavenly voice; they are conferring with him, not vice versa—what was suggested at the baptism should now be clear: the Son *agapētos* is the "only" or "unique" Son (see Gen 22:2, 12, 18 LXX; BDAG 7ab). A father's love for such a son is fathomless, precisely because there is no other. What Jesus' disciples should obey is left unspecified, thus all-encompassing. In Mark's immediate context, what they must heed is God's design for the Son of Man's suffering and vindication (8:31), their adoption of his way (8:34-35), restraint on reporting their vision until after the resurrection (9:9), and assurance that all proceeds according to divine plan (9:12-13).

Why "Elijah with Moses" (9:2)? One can speculate. Moses himself had reflected the divine effulgence when proximate to God's glory over the tabernacle (Exod 34:29-35); like Moses, Elijah had experienced a theophany upon Sinai/Horeb (1 Kgs 19:8-18). A cloud descended over Sinai (Exod 24:16); a voice spoke to the prophet on Horeb (1 Kgs 19:12-13). In Malachi 4:4-5 Moses and Elijah are explicitly linked as tandem heralds of the LORD's day. By the first century C.E., a parallel between the lives of Moses and Elijah had become sufficiently well established in Jewish tradition that Elijah appears as Moses *redivivus*.

On its face Peter's confused, frightened suggestion to Jesus (Mark 9:5-6) that three tents be built for him and his interlocutors seems to refer to the Feast of Booths, or Tabernacles (Lev 23:39-43), a popular harvest festival. While Josephus remembered such thanksgiving celebrations as occasions for political agitation (*Ant.* 13.372-73; *J.W.* 6.300-309), three disciples on a hill do not a riot make, not even potentially. Probably underlying Peter's addled proposal is Israel's religious memory of the wilderness tabernacle as the Lord's "mobile home" (Exod 25:1–31:18; Lev 26:11-12; Rev 21:3) and, by imaginative extension, eternal dwellings for the righteous (Luke 16:9; 2 Cor 5:1). A forerunner and constituent of the Solomonic and Herodian temples, the tabernacle was both liturgical shrine and oracular venue ("the tent of meeting," Exod 27:21; 29:43-44). If Peter intends to contain divine disclosure by creating sacred dwelling places, that hope is dashed: Mark dismisses this proposal (9:6); the supernatural colloquy evaporates (v. 8); and the foursome descends the mount (v. 9). Like Elijah from Horeb (1 Kgs 19:15) and Jesus from the Jordan (Mark 1:12-13), the disciples are redirected into the world (9:9-29), having gotten from God something more than Elijah's "thick silence" (1 Kgs 19:12-13), yet altogether different from that prophet's political marching orders (19:15-18). The Twelve must pay attention to Jesus: the moving nexus and veiled disclosure of divine mystery that asserts, without clear resolution, a supremacy more radiant than any fuller can bleach (Mark

9:3) and a suffering that overshadows like a cloud (9:9). The beloved Son encountered on this mountain is beyond *doxa* (glory). He is, in the most literal sense, *para*dox (Black 2005a).

Disciples Mystified (9:9-13)

The conversation between Jesus and his disciples while descending from their summit meeting (v. 9a) is Mark at his most obfuscatory. The initial gag order recalls others that Jesus has issued (1:34b, 44a; 3:12; 5:43a; 7:36a), this time with a terminus: they may speak of what they have seen after the Son of Man has been raised from death (9:9b). This picks up a thread left dangling from the prediction in 8:31, even though it has nothing directly to do with the transfiguration (9:2-8). The implication—it is no more than that, since Jesus does not elaborate—is that broadcasting the vision on the mount is premature or inappropriate until after his resurrection: another miraculous gift from God of which he will be the recipient. (An alternative interpretation is that both transfiguration and resurrection must be tempered by the Son of Man's ignominious death.) Typically in this Gospel— for good (1:16-20; 6:13; 10:28; 11:1-7; 14:12-16) or ill (14:26-31, 43-54, 66-72)—the Twelve comply with Jesus' order (v. 10a). Obedience in this Gospel never guarantees understanding, however (4:13; 6:36-37, 52; 7:17-18a; 8:14-21); thus, the disciples begin questioning (or "arguing": *syzētountes*: 1:27; 8:11; 9:14, 16; 12:28) "what it means to rise from the dead" (9:10b, most literally translated in NEB, NAB, REB, Lattimore). Of all things they might quibble over, this is one of the least expected: though not universally accepted (see 12:18), resurrection was an intelligible concept for Pharisees and other Jews of that era (see, e.g., Isa 26:19; Dan 12:1-3; Wis 1–6; *1 En.* 22–27, 92–105; *Jub.* 23:11-31; 1QS 3:13–4:26; 1QH 3:19-23; 11:3-14). Mark gives the impression that Jesus' disciples had never before heard of such a thing. When they formulate a question (9:11), it has nothing directly to do with resurrection. Instead, "Why do the scribes say that Elijah must [*dei*] come first?" The Twelve have lately heard of the Son of Man's divine necessity (*dei*: 8:31); some have just seen Elijah in a vision (9:4-5). Nevertheless, the question, posed in the eschatological context suggested by resurrection, seems to imply that they seek Jesus' view of the notion that Elijah, who had ascended to heaven in a whirlwind (2 Kgs 2:1-2), would return before "the great and terrible Day of the LORD" (Mal 4:5-6; cf. *m. Ber.* 1.1; *m.ᶜEd.* 8.7). Jesus accepts the idea that Elijah, "having come first, restores all things" (Mark 9:12a AT). The subject of Elijah is dropped, and a different question is raised: "How then is it written about the Son of Man, that he is to go through many sufferings and be treated with contempt?" (9:12b). Though consistent with the prophecy in 8:31, this is a baffling question: it has nothing directly to do with Elijah (cf. the disciples' non sequitur in 9:10-11), and there is no indication of what scriptures are in view. (Neither is there biblical precedent for the Son of Man's sufferings. For Mark [see also 14:21, 49], to say "it is written" is a way of conveying divine necessity; see Juel 1988, 94-95.) If all that were not confusing enough, Jesus *returns* to Elijah, announcing that he *has* come (presumably in John [1:2-8]—but how did he restore all things?) and that (unnamed) subjects did to him whatever they wished (Mark 9:13a), congruent with (unspecified) scripture (v. 13b; perhaps an allusion to 1 Kgs 19:1-10). There ends this conversation.

Mark 9:9-13 is like 8:14-21: in both, the disciples are preoccupied with something (forgetting bread; ignorance of resurrection) other than what Jesus is cryptically talking about ("the leaven of the Pharisees" KJV; a report after the Son of Man's resurrection). Jesus and his disciples seem to be riding on different tracks, each talking past the other: "Why must Elijah come first?" "How is it written about the Son of Man?" Jesus offers a reply ("How many baskets...did you collect?"/"Elijah has come") whose meaning remains veiled. No wonder that Luke omits this entire episode or that Matthew (17:9-13) deletes Mark's most obscure statement (9:10), abbreviates while clarifying others (Matt 17:11-12/Mark 9:12-13), and draws the obvious conclusion,

reflecting credit on the Twelve: "Then the disciples understood that he was speaking to them about John the Baptist" (Matt 17:13). Also clearer than Mark 9:9-13 is the *Gospel of Thomas* (51): "His disciples said to him, 'When will the repose of the dead come about, and when will the new world come?' He said to them, 'What you look forward to has already come, but you do not recognize it.' "

One might point to such passages as examples of the Evangelist's clumsy construction, as though Mark were a hapless raconteur incapable of telling a joke without bollixing the punch line. Maybe the joke is on us. This Gospel displays abundant evidence of careful construction, from traditional intercalations (table 2) to complex triptychs (table 10). Whatever the *intent* of 8:14-21 and 9:9-13, the *effect* is to confuse the Gospel's readers. Could that be part of the point? Is the Evangelist so dedicated to placing us in the company of bumbling followers of Jesus that he is willing to jeopardize his own authorial credibility?

Prayer in a Faithless Generation (9:14-29)

This pericope is the fourth and final narration of an exorcism in Mark (see also 1:21-28; 5:1-20; 7:24-30; cf. 1:32-34; 3:11-12; 3:22; 6:13). We have seen how such stories convey not only "the deeds of power... done by [Jesus'] hands" (6:2), but many other issues: the freshness of Jesus' teaching (1:27d), the Lord's mercy amidst radical uncleanness (5:2, 3, 11), and the benefits belonging to Gentiles (7:28). The same is true in 9:14-29, of which only three verses describe the exorcism itself (vv. 25-27). Matthew (17:14-20) and Luke (9:37-43a) compress Mark's tale, but excising the details loses much of importance in the Second Evangelist's version.

Though not the last of Jesus' mighty works in this Gospel (see 10:46-52; 11:12-14, 20-21), Mark 9:14-29 sums up much that has occurred in all those preceding it. Amazement attends the miracle (9:15; see 1:27; 2:12; 4:41; 5:15b, 42b; 6:2a, 51b; 7:37), as well as argument (*syzētountes,* 9:14, 16; 3:1-2, 6; 4:37-38; 5:17-19; 6:2-5; 8:11-12) sometimes involving the scribes (9:14;

1:22; 2:2-6). Like other intercessors (1:32; 2:3-5a; 6:54-55; 7:32) who appeal for pity (9:22b; see 1:41; 5:23a), a parent (9:17; cf. 5:22-24a; 7:25-26) pleads for a child who suffers a hideous, chronic condition for which there is no apparent cure (9:18, 20-22; also 1:40; 2:3; 3:1; 5:2-5, 25-26, 35; 8:22-24). When the healing takes place, this father's child, given up for dead, is "lifted up" by Jesus and able to stand (9:26-27), the same as Jairus's daughter (5:39b-42a). The unclean spirit in 9:17c prevents the son from speaking; with rebuke (*epitemēsen*; cf. 8:30, 32-33) Jesus addresses the "spirit that keeps this boy from speaking and hearing" (9:25c). Deafness, speech impediment (7:32a, 37b), and blindness (8:22) have characterized the infirm whom Jesus has healed near this Gospel's center—precisely the point where the Twelve themselves have become increasingly blind (6:49; 7:18; 8:33) or tongue-tied (8:17-21, 32; 9:6, 11) toward their teacher. Though exorcisms have been within their reach (6:13), here (9:18c, 28) the disciples prove incapable, corresponding with the deterioration in their understanding of Jesus (8:14-16, 32b; 9:33-34; 10:13, 35-41).

In 9:14-20 Mark stresses two complementary issues: the child's desperate straits and the father's wavering faith. While Matthew tells us that the child "is an epileptic and he suffers terribly" (17:15a), Mark *dramatizes* the urgency with gruesome details. First comes the father's description of his son's condition (9:17c-18b). When the spirit sees Jesus (v. 20b), its victim is convulsed and thrown to the ground, where he thrashes and foams (v. 20c). As with the Gerasene demoniac (5:3-5), the boy's sad case history is presented (vv. 21-22a). Even his cure is terrifying: the spirit shrieks and convulses the child, who is like a corpse (v. 26).

In the face of terror stands faith or its deficiency. Mark 9:14-15 whispers this subject. The multitude's awe on seeing Jesus alludes to the Israelites' fear of Moses' shining visage after he conversed with God on the mountain (Exod 34:29-30; cf. Mark 9:2-8)—which in turn reminds one of Israel's gross infidelity during its leader's absence (Exod 32:1-35). (Could the reference to Jesus' "[seeing] that a crowd came running together" [9:25a] be a throwback to Moses' "[seeing] that the people were running wild" [Exod 32:25]?) Like Moses, Jesus lambastes this "faithless generation" (Mark 9:19a): the disciples' inability to heal the child (v. 18c) recalls the Pharisees' faithless search for a sign (8:11-12). "How much longer" Jesus must put up with this generation (9:19b) chimes with Isaiah's cry: "How long, O Lord" must he proclaim a message that deadens Israel's senses (Isa 6:9-13; cf. Mark 4:11-12)? Though faithlessness has limited Jesus' power (6:5-6a), here he is undeterred (9:19c): "Bring [the child] to me." The father's qualified confidence in Jesus (v. 22) prompts his retort—"If you are able!" (v. 23a)—and his delivery of this pericope's punch line: "All things can be done for the one who believes" (v. 23b; see also 2:5; 11:22-24). From there Mark could easily have moved straight to the exorcism (v. 25). Instead, the father replies with a follow-up plea. Previously he had petitioned, "Help us" (v. 22). Now he cries out specifically for himself: "I believe [*pisteuō*]; help my unbelief [*tē apistia*]" (v. 24). Not only is the child convulsed; so is his father. Both need to be healed. Of that there is no doubt in verses 28-29. If all that mattered were a successful exorcism, the story could have ended at verse 27. Mark adds private discourse between Jesus and his disciples in a house (4:10; 7:17), addressing the *other* spiritual problem: "Why weren't we able to cast it out?" (9:28 AT). "This kind can by no means be driven out except by prayer" (9:29 AT; "and fasting" is a scribal addition in many manuscripts).

Embedded in Jesus' answer to his disciples' query (9:28-29) are two further questions. To what does "this kind" refer? And if prayer is requisite for driving out "this kind," should we infer that the Twelve have not prayed? As to the second question: Jesus' followers have not been praying. Mark has shown Jesus at prayer (1:35; 6:41, 46; 8:6; 14:22-23, 32, 35-36). Jesus teaches his disciples to pray (11:17, 24-25; 12:40; 13:18). But Mark's reader never observes the Twelve praying, even when they are in need (4:37-38; 6:36-37, 48-50a; 8:4; 14:29-31, 50, 66-72). When urged to do so in the hour of Jesus' crisis, they sleep (14:37-41). Prayer is an expression of trust in God, whose ability transcends mortal inability (see 11:22-24). With such faith, all things are possible (9:23b). Without it, nothing is possible.

Yet Mark's understanding of faith is not simplistic. The primary beneficiaries of Jesus' instruction in faith never demonstrate it: they are incorrigibly frightened (4:41; 6:50; 9:32; 10:32; 16:8). Others reaching for faith—Jairus, the hemorrhaging woman, and the epileptic child's father—must grapple with their fear or faithlessness (5:33-34, 36; 9:24). Later even Jesus himself will wrestle with torment (14:33-34); at Golgotha his last words are the psalmist's lament of abandonment by God (15:34; Ps 22:1). After Jesus' burial, he is raised (15:42–16:8), even as he raised a boy thought dead (9:26-27) and a little girl sleeping in death (5:39-42). God's power to restore is reliable in Mark, but such restoration never sidesteps illness, demonism, and death (see Bolt 2004). That power drives straight into their heart to undo them. And that kind of faith comes only through prayer (9:29).

To See and Not Perceive (9:30-37)

The Second Cycle: Through Galilee to Capernaum, the Greatest and the Least (9:30-37)

Like its predecessor, which took place in a particular geographical region (8:27), **the second prediction** of the Son of Man's destiny (**9:31b**) is situated in Galilee (9:30), southwest of Caesarea Philippi. The motif of Jesus' suppressing knowledge recurs (9:30b); this time the reason for muffling is that "he was teaching his disciples" (see also 8:31; 4:10; 7:17).

Compared with those in 8:31 and 10:33-34, the prophecy in 9:31b is the most concise. Only the basic elements are articulated: the Son of Man's delivery into the hands of those who will kill him, and his resurrection after three days. Two aspects are noteworthy. Unlike 8:31, 9:31b highlights betrayal (literally, "being handed over"), a scarlet thread that, beginning with John's arrest (1:14), runs through this Gospel. Another deviation from 8:31 and 10:33-34 is the generality of the Son of Man's betrayers, whose redundancy in Greek is captured in the KJV: "The Son of Man is delivered into the hands of men" (9:31).

In this second cycle Mark flatly asserts the Twelve's *ignorance* of Jesus' saying, compounded by their fear of inquiry (9:32). The disciples' fear of Jesus is another theme pervading this Gospel (4:41; 6:50; 9:6b; 10:32). Mark aligns Jesus' craven disciples with those actively pursuing his destruction (11:18, 32; 12:12); fear intimately associates the betrayer among Jesus' followers (3:19a; 14:10-11, 18, 21a, 42, 44) with the Jewish authorities who deliver one of their kinsmen into Roman custody (15:1, 10, 15; cf. 13:9, 11-12). By contrast, those with faith in Jesus have nothing to be afraid of (4:40-41; 5:33-34, 36).

Fear stymies inquiry that might alleviate ignorance. Thus, it is no surprise that in **9:33-34** the Twelve **radically misunderstand** their teacher, as their deeds and words demonstrate. Arriving in Capernaum (*ad loc.* 1:21; 2:1), Jesus repairs with his followers into "the house," a typical site for much teaching in this Gospel (7:17; 9:28). To those who have asked nothing (9:32b), Jesus poses a sharp question: "What were you arguing about on the way?" (9:33b). The Twelve are at it again (see 8:16-17), divided among themselves like the scribes (2:6, 8; 11:31). Jesus' simple question elicits the Twelve's ambivalent condition throughout the whole of Mark: "on the road" of discipleship (8:27a), at odds with Jesus and one another nearly every step of the way. In contrast with earlier Peter's verbiage (8:29b, 32b; 9:5-6a), here the disciples are mute because they have been debating one another who among them is the greatest. (The Greek text actually reads "who [is] greater," a Semitic construction in which a comparative adjective implies the superlative [BDF 126-29].) Given antiquity's assumptions about status in social groups, the debate is predictable. In Mark's context, however, it is nonsensical, since Jesus is superior to them all. Disregarding their general, the foot soldiers are bickering over their respective ranks.

Though brief, the structure of Jesus' **instruction** (9:35-37) is complex: an aphorism (v. 35b) followed by a pronouncement story, in which the summons of a child (v. 36) sets up two punch lines, the second (v. 37b) an extension of the first (v. 37a). The verbal hinge holding everything together is *to paidion*, "little child" (vv. 36, 37a), which in Greek has the double meaning of "immediate offspring" and "slave." It is a synonym for "servant" (*diakonos*, v. 35b), an assistant who mediates for a superior (BDAG 230a-31a, 750a-51a). Jesus' rejoinder to quibbling over rank is a paradoxical assertion that parallels 8:35 by turning social assumptions inside out: just as the saving of one's life requires its sacrifice for the gospel's sake, so too does primacy in discipleship demand taking a place last of all, as everyone's servant (9:35; see also Matt 20:16; 23:11-12 and, regarding self-subjugation to Torah, *b. B. Meṣ'ia* 85b). The child epitomizes the most subservient in ancient society, those with least status. In Jesus' presence a little child literally has "standing" (*estēsen*, Mark 9:36a: obscured in the NRSV but clear in Goodspeed, NIV, GNT); Jesus' compassionate approbation (v. 36b) recalls his sensitivity to another child's father (vv. 14-29) and Jesus' own standing, at the mount of transfiguration, as God's beloved Son (v. 7). Jesus' embrace also captures a peculiar nuance in the doubled saying in 9:37, which reiterates the importance of "receiving"/"welcoming"/"approving" (*dechomai*: BDAG 221ab) "one such child in my name" and, indeed, Jesus himself. Like self-sacrifice for the gospel's sake in 8:34-35, these qualifications for acceptance in 9:37 are important, steering interpretation away from sentimentality: the "last of all and servant of all" (v. 35) is received "in my name" as a disciple of Jesus who evinces the teacher's own belittlement by betrayal (9:31). Welcoming such an ambassador of Jesus is tantamount to receiving Jesus, who himself is a mediating emissary of the one who has sent him (9:37; see also Matt 10:40; Luke 10:16; John 12:44-45; 13:20).

Children will return in this Gospel as exemplary of discipleship (10:13-16), but the emphasis in 9:33-37 is different. Here Mark concentrates the reader's attention not on the child's receptivity (see 10:15), but on the necessity of *a disciple's welcoming other children* in Jesus' name. That is the positive counterpoint of both Jesus' rejection (emphasized in 9:31) and the Twelve's aspersions cast on one another. In other words, the top-to-bottom reversal of rank in 9:35 realigns how listeners should receive those whom they have mistakenly regarded as beneath them (9:34, 36-37): the point developed in the pericopae immediately following.

How Hard to Enter the Kingdom (9:38–10:31)

The next five pericopae (9:38-41, 42-50; 10:1-12, 13-16, 17-31) address various facets of discipleship: its boundaries, internal responsibilities, implications for family, and relationship to wealth. Although other portions of Mark consider responsibilities within society (2:15-17, 23-28; 3:31-35; 7:1-23; 12:13-17, 28-34, 38-40), it is fair to say that 9:38–10:31 presents this Gospel's most concentrated cluster of moral teaching. Here we have not a systematically formulated "ethic" but coherent vignettes of discipleship expressed within the believing community, the family, and a larger social sphere. Discipleship's radical character is maintained, consistent with the mandate to become "last of all and servant of all" (9:35).

"Whoever Is Not Against Us Is for Us" (9:38-41)

In antiquity names were believed to carry the power or character of their owners (see Mark 3:16, 17; cf. Gen 32:22-32; Exod 3:13-14). The use of divine names to force those deities' cooperation was a standard procedure in magical incantations (cf. Mark 1:24-25; 3:11-12; 5:7-13). What is to be made of someone who, without authorization, uses Jesus' name to cast out demons (cf. 6:7, 13; 16:17)? The answer was not obvious to early Christians. Later in Mark, Jesus will warn disciples away from many who would mislead them "in my name" (13:6). In Acts (19:11-20) when seven sons of a Jewish high priest adjure evil spirits "by the Jesus whom Paul proclaims," their endeavor backfires spectacularly. In Mark 9:38 John, one of the Twelve (last seen at 9:2), reports to Jesus the case of an exorcist whom the Twelve have tried to prevent "because he was not following *us.*" In this reason is a trace of arrogance: they have just been quibbling over their own pecking order (9:34) despite the fact that their last attempted exorcism was a faithless failure (9:18, 28-29).

Jesus' response may offer a glimpse into Mark's view of the church. "Bear[ing] the name of Christ" (9:41) bespeaks a time after Jesus' own ministry (see Acts 11:26), as does the claim that "no one...will be able *soon afterward* to speak evil of [Jesus]" (Mark 9:39b, emphasis added). Since in this Gospel's Passion Narrative many do defame Jesus (14:57; 15:29, 32), "soon afterward" seems to point beyond the narrative's frame, into the life of the Markan community. Could later Christian exorcists have incurred slander of themselves and of Christ, as Mark recalls happened to Jesus himself (3:22)? Whatever the case, the view expressed in verse 39 jibes with that in 3:23-27: those who rout evil spirits in Jesus' name are executing "a deed of power" true to his character, most recently exemplified in 9:14-29. They cannot be in league with Beelzebul if they are driving out demons in Jesus' name. Such exorcists are to be welcomed as "one such child in my name" (9:37a), as though welcoming Jesus himself (9:37b). Mark, however, does not stop there. Ascribed to Jesus is a broad-minded attitude toward those outside the disciples' circle: "Whoever is not against us is for us" (9:40)—a positive phrasing of a similar, negative aphorism in Q (Luke 11:23 = Matt 12:30). While Mark knows that those commissioned by Jesus may be rejected (6:11), here the Evangelist presents Jesus as commending in strongest terms ("truly I tell you"; see 3:28; 8:12; 9:1) the reward due anyone who offers disciples so little as a cup of water to drink "because you are Christ's by name" (9:41 AT). Adhering to the spirit of 9:35-37, 9:38-41 stresses gracious reception of anyone whose action, dynamic or modest, genuinely conforms to Jesus' name and character.

Traps and Salt (9:42-50)

Three general qualities of this segment are noteworthy. First, its scribal transmission shows considerable disturbance, some of which surfaces in modern English versions (see Swanson 1995, 152-55). The NRSV's consignment to a footnote of verses 44 and 46, missing from some of the oldest manuscripts, reflects an assessment that later scribes reduplicated verse 48 and twice inserted it into the text. In verse 45 some ancient copyists repeat "into the unquenchable fire," borrowed from the end of verse 43. A range of manuscripts, some early and of high quality, preserve in verse 42 the phrase "who believe *in me*." This could be a textual insertion, following the parallel expression in Matthew 18:6; had the phrase been original, it is hard to imagine why other scribes would have omitted it, as they have. Verse 49 was copied in different ways: "For everyone will be salted with fire"; "For every sacrifice will be salted with salt"; and a third alternative that couples the first and second. The first version has the strongest attestation. Since it is also the hardest to understand, scribes likely introduced into later manuscripts the other two formulations as attempts to make sense of it.

Mark 9:42-50 comprises a chain of sayings, with catchwords as links. Three sayings about an "offending" hand (v. 43a KJV), foot (v. 45a), or eye (v. 47a) have been joined, appended to another that warns against "offending" little ones (v. 42a). "Hell" is another verbal link in verses 43b, 45b, and 47b. After mention of hell's unquenchable fire (v. 48), "fire" attracts a saying about being "salted with fire" (v. 49). The verbal relay continues with different "salt" aphorisms: salt sans saltiness (v. 50a); "have salt in yourselves" (v. 50b). To scour this passage for rigorous logic is a mistake. It is intelligible in a looser, broadly associative way.

Another aspect of Mark 9:42-50 is unmistakable: its stark imagery. The Jesus of this Gospel who has healed bodies that are diseased or deformed is not literally advocating self-mutilation (vv. 43a, 45a, 47a). This is stark language intended to grab listeners by the scruff of the neck and shake them to their senses. Novelist Flannery O'Connor (1925–1964) explained such a strategy:

> When you can assume your audience holds the same beliefs you do, you can relax a little and use more normal means of talking to it; when you have to assume that it does not, then you have to make your vision apparent by shock—to the hard of hearing you shout, and for the almost-blind you draw large and startling figures. (1969, 34)

Mark 9:42-50 uses shock treatment to speak of how a church treats its members—or had better.

Though we have separated the logion beginning at 9:42 from that ending in 9:41, it makes interpretive sense to read these together, without interruption and in sharp contrast:

> "For whoever [*hos gar an*] offers you a cup of water because you bear Christ's name..."
> "But whoever [*kai hos an*] trips up one of these little ones who believe..." (AT).

The basic sense of the Greek word *skandalon* is a trap for catching a live animal (BDAG, 926a; see LXX Josh 23:13; Ps 140:9; 1 Macc 5:4), which shades into a metaphorical pitfall (Rom 11:9; 1 John 2:10). The cognate verb *skandalizō* (NRSV: "put a stumbling block before" [Mark 9:42] or "cause to stumble" [9:43, 45, 47]) conveys the sense of tripping up someone to cause downfall. (The same verb occurs in Mark 4:17, referring to rootless believers who fall away when trouble comes.) The fundamental contrast established in 9:39-41 and 9:42-48 is that between nurturance of Christian believers and infliction of injuries that would cause them to lose their faithful footing. Although Matthew develops the term (10:42; 11:11; 18:6, 10, 14), only in 9:42 does Mark use "little ones" (*tōn mikrōn*) to refer to one's fellow believers. It is conceptually related to the child (*paidion*) who should be received "in my name" (9:36-37). Harming "one of these little ones" invites a punishment *worse* than being hurled into the sea with "a great millstone...hung around your neck" (9:42): *mylos onikos,* a huge grinding stone turned by a donkey (cf. Rev 18:21).

In Mark 9:43, 45, and 47 the refrain of hypothetical stumbling recurs, here with the self as apparent victim. Yet the context (vv. 42, 49c) and content of the aphorisms suggest social responsibility: one may trip up oneself through conduct that harms others. The foot can take you places you dare not go; the hand can reach where it should not; the eye can gaze with evil intent (cf. 7:21-22). Just as amputation of an appendage may be required lest the whole body be destroyed, drastic surgery may prove necessary in emergencies if one hopes "to enter life" (9:43, 45): presumably, eternal life (10:17) or "the kingdom of God" (9:47; see also 1:15; 4:11, 30; 9:1). If one suffering gangrene—whether of the body or of the soul—pretends to wholeness, the only outcome is hell: literally "Gehenna" or "Hinnom Valley" (9:43, 45, 47), a ravine south of Jerusalem that was notorious for pagan infanticide (2 Kgs 23:10; 2 Chr 28:1-14; Jer 7:3-34) and envisioned by later Jews as the place of the wicked's final judgment (Luke 12:5; Jas 3:6; 4 Ezra 7:26-38; Sib. Or. 2.291). Undying worm and unquenched fire (Mark 9:48) were stock images for the destruction of evil (Isa 66:24; Jdt 16:17; Sir 7:17). It is a good, if unanswerable, question whether the imagined "amputations" in Mark 9:43-47 include expulsion of grave offenders from the Christian community for the sake of its comprehensive welfare (see 1 Cor 5:1-13). In any case the jarring images in Mark 9:42-48 harshly restate the fundamental requirement that Jesus' disciples lose their lives for his sake so that they may gain them (8:35-37). By graphically depicting such radical obedience to Jesus, this section of Mark serves a function similar to Matthew's Sermon on the Mount (5:1–7:29; N.B. 5:13, 27-30; 6:22-23; 7:13-14).

Grim prospects yield to the sunnier in Mark 9:49-50. The cryptic proverb in verse 49 makes some sense if one remembers that salt was used as a preservative (Num 18:19; Matt 5:13; Luke 14:34; Col 4:6) and in sacrifice (Lev 2:13; Ezek 43:24). One way to interpret Mark 9:49-50 is to return to 8:34-37 while looking ahead to 13:9-13. "Salt is good": a sacrificial preservative is akin to cross-bearing discipleship, preventing the church from insipidity (9:50ab). The "salt" of self-sacrifice for the gospel promotes a communal peace that quells self-centeredness and one-upmanship (9:50c; cf. 9:33-34, 38).

Marriage (10:1-12)

Jesus departs from "that place" (Capernaum, in eastern Galilee: 9:33), south "to the region of Judea beyond the Jordan"

(10:1; *ad loc.* 1:5). Again the crowds flock to Jesus (10:1b; 8:1; 9:14); "as was his custom, he again taught them" (2:13; 4:1-2; 6:34). As is their custom, the Pharisees test him (10:2a; 8:11; 12:15). The translation, "Is it *lawful* for a man to divorce his wife?" (10:2b, emphasis added), may load the issue more heavily, even ludicrously, than the Greek demands (*exestin*). Since divorce was indisputably legal for Jews and Romans in the first century C.E., there is nothing controversial in such a query. A better translation might be, "They were asking him if [Jesus thought it] right for a man to divorce a woman" (thus Phillips). Jesus lobs back the obvious question: "What did Moses command you?" (10:3). Not unreasonably they paraphrase Deuteronomy 24:1-4: Moses allowed "[a man] to write a certificate of dismissal and to let her go" (Mark 10:4 AT). Moses, Jesus replies, wrote this command for them because of their hardness of heart (10:5), of which the Pharisees have been accused in this Gospel (3:2-5). Reaching farther back into Torah, to the Pentateuch's first book, Jesus cites an amalgam of Genesis 1:27; 2:24; 5:2, which obtains "from creation's beginning":

Mark	Genesis
"God made them male and female" (10:6).	"Male and female he created them" (1:27c).
	"and he blessed them and named them *'adam*" (5:2)
"For this reason a man shall leave his father and mother [and be joined to his wife]" (10:7)	"Therefore a man leaves [*ʿazab*] his father and his mother and clings [*daḇaq*] to his wife,
"and the two shall become one flesh" (10:8a).	and they become one flesh" (2:24).

(A minority of Markan manuscripts lacks the bracketed clause in 10:7. The majority may have added it to create even closer correspondence with Gen 2:24.) Reiterating 10:8a, the primary point lies in Mark 10:8b: *"So they are no longer two, but one flesh"* (emphasis added). That deduction undercuts the premise of the Pharisees' original question, which differentiated the two by hypothesizing divorce. To sharpen the point, Jesus exhorts that no human being (*anthrōpos*) should separate what God has yoked together (v. 9). Divine intent from creation's beginning (v. 6a) trumps a law required by human stubbornness.

As expected (4:10; 7:17; 9:28), in the house the disciples inquire about the matter (10:10). Jesus' teaching (vv. 11-12) is multiply striking. It presupposes as possible—divorce—what has just been enjoined (v. 9). The balanced pair of possibilities ("whoever divorces his wife"/"and if [a woman] divorces her husband") was socially anomalous in a Palestinian context: under Jewish law, a woman could not initiate divorce against her husband, though under Roman law she could. Mark's presentation suggests a Roman modification of Jewish practice (cf. Matt 5:32; 19:9). By OT definition, adultery was a violation only of the husband's right, not of the wife's (Exod 20:14; Deut 5:18; 22:22). By contrast, in Mark 10:11-12 the husband can commit adultery against his wife (thus, too, Matt 5:32; Luke 16:18). By marriage *she* has as much claim on *his* sexuality as he has on hers. If divorce occurs, remarriage by the instigating spouse, male or female, is regarded as adultery—an extraordinarily radical view.

Mark 10:6-8 appeals to the creation narratives (Gen 1:2–2:25; 5:1-32), situating marriage within God's primordial covenant (Mark 10:6a). These traditions emphasize the intrinsic complementarity of male and female, whom God blesses and names *'adam,* "humankind," in one flesh (Gen 2:24b; 5:2). A man's "leaving" his parents and "clinging to" his wife (Gen 2:24a; Mark 10:7) adapt verbs that characterize Israel's departure from her covenant with God (Jer 1:16; Hos 4:10) and the nation's fidelity to God (Deut 10:20; 1 Kgs 11:2; see Terrien 1985). In an old Roman description of marriage, Modestinus (early third century C.E.) may reflect Christian influence: "Marriage is a joining

together of a male and a woman, and a partnership for life in all areas of life, a sharing in divine and human law" (Treggiari 1991, 3-36).

Ancient Israel considered adultery a great sin (Exod 20:14; Deut 5:18, 21), even a capital crime (Lev 20:10; Deut 22:22). It was an assault on the divinely ordained nuclear family (Qoh 6:1-2; Sir 23:22-23), socially treacherous (2 Sam 11:2-27; Job 24:13-16), and a metaphor for the nation's apostasy (Ezek 16:1-63; Hos 1:1–3:5). Roman laws against adultery were not always explicit, and their enforcement was haphazard (Treggiari 1991, 262-319). As children's legal status depended on that of their mother, a wife's adultery was usually grounds for divorce (*Luc.* 38.1); a husband's adultery was more readily excused (*Cael.*). Roman moralists took a dim view of frivolous divorce (*Andr.* 367-68; *Ben.* 3.16.2). Rabbinic schools variously interpreted the "indecent thing" (*^cerwat da<u>b</u>ar*, Deut 24:1-4) as ground for divorce. Shammai's disciples narrowed it to sexual transgressions; Hillelites broadened it to include childlessness, even unsatisfactory fulfillment of domestic responsibilities (*m. Giṭ* 9.10; *b. Giṭ* 90a).

Jesus' strictures were remembered by Paul (1 Cor 7:10-11) and in Q (Luke 16:18 = Matt 5:32). Responding to changed cultural contexts, first-century Christians qualified Jesus' severity (Matt 5:32; 19:9; 1 Cor 7:12-16; Eph 5:21-33). In Mark, Jesus' vision retains its sharpest edge: even if a marriage be legally dissolved owing to "hard-heartedness," divorce ruptures the unity between women and men intended by God since creation. If divorce occurs, serial monogamy perpetuates violation of that intent, injuring everyone. Such radical teaching is congruent with radical discipleship, articulated in 8:34–9:1 and 9:42-50. Mark 10:2-4 has in view the power to escape from marriage, not abusive conduct that threatens a spouse's life while undermining marriage itself. In a society where a woman's dowry could be compromised by divorce, marriage provided social security. Divorce, if it comes, carries with it personal, social, and theological consequences: the pain of amputation (cf. 9:43, 45, 47), dissolution of mutual peace (9:50cd), and temporary defeat of the unity that a creative God has always intended for all of creation (10:6a). Discipleship stakes a beachhead on an "adulterous and sinful generation" (8:38), still held captive and in need of rescue (see Via 1985, 101-27).

Children (10:13-16)

Curiously, Mark 10:1-12 never refers to fertility as a reason for marriage's blessedness (Gen 1:28ab). Still, children's reappearance (Mark 9:36-37, 42) here follows naturally from marriage.

Mark 10:13-16 is a vignette encapsulating a memorable saying of Jesus (cf. 2:15-17; 3:31-35; 12:13-17). Typical of Markan style, an indefinite "they" (cf. 1:21-32) "were bringing" to Jesus (6:27-28; 7:32) "little" (5:23, 41-42) children (10:13a). Jesus' touch, to heal or bless (10:13a; cf. Gen 48:14-16; see Daube 1956, 224-46), is a Markan common motif (1:41; 5:23; 8:22). In character, his disciples "rebuked" (*epetimēsan*: KJV, RSV, NIV) this attempt (10:13b; cf. 8:32-33). Jesus repudiates his disciples' conduct (10:14a), which triggers his pronouncement that the children should come to him without obstruction (*mē kō-luete*; cf. 9:39a). His justification: "The kingdom of God is for such as these" (10:14b AT; cf. 9:42, 47). To this assurance is added a prophetic warning (see 3:28; 8:12; 9:1), whose spirit Cassirer captures: "Indeed, I can give you solemn assurance of this. He who does not accept the kingdom of God in the way in which a child would, will never find entry into it" (10:15). Jesus repeats an earlier action (9:36): embracing a child (10:16a). One may interpret the imperfect verb as suggesting that Jesus customarily blessed them by laying his hands on them (10:16b). This may be Mark's tenderest depiction of Jesus. The wording implies that it was no one-time occurrence.

Left ambiguous is the way in which a child receives God's kingdom (10:15). Previously, Jesus counseled his disciples to receive such children in his name (9:37), which they have immediately failed to do (10:13). In 10:14-15 the stress shifts to *becoming like* a child. A disciple of Jesus can never hope to enter the kingdom, apart from childlike receptiveness. In antiquity a child connotes many qualities: among others, neediness (Plutarch, *Life of Antony* 9.40.9), innocence (*Herm. Sim.* 9.29), humility (*Hom. Act.* 30.3), immaturity (*Diatr.* 3.24.8), and economic worthlessness (Oepke 1967). What is Mark driving at? A more confident verdict can be returned after considering Jesus' next encounter.

Wealth (10:17-31)

This segment comprises two scenes: an exchange between Jesus and a new supplicant (vv. 17-22) with a subsequent conversation between Jesus and his disciples (vv. 23-31).

Scene One: Jesus and His Petitioner (vv. 17-22). Proceeding on "the way" (thus, KJV, NIV, GNT; a reminder of "the way of discipleship" [6:8; 8:27; 9:33]), Jesus is met by one whose character is neatly sketched. Running and kneeling before Jesus (1:40; 5:6, 22, 33; 7:25), this one compliments him and asks what he may do to inherit "eternal life" (10:17). Rejecting the compliment, Jesus avers that God alone is good (v. 18). Unflustered to maintain Jesus' goodness or sinlessness (cf. Matt 19:17; John 8:46; 2 Cor 5:21; Heb 7:26; 1 Pet 2:22), Mark typically highlights God's gospel (1:14) and power (9:1; 12:24-27), will (3:35; 8:33; 10:9) and commandment (7:8-9, 13): the one God (12:29-30) who deserves glorification (2:12; 5:19). "Life" or "eternal life" is mentioned in Mark only four times (9:43, 45; 10:17, 30). In all these cases it overlaps "the kingdom of God" (see 9:47, 10:23-25). The notion of indestructible life, transcendent blessedness as God knows it, rarely creeps into the LXX (e.g., Prov 9:6; Job 19:25; Dan 12:2) but is well developed in later Judaism (e.g., Wis 5:15; 2 Macc 7:9; 4 Macc 15:3; *Ps. Sol.* 3:16; 15:15; *T. Ab.* 5.20). Some early Christians write of future blessedness as presently intelligible (esp. John; also Col 3:3-4; 1 Tim 6:12, 19; 2 Tim 1:1); others differentiate the two, as does Mark 10:30 (1 Thess 2:19; 2 Tim 2:10; Rev 20:4-5).

Jesus' response (Mark 10:19) is impeccably orthodox: adherence to the Decalogue, of which the fifth (Exod 20:12 = Deut 5:16; cf. Lev 19:3), sixth (Exod 20:13 = Deut 5:17), seventh (Exod

20:14 = Deut 5:18), eighth (Exod 20:15 = Deut 5:19), and ninth commandments (Exod 20:16 = Deut 5:20) are stipulated as representative. "You shall not defraud" (Mark 10:19) is omitted from some manuscripts, presumably because the scribes recognized its absence from the Decalogue (see also Matt 19:18-19; Luke 18:20). All these commandments bear on righteousness within the community of faith, congruent with this section's focus on discipleship. The same concerns arise throughout Mark: honoring father and mother (7:10), deceit (7:22; 14:11-12, 44-45), adultery (10:11-12), theft (11:17c), false witness (14:56), and murder (15:13-15). Jesus' interlocutor has kept all these commandments "since my youth" (10:20): a vague intimation that he just might qualify as a child who receives the kingdom (v. 15). Such hope is extended a moment more by Jesus' affectionate reaction (v. 21a), which harks back to his embrace of children (v. 16). Only one thing is lacking (v. 21b): selling what he has, giving the proceeds to the wretchedly poor, and following Jesus (v. 21; cf. 1:17; 2:14). Jesus' gaze (10:21a) meets the man's visage: "The one appalled by the word went away in grief" (v. 22a AT). The participle *lypoumenos* (grieved) suggests mourning; *stygnasas* is dismay that slides into gloom, as a pall is draped over a coffin's lid. Only now do we learn the reason: "He had many possessions" (v. 22b)—crucial information withheld by Mark until the last moment.

Scene Two: Jesus and His Disciples (vv. 23-31). When Jesus "looks around" before saying something, a hammer is about to fall (see, e.g., 3:5, 23; 5:32; 8:33). The same is true in 10:23: how hard it will be for those enjoying wherewithal to enter God's kingdom. The rich have the means to make things happen. The disciples are thunderstruck (10:24a; 1:27; 10:32) and dumbfounded (10:26): if the rich cannot, "Then who *can* be saved?" With greater generality and affection (*tekna*, "children"), Jesus reiterates his lament (10:24b). The wealthy have a harder time making it into God's kingdom than a camel in squeezing through a needle's eye (v. 25), a comical metaphor that Origen also remembered from the *Gospel of the Nazarenes* (*Comm. Matt.* 15:14). Scribes ancient and modern rationalize the simile: some change *kamēlon* (camel) to *kamilon* (cable); others imagine a narrow passageway in Jerusalem called "the needle's eye" (branded by Taylor [1981, 431] as "exegetical fantasy"). Mark 10:25 intends hyperbole to make its point, as 10:27 confirms: what is impossible for humans is not so for God. Although divine omnipotence was debated in antiquity (Dowd 1988, 78-92), Israel's trust in God to do the impossible pervades the OT (Gen 18:14; Job 42:2; Zech 8:6).

Only in Mark 10:24 does Jesus address his disciples as *tekna*. They are children, not unlike those they impeded from approaching Jesus (10:13). The Evangelist sets before the reader two improbable claims side by side, teasing out the meaning of each in relation to the other: "Whoever does not receive the kingdom of God as a little child will never enter it" (10:15); "How hard it will be for those who have wealth to enter the kingdom of God" (10:23).

What the child lacks that the rich have is the power to make things happen. In the economy of God's kingdom, the advantage a child enjoys is the helplessness to do what only God can do for him or her (10:27). En route to gaining the whole world (8:36), the man with possessions has become incapacitated (10:17-22): because *they* possessed *him*, he forfeited the very life he was seeking (10:17; cf. 4:18-19). For one who wanted to save his life on terms other than the gospel's (8:35), there could be neither yield (4:19) nor profit (8:36). Only a camel can be threaded through a needle, only the helpless can enter eternal life, because things divine and not human propel *God's* kingdom (8:33b). In effect, Mark speaks of "the grace of our Lord Jesus Christ, that though he was rich, yet for your sake he became poor, so that by his poverty you might become rich" (2 Cor 8:9 RSV). Mark 10:13-27 drains every vestige of sentimentality that might be slathered on Paul's testimony. Grace is an impossible possibility.

Mark 10:28 presents one of the few instances that a member of the Twelve speaks accurately to the point at issue. Simon Peter, often representing others (1:36; 8:29, 32b; 9:5), insists that the Twelve have done what the rich man (10:27) could not: they "have left everything and followed" Jesus (v. 28)—the clear implication in 1:16-20. Unlike the disciples' other protests (8:33;

9:33-35; 10:13-14, 35-45), Jesus upholds Peter's. Using a vow with prophetic solemnity ("Truly I tell you": 3:28; 8:12; 9:1, 41; 10:15), Jesus assures him that whatever is relinquished "for my sake and for the sake of the good news" (also 8:35) will be reimbursed in kind, one-hundredfold "in this age" (10:29b-30a). Their future recompense will be qualitatively superior: "in the age to come eternal life" (v. 30b), the very thing Jesus' questioner was seeking (10:17). The concluding maxim in 10:31 inverts a saying of Jesus also remembered in Q (Luke 13:30 = Matt 20:16; cf. Mark 9:35). The man of great means (10:22) is among many of this age who are first and will be last; the child (10:14), now last, will be first in the age to come.

Jesus' assurance of reward to his disciples (10:29-30) is noteworthy in many respects. (1) There is fulfillment awaiting those who have left all to follow Jesus (8:35b; 9:1, 41; 10:14; 13:13b, 27; 14:8-9). Discipleship is hard, but it is not futile. (2) Compared to those envisioned elsewhere in Jewish apocalypticism, the recompense Jesus promises is modest, lacking the grandeur of *4 Ezra*'s seven orders of blessedness (7:88-98) or Matthew's vision of the Twelve enthroned as Israel's judges (19:28: cf. Rev 3:21; 4:4). (3) The sacrifices and compensations in Mark 10:29-30 are *familial* (cf. 9:42–10:12). "Fields" are included (10:29, 30), but at the forefront are "houses": not real estate, but "brothers or sisters or mother or father or children" (v. 29). The Zebedee brothers (1:18-20) and Jesus himself (3:21, 31-33) depicted such loss. As in 3:34-35, so also in 10:30: those who have suffered rupture from their families by following Jesus will be bountifully reintegrated into other families. (Consistent with 10:2-9, Jesus does not stipulate a disciple's leaving a wife or a husband.) (4) If one compares family members lost in 10:29 with those gained in 10:30, one figure is missing from the second roster: "fathers." This is an extraordinary omission, striking at the root of Roman *patria potestas*: power uniquely residing in the *paterfamilias*, the household's father. At least theoretically, the father exercised power of life and death over his children, whom he could dispose in marriage, dispossess of property, and even sell without their consent (see Treggiari 1991, 15-16). In the new family promised by Jesus there is no such figure, because there is no place for such "great ones" who "are tyrants over" others (10:42-43a). (5) While the age to come promises eternal life (10:30c), in this age "persecutions" are added even to the abundant rewards of sacrificial disciples (10:30ab). Such incongruity is typically Markan, who marches his readers up to the expected cliché—in this case, the rewards of discipleship—only to pull the rug out from under them (cf. 4:10-12, 30-32; 8:14-21; see Tannehill 1975, 147-52).

To Drink the Cup (10:32-52)

The Third Cycle: Going Up to Jerusalem, Becoming a Slave to All (10:32-45)

Adhering to the pattern established in 8:27 and 9:30b, the third prediction of what awaits the Son of Man is geographically located: "on the road, going up to Jerusalem." As elsewhere, "road" or "way" is both literal (1:2; 2:23; 4:4; 6:8) and metaphorical (1:3; 4:15; 10:52; 12:14). Because "Jerusalem" is associated with hostility in Mark (3:22; 7:1), it is no wonder that those following him are "amazed" and "afraid" (see also 4:41; 5:36; 6:50; 9:15, 32; 16:5-6, 8).

Mark 10:33-34 is by far the most detailed **prophecy** of the three in this Gospel's triadic cycle (see table 10). Indeed, it epitomizes Mark's Passion Narrative.

Table 13: *The Third Passion Prediction as Synopsis of the Passion Narrative*

The Prediction (Mark 10)	*The Passion Narrative (Mark 11–16)*
"Going up to Jerusalem" (v. 33a)	Entry and returns to Jerusalem (11:1, 15, 27)
Being "handed over" (v. 33b)	The destiny of Jesus' disciples (13:9, 11, 12)

	Judas's treachery (14:10-11, 18, 21, 41-42, 44)
	Rendition of Jesus to Pilate (15:1, 10, 15)
"To the chief priests and the scribes" (v. 33b)	Present in the temple (11:18, 27); before (14:1), at (14:43), and after the arrest (14:53); after the Sanhedrin trial (15:1, 31)
Who "will condemn him to death" (v. 33c)	The plot and its realization (11:18; 14:1, 64)
"Then they will hand him over to the Gentiles" (v. 33d)	Pilate (15:1)
"They will mock him, and spit upon him, and flog him," (v. 34ab)	The Sanhedrin (14:64) and Roman cohort (15:15-20)
"And kill him" (v. 34c)	Death by crucifixion (15: 24, 37)
"And after three days he will rise again" (v. 34d)	Announcement of the resurrection (16:1-8)

As in 8:31 and 9:31, repudiation and betrayal return in 10:33a, alongside collusion of Jewish authorities and humans in general (10:33b). Mark 10:33-34 details the "great suffering" the Son of Man must suffer. That others will "kill" (*apokteinō*) him is simply asserted in all three prophecies; all simply state his rising again (*anistēmi*) after three days (see table 10). Unlike its predecessors (8:32; 9:32), Jesus' prediction in 10:33-34 ends without editorial comment.

The reader is accustomed to the Twelve's immediate **rejection or misconstrual** of Jesus' teaching (8:32-33; 9:33-34); sadly, in **10:35-37** they run true to form. Here the sons of Zebedee express their befuddlement. With Simon and Andrew, they were the first whom Jesus called (1:16-20); these four reappear in Mark as members of an inner circle within the Twelve (3:16;

5:37; 9:2; 13:3; 14:33). As Peter took Jesus aside for rebuke (8:32b), James and John also distance themselves from the pack (10:35). Both times this attempted separation is thwarted. At 8:33-34 Jesus encompasses the full circle of disciples. At 10:41 the other ten interpose themselves.

Unlike 9:33-34, which indicates bickering over rank while leaving sordid details to the reader's imagination, 10:35-37 dramatizes James and John's attempt to ingratiate themselves with Jesus. They "come forward" (v. 35a), which, after Peter's having been put back in his place *behind* Jesus (8:33a), already signals trouble. Their request—"Teacher, we want you to do for us whatever we ask of you" (10:35b)—is in many ways problematic. (1) It is an unbridled petition for patronage; nowhere in Mark has Jesus granted a request made in that manner. (2) The petition is made without qualification. Not only does this put Jesus on the spot (see also 8:11-13); it is abstracted from the context of faithful prayer that Jesus insists upon (9:29; 11:22-25), consistent with the attitude adopted by sufferers who have sought his help (2:5; 5:34, 36; 9:23-24). (3) Their appeal to be seated on either side of Jesus "in [his] glory" (10:37; 13:26) disregards everything Jesus has emphasized in the Son of Man's destiny, which is concentrated on rejection, suffering, and death (8:31; 9:31; 10:33-34). (4) Mark's reader has heard James and John's request before: it paraphrases Herod's disastrous impetuosity to Herodias's daughter (6:22-23). James and John are acting the way this world's rulers throw their weight around, which in part accounts for the poignancy in Jesus' reply in 10:42. Even worse: they are requesting places of supreme honor ("at your right hand"), to which only the Lord's regents are entitled (Ps 110:1; Mark 14:62c). (5) In a lacerating irony soon to become manifest, those positions on Jesus' "right and left" are assumed by faithless ones crucified with Jesus (15:27, 32b) after all of the Twelve have fled (14:27a, 50-52). Instead of reckoning with the sheer otherness of Jesus as God's Son (4:35-41; 6:45-52; 9:2-8), members of the Twelve continue to jockey for their teacher's special consideration.

Jesus' initial response is that the brothers do not know what they are asking (10:38a): a safe deduction, since perspicuity is hardly the Twelve's strong suit (4:41; 5:31; 6:52; 7:18a; 8:14-21; 9:6; 14:31). In riddling speech (4:34a) he inquires of their ability "to drink the cup that I drink, or be baptized with the baptism that I am baptized with" (10:38). These metaphors are multivalent. They are vaguely "sacramental" (see Rom 6:3; 1 Cor 10:16, 21; 11:25-28; *Did.* 9.1–10.7; *Trad. ap.* 20-21, 23-24), and very early both the Lord's Supper and baptism were interpreted as participation with Jesus in his death (Rom 6:3-4; 1 Cor 11:25). In Mark (1:14; 6:14-29; 9:9-11) baptism has acquired an ominous connotation because of John the Baptist's capture and execution. In the OT "cup" can symbolize either joy and salvation (Pss 23:5; 116:13) or woe and judgment (Ps 11:6; Isa 51:17, 22). Given the mixed signals already established between Jesus and the Twelve (8:14-21), the reader of 10:38-39 can reasonably intuit the same here: the Zebedee brothers confidently affirm their capability (v. 39a) because they think of benisons that accompany exaltation with Jesus in glory (v. 37). Jesus, for his part, speaks of a cup and of a baptism with baleful consequences (v. 38; see also 14:38; Luke 12:50; John 18:11). However confused they may be, Jesus does not deny for his followers a cup and a baptism: suffering for the gospel's sake (Mark 10:39b; 8:34-35; 13:9-23). What he does deny them are those requested places of honor. These are not his to grant, but instead belong to those for whom they have been prepared (10:40: a divine passive [8:31; 9:31; 10:33]). That is a christological and theological statement of major importance. To the very end Jesus refuses any authority that has not been consigned him by God (see also 9:37b; 11:17; 12:6-7; 14:21a, 49b), whose will is absolutely final (3:35; 10:6-9, 27; 12:17a, 27a, 29-30; 14:25, 36, 49b).

Naturally, the other ten in Jesus' entourage take umbrage at the Zebedees' maneuvering (10:41). Jesus does not put James and John on the spot as they did him. Nor does he defend their action. Instead, he reunites the Twelve for **teaching** about authentic discipleship (**vv. 42-45**). He draws a contrast not with Jewish officialdom (8:31; 10:33) but with arrogant, tyrannical

Gentiles (v. 34). Putting the matter that way does two things at once. First, by broadening his critique, Jesus indicates that the root of evil lies not in Jewish opponents but in fundamentally human assumptions (cf. 7:20-22, 9:31), including those of Gentiles to whom the Son of Man will be handed over (10:33b; see Kaminouchi 2003). Second, "the many" whom the Son of Man serves includes but is not limited to Israel (7:24-37; 10:45). ("Many" need not imply exclusivity; it can also suggest a comprehensive object, as in Isa 53:12; Rom 5:15, 19; see Evans 2001, 122-23.) This world's construction of authority, which James and John have projected onto the end time (v. 37), is altogether erroneous. Status relations determined by the Son of Man upend conventional expectations (v. 43, essentially reiterating 9:35). In 9:36-37 the "servant" (*diakonos*) is aligned with "a little child" (*paidion*); in 10:44 the "servant" slides into "everyone's slave" (*pantōn doulos*)—an even more intensive self-derogation. Though slavery in antiquity connoted different things, depending on one's social station (Martin 1990, 1-49), the privileged regarded slavery a despicable form of life (*Ep.* 47.17). In Mark 10:44, by contrast, the status of slavery has become radically *normative* for Jesus' disciples. Unlike James and John (and the rest of the Twelve), whose imagination has shrunk to a client's bid for promotion by a patron, the Son of Man has come not to be served but to serve (10:45a). That service is giving his life as "a ransom [*lytron*] for many" (10:45). This metaphor is contextually significant. In the OT a *lytron* is the compensation required to redeem a slave or prisoner of war out of bondage (e.g., Exod 21:8, 30; Lev 25:47-52; Num 3:45-51; see A. Y. Collins 1997b). In Mark the Son of Man does not present himself as a new master; he is, instead, the release of others from their enslavement (14:24b). While this image does not recur in Mark as often as in some biblical books (e.g., Isa 43:1-7; 44:21-23; 52:13–53:12; Rom 3:23-25a; Heb 9:12, 15; 1 Pet 1:18-19), it remains an undeveloped aspect of Markan soteriology. Instead of elaborating a doctrine of atonement, the Second Gospel, like Deutero-Isaiah, plants seeds from which later theological developments flourish (Telford 1999, 194-95).

Postlude: A Blind Man at Jericho (10:46-52)

The final pericope in Mark's central section is this Gospel's last healing story. It mirrors the cure of another blind man (8:22-26), the passage that opened this section. The tale's basic structure is familiar; the interest lies in its unexpected twists.

The setting is Jericho (v. 46), a city in the Jordan Valley about twenty miles northeast of Jerusalem. Leaving the town with his disciples, Jesus is attended by the typical crowd (e.g., 5:21, 24; 6:34; 8:1; 9:14). Seated on the roadside (literally, "by the way" [4:4, 15]) is a blind man, begging (10:46; certainly not "lord[ing] it over" anyone [10:42]). Besides Jairus, the synagogue leader who pleads for his daughter (5:22-23), Bartimaeus (Aram., "Timaeus's son" [cf. 3:17b; 5:41; 7:11, 34]) is the only named beneficiary of Jesus' healing in this Gospel. He has heard of "Jesus the Nazarene" (10:47a AT), a rare identification in Mark (1:24; 14:67; 16:6). Unlike his counterpart at Bethsaida (8:22), Bartimaeus is not a passive figure: repeatedly he cries out, "Jesus, Son of David, have mercy on me!" (10:47-48). Though Mark occasionally mentions David (2:25; 12:36) or David's kingdom (11:10) or even David's son (12:35), only here is Jesus addressed as "Son of David" (cf. Matt 1:1; Rom 1:3; Rev 22:16). David was considered the Lord's special designate (2 Sam 7:4-17; Ps 89:3-4); the DSS and the *Psalms of Solomon* (17:32) expected an eschatological messiah of the Davidic line. Therapeutic powers were sometimes associated with David's Son (Matt 9:27-31; 12:22-23). Nevertheless, in Mark 12:35-37 Jesus will question the title's pertinence or adequacy with reference to the Christ. Bartimaeus can be forgiven: he is blind. In Jesus he recognizes someone important, even though his perception is blurred. Similarly, Bethsaida's blind man saw people who looked like walking trees (8:24).

Having prepared the reader for a miracle story, Mark deftly turns this into a vignette of discipleship (see Olekamma 1999). The harsh reprimand (*epetimōn*) of the needy (10:48a) recalls the disciples' rebuke (*epetimēsan*) of little children (10:13); now, as then, Jesus insists on receiving the petitioner (10:14; 49). Jesus' call of Bartimaeus (10:49a) echoes Bartimaeus's call of him: a persistent appeal, like that of a hemorrhaging woman who also had to fight her way to the healer through a crowd (5:24b-28). Jesus diverted his attention to her (5:30); for him, he stands still (10:49a). Yet another call is the crowd's to Bartimaeus: "Take heart; get up, he is calling you" (10:49b; cf. 6:50 and 9:35a, directed to Jesus' disciples). "Throwing off his cloak" (10:50a) recalls the encumbrances that Jesus' disciples should shed (6:8-9; 13:16). Jesus' question to Bartimaeus (10:51a) is identical to that which he has posed to James and John (10:36). Whereas they blindly plumped for glory (8:18a; 10:37), Bartimaeus insightfully addresses "my teacher" (*Rabbouni*): "Let me see again" (10:51). Unlike the Twelve (10:38a, 41), this man knows what he is asking; his question springs from restorative faith, as Jesus acknowledges (10:52a; 5:34a). Bartimaeus immediately gets just what he requested: he sees again (10:52b). He moves from the wayside (v. 46b) *onto* "the way," following Jesus—Mark's capsule metaphor for discipleship (1:18; 2:14; 8:34; 10:21, 28; 15:41). With the teacher at the head and his disciples in tow, Bartimaeus leads the reader into Jerusalem (11:1; Malbon 2000, 70-99). How many disciples will follow Jesus *out* of the city remains to be seen.

APPOINTMENT IN JERUSALEM (11:1–13:37)

To this point in Mark, various persons have come from Jerusalem, Judea's capital (1:5; 3:8, 22; 7:1). At 11:1 Jesus arrives in "the city of the great King" (Ps 48:2), which he never leaves for long. Chapter 11 exhibits a strange oscillation: Jesus comes to the city (vv. 6-11a, 15a), leaves it (vv. 11b, 19), and returns to it from Bethany (vv. 12, 27; see also 14:3, 13, 16). Though Jerusalem exerts a gravitational pull, Jesus is never at home there. Here he shall die (10:33-34).

Because Jerusalem marks a narrative turning point, Mark arranges this material with care:

11:1-26: Jesus makes his way to the temple, the city's cultic and political center.

11:27–12:44: Jesus commandeers the temple as the site for controversial teaching.

13:1-37: Jesus bids farewell to the temple and to his disciples on the eve of his capture.

Obviously central in these segments is the temple, the venue for Jesus' instruction and the locus for imminent destruction. Its shadow falls across Jesus' deeds and words throughout 11:1–13:37, even as it will overshadow the Evangelist's account of Jesus' arrest (14:49), his trial by Jerusalem's Sanhedrin (14:58), and his subsequent crucifixion (15:29, 38). In spite of the joy and beauty associated with the "house of the LORD" in the OT (Ezra 3:11; 7:27; Pss 27:4; 92:13; 122:1), in Mark, Jesus' destruction is bound up with the temple's own.

Clearing a Path into the Temple (11:1-26)

Entering the City (11:1-11)

Preparations for Jesus' Entrance to Jerusalem (11:1-6)

Mark 11:1-6 describes preparations for Jesus' entrance to Jerusalem. The setting (v. 1) is Bethphage (whose location is uncertain) and Bethany (two miles southeast of Jerusalem: see John 11:18), at the Mount of Olives: a high hill east of the city (Ezek 11:23), associated with its defeat (2 Sam 15:15-30) and Israel's hope for God's end-time triumph (Zech 14:4). The significance of "a colt [or 'young donkey'] that has never been ridden" (v. 2a) is obscure. The animal may allude to a humble king's conveyance (Zech 9:9); its having never before been ridden may allude to unyoked beasts consecrated for God (Num 19:2; Deut 21:3; 1 Sam 6:7). Except for its occurrence in a text of dubious provenance (16:19-20), verse 3 is the only place in Mark where Jesus refers to himself as "the Lord," although it is suggested elsewhere (2:28; 12:36-37; 13:35); at least one supplicant has so addressed him (7:28). Usually when Jesus speaks of "the Lord," he refers to Israel's God (12:9, 11, 29-30; 12:36; 13:20; probably 5:19). Congruent with Samuel's commission for a pair of asses to confirm Saul's anointing as "prince over his people Israel" (1 Sam

10:1-8 NEB), Mark 11:2-4 suggests an acknowledgment of Jesus' authority and prophetic prescience. In verses 3b-6 all unfolds, just as Jesus predicted (a motif that recurs in 14:13-16). When Israel's hidden Messiah enters the royal city, he does so in a manner no one would expect unless they are attuned to a particular scriptural frequency. Apart from that, a simple act is draped in mystery.

Entrance into Jerusalem (11:7-10)

After the disciples return with the colt and seat Jesus upon it, his entrance into Jerusalem commences (11:7-10). A family of ancient Jewish stories details the entrance of a heroic figure after a military conquest (Catchpole 1984). One example among many (1 Macc 4:19-25; 13:43-51; *Ant.* 11.325-39; 16.12-15; 17.194-239) is Judas Maccabeus's return to Judea following a triumphant, albeit bloody, campaign (1 Macc 5:45-54; *Ant.* 12.345-49). The details vary, but the format is typical: following victory, a military champion enters a city, attended by joyous acclamation, and offers cultic thanksgiving, often at a temple.

Jesus' entry to Jerusalem recalls this pattern, with important modifications. Replacing military conquest is Jesus' peaceful ministry. Upon entrance Jesus does not perform the usual cultic ritual. In all of the Gospels save Mark, adulation is focused on Jesus himself (Matt 21:9a; Luke 19:38a; John 12:13b). Mark's account is subdued. A celebrative aura persists: the spreading of cloaks and branches (11:8) is common in Israel's festal processions (2 Kgs 9:13; 1 Macc 13:51; 2 Macc 10:7). In the multitude's praise a touch of the martial genre lingers: "Blessed is the one who comes in the name of the Lord" (Mark 11:9b) quotes Psalm 118:26a, a thanksgiving for military deliverance. "Hosanna" (Mark 11:9b, 10b)—"Save now"—is a liturgical formula for God's praise (Ps 118:25a). In Mark 11:10 the object of praise is general, not concentrated on Jesus: "Blessed is the coming kingdom of our ancestor David." Jesus himself has proclaimed "the kingdom of God" (1:15; 4:11, 26, 30; 9:1, 47; 10:14-15, 23-25) apart from bellicose connotations. Blind Bartimaeus addressed his healer as David's Son (10:47-48), though Jesus himself will challenge that identification (12:35-37).

Aftermath (11:11)

The most surprising twist in the conventional pattern lies in the aftermath of Jesus' procession. Here one expects the hero's performance of some ritual act of thanksgiving. In 11:11 Jesus visits the temple—but does nothing more than "look around at everything." It is late and he leaves, returning with his disciples to Bethany. Far from exercising royal prerogatives, Jesus acts like a desultory tourist. The Evangelist has steered readers to another climax, only to snatch the carpet out from under them (see also 4:30-32; 5:40-43; 6:45-52; 10:29-31). Such narrative subversion matches the character of the gospel that Jesus preaches (10:13-31, 42-45). "Mark uses every strategy to say two things at once: yes, this is the Messiah, the greatest of miracle workers, the Son of God, but, no, that does not mean at all what you thought it meant" (Placher 1994, 14). Mark has not narrated a "triumphal entry." He has lampooned it.

Strange Episodes at the Temple (11:12-25)

Though some voices dissented (e.g., *Sib. Or.* 4.24-30), much ancient Jewish literature favored the temple, its priests, and their practices. *The Epistle of Aristeas,* Josephus (*Ag. Ap.* 1.32), and Philo (*Spec. Laws* 1.66-345) write lovingly of temple sacrifice, with a piety they attribute to Jews in Judea and throughout the Diaspora. The same is true of the DSS: sectarians at Qumran respected the temple and its practices; what they disparaged was the contemporary priesthood (CD 4.18; 5.6-8; cf. *Pss. Sol.* 8.9-15; see Sanders 1992, 147-69, 279-303).

Jerusalem's second temple, the acme of Herod the Great's building projects, was not a building; it was a vast complex (*J.W.* 5; *Ag. Ap.* 2.102-19). One estimate of the area enclosed by its walls is about 169,000 square yards or 35 acres (Safrai 1976, 865-907): enough room to have contained about thirteen American football fields. A large area to the northeast comprised the Court of the Gentiles, beyond which lay the Court of the Women, the Court of the Israelites (male laity), the Court of the Priests, and deepest inside, the Holy of Holies, where God was believed to be specially present (*Ant.* 3.215-18; cf. Matt 23:21). Each of these courts was separated by a portico, wall, or parapet; within the Holy of Holies there were additional partitions, through which only priests actually presiding at sacrifice could pass (for pictorial reconstructions, see Perkins 1995, 662). Mark tends to use the term *hieron* in contexts where the entire temple complex is in view (11:11, 15, 16, 27; 12:35; 13:1, 3; 14:49), with *naos* referring to the sanctuary within the temple (14:58; 15:29, 38).

Priests offered sacrifices twice a day, at early morning and during the afternoon (*Ag. Ap.* 2.105). According to Philo (*Spec. Laws* 1.197), sacrifice was intended to praise God (burnt offerings; Sir 50:1-18), to acquire blessings or "good things" (shared sacrifices; Sir 50:19-24), and to atone for trespasses (sin offerings; Heb 9:22). These motivations resolved into one: the preservation of Israel's communion with God. Ritual expression of this faith was typically through the offering of a domesticated animal's blood: because life resides in the blood, and the blood (= life) belongs to God (Lev 17:1-16), the sacrificial victim was a vicarious expression of Israel's giving of its life to its Creator.

In 11:12-25 the reader encounters some of Mark's most baffling pericopae: Jesus' cursing of a fig tree and his disturbance of the temple's routine. Their intercalation is a key to their interpretation (see table 2). The Evangelist sandwiches one episode (vv. 15-19) into another's framework (vv. 12-14 + 20-21), prompting Jesus' teaching about faith and prayer (vv. 22-25). Mark has intricately interlaced some very different materials.

- The Evangelist begins by setting the clock. On Jesus' second day in Jerusalem he pronounces judgment (v. 12); "early" on the following day (v. 20) the action resumes from the previous evening (v. 19).
- They "go out" from Bethany (v. 12); they "go into" Jerusalem" (v. 15).
- Jesus' viewing of the tree from a distance, followed by closer

inspection (v. 13a), is echoed by his general survey of everything in the temple the day before (v. 11), followed by direct
engagement with its practices (v. 15).

- Destruction lies at the heart of both stories: Jesus pronounces judgment on both the tree (v. 14a) and the temple's
proceedings (vv. 15-17). Correlatively, the chief priests and
scribes seek to destroy Jesus (v. 18a).
- In both cases Jesus' judgment is thoroughgoing. He allows
no one to carry a vessel through the temple (v. 16); the tree is
withered to its roots (v. 20).
- Preclusion (*ouk ephien*) of cultic observance (v. 16) is contrasted with forgiveness (*aphiete, aphē*) among disciples
(v. 25).
- In both tales audiences are stunned by the results: the enrap-
tured crowd in the temple (v. 18b); Peter upon discovering
the withered tree (v. 21).
- In the framing episode Jesus "answers" the tree and his disciples (*apokritheis*, vv. 14a, 22); both episodes end with teaching (vv. 17, 18b, 22-25).
- Betrayal of the temple's proper function is ascribed to its visitors (v. 17); the disciples are exhorted to practice faithfulness
(vv. 22-24).
- The temple was intended as "a house of prayer" (*oikos
proseuchēs*, v. 17a); Jesus mandates of his followers confident, forgiving prayer (*proseuchesthe, proseuchomenoi*,
v. 25).
- "This mountain['s]" being taken up and thrown into the sea
(v. 23a) adverts to the mount on which the temple rests.
- The insularity of the temple's proceedings (v. 17c) stands
over against the boldness with which Jesus claims his disciples' petitions have been answered in their very asking
(v. 24).

The threads braiding 11:12-14 + 20-25 and 11:15-19 are unmistakable: Mark intends for these episodes to comment on each
other. What are they driving at?

Jesus' Cursing of a Fig Tree (11:12-14)

Jesus' cursing of a fig tree (11:12-14) is a weird story in substance and in form. To this point in the Gospel, Jesus has used his power only for restoring that which is out of joint; here, for the first and only time, that *dynamis* is used for a bane (v. 14a), not for a boon.

In the OT fig trees evoke many associations. Approaching Palestine, traveling Israelites welcomed the sight of fig trees (Num 13:23; Deut 8:8), whose large leaves afforded shade from the sun (Gen 3:7; cf. John 1:48, 50). In early spring, green fruit emerged from the previous season's branches (Song 2:13; Isa 34:4). Fig trees symbolize prosperity and peace (1 Kgs 4:25; 2 Kgs 18:31 = Isa 36:16; Joel 2:22; Mic 4:4; Hag 2:19; Zech 3:10); their loss or destruction is a conventional sign of prophetic judgment and national distress (Isa 28:3-4; Jer 8:13; Hos 2:12; Joel 1:7, 12; Amos 8:1-3; Mic 7:1). The Lord God planted Israel like a fig tree; when its fruit turned bad or was absent from the branch, divine judgment had occurred or was impending (Telford 1980, 128-204).

With this panorama in place, details in Mark 11:12-14 arrest one's attention. (a) Hungry, Jesus *wants* to find a fruitful tree (v. 12). (b) From afar its leafiness *suggests such a possibility,* which on closer inspection goes unsatisfied (v. 13a). (c) Though in leaf, there was *merely a chance* that he might find anything in it (*ei ara ti eur sei en autē,* v. 13b). (d) The tree has *only leaves, no fruit* (v. 13ab). (e) Absence of fruit owes to the fact that "it was not the season [*kairos*] for figs" (v. 13c). In Mark the term *kairos* refers not just to botanical season but to an eschatologically pregnant time of history's intervention by God's kingdom (1:15; 4:17; 10:30; 12:2; 13:33). It is no time for figs; it is time for something else. (f) Jesus' judgment has *lasting impact* (v. 14a), with a condemnatory promise *for disciples to hear* (v. 14b). At this point, Mark does *not* report the fig tree's fate. More must unfold before that can be confirmed and understood.

Jesus Upsets the Temple's Daily Routine (11:15-19)

The tale in Mark 11:12-14 is odd; so is the episode it introduces (11:15-19). Jewish families could not have been expected
to bring sacrificial offerings to the temple (see Luke 2:4, 22-24);
accordingly, animals were provided for purchase on site. Where
such sales took place is uncertain: whether in the outermost area
of the Court of the Gentiles or in shops outside the temple gates
(Sanders 1992, 85-88). Far from an irregular breach of religious
piety, the vending and purchase of sacrifices were commonplace,
legitimate, and necessary for cultic rituals to take place. Except
for Jews who believed that illegitimate functionaries were con-
ducting cultic affairs (1QpHab 12:8-10), there is scant evidence
suggesting that Jerusalem's priests were engaged in anything dishonest. To the contrary: while Titus's legions looted the temple
before burning it down (70 C.E.), "the priests carried on their
religious service uncurtailed, though enveloped in a hail of mis-
siles . . . [and] massacred at the altar" (*J.W.* 1.148). Jesus does not
upbraid vendors for illicit activities; he drives out *both* sellers
and buyers (11:15), forbidding *any* vessel to be carried through
the temple (11:16). With Rome's Antonia Fortress located just
outside the temple complex, it is hard to imagine Jesus eluding
arrest on the spot had his actions ignited a full-scale riot. To
some degree, at least, Jesus upsets the temple's daily routine
(11:15-18).

Why did Jesus do this? The answer lies in his obscure teaching
(11:17a), which quotes Isaiah 56:7 LXX with a rough paraphrase of Jeremiah 7:11 LXX (11:17b). The biblical contexts for
these quotations are important. Isaiah 56 is an expansive vision
in which, following Israel's restoration in 538 B.C.E., both native
Jew and proselyte would be united to one another and to the
Lord, whose reconstructed temple would be called "a house of
prayer for all the nations." To this hope Mark yokes an accusation from Jeremiah's temple sermon. Before its collapse in 586
B.C.E., disobedient Israelites assumed that they could repair to the
temple for protection, just as thieves hide in their lair. Not so,
preached Jeremiah: as God destroyed Shiloh's shrine five hun-

dred years before, so too would Solomon's temple fall (Jer 7:8-15). Evidently, the assumption on which the temple's existence and practice were predicated—the Jews' consecrated separation from the nations—is fallacious. Properly understood (by way of Isa 56:7), God's house should be one of prayer *for all the nations*. Because the religious have come to regard it not as a universal beacon (Isa 66:18-21) but as a hideout ("a den for *lēstai,*" nationalist bandits: *Ant.* 14.15; 15.10; *J.W.* 1.16), the second temple will be destroyed as assuredly as was the first (Barrett 1975). Signifying the temple's destruction, Jesus made a prophetic statement by overturning its tables and its visitors' expectations (Mark 11:15-16), much as Jeremiah shattered a potter's flask to demonstrate that the Lord would break Jerusalem and its people (Jer 19:1-15). Jeremiah was immediately arrested, beaten, and thrown into the stocks (Jer 20:1-18). For a time Jesus evades capture because the crowd is spellbound by his teaching (Mark 11:18-19).

Laminating the story of Jesus' protest in the temple inside his cursing of the fig tree creates a complex, allusive effect. The tree's leafiness may match the temple's commerce: things appear normal, healthy, and productive, though both may be fruitless. The possibility that Jesus might find figs on the tree (11:13b) may bleed into 11:17: though he entered the temple looking for a promise fulfilled for all the nations, instead Jesus may have found religious parochialism (cf. 7:1-23). It is not the season for figs (11:13b); the temple's own season (*kairos*) has also come to an end. If by Jesus' word the tree will remain forever fruitless (11:14a), then by his deed the temple will never again know business as usual. The reader gropes for meaning alongside the narrative's figures. Disciples are listening (11:14b). Jesus' teaching enthralls the crowd (11:18b). There is still more to learn.

The Tree Withered (11:20-21)

Mark 11:20-21 inserts the second slice of a sandwich built in 11:12-14. On Jesus' third day in Jerusalem, the rabbi and his disciples pass by the fig tree he had cursed. The tree is now withered to its roots, as Peter remembers events of the day before (v. 21a; cf. 14:72). Why does the Evangelist wait until now to finish this story? It creates suspense. Mark has left the reader dangling since 11:14: Will Jesus' judgment be fulfilled? After a time it is proved true (v. 20). If Jesus' complementary judgment on the temple's practice has not yet been fulfilled, the reader has good reason to conclude that in time it too will be.

Trusting Petition (11:22-25)

The lag between prophecy and fulfillment also opens the door to Jesus' teaching (11:22-25) on trusting petition. In these verses the flow of thought is not rigorously logical; they appear to have been linked together by catchwords (cf. 9:42-50): "faith" (*pistis*) or "believe" (*pisteuō*) in verses 22, 23, and 24; "pray" in verses 24 and 25 (cf. "prayer," *proseuchē,* in v. 17b). Because of their disjointed character, there is much confusion in these verses' textual transmission. Several manuscripts read, "if you have faith" (*ei echete*); a majority read, "have faith" (*echete*): a hard case to adjudicate, based solely on manuscript evidence. Most English versions translate the disputed words as a simple imperative (KJV, RSV, NIV, NEB, NAB, NRSV); between the two alternatives there is little material difference. Verse 24 presents a more interesting problem: a majority of Greek manuscripts read, "believe that you may receive" (KJV, Lattimore) or "will receive" (Goodspeed, Moffatt, NAB, NRSV, REB); yet some of the finest codices read, "believe that you have received" (RSV, NIV, JB, GNT, Cassirer, NEB ["it is happening"]). The latter is more likely to have been original: theologically it is the more difficult claim (cf. Matt 21:22.) After verse 25, a number of later manuscripts include a verse that, in the NRSV footnote, is numbered 26: "But if you do not forgive, neither will your Father in heaven forgive your trespasses." Probably this is a later addition, inserted to complement its positive assertion in 11:25 (cf. Matt 6:14-15).

"Have faith in God" (Mark 11:22) is an elliptical response to Peter's observation of the fig tree's withering. It is, however, intelligible: if the temple is on the brink of collapse (vv. 15-17), then one must redouble faith in God. Moreover, it takes confidence to pronounce judgment on a tree, or on the temple; it is such trust in God's power to overcome seemingly unconquerable obstacles that verse 23 encourages (cf. Matt 17:19-20 = Luke 17:5-6). Mark 11:23 is underscored by one of Jesus' firm prophetic assurances (cf. 8:12; 9:1, 41; 10:15, 29). The opposite of utter confidence is "a divided heart" (11:23b AT): a rift within the seat of religious discernment (2:6, 8; 7:6, 21; cf. 12:30, 33). In verses 24-25 the importance of trusting God is correlated with prayer (*proseuchesthe*), petition (*aiteshte*), and forgiveness (*aphiete*). Prayer while standing (v. 25) was customary in Jewish worship (1 Kgs 8:14; Neh 9:4; Ps 134:1; Matt 6:5; Luke 18:11, 13). Mutual forgiveness within the community of disciples is not merely mandated (9:42-50; 10:42-44); it is built into the relationship between the children of God and their heavenly Father (Matt 6:12 = Luke 11:4). On the Day of Atonement the high priest would confess Israel's trespasses and beg God's forgiveness while glorifying the divine name. The temple may totter; prayer must persist. Most striking of all is 11:24: the very acts of prayer and petition, expressions of trust in God, assure the supplicant's receipt of what is requested (5:34-36; 9:23-29; cf. 1 John 5:14-15).

◊ ◊ ◊ ◊

Interpretation of Mark 11:1-25 has been crippled by slogans attached to its constituent parts: "the triumphal entry," "the cleansing of the temple," "the lesson of the fig tree." We have seen that Jesus' entrance into Jerusalem (vv. 1-11) is not as glorious in Mark as in the other Gospels. Likewise, "the temple's cleansing" is bound to mislead interpreters if, in Mark's view, there was in the temple nothing dirty. Nor does this fig tree teach a single "lesson": instead, Jesus' judgment on both tree and temple raises deeper questions about prayer.

Most obvious in 11:1-25 is Mark's continued subversion of what one expects of a Messiah. Entering David's City on an ass, assaulting the normal routine in Herod's temple, Jesus does not act as tradition and common sense suggest he ought to. Jesus turns the tables on everyone, registering as a special threat among the cultic custodians of Israel's piety. The latter are in no mood for forgiveness (11:25); they want this fellow dead (11:18). Eventually, they will succeed (14:63-64; 15:31-32)—but not before their adversary has relocated the temple's center away from the altar, onto his own teaching (11:27–12:44).

"The cleansing of the temple" gets Mark's point backward. Jesus does not purify the temple. By bringing "all the nations"—Gentiles—back into its purview (11:17a), Jesus *pollutes* the temple, at least in popular imagination. Mark began unraveling that perception in 7:1-37: "It is what *comes out* of a person that defiles" (v. 20, emphasis added). Conventional lines between clean and unclean have been obliterated (7:19b). Reclaiming the prophets' judgment of the temple's intent and practice, Jesus has not in fact profaned God's house; rather, the priests' certified vendors and brokers have made of it a bandits' refuge (11:17). All this may seem irrelevant to modern readers. It is not. In Mark, Jesus assails a system that has made God the patron of its users. When scripture is cited to admit "the unwashed," the religious are always enraged. When the heart of that system is judged defunct, the pious are stripped of their security and have no place to run—except to God.

That is why this section of Mark ends as it does: "Trust God" (11:22 AT). From the temple's inception and through its revivification, prayer, not only ritual sacrifice, was the temple's raison d'être (1 Sam 1:1-28; 1 Kgs 8:30-51; 2 Kgs 19:14-37; Jdt 4:9-15; 2 Macc 3:15-40). After the second temple's destruction in 70 C.E., Rabbi Eleazer wondered if, for Israel, "the gates of prayer were locked," "an iron wall divid[ing] Israel and their Father in heaven" (*b. Ber.* 32b). In time rabbinic Judaism decided that this was not so: the synagogue, the place of prayer and study of Torah, would serve as a metaphorical temple. By the first century's end, most Christians concluded that Jesus' teaching had reoriented faith and prayer, even toward the Teacher himself. Mark 11:27–12:44 is headed in that direction.

Holding Court in the Temple (11:27–12:44)

Mark's next segment consists of eight pericopae:

11:27-33: The question of Jesus' authority
12:1-12:   The parable of the vineyard
12:13-17: The paying of Caesar's taxes
12:18-27: The validity of belief in the resurrection
12:28-34: The first among the commandments
12:35-37: The question of David's "Son"
12:38-40: A warning about the scribes
12:21-44: The widow's mite

The Evangelist distinguishes the first five in this series from the last three. Various groups or individuals provoke the teaching in 11:27–12:34. At 12:34b Mark creates a break: "After that no one dared to ask him any question." In 12:35-44 Jesus takes the initiative.

This material faces backward and forward. Five controversies in the temple (11:27–12:34), barbed with pronouncements (12:35-37) and observations (12:34-44), recall five chain-linked Galilean controversies (2:1–3:6). Mark 11:27–12:44 also anticipates what follows in 13:1-37: both segments arise from prophetic acts (11:14, 15-16) or utterances (11:17, 23; 13:1-2), implying or asserting the temple's demise. On the Mount of Olives (13:3) Jesus instructs his disciples about events attending that catastrophe. While the temple stands (11:27b) Jesus sits within its precincts, educating an audience broader than his entourage (11:18b; 12:12a).

Several motifs are clustered in Mark 11:27–12:44. The preoccupation that opens this section is the nature of Jesus' authority (11:27). The answer: Jesus is "a beloved son," destined for execution (12:6-8), and a true teacher (12:14, 19, 32), destined for recognition as David's Lord (12:36-37). Correlative with this christological concern is Mark's interest in situating Jesus vis-à-vis recognizable groups within Judaism of his day: chief priests and elders (11:27), Pharisees and Herodians (12:13), Sadducees

(12:18), and scribes (11:27; 12:28, 38). Each of these parties had a distinctive view of what Judaism should be in the early decades of the first century C.E. How do Jesus' views compare with theirs? The battle of theological ideas is waged on scriptural grounds. Repeatedly in chapter 12 an interlocutor quotes or alludes to the Bible. Here, as elsewhere, the Evangelist seems to be moving toward fresh theological positions by "merging scriptures" (Kee 1977, 45-49).

At stake in these issues are two primary questions: Who is God, and on what basis shall the people of God conduct their lives? That these questions should be debated in the temple precincts is altogether fitting, because the entire sacrificial system was designed to preserve the community's integrity in its communion with God. With that cultic system in jeopardy (11:15-17; 13:1-2), reassessment of that communion and community is imperative.

Jesus Challenged (11:27–12:34)

Most of this subsection's five segments amount to a sinister quiz show: *Stump the Rabbi*. Throughout Mark, others have sought out Jesus: his disciples (1:35-38; 7:17-23; 9:38-41; 10:35-45) and people who need healing (1:21-34; 3:7-12; 5:1-34; 7:32-37). What sets 11:27–12:34 apart is its characters' repeated hostility toward the teacher as they accost him in the temple. Most of these interlocutors are not seeking help (11:31; 12:12-13, 18). Instead, they are challenging Jesus or trying to trip him up. The construction is suspensefully entertaining: various opponents set traps. How will Jesus avoid springing them?

A Question of Authority (11:27-33)

For the third time in as many days (11:11, 15), Jesus and his disciples return to Jerusalem and its temple (11:27ab), where he provokes a question of authority (11:27-33). Unlike the day before, Jesus instigates no dramatic outburst (11:15-16); he is simply "perambulating" (v. 27b AT). The "chief priests, the scribes, and the elders" seize the occasion (v. 27b). All of these figures have already appeared on the Markan stage, though, until now, only in Jesus' first prediction of the Son of Man's destiny (8:31) were they allied. The scribes were among the first representatives of "official Judaism" to challenge Jesus (*ad loc.* 2:6, 16); throughout this Gospel, they have so persisted (7:5; 9:14), sometimes making the trip from Jerusalem to do so (3:22; 7:1). They and the chief priests are in cahoots to destroy Jesus (10:33; 11:18). Though "the tradition of the elders" has been an object of Jesus' critique (7:3, 5), the elders themselves become prominent only in Mark's later chapters, always associated with chief priests and scribes (11:27; 14:43, 53; 15:1). In line with the OT (Lev 4:13-21; Num 11:16-23; Deut 21:1-20) Israel's elders were venerable representatives of the community (see 1QS 6:9; 8:1–9:2; Acts 15:2-6, 22-23; *m. 'Abot* 1.1). "Chief priests" likely supervised their subordinates' hearing of confessions and offering of ritual sacrifices (*Let. Aris.* 92-95). "Scribes" were considered learned in Torah and socially prominent (Sir 38:24–39:11; *Ant.* 12.3.3). It makes sense that these dignitaries would seek out Jesus to ask "by what authority" he acted as he did in the temple (presumably, referring to his actions in Mark 11:15-17). Chief priests, scribes, and elders were acknowledged as responsible for the temple's proper conduct. Their repeated questions of Jesus in verse 28 are not impertinent. They were entitled to know.

Without impugning their authority, Jesus responds by asserting his own in a rabbinic counterquestion (v. 29; cf. 2:25-26; 7:6-13; 10:3). Notice the twist: directly interrogated, Jesus offers neither direct explanation nor defense of his conduct. Instead, by countering with his own pointed question (*"You* answer *me"*: 11:29b, 30b AT), he continues to wield the very authority that Jerusalem's leaders have disputed. He will give them an answer if they answer him first (v. 29a). The substance of his question is intriguing: the authority by which John baptized. Was it heavenly or human (v. 30a)? The leaders' first response—typically, for Mark—is to bicker among themselves (v. 31a; cf. 2:6; 3:4; 9:10). By this it becomes clear that, before Jesus, their authority is crumbling. Moreover, the nature of their internal argument is revealing: they weigh the political calculus in assessing John's baptism. Whatever their reply, they risk undermining their position (11:31-32). To discredit John would be dicey: according to Josephus (*Ant.* 18.117-18), Mark himself (1:2-8; 6:14-29; 8:28), and other NT writers (Matt 21:32; Luke 1:1-80; 7:28-30; Acts 19:1-7), John and his baptism of repentance were deeply esteemed.

As many politicians are wont, they split the difference and cop a plea of ignorance (v. 33a). Jesus' retort—"Neither will *I* tell *you* by what authority I am doing these things" (v. 33b, emphasis added)—is *triply* barbed. First, his interrogators are in no position to reject his reply as evasion, since they have just evaded a straight answer. Second, having confessed inability to adjudicate John's credibility, they have effectively disqualified themselves from judging that of Jesus. Finally, by pleading ignorance because of popular repercussions, his accusers reveal where they believe *their own authority* ultimately resides—not in "heaven" but in the view of "mortals," the multitude whose displeasure they fear (v. 32a). By their own deeds and words the temple's custodians have impeached their own authority. Because they will not or cannot accept that their defendant's power is heavenly (v. 30a), their judgment of both John and Jesus is truer than they recognize: "We do not know" (11:33a). Later, at the high priest's house, Peter will offer the same ironically disingenuous but accurate response (14:68a).

The Vineyard Owner and His Tenant Farmers (12:1-12)

Jesus begins to speak (12:1), presumably to "the chief priests, the scribes, and the elders" (11:27), "in parables" (12:1; 3:23; 4:2). In the story of the vineyard owner and his tenant farmers (12:1-12), the scripturally knowledgeable reader would recognize the opening lines, reshuffled, of Isaiah's "Song of the Vineyard" (5:1-7).

Isaiah 5:1-2 (LXX)	Mark 12:1
kai phragmon periethēka	*kai peritēken phragmon*
(and he had put a hedge around it)	(and he surrounded it with a hedge)
kai epheyteusa ampelon)	*ephyteusen ampelōna*
(and he planted a vineyard)	(he planted a vineyard)

kai ōkodomēsa pyrgon
(and he built a
watchtower)
kai prolēenion ōryxa
(and he hewed a pit)

kai ōkodomēsen pyrgon
(and he built a watchtower)

kai ōryxen hyplēnion
(and he dug a vat)

Isaiah's ballad is set in a minor key: "My beloved" did every-thing possible to cultivate choice fruit, but the vines yielded noth-ing but sour grapes (5:1-2). Jerusalem's citizens and Judah's inhabi-tants are invited to pass judgment on themselves: What more can be done to cultivate a vineyard that yields nothing but a sour crop (5:3-4)? Nothing. All the loving protection, the hedge and its wall, shall be torn down and trampled; the vines shall be laid waste, bereft even of rain (5:5-6). The final chorus interprets the whole:

> For the vineyard of Lord Sabbaoth is [the] house of Israel, and the Judahite is his beloved planting. [The Lord] waited for the doing of justice, but [the Judahite] made lawlessness and no righteousness—but [only] a cry (Isa 5:7 LXX AT).

That is the song one might have expected, but Jesus offers a variation on it. The big change lies in an absentee landlord's hir-ing of *geōrgoi* (Mark 12:1): "farmers" (NIV), "vine-growers" (NEB), or "tenants" (JB, RSV, NRSV). The term's basic meaning is "soil-tillers," though "tenant farmers" (NAB) or "sharecrop-pers" would be an appropriate translation. In Isaiah 5 there is no comparable figure, and for Mark's interpretation it is crucial that readers recognize the switch: Jesus is *not* singing the same old prophetic ballad of Israel's infertility in righteousness (also Jer 2:21; Ezek 19:10-14; Hos 10:1). Instead, this parable concerns the dynamic interaction of the planter (God) and the hired hands (Israel's leading custodians) to whom the vineyard has been leased. The latter may have expected the sad hymn from Isaiah's songbook. What they get is something more.

COMMENTARY

Interpreters drilled by Jülicher (1899) to repudiate allegorization of Jesus' parables may be troubled by Mark 12:1-12 (= Matt 21:33-46 = Luke 20:9-19; see A. Y. Collins 2007, 541-44): a parable shading into allegory. Some parables do this (e.g., Ezek 34:1-31). By the time the Evangelist received the parable, the quotation of Psalm 118:22 may already have been attached, though we cannot be certain: *ben* (son) and *'eben* (stone) create a neat pun in Hebrew, though not in Aramaic or Greek.

◊ ◊ ◊ ◊

Unlike Isaiah 5:1-7, Mark 12:2 suggests that the owner's vineyard has been fruitful because he sends for some of the crop *tō kairō* ("when the season came"). The term *kairos* strikes an eschatological tone (1:15; 10:30; 11:13; 13:33). The owner's deputy is a slave or servant, *doulos*: a term used to describe OT prophets (Jer 7:25; 25:4; Amos 3:7; Zech 1:6). That this is the term's likely connotation in Mark 12 is suggested by the terrible brutality that one slave after another suffers at the sharecroppers' hands (1 Kgs 18:12-13; 2 Chr 24:20-22; 36:15-16; Neh 9:26). Two details are noteworthy in Mark 12:3-5. Violence escalates: the first emissary is beaten and sent back empty-handed (v. 3); the second is "brained" (*ekephaliōsan*) and shamefully abused (v. 4); still another is murdered (v. 5a); "many others" are beaten or killed (v. 5b). One might bemoan Mark's maladroit storytelling: Doesn't the Evangelist know that in folk tales things properly happen in threes (cf. Matt 21:34-37; *Gos. Thom.* 65-66)? Of course Mark knows this (see 14:32-42, 66-72). By modifying the genre's predictable form, the Evangelist underscores the farmers' outrageous malice. The other detail that emerges from 12:2-5 is the owner's patient endurance of persistent disrespect.

The climax (*eschaton*, "finally": v. 6) arrives with the owner's attempt to receive his due by dispatching his "beloved son" (1:11; 9:7), whom the farmers will surely respect. The result is the opposite: considering the son "the heir," they kill and throw him out, hoping to inherit the vineyard (12:7-8). Whether first-century Jewish law would have supported such a perverse aspiration is debated (Jeremias 1972, 74-76; Marcus 2009, 803-4) and beside Mark's point, which is the homicidal rapaciousness of tenants without a genuine claim of ownership. The *geōrgoi* behave as one might expect of *lēstai,* violent brigands (11:17). The true owner's last resort is a foregone conclusion: destroying the tenants and transferring the property to others (v. 9). Mark does not draw Matthew's conclusion (21:43): "the kingdom of God will be taken away from you and given to a people that produces the fruits of the kingdom." Maybe that is not Mark's intent (contra Schweizer 1970, 241; Hooker 1991, 276). Perhaps Mark insists that after its overweening leaders are disinherited, God will award custody of Israel to more faithful stewards, Jewish or Gentile ("all peoples": 11:17a).

The quotation of Psalm 118:22-23 in Mark 12:10-11 draws together the parable's chief protagonists at an implied christological crux. Day laborers have rejected the very stone (the Son) that the Lord (the architect) has chosen as his keystone. Does Mark suggest that Jesus is the cornerstone for a new temple (= the church), to replace another that is tottering? That may go too far: Mark is more graphic in its anticipation of the existing temple's *demise* (13:2; perhaps 15:38) than of a restored temple's *recreation.* The use of Psalm 118:22-23 in Ephesians 2:20 and 1 Peter 2:7 is headed in that ecclesiological direction, even though Acts 4:11 is not. (For an alternative view, see Gray 2008.) The primary point in Mark 12:10-11 is the double-barreled contrast between (a) God's purposes and those of the temple's hierarchy, which pivots around (b) their starkly opposed assessments of Jesus. Of that 12:12 leaves no doubt. For a change (cf. 4:13) the point of a parable is unmistakable: in veiled, unmistakably scriptural terms, Jesus has answered the question about his authorization (11:28) and challenges Jerusalem's religious leadership in the strongest terms (12:2-8). Their position is as untenable (12:9) as the institution over which they preside (11:14-21). Their response—recognition that inflames heightened hostility (12:12)—demonstrates the power of Jesus' parables to confound those whose hearts are already hardened (4:11-12; 6:52).

Paying Caesar's Taxes (12:13-17)

The second round to catch Jesus out falls to "some Pharisees and some Herodians" with a devious question about paying Caesar's taxes (12:13-17). The framing of this classic paradigm (Dibelius 1935, 56) offers interesting details. Mark indicates (v. 13) that these questioners are proxies for those momentarily stifled (11:27). Why these substitutes? When the temple and its priesthood collapsed after 70, the Pharisees steered Judaism into a new phase culminating with the rabbinical schools. Historically, they were the ones who assumed proprietorship of God's vineyard after its *georgoi* were destroyed (12:9). We have met the Herodians once before (3:6), associated with Pharisees scheming to destroy Jesus. Of Herodians, Josephus says little (*J.W.* 1.319, 326; *Ant.* 14.450). While evidence is sparse, Herodians appear to have been Jewish partisans of the Herods, client-rulers of Galilee or Judea, perhaps reasoning that indirect Roman rule was preferable to direct Roman oversight. The Herodians may have been pro-Roman since, to retain their influence, the Herods themselves backed Rome (Smallwood 1981, 263-64; Richardson 1996, 259-60). Throughout their history, the Pharisees appear to have been politically adaptable (Neusner 1979, 143-54). By the time Mark was written, they may have been reemerging as a political force.

The Pharisees and Herodians are bent on ensnaring Jesus (12:13). In verse 14 the Evangelist gives them an extended setup, whose verbosity is a masterpiece of slimy fulsomeness: "Teacher, we know you are true; you don't care what others think; you're no respecter of persons; with simplicity you teach God's way" (AT). (Compare their commissioners [11:27], who care very much what people think [vv. 31-32].) This is a neat example of the irony with which Mark's Passion Narrative will be layered thick: though the speakers have accurately epitomized Jesus' character, not for a moment do they believe what they say. Jesus is discerning: he recognizes their blather as hypocrisy (*hypokrisis*, v. 15a) cajoling him to lower his guard (v. 15b). Their bait: "Is it lawful to pay taxes to the emperor, or not?" (v. 14). The *kēnsos* was a poll tax (BDAG 542b). Hard-pressed Jews had long known heavy taxation, which grated under an empire whose principal income came from taxes levied outside Italy (Sanders 1992, 146-69). The imperial per capita tax forced Jews to pay tribute to an occupying power that was religiously illegitimate yet politically inescapable. Therein lay the trap: if Jesus were maneuvered into sanctioning payment, his piety would be compromised. If he advocated nonpayment, sedition was suggested. His request for a denarius before answering (12:15b-16a) has been interpreted as either stalling for time or tricking a Jew into revealing his possession of pagan currency. The former is psychologistic; the latter, a non sequitur: the reason for the exchange (*kollybistoi*, 11:15b) in the Court of the Gentiles was to divest oneself of imperial currency. The presentation of the denarius is key to interpreting Jesus' famous reply (v. 17a). The coin, a laborer's daily wage, was likely inscribed "Tiberius, Emperor, Son of the Divine Augustus," embossed with an image (*eikōn*, v. 16) of Caesar's head. As the Herodians connived to hear, Jesus does not advocate treason: Caesar is entitled to his own. Neither does Jesus countenance idolatry or abrogation of Jewish monotheism: God is entitled to "the things that are God's," which for pious Pharisees would include *everything,* without exception. All creatures of the one Creator are themselves made in the image of God (Gen 1:27; 9:6), as Rabbi Akiba would later assert: "Beloved are humans, because they were created in God's image" (*m. 'Abot* 3.15). Therefore, ultimate tribute (pun intended) belongs solely to God. Left to the reader's judgment is whether marvel at this reply (Mark 12:17b) arises from appreciation of, or frustration by, Jesus' discernment.

Belief in the Resurrection (12:18-27)

Enter the Sadducees, for the first and only time in Mark. They denied resurrection from the dead (12:18). That datum corresponds with Josephus's comparisons of Pharisaic and Sadducean schools of thought (*J.W.* 2.8.2-14; *Ant.* 18.1.2-6) as well as Luke's comments in Acts (23:6-8; see Meier 2001, 389-487). In Mark 12:18-27 some Sadducees adopt a roundabout gambit to challenge Jesus on validity of belief in the resurrection. This is a different challenge from those witnessed in 11:27–12:17, which have struck near the heart of contemporary Jewish conduct, cultic or political. From Mark's point of view, however, the Sadducees' question touches on God's power and directly assails the credibility of Jesus' teaching about the Son of Man's resurrection (8:31; 9:9-12, 31; 10:34). The basis for their attack is what "Moses wrote for us" (12:19) regarding levirate marriage: the ancient custom whereby an unmarried brother was obligated to marry his deceased brother's childless widow in order to raise surrogate offspring (Deut 25:5-6). The torturous test case presented to Jesus is that of a widow who outlives seven childless brothers before dying herself (12:20-22). "In the resurrection whose wife will she be? For the seven had married her" (v. 23).

As expected, Jesus' answer is ingenious. First, he slams his questioners' scholasticism as errant in its assumptions (v. 24). Second, he implies that their refusal to believe in resurrection has led them to mistake the character of postmortem life (v. 25; cf. 1 Cor 15:35-58, which associates resurrection with "spiritual bodies"). If the matter ended there, it would be only one teacher's opinion against others'. To cap his riposte, Jesus argues scripturally (v. 26a), as his adversaries have done, by reaching more deeply into Torah for an *earlier* Mosaic precedent (cf. 10:4-8): God's self-identification at the burning bush as "the God of Abraham, the God of Isaac, and the God of Jacob" (Exod 3:6a; Mark 12:26b). The point is that God spoke of his enduring authority over three patriarchs who, by the time of Moses, had long since died. If God *remains* their father, then it follows that in some sense they must still be alive (cf. Luke 16:19-31): "He is God not of the dead, but of *the living*" (Mark 12:27a, emphasis added)—a point the Sadducees could hardly have denied. For this reason, Jesus reiterates, his interrogators have altogether strayed from Scripture's deeper intent and from the truth of the matter (v. 27b; cf. v. 24).

"Which of the Commandments Is First of All?" (12:28-34)

Round One: chief priests and scribes and elders (11:27–12:12). Round Two: Pharisees and Herodians (12:13-17). Round

Three: Sadducees (12:18-27). The reader is braced for Round Four; the prospects are no more auspicious. Amid controversy (v. 28a) another interlocutor steps forward. Because he is a scribe, that spells trouble (see 2:6; 3:22; 8:31; 10:33). Yet Mark has in store another surprise (12:28-34). This scribe admires Jesus' teaching (12:28b). Unlike the Sadducees' *amplificatio ad absurdum,* he asks a serious question: "Which of the commandments is first among all?" (v. 28c AT). In later Jewish literature this matter would lie near the rabbis' hearts (Chilton et al. 2010, 383-86), and their answer would be much the same as Jesus' (*m. Ber.* 2.2, 5; *Sipra* Lev 19:18; *b. Ber.* 61b). In Mark 12:29-30 Jesus repeats the Shema, "Hear, O Israel": the supreme dictum, from Deuteronomy 6:4-5. Jesus expands it: "The Lord our God," the one Lord, should be loved with wholeness of heart (*kardia,* "the inner compass"), life (*psychē*; see Mark 3:4; 8:35-37; 10:45), strength (*ischys*)—plus discerning intelligence (*dianoia*). Inseparable from this command is a second: love of neighbor as oneself (12:31a; Lev 19:18; cf. Rom 13:9; Gal 5:14; Jas 2:8; *Spec. Laws* 2.63; *T. Iss.* 5.2; *T. Dan.* 5.3). According to Rabbi Akiba, something like this conflated command is "the whole Torah; the rest is commentary" (*b. Mak.* 23b-24a; cf. Mark 12:31b). Likewise, Irenaeus (*Haer.* 4.16.3) regards love of God without injury of neighbor as "the meaning of the Decalogue." Jesus' reply to this scribe could not be more orthodox.

And so this scribe accepts it, complimenting the teacher for his accuracy (12:32a), accenting God's oneness (v. 32b), repeating the Shema's core (v. 33a), and adding his own gloss: the greatest of the Torah's double commandment "is much more important than all whole burnt offerings and sacrifices" (Mark 12:33b; 1 Sam 15:22). Whole burnt offerings and sacrifices are what priests offered in the temple, whose apparatus Jesus has undermined (11:15-19) and whose massive structure will soon be demolished (13:1-2). In a sense 12:28-34 is a companion piece for 7:24-30: each presents Jesus in genuine give-and-take with a strong petitioner demonstrating perspicacity that Jesus honors. For Mark the scribe's reply bespeaks discernment (*nounechōs,*

12:34a; note the addition of *dianoia* in v. 30b), and so Jesus replies in kind: "You are not far from the kingdom of God" (v. 34a). Were this scribe's approach to God's kingdom any closer, would he then be a disciple of Jesus? Apparently so—here all debate in the temple lurches to an end (v. 34b). His debaters have challenged his authority, tried to outfox him, fenced with him over Scripture, and finally addressed him with straightforward approbation. To cut any deeper would reach the marrow of discipleship.

◊ ◊ ◊ ◊

Nowhere in Mark does Jesus say more about God's character than in 11:27–12:34 (Donahue 1982). The Evangelist's presentation is simultaneously climactic and circular. The issues put to Jesus intensify: from his authority in general (11:28; 12:9) to his assessment of religious and political entanglements (12:14b-15a); through his ability to interpret Scripture (12:19a, 23) to his first principles for biblical interpretation (12:28c). What the beginning of this segment suggests (11:30, 33; 12:1-9) is spelled out in Israel's Shema (12:29, 32), the capstone beyond which little needs to be added. Yet this capstone converges with "the cornerstone" that Israel's Lord has set in place: the beloved Son (12:6, 10-11). The truth about God is trustworthy because of its truthful delivery by Jesus, the target of all questioners in 11:27–12:34. There lies the circularity: this segment opens with dispute of Jesus' authority (11:28) and ends with a declaration of his proximity to God's rule, which silences all critics (12:34).

What does one learn from Jesus about God? (1) God never abandons his "planted vineyard" (12:1-2). Repeatedly, God has dispatched servants, John the Baptist (11:30) and other prophets (12:2-5), to receive the vineyard's fruit ("a baptism of repentance for the forgiveness of sins" [1:4]). (2) When Israel's trustees have betrayed the trust vested in them, God has judged and abolished their stewardship, delivering it into others' hands so that the vineyard may yet prove fruitful, that the edifice may stand secure (12:9-11). (3) A choice between theocracy and worship of empire is false: Caesar receives his due but not more, for Caesar and God are neither identical nor interchangeable (12:17a). (4) It is ridiculous to speculate how many husbands can dance with a common wife in the afterlife (12:25). Resurrection is a claim about the living God's power to remain faithful, in life and in death, to those claimed for an everlasting covenant (12:24, 26-27a). (5) The motor driving Scripture and those who would align themselves with its realization is the confession of Israel's one God, to be loved with every human faculty to such a degree that it spills into love of the neighbor as one loves oneself (12:29-31). No religious practice, however honorable (12:33b), can approximate fulfillment of these two commandments. (6) What more, then, is required to enter God's kingdom (12:34a)? For Mark it is discipleship in the way of God's beloved Son, whom God has sent and to whom attention must be paid (9:7b; 12:6). Lacking correction by this Christ (12:35), ritual turns insular (11:17), religion suffocates in hubris (12:3-8), society bends toward anarchy or political idolatry (12:14d-15a), and Scripture is twisted into intellectual Tinker Toys (12:18-24). Unless Jesus exposes their pitfalls, religious leaders turn cowardly (11:31-32), vicious (12:2-8), hypocritical (12:15b), and wrongheaded (12:24, 27b).

Because Mark is a story about Jesus and about his disciples, 11:27–12:34 stands as an important set of cautionary tales. Chief priests and scribes and elders, Pharisees and Herodians and Sadducees, have long since exited the historical stage; the attitudes they reveal in Mark about human religiosity remain alive and sick—and as much endemic among Christians as everyone else. There also remains the scribe who asks serious questions and speaks wisely (12:28, 34a). Readers who leave this portion of Mark with self-congratulation, pleased by their superior sensibility, have entirely missed the point. The question that Jesus put to the discerning scribe stands: How far from God's kingdom is Mark's reader?

Jesus Challenges (12:35-44)

In the next ten verses Jesus is the actor, not the reactor. No longer does he reply to others' questions (11:28; 12:14, 23, 28); now it is his turn to challenge his listeners (so also 12:9-11). It is seductively simple to read Mark 12:35-44 as three brief pericopae linked only by some recurring key words: "scribes" (vv. 35, 38; cf. vv. 28, 32) and "widows" (vv. 40, 42, 43). The temptation should be resisted. If 11:27–12:34 is Jesus' most concentrated instruction on the character of God in Mark, then 12:35-44 spells out its implications for understanding Christology (vv. 35-37) and discipleship (vv. 38-44). The double commandment in 12:29-31 swivels between these two segments, assisting the reader to interpret them complementarily. The imperative to love Israel's one God without reservation (12:29-30) is predicated on understanding who that God is: the Deity who meets us in 11:27–12:34. To love one's neighbor as oneself (12:31a) requires genuine attention to that neighbor (12:38-44), exemplified by "David's Lord" in 12:35-37.

David's Son (12:35-37)

The first of Jesus' rejoinders (Mark 12:35-37) presents a christological puzzle. Socratically (Daube 1956, 151-57), Jesus asks how the scribes claim that the Christ is David's son (12:35) when David himself (vv. 36a, 37a) resisted that association while singing Psalm 110:1 under the Holy Spirit's sway (Mark 12:36). In that psalm (so the reasoning goes), "The LORD [God] says to my [= David's] lord, / 'Sit at my right hand'" (Ps 110:1a/Mark 12:36b). If David addresses someone as "Lord," then that Lord cannot be David's subordinate (12:37). Mark seems to deny the validity of Davidic Christology: if the Lord is lord over David, then that Lord cannot be David's son. This is a defensible position, though out of sync with most of the NT: from Matthew (1:6, 20; 9:27; 21:9, 15), through Luke (1:27, 32, 69; 2:4) and Acts (2:30, 36; 13:22-23, 31-39), to Paul (Rom 1:3) and Revelation (22:16).

For all its deviation at this point from much NT Christology, 12:35-37 is consistent with Mark's few references to David elsewhere (2:23-28; 10:47-48; 11:10). In the first-century B.C.E. *Psalms of Solomon* (17:1-51) and at Qumran (1QSb 5:21-28; 4QFlor 1:1–2:13), Davidic sonship had come to connote military triumph in an earthly kingdom (Nickelsburg 1981, 207-9; J. J. Collins 1995, 49-73). The Second Evangelist wants no part of that (8:29-33; 11:1-11; cf. John 7:40-44). Although other NT authors apply Psalm 110 to the risen Christ (Acts 2:34-35; 1 Cor 15:25; Heb 1:13), nowhere does Mark imply fulfillment of the psalmist's promise that the king's enemies will be seated "beneath his feet" (RSV, NIV, REB) or "as a footstool" (KJV, Moffatt, Cassirer). Such a claim of consummated victory would be impertinent in Mark 11:1–12:34, wherein Jesus remains in contest with his adversaries.

Rarely in Mark (9:41; 11:3)—and then only to disciples fumbling on the outskirts of his intent—does Jesus identify himself as "Christ" or "Lord," though he may accept such identifications that others make (8:29-30; 14:61-62a). His exaltation (12:36d) will not occur apart from his rejection and murder (12:7-8, 10-11). Perhaps for that reason a Davidic messiahship simply cannot be made to fit Jesus in the Second Gospel (12:35, 37). It is hard to know what to make of the comment that Jesus' large audience heard him *hēdeōs*—"gladly" (RSV), "eagerly" (NEB), "with delight" (NRSV), or "with pleasure" (Lattimore). Such a response for a time keeps at bay Jesus' arrest (12:12). If his listeners comprehended the truth about Jesus as the suffering Son of Man (8:31; 9:31; 10:33-34), would they be so delighted?

Warnings about the Scribes (12:38-40)

To judge by his warnings (12:38-40), what disturbs Jesus about the scribes? It is the corruption or dereliction of their responsibility: ostentatious piety (v. 38), delight in honor (v. 39), and windy prayers while "devour[ing] widows' houses" (v. 40b). The latter charge is obscure; without corroborative evidence it is mischievous to guess what some may have done. (Matt 23:1-36 and Luke 11:37-44 shift this blameworthy conduct from scribes to Pharisees.) In any case some malefactors' conduct should not be generalized: in rabbinic tradition "To rob widows and orphans is to rob God" (*Exod. Rab.* 30.8 on Exod 22:22). This view is a hallmark of OT theology: widows, among Israelite society's most vulnerable members, were to be protected and assured legal restitution (Exod 22:22-25; Deut 24:17). When not, the prophets were withering in their judgment (Isa 10:1-2; Zech 7:10; Mal 3:5; cf. Ps 94:1-7; Wis 2:6-11). So, too, Jesus sides with the weakest. "The widow" must be protected, especially when society's protectors default their responsibilities most duplicitously. Like Ezekiel (34:1-31), the Son of Man prophesies against Israel's traitorous shepherds: "They shall receive more abundant condemnation" (Mark 12:40b AT).

A Widow in the Temple (12:41-44)

By contrast, appropriately, a widow in the temple has the last word (12:41-44), even though she says nothing and Jesus interprets her contribution (a motif Mark will duplicate in 14:3-9). Concluding his instruction in the temple, Jesus is seated opposite the *gazophylakion* (12:41a, 43b), which could refer either to the temple's treasury, a chamber that abutted the Court of the Women, or to a receptacle for offerings located in that precinct (John 8:20). "And many rich were throwing in big [money]" (Mark 12:41b AT). Among this throng, Mark twice refers to "one widow, a poor one" (vv. 42, 43). Her offering is "two *lepta*"—the smallest copper coins then in circulation—"that equal a [Roman] *quadrans*" (v. 42 AT), whose value was one-sixty-fourth a denarius, a laborer's daily wage (12:15b). In the social scheme of the temple's proceedings, this seems no big deal, but as always, Jesus uses an unconventional measuring stick. Calling the poor widow's deed to his disciples' attention (v. 43a), he utters a prophetic announcement using the attention-arresting formula, "Truly I tell you" (v. 43b; cf. 11:23): she has contributed to the temple "more than them all" (AT). Jesus' evaluative scale is not absolute but proportionate to circumstance: all others have donated droplets of their overflow, while from her destitution she has withheld nothing. She has thrown in everything she has, "the whole of her life" (*holon ton bion autēs*, v. 44 AT). (The term *bios* embraces both "life" and "livelihood" that supports it.) Whereas the receptive scribe was "not far from the kingdom of God" (12:34a), this poor widow has apparently entered it: no one in Mark's Gospel receives from Jesus higher commendation than this. *What a waste,* one thinks: *the temple is due for destruction* (11:12-21; 13:1-2). Lacking all social support, this poor widow gives up all she has, throwing herself unreservedly into a lost cause—but so do the Son of Man (10:45; 11:22-25) and the vineyard's owner (12:1-11).

The demands of discipleship are played out in the real world of power differentials. For all their differences, the ancient and modern worlds tend toward the same equations: the more money one has, the higher the status; the higher one's status, the greater one's power. Mark 12:35-44 turns these assumptions inside out. This section begins by overturning the reader's belief that Jesus is "David's son," a victor in the Davidic mold. No, he is not: Jesus is David's *Lord* (12:37a) and, therefore, redefines what it means to be "the Christ" (12:35). The adversaries of David's Lord are not yet subject to his authority (cf. 12:36). That is evident in the temple (11:27–12:34). It will become even clearer in the Passion Narrative (14:1–15:47).

Jesus' power is not drawn from the rich apparatus around him (12:41): the "house of prayer for all the nations," withering like fig leaves on a dead branch (11:17b, 21). His power is not that of teachers who devour poor "houses" while parading their status within influential circles (12:38-40a). Jesus' power lies in *his ability to give it up.* That is why the widow who can sacrifice her whole life by divesting herself even of her poverty becomes, in this Gospel, a model disciple (12:43-44; cf. 8:34-37; 10:17-31; see Malbon 2000, 166-225). All others gave from their abundance (*perisseuontos*, 12:44a). As a perceptive scribe has just noted, there is no gift more abundant (*perissoteron*) than complete love for God and for one's neighbor (v. 33). This is no maudlin precept. It is the principle of God's judgment: the living (v. 27), demanding (v. 17), righteous (v. 9) God who seats his faithful Messiah (vv. 35-36), unseats rapacious scribes (v. 40b), watches over widows (vv. 41-44), and renders accounts payable by this world's principalities. To the latter subject Jesus directs his final speech to his disciples.

Jesus' Farewell (13:1-37)

Chapter 13 contains Jesus' longest uninterrupted discourse in Mark. It should be considered (a) in its immediate context, (b) as a literary genre, and (c) topographically. This material also invites (d) consideration within the context of ancient apocalyptic literature.

(a) Mark 13:1-37 extends a carefully patterned block of teaching introduced at 11:22:

> 11:22-25: Prompted by Peter (v. 21) *outside* the temple, Jesus instructs his disciples about faith.
> 11:27–12:44: *Inside* the temple, Jesus teaches "the things of God" (v. 17a).
> 13:1-37: Prompted by his followers (vv. 1, 3) *outside* the temple, Jesus instructs his disciples about God's climactic judgment.

Thus, 11:22-25 and 13:3-37 serve as bookends: in both, Jesus teaches his disciples outside the temple, facing the prospect of its imminent destruction (11:15-21; 13:1-2).

Not only is the temple's demise imminent; so, too, is Jesus' own. Immediately after the Olivet Discourse, the plot for his arrest is consummated (14:1-11). Laden with dark images and phraseology recurring in chapters 14–15, chapter 13 decelerates the narrative and prepares the reader for Mark's Passion Narrative.

(b) On the eve of Jesus' execution, Mark 13:5b-37 functions as an *Abschiedsrede*: a "farewell address of a great man before his death." This is a familiar ancient genre: Genesis 49:1-33 (Jacob);

Deuteronomy 31:1–33:29 (Moses); Joshua 23:1–24:30 (Joshua); 1 Samuel 12:1-25 (Samuel); 1 Kings 2:1-9 and 1 Chronicles 28:1–29:5 (David); Tobit 14:1-11 (Tobit); 1 Maccabees 2:49-70 (Mattathias); not fewer than four leave-takings by Socrates in Plato's *Apology, Crito, Phaedo,* and Xenophon's *Memorabilia* (4.7.1-10); *1 Enoch* 91–105 (Enoch); Acts 20:18b-35 and 2 Timothy 1:1–4:22 (Paul). A second-century B.C.E. corpus comprises stylized *Testaments of the Twelve Patriarchs.* Jesus' farewell discourse in John 14:1–17:26 serves the same purpose.

(c) The setting for Mark 13:1-37 is the Mount of Olives (vv. 1-2; *ad loc.* 11:1-11), opposite the temple. We have considered that structure's interior (*ad loc.* 11:12-25); the disciples' expression of awe (13:1) invites comment on its exterior. In the eighteenth year of his reign (20 B.C.E.) Herod began reconstruction of the temple, "assuring his eternal remembrance" (*Ant.* 15.11.1). Finishing touches were applied ca. 61 C.E., about a decade before its destruction during the Romans' siege of Jerusalem (70 C.E.; *J.W.* 5.7.2–6.4.3). The platform on which the temple sat exceeded every extant complex in Western antiquity (Peters 1985, 79). Its edifice was built of hard white stones (*Ant.* 15.11.2), soaring some 164 feet into heaven and covered on all sides with massive golden plates. "The outside of the building lacked nothing to astonish the mind or eye" (*J.W.* 5.222). Today's visitors to the temple's Western Wall (the Wailing Wall, a remnant still standing) can observe building blocks whose weight ranges from two to nearly four hundred tons.

(d) Since the nineteenth century, scholars have referred to Mark 13 as "a little apocalypse." Nowadays scholars do not concur on what constitutes "apocalypticism" and what qualities a document should exhibit to be reckoned "apocalyptic" (Beasley-Murray 1993, 1-109). For instance, Jesus adverts to a supernatural world, inhabited by the Son of Man and his angels (13:26-27), but he neither conducts a tour of that cosmos (*1 En.* 72–82) nor discloses visions of it after ascending to heaven (*Apoc. Ab.* 15–29). He mediates a revelation, but not as an otherworldly being (cf. *4 Ezra*). While there are points of theological intersection between Mark 13 and Revelation, the latter belongs to a different genre.

Though quoting or alluding to prophetic books, Mark 13 is not a thorough interpretation of Isaiah, Daniel, or any other OT book; nevertheless, it does resemble some "historical apocalypses" that envision stressful events in their authors' days (Dan 7–12; *Jub.* 23:16-32; *1 En.* 83–90; see Nickelsburg 1981, 71-99). Mark 13 offers prophetic encouragement and admonition to disciples, adopting an eschatological perspective that, as we shall see, is scripturally grounded and apocalyptically tinctured.

A Terrifying Prospect (13:1-2)

Because Jerusalem's temple was stupendous, Jesus' insistence (v. 2) is frightening: "Here *by no means* [*ou mē*] will stone upon stone be left [standing], as *assuredly* [*ou mē*] it will be pulled down" (AT). Mark's wording is less graphic than Luke's (19:43-44; *J.W.* 5.21–6.4.1); one cannot say with certainty whether Mark knows of the temple's destruction as a fait accompli or whether that event looms on the Evangelist's horizon. (See the Introduction, "What We Can Infer: Date.")

Two Questions for the Teacher: Of Sign and Season (13:3-4)

Jesus' prediction supports an interpretation of 11:15-19 as a veiled prophecy of the temple's imminent ruin (cf. Jer 26:6, 18; Mic 3:12, regarding the Solomonic temple). On the Mount of Olives in private consultation (v. 3; cf. 4:34), Peter, James, John, and Andrew express anxiety (v. 4). Here members of the Twelve are cast in a favorable light: they trust Jesus to know answers to their questions. Still, their assumptions are flawed. First, they want to know the catastrophe's timing. Second, they ask for a single sign. Jesus' reply expands the scope of their second presupposition and reverses in importance the order of their queries.

Reply to the Disciples: Warning, What to Watch for, and When (13:5-37)

"Beware" (13:5): General Earthly Troubles (13:6-8)

Jesus' response opens with a warning, which may be addressed as much to Mark's readers as to four disciples:

"Beware that no one leads you astray" (v. 5). The first of many indicators is described as general earthly troubles (vv. 6-8): a proliferation of impostors, wars and rumors of wars, the rise of nations against nations and kingdoms against kingdoms, local earthquakes and famines. While sociopolitical turbulence is common in prophetic portents (Isa 19:2; 2 Chr 15:6; Jer 22:23), first-century Jews and Christians could have experienced such civil unrest as Mark depicts (Luke 17:23; Acts 5:36-37; 21:38; Rev 6:8; 11:13). The self-predication, "I am he!" (*egō eimi,* Mark 13:6), is oddly oblique, though the Markan context offers interpretive help: deceivers will come "in [Jesus'] name"; elsewhere Jesus has so identified himself to frightened disciples (6:50b). The implication is that disciples may expect the rise of unreliable interlopers, passing themselves off as those speaking on Jesus' authority at times of crisis. All these things are to be taken in stride: "Do not be alarmed." Such phenomena lie within God's province; none is proof that the end has come (v. 7; cf. 2 Thess 2:1-12). These are but the beginning of the world's "birth pangs" (v. 8b; cf. Rom 8:18-22).

Particular Earthly Calamities Experienced by Believers (13:9-13)

Further signs must unfold: particular earthly disasters experienced by believers (vv. 9-13). The focus is sharpened on what Jesus' followers may undergo and of what they should "beware" (v. 9a). These tribulations culminate in arrest and delivery into the hands of hostile authorities. The key word is *paradōsousin* (vv. 9b, 11, 12), "betrayal" or "handing over," much as John the Baptist experienced (1:14) and Jesus himself will know (3:19a; 9:31; 10:33; 14:41). The ensuing torments are concentrated on Jesus' disciples: "bearing witness on my account" (v. 9b AT), "hated by all because of my name" (v. 13a; cf. Matt 10:21-22; John 15:18-21). The Roman historian Tacitus attests to such hatred of Christians (*Ann.* 15.44). The agents of the disciples' arrest are at first unspecified (Mark 13:9b, 11a), but soon all too painfully particularized: siblings, parents, and children intent on putting one another to death (v. 12). Interfamilial betrayal is a stock prophetic motif (Mic 7:6); still, such divisions occurred among first-century Christians (John 9:18-23; 16:2). The venues for persecution will be judicial (local Jewish tribunals, *synedria*), religious (*synagōgas*), and political (governors and kings; Mark 13:9b). Jesus alleviates this dismal picture. (1) Witness to him shall not be quashed by his followers' trials: "The good news must first be proclaimed to all nations" (v. 10; see 1:1, 14); by implication, that project will be guided by God (cf. Isa 49:5; 52:10; Mark 16:20; Rom 1:5-17; 11:11-32; Eph 3:1-10). (2) Disciples are assured that they will not face their persecutions unaided: God's spirit will supply them what they need to say in their hour of trial (Mark 13:11b; cf. John 14:26). (3) Whatever they endure, God will ultimately vindicate (Mark 13:13b; Rev 2:10). (4) In this comprehensive light Jesus' followers should not be anxious beforehand (Mark 13:11a). This segment of Jesus' discourse pulls no punches in what awaits his disciples; neither does it give them reason to despair.

Extraordinary Tribulation and How Humans Will Respond (13:14-23)

So far "the signs" of strife have been this-worldly, albeit horrendous. Attention is turned in verses 14-23 to such extraordinary tribulation as the world has never seen (v. 19) and how humans will respond to it. Its trigger will be "the desolating sacrilege [*to bdelygma tēs erēmōseōs*] set up where it ought not to be" (v. 14a). "Let the reader understand" (v. 14a) is as mysterious as that which it purportedly explains, though Matthew's interpretation (24:15) makes sense: in Daniel (9:27; 11:31; 12:11) "the desolating abomination" refers to an infamous desecration by the Seleucid king Antiochus IV (175–164 B.C.E.), who amid a full-scale Jewish pogrom plundered the temple (1 Macc 1:21-24), desecrated its vessels (2 Macc 5:15-16), and set up an "appalling abomination" on its altar (1 Macc 1:54). In the first century Antiochus was no longer on the scene, though the Romans were. Mark alludes to some sociopolitical catastrophe, in whose face Jesus' counsel is, quite literally, to "head for the hills," Judea's mountainous terrain (13:14). Mark 13:15-17 accents alacrity, immediate response, prayer, and pity for pregnant and nursing mothers unable to flee without encumbrance. If chaos came in winter (v. 18), heavy rains would impede travel.

Adhering to a pattern established in verses 9-13, verses 19-23 segue from dire prophecies to reassurances. (1) As awful as such incomparable tribulation will be (v. 19), at least it shall be so blatant that it is impossible to mistake (cf. Dan 12:1; Rev 7:14). Moreover, (2) God will curtail the suffering (v. 20). (3) In the OT "the elect whom [the Lord] chose" refers to Israel (Ps 105:6; Isa 42:1; 43:20; 65:9); in the NT the term usually indicates the church (Rom 8:33; Eph 1:4-5; Col 3:12; 2 Tim 2:10; 1 Pet 1:2). Mark 13:20 may connote both. Unlike some apocalyptic texts, "Jesus speaks of an 'elect' but not a 'damned,' of an ingathering but not a sorting out" (Sabin 2002, 145). (4) The reemergence of pseudo-christs and pseudo-prophets (cf. 13:6)—misleading followers, conjuring spurious "signs and wonders"—is predictable (vv. 21a, 22, 23b KJV). These are commonplace nuisances in biblical tradition (Deut 13:1-3; Matt 7:15-23; 2 Thess 2:9-10; Rev 19:20). (5) Most reassuring are Jesus' corrections *before* disciples wander off course: "Don't you believe it—just watch out" (vv. 21b, 23a AT).

Particular Supernatural Responses to the Great Tribulation (13:24-27)

The grand finale: specific supernatural responses to this awful tribulation (vv. 24-27). Mark's language draws from OT portrayals of "the day of the LORD." Among other examples (Isa 13:10; 34:4; Joel 2:10), Ezekiel 32:7-8 (NJPS, alt.) is representative:

When you are snuffed out,
I shall cover the sky
And darken its stars;
I shall envelop the sun with clouds
And the moon shall not give its light.
All the lights that shine in the sky
I shall darken above you;
And I shall bring darkness upon your land
        —declares the Lord GOD.

After such celestial convulsions, "they"—presumably everyone, but especially those having endured faithfully to the end (Mark 13:13b)—"will see 'the Son of Man coming in clouds' with great power and glory" (13:26). This is Mark's second prediction of the advent of the Son of Man (see 8:38; 14:62; also table 12), an apocalyptic figure at least as old as Daniel (7:13-14; *ad loc.* 8:38). Mark 13:26-27 offers the most detailed presentation of this Son of Man.

Table 14: *The Apocalyptic Son of Man in Mark*

Mark 8:38	*Mark 13:26-27*	*Mark 14:62*
...	And then they will see	And you will
the Son of Man will be ashamed of him	the Son of Man (AT)	see the Son of Man
when he comes	coming in the clouds	coming with the clouds of heaven
in the glory of his Father with the holy angels	with great power and glory; and then he will send the angels, and they will gather together the elect out of the four winds from earth's bound unto heaven's bound	seated to the right of power

---

In none of these predictions does Jesus explicitly identify himself as the Son of Man, though Mark probably intends that identification (see 2:10, 28; 9:9, 12). Common to all three is the affirmation that "the Son of Man will come." From there they diverge in emphasis: 8:38, the contrast of shame and glory; 14:62, power; and 13:26-27, the elect's reclamation. Mark

13:26-27 conflates elements in 8:38 ("angels," "glory") or 14:62 ("see," "clouds," "power"). The second clause of 13:27, pertaining to the angels' commission, appears in neither 8:38 nor 14:62. That clause unlocks the function of this second prediction: amid terrible stress a supervisory Son of Man and his messengers will rescue God's elect. From the four winds to heaven and earth's farthest bounds (cf. Deut 13:7; 30:3-4), none so chosen shall be lost: a pervasive biblical hope (see Isa 11:1, 16; Ezek 39:25-29; Zech 10:6-12; 2 Bar. 5:5-9; 1 Thess 4:15-17). As in previous segments verses 24-27 balance horror and encouragement.

To this point Jesus' response to a question of "the sign" (Mark 13:4b) has been fourfold:

Table 15a: *The Structure of Jesus' Address in Mark 13*

A. General earthly calamities to be experienced by all (vv. 6-8)

B. Particular earthly calamities to be experienced by believers (vv. 9-13)

C. Particular human responses to the calamitous great tribulation (vv. 14-23)

D. Particular supernatural responses to the great tribulation (vv. 24-27)

This arrangement displays great care. Jesus does not speak of random signs or troubles. Instead he advances from familiar, abstract disturbances—which are but the beginning of the world's labor contractions (vv. 6-8)—through more intense, personal suffering (vv. 9-13) that culminates in breathtaking, cosmic turbulence (vv. 24-27). At 13:27 this speech reaches its emotional climax. From there until its end, the address proceeds with quieter caution. Doubtless this literary arrangement reflects one of Mark's theological convictions: the need for Christians to remain calm under eschatological pressure.

In 13:4 the disciples ask two questions. After a pointed caution (v. 5), Jesus answers the second (vv. 6-27). In verses 28-37 it remains for him to address the first: "When will this be?" That reply is in two parts, extending the topical arrangement of verses 6-27:

Table 15b: *The Structure of Jesus' Address in Mark 13 (continued)*

E. Predictable imminence and assurance of the time (vv. 28-31)

F. Unpredictable suddenness and ignorance of the time (vv. 32-37)

Reliable Imminence (13:28-31) and the Unknowable Time (13:32-36): "Watch" (13:37)

The address ends as percussively as it began: "Watch" (v. 37 KJV, recalling v. 5: "Beware"). As in Mark 9:42-50 and 11:22-25, the reader detects in 13:28-37 counsels on discipleship that are linked by key words: "these things" (vv. 29, 30); "pass away" (30, 31); "doors" (or "gates," NRSV) and "doorkeepers" (vv. 29, 34); and "beware," "watch," or "keep awake" (vv. 33, 34, 35, 37). Mark may have drawn on traditions in which these links had been forged. In any case they provide the Evangelist's audience subliminal points of thematic coherence.

As noted at 11:12-14 (*ad loc.*) figs and fig trees are common biblical images for the imminence or certainty of God's judgment of a religiously sterile Israel. Previously in Mark (11:12-14, 20-21), a fig tree was associated with judgment on the temple. In 13:28a Jesus invites his disciples to "learn the parable from the fig tree" (AT). Common to both 11:12-14 and 13:28 is not only a fig tree but the correlation of its leaves or branches with a certain season (*kairos*, 11:13b), interpreted eschatologically. When fig leaves appear, summer is near. When disciples witness the things that build to a climax in 13:6-27, something or someone is "near, at the very gates" (v. 29). Exactly who or what might be near is vague. (The implied subject in the verb *estin* could be a person or a thing.) The primary point in 13:28-31 is reliable imminence. Jesus underlines this with prophetic emphasis: "Truly I tell you [see also 9:1; 11:23; 12:43], this generation will not pass away until all these things have taken place" (v. 30). In 8:12 Jesus was equally emphatic that "this generation" would not receive a sign, but there he was speaking to faithless adversaries. Here, addressing anxious disciples, he speaks of signs (13:22) whose import properly orders their perception. Verse 31 drives home reassurance: though heaven and earth pass away, his promise is enduring and dependable.

There is an immediate qualification (vv. 32-36): the precise time is unknowable but will be unpredictably sudden. "That day" (v. 32) harks back to "the day of the LORD" (Isa 2:12; Jer 46:10; Amos 5:18-20; Zeph 1:14-18); "that hour" refers to God's appointed time for consummating the age (cf. Dan 8:17-19). Only God knows that day and that hour, unseen by the angels and even "the Son" (the only occurrence in Mark of Jesus' simplest self-reference; cf. Matt 11:27 = Luke 10:22). A concluding parable illustrates caution (Mark 13:34-36): a person may leave home, leaving slaves (*douloi*) in charge and his doorkeeper on watch. None knows exactly when "the master of the house" will return, but all must stay awake: whether at evening, midnight, cockcrow (three in the morning), or dawn—the four nocturnal watches of Rome's *vigilies urbani* (police or firefighters; Dio Cassius, *Roman History* 55.8). The moral: "Watch, stay alert: for you do not know when the time [*kairos*] is" (Mark 13:33 AT; cf. Matt 25:1-30; Luke 12:35-46; Rom 13:11-14; 1 Thess 5:1-11). By inquiring when these things will be (Mark 13:4a), the disciples have not asked the truly important question. It is not a matter of identifying the season or clocking the hour. These are indeterminate. The substantive issue is discerning, vigilant discipleship in the meantime. Jesus' final word is addressed not merely to four disciples but to all: "Keep awake" (*grēgoreite*, v. 37; see Geddert 1989).

Recent investigations of Mark 13:1-37 bespeak modern scholars' attempts to reconstruct a traditional source on which this
chapter has been based, or its precise historical context (both
summarized in Balabanski 1997, 55-134). Such questions, while
interesting, miss Mark's emphases just as much as the disciples'
queries in 13:4. There are three main points of stress.

(a) Considered *christologically,* this chapter is fascinating.
Nowhere else in Mark does Jesus speak at such length, with such
authority and empathy toward his disciples, about "the last
things." Many aspects of the address remain obscure—in some
cases necessarily so (vv. 32-33)—yet much is surprisingly clear.
Even the parables in verses 28-29 and 34-36 are not confounding
riddles (cf. 3:23-30) but homely illustrations of critical issues. It
is as though Mark knew that, already in the mid-first century,
there was enough speculative, apocalyptic claptrap in circulation
that corrective clarity was called for.

Jesus' authority is revealed not merely by the fact that after
13:4 he is the only speaker, but also by his repetitive exhorta-
tions, predictions, commissions, and pronouncements. On the
other hand, Mark lays Jesus' credibility on the line in verse 31 (a
prediction that, on its face, could be disproved over time) and
stresses the limit of the Son's knowledge (v. 32). Recalling 12:35-
37, Mark draws the Son into closest alignment with the Father,
while preserving a distinction between them (see 2:7-9; 10:18;
12:29, 32; 14:36).

Chapter 13 is a dress rehearsal for the Passion Narrative
(chapters 14–15). In both segments the reader encounters common themes: abrogation of the temple's holiness (13:2, 14a;
15:38), believers "being handed over" to hostile authorities
(13:9, 11-12; 14:11, 41; 15:1, 10, 15), Jesus' prescience of how
matters will unfold (13:23; 14:13-16, 18, 27, 30), "the hour['s]"
approach (13:11, 32; 14:35, 37, 41; 15:33-34), the need for disciples to "watch and stay awake" (13:5, 9, 33-35, 37; 14:35, 37-
38), the importance of prayer (13:18; 14:32, 35, 38, 39), a tension between "flesh" and "spirit" in the moment of trial (13:11,
20; 14:38), and a predicted vision of the coming Son of Man
(13:26; 14:62). The next two chapters will demonstrate how

right Jesus was: "I have already told you everything" (13:23b).

(b) *Eschatologically,* Mark 13 intends to cool apocalyptic fervor rather than raise its temperature. Thus, the teacher's repeated counsels not to be alarmed (v. 7), not to worry (v. 11a), not to be gulled (v. 21); to hold fast under fire (v. 13b), and to trust the Holy Spirit (v. 11b) and God (v. 20) and the Son of Man (vv. 26-27) and Jesus himself (vv. 30-31). A similar calm is conveyed by the speech's clear organization, which offers worried listeners consistent points of orientation while grappling with equivocal circumstances (Black 2001b). Though often distorted, the intent of Mark 13 is not to gin up fanaticism. Rather, its eschatological perspective performs two functions vital for the beleaguered. First, it locates what they are enduring, and its geopolitical causes, on a panoramic canvas. Everyday reality is not denied; it is grounded in a comprehensive scriptural vision. Second, a healthy eschatology offers counsel against despair and stimulus for hope in the Lord to whom final victory belongs. Such things may not register among many North American Christians, cushioned by law and custom, to worship without fear. In countries like China, Saudi Arabia, and the Sudan—where believers have been imprisoned, enslaved, tortured, or executed for publicly expressing Christian faith—Mark 13 would be read with different eyes.

(c) The four disciples ask their teacher for an apocalyptic timetable (vv. 3-4). Jesus gives them something else: a mandate for *faithful discipleship* in excruciating times. The surprise in the Olivet Discourse lies not in its predictions but in its insistence on what Jesus' disciples should do when things fall apart: namely, bearing witness to him (v. 9b), preaching good news to all nations (v. 10), relying on spiritual resources that surpass their own (v. 11), suffering for the gospel's sake (vv. 9a, 12-13), discerning when to stand and when to flee (vv. 9, 11, 15-16), and staying on constant alert when the Lord leaves them (vv. 34-36). All these responsibilities, consistent with Jesus' teaching throughout Mark (6:7-13, 37a-42; 8:6-8; 8:34–9:1; 9:33-50; 10:35-45; 11:22-26), remind the reader that the destiny of the Son of Man and of his followers is inextricably entwined (see Donahue 1983).

HAUNTED: JESUS' FINAL SUFFERING (14:1–15:47)

We come to Jesus' betrayal and arrest (14:1-52), arraignment (14:53–15:15), execution (15:16-41), and burial (15:42-47). So sketched, this segment has all the appeal of a grocery list.

The flesh for these bare bones is something else. Kähler (1964, 80n11) famously typed Mark a Passion Narrative with an extended introduction. Like any caricature, Kähler's was based in reality: the whole of Mark strides to this climax; apart from it the Gospel's first thirteen chapters are unintelligible. Marxsen (1969, 32) opined that Mark composed backward: all the Gospel's thematic roads end at Golgotha. It is as though the Evangelist took as his starting point Paul's witness to the fundaments of the apostolic proclamation (1 Cor 15:3-4), then developed its details into a narrative, advancing to Easter while recapitulating how Jesus had arrived at his ordained destination. Unlike Paul's testimony, Mark's account of Jesus' passion (or "suffering," from the Gk. *paschō*) touches on (14:24) but does not explain the expiatory significance of Jesus' death. Conversely, what Paul's précis lacks is just what Mark stresses: the portentous details leading to Jesus' death (Black 1996).

All of the NT Gospels concentrate on the Passion Narrative. Most likely, Matthew and Luke independently elaborated Mark's framework. Whether the Fourth Gospel knew and used the Second is a more controversial question; still, John is closer to Mark in the Passion Narrative than elsewhere. Table 16 sorts some of the particulars so that Mark's presentation may be better identified.

A musical analogy may clarify the technique in Mark's Passion Narrative: Prokofiev's' suite *Lieutenant Kijé* (1933). Its final movement begins and ends with the same plaintive trumpet call that announced the lieutenant's birth (in the first movement), then interweaves themes that the composer has associated with important moments throughout Kijé's life: his courtship (the second movement), his wedding (the third), and a sleigh ride's exhilaration (the fourth). The suite's last movement, as Kijé goes to his grave, relives the entire story with musical reminiscences that wander in and out of the listener's ear. So it is with Mark's Passion Narrative. Chapters 14 and 15, plus the coda in chapter

Table 16: *The Events of the Passion Narrative in the Four Gospels*

Episode	Matthew	Mark	Luke	John
1. *The Conspiracy against Jesus*	Proximately forecast by Jesus; hatched but temporized by chief priests, elders, and Caiaphas, two days before Passover	Hatched but temporized by chief priests, and scribes, two days before Passover	Hatched by chief priests and scribes, soon before Passover	Hatched by chief priests, Pharisees, Sanhedrin, and Caiaphas, after the raising of Lazarus
2. *Jesus' Anointing*	On the head, by a woman, at Bethany in the house of Simon the leper; indignation of the disciples	On the head, by a woman, at Bethany in the house of Simon the leper; some were indignant	[*Cf. 7:36-50:* On the feet, by a woman who was a sinner, at the home of Simon the Pharisee; Simon slently indignant]	On the feet, by Lazarus's sister Mary, in Bethany, six days before Passover; Judas was indignant
3. *Judas's Collusion*	Strikes a deal with the chief priests, for thirty pieces of silver	Strikes a deal with the chief priests, with their promise of money	Under Satan's sway, strikes a deal with the chief priests and temple captains, with their promise of money	Under the devil's sway
4. *Preparation for the Passover*	After their inquiry, Jesus instructs the disciples to prepare the Passover at the home of a certain man	After their inquiry, Jesus dispatches two disciples to prepare the Passover in the upper room of a householder	Jesus, initiating preparations, dispatches Peter and John to ready the Passover in the upper room of a householder	[Passover is not yet at hand: see John 18:28]

Episode	Matthew	Mark	Luke	John
5. Response to the Prediction of the Twelve's Defection	Judas: "Surely not I, Rabbi?" Jesus: "You have said so."	The disciples: "Surely not I?"	General questioning among the disciples	Simon and the Beloved Disciple press for an answer; Jesus triggers Judas's exit from the table
6. Institution of the Supper	Bread; cup	Bread; cup	Cup; bread [+ cup after supper, in a large number of variant texts]	[No words of institution; Jesus washes the disciples' feet]
7. Prophecy of Peter's Denial	After singing a hymn, en route to the Mount of Olives	After singing a hymn, en route to the Mount of Olives	During the supper, in the course of Jesus' final instructions to the disciples	During the supper, in the course of Jesus final instructions and lengthy farewell to the disciples
8. Jesus with His Disciples	Gethsemane: Jesus' anguish and the disciples' sleep	Gethsemane: Jesus' anguish and the disciples' sleep	Gethsemane: Jesus' anguish, the ministering angel, the disciples sleep	Jesus and the disciples across the Kidron Valley; neither Gethsemane, Jesus' agony, nor the disciples' sleep described
9. The Posse's Arrest of Jesus	Judas, with a crowd from the chief priests and elders	Judas, with a crowd from the chief priests, scribes, and elders	Judas, a crowd, the chief priests, captains of the temple, and elders	Judas, Roman soldiers, officers of the chief priests, and the Pharisees
10. A Jewish Interrogation	Nocturnal trial by the Sanhedrin; some agreement in false testimony	Nocturnal trial by the Sanhedrin; no agreement in false testimony	Nocturnal stay at high priest's house; diurnal trial by Sanhedrin	Nocturnal questioning by Annas, who hands Jesus over to Caiaphas

Episode	Matthew	Mark	Luke	John
11. *Peter's Denial*	With some variation in detail, all four Gospels agree that Jesus is denied by Peter in the court of the high priest's house.			
12. *Jesus Is Mocked*	By the Sanhedrin	By the Sanhedrin	By his captors	By the Roman officer
13. *Charges Brought against Jesus*	Ability to destroy the temple; "Are you the Christ, the Son of God?"	Threatened destruction of the temple; "Are you the Christ, the Son of the Blessed One?"	"If you are the Christ...", "Are you the Son of God?"	Jesus questioned about his teaching
14. *Jesus' Response*	"You have said so."	"I am."	"You won't believe..."	"I have spoken openly..."
15. *The Verdict*	Blasphemy; sentenced to death	Blasphemy; sentenced to death	Sufficient testimony	"A criminal" (18:30)
16. *Referral to Roman Jurisdiction*	To Pilate	To Pilate	To Pilate	To Pilate
17. *Fate of Judas*	Self-inflicted death by hanging		[Death from a fall: Acts 1:18]	
18. *Pilate's Question and Jesus' Response*	All four Gospels agree that Pilate asks Jesus, "Are you the King of the Jews?" Jesus answers (in the Synoptics), "You say so" / (in John), "You say that I am a king."			
19. *Referral to Galilean Jurisdiction*			To Herod Antipas	
20. *Offer of a Prisoner's Release*	All four Gospels agree that, given the choice, the crowd prefers to have the insurrectionist Barabbas released instead of Jesus.			
21. *Pilate's Response; His Audience's Response*	Pilate washes his hands; "His blood be on us..."			

Episode	Matthew	Mark	Luke	John
22. *Treatment of Barabbas and Jesus*	Pilate releases Barabbas; Jesus is flogged	Pilate releases Barabbas; Jesus is flogged	Pilate releases Barabbas; no flogging of Jesus	[Implied release of Barabbas;] Jesus is flogged
23. *Jesus Mocked as King of the Jews*	By the Roman soldiers	By the Roman soldiers	By Herod and his soldiers [see #19]	By the Roman soldiers
24. *The Way to the Cross*	Simon of Cyrene carries Jesus' cross	Simon of Cyrene carries Jesus' cross; Jesus	Simon of Cyrene carries Jesus' cross; Jesus addresses the "Daughters of Jerusalem"	No mention of Simon of Cyrene; Jesus carries his own cross
25. *The Crucifixion*	All four Gospels agree that Jesus is crucified between two others and that the soldiers cast lots for Jesus' garments.			
26. *Jesus' Last Words from the Cross*	"My God, my God, why have you forsaken me?"	"My God, my God, why have you forsaken me?"	["Father, forgive them, for they do not know"; omitted from some textual witnesses] "Today you will be with me in Paradise." "Father, into your hands I commend my spirit."	"Woman, here is your son." "I am thirsty." "It is finished."
27. *A Soldier's Response*	Centurion: "Truly this man was God's Son."	Centurion: "Truly this man was God's Son."	Centurion: "Certainly this man was innocent [or 'righteous']."	One of the soldiers pierces Jesus' side.

Episode	Matthew	Mark	Luke	John
28. *Present at the Crucifixion*	Women from Galilee, watching from a distance: Mary Magdalene, Mary the mother of James and Joseph, and the mother of the sons of Zebedee	Women from Galilee, watching from a distance: Mary Magdalene, Mary the mother of James the younger and of Joses, and Salome	Women from Galilee, watching from a distance	Women at the cross: Jesus' mother, and his mother's sister, Mary the wife of Clopas, Mary Magdalene; also the Beloved Disciple
29. *The Burial of Jesus*	All four Gospels agree that Jesus was buried in a *new* tomb [not explicit in Mark] by Joseph of Arimathea [also by Nicodemus in John]. The Synoptics agree that those who were last at the tomb were the women.			

16, are haunted by reminders of everything in this Gospel that has gone before. If one pays close attention to *how* Mark tells his tale, one is best positioned to understand *what* Mark is driving at.

Unfolding according to Plan (14:1-52)

From the beginning Mark has emphasized that nothing in Jesus' story has happened by accident or blind fate. Israel's Scriptures have provided the template (e.g., 1:2-3, 11; 6:14-50; 11:17; 12:1-11). All the NT's authors believed that Jesus' advent as the Messiah was in accordance with the Scriptures (9:12-13; 1 Cor 2:6-16; Eph 1:3-14). God has been the unseen agent governing all things to divine ends, with the unwitting collusion of human subjects (*ad loc.* 8:31; 10:33-34; 13:7, 10). "[Such stories as Mark recounts] locate us in the very midst of the great story and plot of all time and space, and therefore relate us to the great dramatist and storyteller, God himself" (Wilder 1964, 57). Contrary to appearances, the end of Jesus' life is no tragedy. The gospel receives its warrant from God, whose will cannot be trumped and whose providence is impossible for mortals to overturn. With the crucial exception of Jesus, the story's human characters are incapable of recognizing the divine intent in those events in which they participate. None is a mere marionette, twitching from puppet strings: Peter (14:29, 31) and the high priest (14:63-64) and Pilate (15:15) believe themselves in control. Yet their perspective on the divine vista is foreshortened, unreliable, and dim. The reader, beneficiary of the Evangelist's guidance, can better interpret what is really happening. That advantage creates the condition for appreciating the deep irony in Mark's narrative: characters acting and speaking in ways profoundly correct, or sometimes incorrect, without recognizing their significance. The entire Gospel is punctuated by such irony; at its climax, it crashes in relentless waves. So forceful is this ironic intensity that at times it may seem too much to bear.

A Noble Act amidst Treachery (14:1-11)

The Second Evangelist is a master of narrative placement: the right episode positioned at the story's most powerful point. Luke placed the legend of Jesus' anointing at a point early in his account of Jesus' ministry (7:36-50; see table 16 #2). Why did Mark tell this story just here, prefaced by a note that it was two days before the feasts of Passover and Unleavened Bread (14:1)? The likeliest answer: Mark bookends his account of Jesus' final days with stories about *his disciples' reaction* to them. If one considers the juxtaposition of this narrative segment's beginning (14:1-11) with its end (15:40–16:8), the method is plain: from start to finish the Evangelist is making a statement about preparations for Jesus' burial (14:8; 16:1), contrasting the conduct of faithful women (14:3; 15:40-41, 47) with that of the feckless Twelve (14:10, 50, 66-72).

The Anointing of Jesus (14:3-9) and Conspiracy for His Arrest (14:1-2, 10-11)

At 14:1-11 Mark enfolds the anointing of Jesus (14:3-9) within a conspiracy for his arrest (14:1-2, 10-11; see table 2). This narrative sandwich creates a series of simultaneous contrasts, pointing up complementary aspects.

- Both stories are introduced by reference to a banquet (vv. 1a, 3), a customary occasion for conviviality that is marked here by turbulence (vv. 1b, 4).
- The chief priests and scribes proceed by stealth (v. 1b); the dinner attended by Jesus is a public affair (v. 4a).
- The temple hierarchy (v. 1b) may stand in contrast with "the house of Simon the leper" (v. 3; see table 16 #2). So identifying the host reminds us that, to the end, Jesus traffics with those on society's margins.
- An unnamed woman (v. 3) does for Jesus "a beautiful thing" (v. 6 AT) for which she suffers others' reproach (v. 5b). Immediately afterward, Judas (by name) commits treachery with murderous authorities (vv. 2a, 10), gladdening their hearts (v. 11a).

- Both scenes play upon money: the extraordinary cost of the woman's ointment (v. 3), used in honor of Jesus; the bribe promised Judas for Jesus' betrayal (v. 11).
- The woman's public anointing of Jesus' head (see table 16 #2) suggests royal acclamation (cf. Judg 9:8; 1 Sam 15:1; 16:3, 12; 1 Kgs 1:34; 19:16). The only times in Mark when Jesus is addressed by others as "king" are at his trial (15:2, 9, 12, 18) and execution (15:26, 32)—the point to which machinations are driving (14:1, 10).
- Jesus' interpretation of his anointing is that of preparing his body for burial (v. 8). The chief priests collude with a traitorous disciple to expedite his teacher into the grave.
- Both stories end in poignant irony. Though the reader never learns the name of the woman who did "what she could" (v. 8), Jesus declares that what she has done will be remembered wherever the gospel is preached (v. 9). Because of Mark, it has been. Judas also did what he could. For that, neither has he ever been forgotten.

Mark sets the clock at "two days before the Passover" (14:1a). If one counts forward from the temporal indications in 11:1, 12, and 20, the events now narrated occur on Jesus' fourth day in Jerusalem. Two days prior to Passover would have been Wednesday, 13 Nisan (March–April), which was and remains the annual celebration of God's liberation of Israel from captivity (Exod 12:1–13:16). The Passover feast was conjoined with the seven-day harvest festival of Unleavened Bread (2 Chr 35:17; Ezek 45:21-24). In spite of the priests' and scribes' concern that it not occur during the festival (14:2), Jesus' arrest does occur on Passover evening in Mark (14:12-50). Mark's association of Passover with the religious leaders' scheming intimates another irony: Passover is Israel's signal remembrance of its freedom from foreign oppression. In Mark as in all the Gospels (esp. Luke 23:12; John 19:15), this Passover will be remembered for its shotgun wedding of Israel's hierarchy with their Roman overlords because of a perceived need to destroy Jesus.

The appearance of malicious scribes and chief priests (Mark 14:1b) is no surprise (cf. 3:6; 8:31; 11:18; 12:12). Nor is Judas Iscariot's presence a shock (14:10; cf. 3:19a), though the Evangelist never explains why or exactly what he betrayed. The most mysterious figure in 14:1-11 is the woman. Who is she? Why does she do what she does, in the manner detailed?

The interpreter's problem is twofold: one knows too much that is irrelevant to Mark's narrative and too little that is pertinent. Like the so-called "rich young ruler"—an amalgam supported by none of the Gospels (cf. Mark 10:17-23; Matt 19:16-20; Luke 18:18-30)—in popular religious imagination the woman who anointed Jesus has become compounded of aspects from all four Gospels without exactly resembling any of them (see table 16 #2). In Mark 14:3-9 this woman is anonymous. She is an object of reproach not because she is presumed to be louche (cf. Luke 7:37) but because of the wealth her onlookers think she is squandering (vv. 4-5).

Though elite women in antiquity may have welcomed guests to their households by showering them with gifts, that evidence is spotty and better attested for fifth-century B.C.E. Greek homes than for their first-century C.E. Jewish counterparts (Sawicki 2001). An *alabastron* was a small glass bottle with a stopper; *myron nardou,* an ointment or perfume extracted from the vegetable oil spikenard. The implements of Jesus' anointing are vaguely erotic or could have registered as such: an *alabastron* figures in the sexual politics of Aristophanes' *Lysistrata* (ll. 937-58); *myron* appears to have been a conventional gift among Greek lovers (Esth 2:12; Song 3:6; 5:5); spikenard arouses inamorati in the Song of Songs (1:12; 4:13, 14). Mark makes nothing of such connotations, though these details might suggest another contrast: the woman's affection and Judas's defection. The unguent is *pistikēs,* variously translated as "liquid" (Goodspeed), "unadulterated" (Cassirer), and "pure" (RSV, NEB, NIV). (The NRSV punts by offering no translation of it whatever.) Like *pistis, pistikēs* probably derives from the Greek root *peithō,* which carries such connotations as "faithful," "convincing," or "durable." This balm is expensive: its estimated value, over three hundred denarii, would have covered a day laborer's wages for nearly a full year (*ad loc.* 6:37). Myrrh is associated with death and funerals (15:23): as elsewhere in Mark (1:14; 8:35; 13:9-10), the gospel is embedded in suffering that God's will be done. Defending the woman's gift, Jesus' rejoinder touches on all these aspects. It anticipates his interment (14:8); its value betokens something beautiful (v. 6); what she has done for him will endure in memory (v. 9), like her perfume's pungency. Simultaneous with Jesus' commendation, a member of the Twelve, who ought to be doing for Jesus something beautiful, ensnarls himself in a heinous plot against his teacher (vv. 10-11). Judas's discipleship exhibits no more staying power than will his colleagues' (14:27, 50).

Neither here nor in Mark 10:21 does Jesus dismiss the poor's needs (cf. Deut 15:7-11; Ps 82:3-4; Amos 2:6-7; Jas 2:5-6). He qualifies that imperative, however, by coordinating its practice to primary recognition of himself as the kingdom's herald in a unique time, or *kairos.* Every moral injunction is subject to a deeper awareness of God's intent (3:1-6; 7:1-13; 10:2-9). It is fitting that the bridegroom be so honored, for he is soon to be taken away (2:18-22).

As in the present day, benefaction in antiquity was publicly honored. Rare is the philanthropist who refuses credit for the foundation she has established or for the buildings he has funded. Mark 14:1-11 upsets the way its audience evaluates fame. Bethany's most generous of women has never been forgotten, although she has remained anonymous.

The woman in Mark 14:3-9 is a spiritual sister of the nameless widow in 12:41-44, who gave her whole living. Not merely are both incredibly generous. The causes to which they have committed themselves—Jerusalem's temple and God's Messiah—will soon appear irretrievably lost (13:1-2; 14:8b). Nor is there the slightest indication that either woman is conscious of the full import of her donation. Both have done what they could (14:8a). In both cases only Jesus can assay the gift's genuine value and interpret it for his followers.

The Last Passover (14:12-31)

Jesus' final meal with the Twelve comprises four balanced vignettes:

> A. The preparation for the feast (vv. 12-16)
> B. Prediction of betrayal (vv. 17-21)
> A.' Instituting the Lord's Supper (vv. 22-26)
> B.' Foretelling the Twelve's desertion (vv. 27-31)

The Preparation for the Feast (14:12-16)

The preparation for the feast raises another of Mark's calendrical anomalies (cf. 14:2). The first day of Unleavened Bread (v. 12; usually 15 Nisan) seems inconsistent with 14 Nisan, when the Passover lamb was sacrificed (Exod 12:1-20; see table 16 #4). At any rate the details unfold intelligibly. The meal's preparations require attention (14:12). Recalling 11:1-7 (ad loc.), the reader needs only a single verse (14:16) to know that all eventuates as Jesus promises his messengers (vv. 13-14). (Seers and water carriers are typically conjoined in the OT: Gen 24:10-21, 42-49; 26:17-33; 1 Sam 9:11.) Down to the finest detail, Jesus displays extraordinary prescience of how his last night will unfold (8:31; 9:31; 10:33-34). Mark's reader is primed to believe Jesus' later predictions (14:17, 27, 30), however objectionable they may strike his closest companions (14:19, 29, 31).

Jesus' Climactic Prediction of Betrayal (14:17-21)

Jesus' decisive announcement occurs after all have taken their places (literally, "were reclining": the customary posture at ancient banquets). Exactly how Jews celebrated Passover in the early first century C.E. is irrecoverable. The Mishnaic tractate Pesahim (Feast of Passover, late second century C.E.) codified the ritual's preparation and procedure as the rabbinic authors believed it ought to have been observed: the serving of seasoned lettuce, unleavened bread, and roasted lamb with nuts, fruits, and bitter herbs; cups of wine served in contemplative sequence, punctuated by the father's explanation of the feast's religious import (*m. Pesaḥ* 10.1-9; Danby, 150-51). Neither Mark nor any of the Gospels offers such details of Jesus' final meal with the Twelve. Borrowing on Israel's thanksgiving for God's redemption, that feast was transmogrified by and for Christians into a theologically cognate yet different commemoration: Jesus' last supper with his followers.

Participants at Passover were reminded that God kept faith with Israel during its Egyptian captivity. What Jesus says in Mark is startling: a promise of faithless betrayal (14:18). *Amēn* ("truly") denotes emphatic prophecy (e.g., 11:23; 12:43; 13:30; 14:9, 25, 30). The wording of Jesus' prediction is without precedent in the Gospel: although he has spoken generally of the Son of Man's betrayal (9:31; 10:33), this is the first time that Jesus has aimed a finger at one of the Twelve (cf. 3:19; 14:10-11).

The finger is pointed—yet no particular identification is made. Of all the Gospels, Mark is less concentrated on Judas's defection (cf. Matt 26:25; Luke 22:3; John 13:21-30), even though it is not denied (see 14:41-42, 44). Likewise, Mark's version of the disciples' reaction stands apart: "They began to be distressed and to ask him, one by one, 'It isn't me [*mēti egō*], is it?'" (14:19 AT; cf. Luke 22:23; John 13:22). That response is ambiguous. It *could* mean as Matthew interprets (26:22): each of the Twelve believed himself capable of betrayal but with rueful reverence hoped otherwise. Alternatively, Mark may be suggesting that each knew himself culpable, potentially or in fact, and fell into grief upon realizing he had been spotted. (The framing of their question in Greek, both in Mark and in Matthew, invites a denial that could be refuted.) Without resolving the question at this time, Jesus leaves open more than one possibility: the suspect is one of the Twelve, who is dipping with him into a dish (14:20). That could be any of them. Some manuscripts render verse 20 as "the one dipping...into the one [and only] dish." The shorter reading has more varied and slightly stronger support; the longer is probably a theological intensification of the treachery involved.

Jesus' charge carries higher social voltage than modern Western audiences might appreciate. The most execrable setting for a trusted confidant to knife his host is at the dinner table: in Eastern culture, the place where associates become family (cf. Ps 41:9). Jesus sums up his allusive yet pointed prophecy by referring to himself as "the Son of Man" who must proceed "as it has been written about him" (14:21 AT): a way of expressing the divine purpose that Jesus must suffer for others (8:31; 9:31; 10:33, 45; see table 12). Yoked with that immutable reality are baleful consequences for "that man" (*tō anthrōpō ekeinō*) by whom "the Son of Man" (*ho huios tou anthrōpou*) is betrayed. God's will provides no excuse for human evil. Mark makes no attempt to square the interactive circle of divine and human agency. Nevertheless, culpability rests on the betrayer's shoulders, so much so that it would have been by far finer for such a one never to have been born. As in 9:42-50, so here: adherence to Jesus is a serious business, and default carries catastrophic cost.

The Institution of the Lord's Supper (14:22-26)

Allusion to Passover (v. 22) slides into the institution of the Lord's Supper (14:22-26). Jesus has already presided over two other banquets (6:31-44; 8:1-10); there (6:41; 8:6), as here (14:22), his actions are similar: he "took, blessed, broke, and gave" bread (*arton,* in all cases). What he has done for the multitudes he now does for the Twelve (see table 6). On this occasion there are important differences. Here Jesus identifies a loaf with his body (*to sōma*), which they are to take at his offering. In Greek, as in English, the body is a flexible metaphor: "my personality" or "my essential selfhood" may capture some of the nuances here (cf. 1 Cor 10:17). Some Aramaicists judge that the term *guphî* (myself) functioned similarly in Jesus' native tongue (Cranfield 1959, 426; cf. Bultmann 1951, 194: "man does not *have* a *sōma*; he *is* sōma"). Earlier Jesus has spoken of his self-sacrifice for many (10:45); now it is specially focused for the sake of his followers—the very ones just implicated in his betrayal.

That sacrifice is elaborated. Predictably at Passover, Jesus gives thanks over a cup and gives it to all his companions to drink (14:23). Unpredictably, he associates its contents with "my blood [*to haima mou*] of the covenant, which is poured out for many" (v. 24). This resonates with Jesus' characterization of the Son of Man's service as a giving of his life that others may be freed (10:45). At this supper those beneficiaries are his disciples, though not to others' exclusion. Ratifying covenants with shed blood is a classic OT practice (Exod 24:6-8; Zech 9:11; see Ossom-Batsa 2001). The issue is not one of "God's bloodthirstiness," which misunderstands Jewish sacrificial practice. "For the life of all flesh—its blood is its life" (Lev. 17:14a NJPS): the blood of the sacrificial animal serves as a proxy for the worshipers' lives, rendered to their Creator and Sustainer (Lev 1:1–7:37; 16:1-34; Mark 11:12-25 *ad loc.*). In 14:24 Jesus' blood is identified with "the covenant" (or, in a less likely reading probably dependent on 1 Cor 11:25 and Luke 22:20, "the *new* covenant"; cf. Jer 31:31). Jesus identifies himself—his *sōma*, his *haima*—with the Passover sacrifice (cf. 1 Cor 5:7b). His sacrifice is free flowing, "poured out" (*ekchynnomenon*) in the same manner that the woman in Bethany lavished on him her fragrant ointment (*katecheen*: 14:3). The sacrifice is imminent: with prophetic insistence ("*Amēn* I say to you": v. 25), Jesus assures them that this is his last taste of the vine's fruit until drinking it anew in the eschatological age, sometimes envisioned as a magnificent banquet (1 Chr 12:38-40; Isa 25:6-8; Matt 22:1-4). On that somber, hopeful note, they sing a hymn and depart for the Mount of Olives (14:26; cf. 11:1; 13:3).

Jesus' Final Prediction of the Twelve's Desertion (14:27-31)

Passover's celebration (14:22-26) closes the circuit opened with its preparation (vv. 12-16). Jesus' final prediction of the Twelve's desertion (14:27-31) locks the foretelling of his betrayal (vv. 17-21). Mark 14:27a clarifies what 14:18 implied: all the Twelve will "desert" or "stumble" or "fall away" (*skandalisthēsesthe*)—just as the rootless fold under pressure (4:17), as his countrymen have been offended by him (6:3c), and as disciples are in perpetual jeopardy of doing (9:42-43, 45, 47). In 14:27b a quotation from Zechariah 13:7b (LXX) drives the message home. Rocky soil is not fertile because it cannot withstand hardship (4:16-17). One such "rock"—Peter (*petros*, 3:16), the Twelve's customary spokesman (8:29, 32-33; 9:5; 10:28; 11:21)—twice repudiates Jesus' prediction of his threefold defection before the cock has twice crowed that very night (14:29-31a). Peter's peers join with him in a third, equally strong repudiation of this prophecy (14:31b). Jesus holds fast to his forecast, promising his own postmortem fidelity in Galilee (14:28; cf. 16:7). The mind reels at entwined ironies past and to come: Jesus' injunction that his followers must deny themselves (8:34); their precipitate refutation of their imminent denials of Jesus; Jesus' denial of himself—his giving of his own life—out of enduring loyalty to those who will presently prove traitorous.

Mark 14:1-31 encapsulates much of the Gospel's entire theology. *Theologically*—as conveyed through Scripture—all proceeds, as it must, by God's ordination (14:21, 27). *Christologically*, Jesus reveals himself perfectly prescient and aligned with that plan, awful though reliable it be (14:8-9, 13-15, 18-21, 27, 30). *Soteriologically*, the goal of Jesus' self-sacrifice is freedom for others (14:24). While neither accented, as does Paul (Rom 3:21-26), nor explicated in Hebrews' detail (8:1–10:39), Mark holds the view of Jesus' death as a liberating atonement for sin. *Anthropologically*, in 14:21 the Evangelist balances on a razor's edge the convergence of divine will with human responsibility. By asserting both without dissolving one into the other, Mark maintains their unfathomable interaction. *Ecclesially*, Jesus' adherents prove themselves motley in discipleship. In matters of smaller consequence, members of the Twelve obey their teacher (14:12-16). At critical junctures they bluster (14:29, 31) or already have conspired to betray him outright (14:10-11). Ironically, the most faithful disciple in this portion of Mark is none of the Twelve, but a nameless woman who does for

Jesus a beautiful thing (14:3-9; cf. 9:38-41). Neither here nor elsewhere does Jesus' fidelity to his followers depend on their faithfulness to him (14:28). *Eschatologically,* Jesus' reminder at supper of the kingdom of God (14:25)—the heart of his preaching in Mark (1:14-15; 4:11, 26-32; 10:14-25; 12:34)—recalls chapter 13, casting events to come in an apocalyptic context.

Jesus' words at his last supper are as old as Christian oral tradition (cf. 1 Cor 11:23-25; *Did.* 9.1-5), to which Mark himself was indebted. Once introduced, those words appear to have been locked into Christian liturgy with regional variations. Most early Christians veered away from the Synoptics' presentation by disjoining the supper from Jewish Passover (Jeremias 1966, 40-88). The wording of the supper's liturgy and its more frequent observance indicate that Christians fast transformed a rite of Jewish origin into a ritual distinctly their own. To this day Jewish celebration of Passover does more than recount a critical moment in Israel's history; that event of divine deliverance is reinstantiated in the community's life: "Blessed art thou, O Lord our God, king of the universe, who has kept us alive, and sustained us, and enabled us to reach this season" (Glatzer 1996, 21). Likewise, in Mark the remembrance of Jesus' self-identification with the bread and the cup revivifies the teacher's covenantal pledge to pour himself out for many. "[Jesus] has been remembered in the certainty that he remained exactly what he had been [in his mortal life]" (Dahl, 1976, 28).

Anguish, Arrest, and Abandonment (14:32-52)

Just as the supper has been framed by corresponding presentations of Jesus' fidelity (14:22-25, 30) and the disciples' incipient defection (14:10-11, 27, 29-31), the story of his apprehension (14:43-49) is enclosed by contrasting depictions of Jesus' torment (14:32-42) and his followers' fecklessness (14:50-52). The Evangelist heightens the tension of Jesus' arrest by concentrating the reader's attention on how Jesus and the Twelve *react* to it. The contrast could not be sharper.

Gethsemane (14:32-42)

The scene shifts to Gethsemane (14:32-42), a "place" at Olivet (14:26). (Only John [18:1] identifies the area as a garden across from the Kidron Valley.) Its location is unknown; many archaeologists situate it on the slope of the Mount of Olives, above the road running from Bethany (14:3) to Jerusalem. In Hebrew and Aramaic *Gethsemane* may be translated as "oil press." The area may have been cultivated for its olives, whose oil was extracted for sale. On the evening of Jesus' capture no fruit was strained— but he was.

Jesus' purpose in bringing them here is to pray (14:32): an activity in which he is regularly engaged, usually in "lonely places" (1:35; 6:41; 8:6), and about which he has taught (11:23-25; 13:18). Neither in 14:38 nor anywhere in Mark are the Twelve shown at prayer (cf. 9:28-29). As elsewhere (5:37; 9:2; 13:3) Jesus invites Peter, James, and John to remain with him, "to keep awake" (*grēgoreite*: 14:34)—just as he instructed them during a previous visit to Olivet (13:33, 35, 37). The motivation for Jesus' prayer in Gethsemane is deep anguish, detailed at great length: he begins to be utterly dismayed and distressed, in deep grief (*perilypos*; more enveloping than the Twelve's disturbance [*lypeisthai*] in 14:19) and with a soul troubled unto death (vv. 33-34; cf. Pss 42:5, 11; 43:5). Removing himself from them, Jesus prays that, if possible, he might be delivered from "the hour" (*hōra* [14:35], whose eschatological quality surfaced in 13:11, 32). Only here in Mark (14:36a), and nowhere in the other Gospels, Jesus addresses his petition to God as *Abba*: in Aramaic, an intimate form for "Father" (translated by Mark for the reader; cf. 5:41; 7:11, 34). "For you all things are possible": a reminder of Jesus' teaching to the epileptic child's father (9:23) and to the Twelve (10:27; 11:23). The petition is pointed— "Divert this cup from me" (14:36b AT; evocative of the cup from which Jesus must drink [10:38b])—yet qualified: "Yet, not what I want, but what you want" (14:36c). Jesus' request is contextualized by insistent trust that God's will must finally override all others' (see 11:22, 24). Jesus repeats this prayer (14:39), perhaps twice (14:41). Though not the last (15:34), this is the first time that Mark permits us to overhear a prayer by Jesus; nowhere else are the utterances so insistent.

Interrupting his prayer, three times Jesus returns to his waiting trio; each time he finds them asleep (14:37a, 40a, 41a) when they ought to have been awake and watching (vv. 37-38a), as the servants and doorkeeper in Jesus' parable are expected to stay alert for their master's return (13:33-37). Jesus chastises Simon for being unable to stay awake even for an hour (14:37), exhorting him to beware "the time of trial" (v. 38a). An eager spirit (*pneuma*), which Peter has just expressed (v. 29), is no match for human weakness ("flesh" [*sarx*], v. 38b; cf. Isa 40:6). On his second return Jesus finds them still asleep, not knowing what to say (14:40; cf. 9:6). The third and last time Jesus chastises their continued rest, announcing that "the hour" has arrived for the Son of Man to be betrayed into sinners' hands (14:41). The time for fortifying prayer has passed: they are roused from slumber to go with him to meet his betrayer (14:42). The tripartite structure—three long prayers by Jesus with three returns to somnolent disciples—is a familiar storytelling technique. Here, for the first time in his Gospel, Mark employs it to dramatize Jesus' dark night of the soul and his intimates' incapacity to support him in its awful duration. These three, and by implication all of the Twelve, have already begun to fall away from their teacher, just as he foretold (14:27).

To this point in Mark, Jesus has responded with compassion to those in terrible distress. At Gethsemane, Jesus *enacts* the grief that others have displayed. One may compare, in table 17, Mark's intercalated tales of Jairus's daughter (5:21-24a, 35-43) and the hemorrhaging woman (5:24b-34).

By correlating Jesus and Jairus, hemorrhaging woman and dead child and crucified Messiah, Mark suggests that physical torment and spiritual anguish, flesh and spirit (14:38), are different dimensions of an interconnected whole, which humans can alleviate but only a loving God—"*Abba*, Father"—can finally restore (Rom 8:15; Gal 4:6).

Table 17: *Four Sufferers in Mark: Jairus, His Daughter, the Menorrhagic Woman, Jesus*

Narrative Element	5:21-24a, 35-43	5:24b-34	14:32-42
1. *Jesus' shift in location*	v. 21 (sea crossing)	v. 24b (following Jairus)	v. 32 (to Gethsemane)
2. *Presence of "children"*	vv. 39-40 (Jairus's child)		vv. 40-41 [cf. 10:24, *tekna*]
3. *Peter, James, and John*	v. 37		vv. 42-43
4. *Obtuseness*	v. 40a (mourners' laughter)	v. 31 (disciples' protest)	vv. 34, 37-38, 41 (slumber)
5. *Hopelessness*	vv. 23a, 35 [[near] death]	vv. 25-26 (incessant bleeding)	v. 34a (grieved unto death)
6. *Fear*	v. 36 (Jairus: *phobou*)	v. 33 (the woman: *phobētheisa*)	v. 33 (Jesus)
7. *Falling to the ground*	v. 22 (Jairus: *piptei*)	v. 33 (the woman: *prosepesen*)	v. 35 (Jesus: *epipten*)
8. *Familial language*	v. 23 ("little daughter")	v. 34 ("daughter")	v. 36 (" *Abba*, Father")
9. *Plea for relief*	v. 23b	vv. 27-28	vv. 36, 39, 41
10. *Perception of the way forward*	v. 26 (Jesus' encouragement)	vv. 28, 33a	[8:31; 9:31; 10:33-34]
11. *Withdrawal and advance*	vv. 38a, 40 (mourners/Jairus)	vv. 32, 33b (the woman)	vv. 36, 41-42 (Jesus)
12. *Apocalyptic ambience*	vv. 41-42 ("get up")	v. 34 ("peace")	vv. 36 ("cup"), 41 ("hour")

And immediately they led [a Jewish martyr] to the wheel, and while his vertebrae were being dismembered upon it he saw his own flesh ripped around and drops of blood flowing from his entrails. When he was about to die he said, "We, you most abominable tyrant, suffer these things for our godly training and virtue; but you, for your impiety and bloodthirstiness, will endure unceasing tortures." (4 Macc 10:8-11 AT; see also 11:9-12, 20-27; 16:25; 17:11-22)

Chastisements are precious. (attributed to Rabbi Akiba in *b. Sanh.* 101a; *b. Ber.* 5a-b)

If Mark's audience expected Jesus to confront his imminent death with equanimous nobility, then the story of Gethsemane is confounding.

Along with the account of his death (15:33-37), Mark 14:32-42 renders with harsh clarity a crisis in Jesus' faith, exposing his distress on the canvas of earlier stories of healing that highlight humans' need for faith. God may be trusted to restore crushed souls, ruptured wombs, breathless bodies—the collapse of social bodies, as well (10:28)—though that restoration take years (5:25), though death be inescapable (5:35), betrayal inevitable (14:41b-42), and afflictions unavoidable this side of the age to come (10:29-30). At Gethsemane, Jesus himself demonstrates what, for Mark, is the sufferer's appropriate response: faith, evinced by prayer, which penetrates anguish. Mark's Jesus is God's Son, as obedient as he is beloved, a little child able to enter the kingdom (10:13-16), the servant of divine sovereignty that none of his disciples proves to be (9:33-37).

Does Jesus' conduct in 14:32-42 flout his earlier teaching about God, for whom nothing is impossible (10:27), and faith-filled prayer to that God (11:22-25)? Some interpreters (see Dowd 1988) find in Mark a paradox acknowledged but never resolved. Others (see Garrett 1998) think the paradox is more apparent than actual: at Gethsemane, Jesus epitomizes "one who in every respect has been tested as we are, yet without sin" (Heb 4:15; see also 5:7-8). Yet Mark never explicitly sides with antiquity's conventional view that suffering teaches obedience, which

God will reward (Prov 3:11-12; Rom 5:3-4; Heb 10:32-34; Jas 1:2-18; 1 Pet 1:6-7; 4:1-19).

A more satisfying exegesis attends to what the Evangelist says—and does not say. Nowhere does Mark suggest that God afflicts mortals to toughen their obedience, refine their faith, or teach them endurance. Contrary to Akiba, chastisements are not precious: God is no punishing agent, and affliction is terrifying. No one in Mark, least of all Jesus, faces death with heroic dignity. At Gethsemane he steadfastly prays to "*Abba,* Father," whose will is acknowledged at that moment when divine mercy is invisible. It is one thing to ask whether God can make a mountain too heavy to lift. The real question is why Jesus *refuses to ask* God to move the mountain that must remain fixed (cf. 11:22-24). Having reached the Passion Narrative, readers can intuit an answer: through prayer, Jesus has become a little child who can lose his life for the gospel (10:15), if God's will demands—for only by doing so can his life, like others', be made whole (8:34-38). At Gethsemane the teacher trusts that what he has received is what he has finally asked for: that God's will be done (14:36; see 11:24). Returning to those who failed him, he does not fault them for their incompetence (14:41-42; see 11:25). Readers of 14:32-42 have not experienced any expansion of humanity's moral and spiritual faculties. Instead, they have been reawakened to what they learned at Caesarea Philippi (8:33-38): only through suffering can they learn discipleship to this Messiah, the Son of Man from whom the cup could not pass and who finally wanted it no other way (Black 2005b).

Jesus' Arrest (14:43-49)

"Immediately, while he was still speaking" (14:43), Judas appears with a mob intent on Jesus' arrest (14:43-50). Verses 42 and 43 create simultaneity, as though Jesus' very utterance has invited the posse onstage. Mark's mention of Judas creates a pivotal link. His presence as "one of the twelve" (v. 43) closes a circuit opened by three other named followers who have defaulted on Jesus in Gethsemane (14:33, 37, 40, 41). Judas appears as leader of a crowd (*ochlos*), a term used in Mark thirty-six times. Throughout the Gospel, Jesus has attracted crowds (4:1; 5:21; 6:34; 7:14, 17; 8:1; 9:14). Occasionally they have proved a hindrance (2:4; 5:24, 27, 31), even threatening (3:9, 20). Sometimes a crowd has intimidated Jesus' adversaries (11:18, 32; 12:12). Mark's crowds are true to life: mobs are naturally fickle. From 14:43 until the Gospel's end, whenever a crowd appears, it will turn against Jesus. Here they are agents of Jerusalem's religious hierarchy, the constituency predicted by Jesus to betray the Son of Man (8:31; 10:33); their carrying of weapons on a feast day is legally dubious, foreshadowing many irregularities that will attend Jesus' trial (14:55-65). In Mark's second half the chief priests are conjoined with scribes as Jesus' mortal enemies (11:18; 14:1); with the elders they issued the first challenge to Jesus' authority in the temple (11:27). As Mark tells it (14:44), the betrayer has prearranged a signal to identify Jesus, as though the posse would not recognize him or might seize the wrong man. Only Mark inserts a curious qualifier to describe Judas's intent: that his teacher be apprehended and led away *asphalōs* (14:44). The Evangelist's intention is not clear, an uncertainty mirrored in various English versions: "under guard" (NIV, GNT, NRSV), "carefully" (Lattimore), "securely" (NAB), and "safely" (KJV, Moffatt, NEB). While Mark has nothing good to say of Judas (3:19a; 14:10), neither does he demonize the disciple (cf. Luke 22:3; John 13:2). Mark may intend that Judas wants the arrest made securely, without slipup. All proceeds as the conspirators prearranged (14:44-46). Identifying the alleged culprit with a kiss is most ironic, since a rabbi would be entitled to receive such affection from a disciple (Prov 27:6; Luke 7:38). "Rabbi" (like *Rabbouni* in 10:51) is one of the few Aramaic terms that Mark does not translate. Evidently he saw no need.

Drawing a sword, an unidentified bystander slices off the ear of the high priest's slave (14:47). This detail provides contrast for Jesus' reminder (14:48-49a) that he could easily have been apprehended while teaching in the temple (cf. 11:27–12:44). Another ironic touch: he is being captured as a would-be "bandit" (*lēstēs*). Jesus is no revolutionist, but he likened those buying and selling in the temple to brigands who hide out in their lair (11:17). That his arrest has been deferred until now is attributed to divine ordination (14:49b). That decree corresponds to this pericope's beginning: the mob's arrival at the moment Jesus has announced, "The hour has come" (14:41-43).

Mark's version of Jesus' arrest differs from the other Evangelists' (Matt 26:47-56a; Luke 22:47-54a; John 18:1-12). In its simple brevity almost as much is said about Judas (14:43-45) as about Jesus (14:46, 48-49): the characteristically Markan touch of using Jesus' conduct as a foil for that of his followers. Even more obvious is Jesus' comparative passivity. After being arrested (14:46), he does nothing save speak of the irony that they have taken him now, not earlier, in fulfillment of Scripture (14:48-49). Mark's portrait of Jesus at his capture recapitulates the outcome in Gethsemane and sets the tone for the rest of the Passion Narrative: having surrendered himself to God's will (14:35-36, 41-42), Jesus no longer asserts himself. Gone is the teacher and healer who has taken the initiative. The three predictions of the Son of Man's destiny (8:31; 9:31; 10:33-34) have placed him entirely at the receiving end of others' actions. From here on, Mark's narrative drives home that stark reality.

His Followers' Abandonment (14:50-52)

After the arrest, Mark could have moved directly to Jesus' trial (thus, Luke 22:54a; John 18:12-13). Because Mark's is as much a story about the disciples as about the teacher, a brief statement of his followers' abandonment (14:50-52) is not surprising. "All of them deserted him and fled" (14:50), as Jesus predicted (14:27) and the trio in Gethsemane have begun to do (14:35a, 37-38, 40-41). Neither Mark nor any of the Evangelists reports that the posse gave chase or attempted to round up Jesus' disciples;

apparently they were not regarded as threats. At 14:51-52 one encounters Mark's most notorious non sequitur: the unnamed young follower who, when seized, tore off naked into the night. What to make of this? Neither Matthew nor Luke nor John includes this anecdote. They probably did not know what to make of it, either. In its immediate context 14:51-52 may best be understood as an elaboration of 14:50: all of Jesus' followers forsook him and fled (Moloney 2002, 299-300). Notice that the young man "was following him," even after his apprehension (v. 51). Mark is preparing the reader for others who temporarily cling to Jesus in defeat—Peter (14:54, 66-72) and the women (15:40-41, 16:1-8)—only to fold under pressure. Naked retreat suggests shame overtaken by panic. Passages like Genesis 39:12 and Amos 2:16 remind one of the humiliation with which Israel regarded public nakedness. Mark 14:50-52 accents the account of Jesus' arrest by sharply contrasting him and his followers: the former demonstrates calm resolve (vv. 48-49); the latter, scattered panic.

◊ ◊ ◊ ◊

Exegetes who strain toward fantastical solutions of the young man's identity in 14:51-52 risk overlooking an obvious possibility: as recounted, sans explanation, the legend is opaque because it is meant to be. "Sufficient doubt about [their] precise application [teases] the mind into active thought," as Dodd observed of Jesus' parables (1961, 5). Mark's is a mysterious story, strangely told: a parabolic Gospel whose comprehension is possible only if pondered comprehensively (cf. 4:34).

"They Will Hand You Over" (14:53–15:32)

This section of the Passion Narrative comprises five scenes. The first three (14:53, 55-65; 14:54, 66-72; 15:1-15) describe trials: two of Jesus, one of Peter. This portion of Mark can be read as a commentary on three predictions that Jesus has made. Two concerned the Son of Man, who must be "handed over into the hands of people" (9:31 AT) and, more explicitly, who must be "handed over to the chief priests and the scribes, [who] will condemn him to death, then handed over to the Gentiles" (10:33 AT). The third prediction referred to Jesus' disciples, who also will be handed over (13:9, 11-12). The key word, obviously, is *paradidōmi*. Usually in the Second Gospel the term is rendered as "betrayal" (13:12; 14:21, 41), specifying Judas as the betrayer (3:19a; 14:10-11, 18, 42, 44). In chapter 15 the word reappears three times with an added nuance: that of the condemned's legal disposition into the hands of his magistrates and executioners (15:1, 10, 15). This nuance is the first the reader encountered in Mark: the beginning of Jesus' preaching "after John the Baptist's handing over" (*paradothēnai*, 1:14 AT). In many ways, of which this is but one expression, the Gospel moves to a conclusion presaged by its introduction. To borrow another of Mark's uses of this term (*paradoi*, 4:29), the fruit is now ripe, though bitter indeed.

The last two scenes of this segment are the soldiers' mockery of Jesus (15:16-20) and his crucifixion by Pilate's decree (15:21-32). Mark 15:6-15 is pivotal: this pericope follows directly from Jesus' transfer to Roman jurisdiction (15:1-5) while taking up another leitmotif that runs throughout 15:6-32: Jesus' kingship, genuine yet repudiated in ways progressively ghastlier—from ironic refusal (vv. 6-15), through abusive humiliation (vv. 16-20), to crucifixion, the ultimate penalty (vv. 21-32). Comprising sequential materials that he surely inherited from tradition, the structure of Mark's composition remains subtle yet firm.

Two Trials, Two Convictions (14:53-72)

"On the night when he was betrayed" (1 Cor 11:23) not one but two interrogations took place at the high priest's house. Mark heightens their interwoven ironies by folding one story, the trial of Jesus (14:53 + 55-65), inside the other, Peter's interrogation (14:54, 66-72; see table 2). Once again, the effect of this juxtaposition, and likely its purpose, is to compare the teacher's conduct with that of his disciples. After examining each of these constituent legends, we shall be in better position to examine their interlacement. ("Legends" is here used in the form-critical sense: memorable tales of religiously significant figures, embellished in their tellings yet with some basis in fact; Dibelius 1935, 104-32.)

The Trial of Jesus before the Jewish Authorities (14:53, 55-65)

The trial of Jesus before Jewish officials (14:53 + 55-65) exposes this Gospel's thorniest historical questions.

◊ ◊ ◊ ◊

Extant evidence of Jewish judicial proceedings during the time of Jesus is slender. Much on which scholars depend is a Mishnaic tractate, *Sanhedrin*, written some two centuries later than the Gospels' Passion Narratives. That document's evidence is historically problematic, for it is uncertain how much reported therein was stylized, and with what degree of latitude actual Jewish court cases proceeded (Sanders 1992, 458-81). Hyperskepticism is unwarranted, however, since it is reasonable to assume that *Sanhedrin* codified something of conventional practice during the centuries preceding its composition. The stipulations in *Sanhedrin* afford a rough, if imperfect, basis for interpreting Mark's account of Jesus' Jewish arraignment.

The tractate *Sanhedrin* is clear that Western modernity's firm distinction between religion and politics does not apply. In Jewish and Roman jurisprudence those social dimensions were indissoluble. Trial of a capital crime, of the kind that Mark and the other Gospels report, did not take place in the high priest's house. "[In Jerusalem] there were three courts: one used to sit at the gate of the Temple Mount, one used to sit at the gate of the Temple Court, and one used to sit in the Chamber of Hewn Stone [in the temple]" (*m. Sanh.* 11.2; Danby, 399). The Fourth Gospel's account is more credible than the Synoptics': it differs by presenting Jesus' interrogation by Annas, father-in-law of Caiaphas, "who was...high priest that year," as an informal questioning (18:13-14, 19-24), not as a full-blown trial before the Sanhedrin, Jerusalem's supreme judicial council (see table 16

#10). According to *Sanhedrin* (4.1), capital crimes could be tried only in daylight hours, which squares with Luke (22:66) and John (18:24, 28ab), though not with Mark (14:53, 55) and Matthew (26:57, 59). Cases involving capital crimes ought not to have been tried during a religious festival (*m. Sanh.* 4.1) like Passover (in the Synoptics; cf. John 18:28c). During the course of such trials, and others less serious, concurrent testimony of multiple witnesses was required for a conviction (*m. Sanh.* 5.2; cf. Deut 19:15), which Mark repeatedly asserts did not occur (14:56, 59). Yet another irregularity: verdicts in capital cases could not be rendered within a single day (*m. Sanh.* 4.1), which in Mark and the other Synoptics is exactly what happens (Matt 26:66; Luke 22:71).

Perhaps the most striking anomaly between *Sanhedrin*'s protocol and the Synoptic reports is the charge on which Jesus is convicted: that he claimed to be the Messiah, "the Son of God" or "Son of the Blessed One" (Mark 14:61; Matt 26:63; Luke 22:67, 70). Viewed historically, this is multiply problematic. "Son of God" (= "of the blessed": Mark 14:61; Matt 26:63; Luke 22:70) was not equivalent to the "Messiah" (cf. Rom 1:4), a title that, as we have noted (*ad loc.* 1:1; 8:29), carried many connotations among various Jews at different times (Schürer 1979, 488-554). Moreover, although the Synoptics' Passion Narratives suggest the contrary, a claim to messiahship was not inherently blasphemous because it did not impugn God's sovereignty. " 'The blasphemer' is not culpable unless he pronounced the Name itself" (*m. Sanh.* 7.5 [Danby, 392]; also Lev 24:16; *m. Yoma* 3.8; 6.2; *m. Sotah* 7.6). Subsequent, self-styled messianic figures were not charged, much less convicted, as blasphemous. In 135 C.E. the esteemed Rabbi Akiba hailed an insurrectionist, Bar Kochba, as Israel's king and Messiah (*j. Ta'an.* 4.68d). A claim of messiahship might be mistaken, misguided, or delusional; Josephus writes of various insurrectionists in Galilee, Perea, and Judea who aspired to kingship (*J.W.* 2.55, 61-62; *Ant.* 17.273-74, 278). That, however, was not ground for capital punishment. Even if, for reasons irrecoverable, someone claiming to be, or attributed to be, the Messiah was subjected to the death penalty, that leaves hanging the question why, under limited jurisdiction ceded by the Roman Empire (Luke 23:6-12; John 18:31; *Ant.* 14.194; 16.35), the Jewish authorities themselves did not execute Jesus by stoning (cf. Acts 7:58, in which Stephen is executed by the high priest's agents). In Jesus' case it is hard to discern a precise connection between a Jewish claim of blasphemy and a subsequent Roman charge of sedition against the empire. This is not surprising: strict correlation of cause with effect is a point at which ancient and modern historians diverge.

Mark mentions (14:58) while leaving undeveloped another point: Jesus' alleged threat against the temple. This contingency is not specified in *Sanhedrin*. As we have seen (*ad loc.* 11:12-19), Jesus was remembered as having threatened the temple, immediately arousing its officials' ire (11:27). So had Jeremiah (26:1-24); so too would a different Jesus, described by Josephus (*J.W.* 6.300-309), who was apprehended, whipped, and released. A solitary pronouncement of judgment against Israel's cultic center was neither blasphemous nor a death warrant. Nevertheless, the temple's destruction recurs in oblique ways in different traditions. The marvel is that an event of such magnitude in Israel's life does not receive concentrated attention anywhere in the NT: its earliest clear reference appears in the early second-century *Epistle of Barnabas* (16.3-4). In both Mark (15:29) and Matthew (27:40) the claim that Jesus promised to tear down the temple and rebuild it in three days is hurled as a taunt. In Acts 6:14 a prophecy of the temple's destruction, attributed to Jesus, is the basis for Stephen's trial. John spiritualizes the temple's collapse and rebuilding by redirecting its reference to "the temple of [Jesus'] body" (2:19-21). The *Gospel of Thomas* (logion 71; probably second century) preserves another variant of the same tradition: "Jesus said, 'I shall destroy [this] house, and no one will be able to rebuild it.'" Considered historically, Jesus' indictment and death are somehow associated with a threat against the temple.

Such is the available evidence. Before returning to Mark, it is also worth asking, as we have of the extant Jewish evidence, the basis for his information. What sources were available to Mark for what transpired at Jesus' trial? How reliable were they? With what Christian prejudices would those traditions have been transmitted? Later the Evangelist characterizes Joseph of Arimathea as "a well-positioned councilor" (15:43 AT), yet that figure is not identified as those among the Sanhedrin, all of whom adjudged Jesus as guilty and fatally culpable (14:64c). On balance a cautious historian may give credence to the general picture. Soon after his arrest, some among Jerusalem's hierarchy questioned Jesus, before transferring the prisoner to Roman custody. In all the Gospels some collusion between Jewish and Roman officials is suggested and probably existed, for reasons left unspecified. The intensity of the drama in Mark 14:55-65 may reflect an early stage of the Gospels' general tendency to whitewash Pilate by staining Jewish officialdom (see Matt 27:24-26; Luke 23:4-5, 13-25; John 19:1-6). Whether Mark's sources were imperfect or the Evangelist has colored the account from an early Christian palette—or both—the impression created by 14:55-65 is that of a kangaroo court, riddled with judicial irregularities.

Mark recounts that, after his capture, Jesus is led first to the high priest (presumably Caiaphas [18–37 C.E.]; see Matt 26:3; John 18:13, 24), who has apparently convoked a meeting of "all the chief priests, the elders, and the scribes" (14:53). The latter three groups were all represented at Jesus' arrest (14:43), after having challenged Jesus in the temple (11:27). The chief priests and scribes were conspirators with Judas (14:1, 10; cf. 8:31; 10:33). That one "high priest" (*archiereus*) is set apart from the others (14:53) suggests that this is the high priest among subordinate chief priests; if so, that is this figure's first appearance in Mark. Historically it makes sense that he would make his first bow here, when matters have escalated to the point that he would be involved. In Palestine at the time of Jesus, the high priest was not only the chief executive officer of the temple; he was also the principal middleman between Israel and the Roman officials, the broker of political affairs between his countrymen and the chief agents representing Rome's occupying forces. When necessary, he would convene subordinate Jewish leaders as the Sanhedrin, the highest judiciary of some seventy judges, to enact his bidding (Sanders 1992, 481). Mark's reference (14:55 NIV) to "the whole Sanhedrin" in Jerusalem implies that it is this highest tribunal.

According to Mark, this body is in no doubt of Jesus' guilt: "[They] were looking [ezētoun] for testimony against Jesus to put him to death" (14:55a). The verb zēteō is an important tip-off: previously those "seeking" or "searching for" Jesus have usually (though not always: 12:28) done so with dubious motives (1:37; 3:32; 9:14, 16), faithless intent (8:11-12; 14:11), or homicidal purpose (11:18; 12:12; 14:1). The latter is clearly in view at 14:55a. No responsible judge would enter legal proceedings with a mind so closed, even warped (Deut 19:16-21; m. Sanh. 3.6-8). Jewish courts meted justice by forestalling divine retribution on the community for injustices left unpunished and by mitigating the community's revenge. That was the point of lex talionis, "an eye for an eye" (Exod 21:24): to tailor a punishment that fit the crime. Mark 14:55a suggests fundamental miscarriage of principle and procedure: the punishment has been predecided, and the council is searching for a capital offense that may be pinned on Jesus. What the judges need is testimony supporting their predetermined conclusions. What they lack is a legal basis (14:55b).

Witnesses for the prosecution give testimony that, though false, cannot be corroborated. Unlike the other Gospels, Mark twice iterates both aspects of these testimonies: they were specious (14:56, 57) and mutually contradictory (14:56, 59). The focus of their false testimony is on Jerusalem's cultic center: "We heard [Jesus] say, 'I will destroy this temple that is made with hands, and in three days I will build another, not made with hands'" (14:58, effectively braiding 2 Sam 7:4-17 with later Christian reflection [Acts 7:48; 1 Cor 3:16; 1 Pet 2:4-6]). In Mark, Jesus has said no such thing, not even when expelling the temple's buyers and sellers (11:15-19). Departing the temple, Jesus predicted to his followers that not one of its stones would be left standing upon another (13:2); he did not say that *he* would demolish it. Whether the witnesses have misconstrued Jesus—as so frequently occurs in this Gospel, among friend and foe (e.g., 1:44-45; 3:22; 4:41; 5:19-20; 6:49-50; 8:17-18, 32b-33; 9:34, 38; 10:35-37)—or are perjuring themselves is left unresolved. Either way the result is the same: false testimony that does not jibe (14:59). The scripturally knowledgeable reader can intuit what Mark does not say: events in the Passion Narrative resonate with Israel's laments that malicious witnesses accuse an innocent without cause (Pss 35:11-12; 109:2-3). As Mark's story unfolds, those reverberations grow louder.

At this point the chief magistrate asks the defendant if he has nothing to say to these charges (14:60). Jesus is silent; regarding this testimony, he has nothing to say (14:61a). Implied is a blending of a Davidic lament with Deutero-Isaiah's testimony to Israel's suffering servant who, like a lamb to the slaughter, is mute before his shearers (Ps 38:12-14; Isa 53:7). The high priest's next question cracks open the trial in a way he cannot understand: "You are the Christ, the Son of the Blessed?" (14:61 AT). In Greek this clause is formulated as a *declaration*; only the context (14:60) suggests that it is put as a question. This is a crucial, deeply ironic statement: in effect, though not by intention, the high priest addresses his prisoner using the very titles of reverence toward Jesus and God that early Christians adopted as central in proclaiming the gospel (Mark 1:1, 11; Matt 16:16; John 20:31; Rom 9:5; 2 Cor 11:31; Eph 1:3; 1 Pet 1:3). Only once earlier in Mark has someone addressed Jesus as the Christ: Peter at Caesarea Philippi (8:29). There the perceptive attribution was immediately silenced by its recipient (8:30). Here—appropriately, on the eve of his death (8:31-32a)—Jesus affirms another's unwitting acclamation: "I am" (*egō eimi*, 14:62a), then unfolds its significance (14:62b). Only once in Mark, at the theophany on the sea (6:50: again, *egō eimi*), has Jesus hinted the Son's intimacy with the Father.

The rest of Jesus' reply blends OT prophecy and early Christian confession in a way that gives the chief justice more than he bargained for. Jesus promises him an apocalyptic advent of the sovereign Son of Man, in a manner that conflates Psalm 110:1 with Daniel 7:13-14:

Table 18: *The Sovereign Son of Man in Old Testament Context*

Psalm 110:1 (NIV)/ (109:1 LXX)	Daniel 7:13-14 (LXX)	Mark 14:62b
The LORD says to my Lord: "Sit at my <u>right hand</u> until I make your enemies a foostool for your feet."	...and behold: upon <u>the clouds of heaven comes</u> [one] as [a] <u>son of man,</u> and as the ancient of days was there [so] also those in attendance came to him.	...and "you will see the <u>Son of Man seated at</u> the <u>right hand</u> of the Power," and "<u>coming</u> with <u>the clouds of heaven.</u>"

Jesus' answer is oblique, to say the least. Mark's readers can make sense of it by assembling pieces scattered throughout the Gospel. (1) For the second time in this Gospel (8:29–9:1), Jesus transposes an assertion that he is "the Christ" into striking pronouncements about the Son of Man's suffering and ultimate vindication. (2) The closest analogue to the valedictory prediction in 14:62 is that which four disciples received at Olivet: an assurance that, after many disasters, an apocalyptic Son of Man would come, trailing clouds of glory and dispatching his angels to gather the elect (13:26-27; see table 14). (3) In spite of that figure's varying connotations in the Gospel—notably the apocalyptic (8:38) and the suffering (8:31; 9:9, 12, 31; 10:33-34)—Mark probably intends an equation of Jesus himself with that Son of Man (2:10, 28; see table 12). The correspondence of 13:26 and 14:62b is close: subsequent to suffering, whether his disciples' (13:5-23) or his own (now assured by accepting a christological claim that triggers his death: 14:61-62a), Jesus will be vindicated as the Son of Man. (4) As such, Jesus will be seated at the right hand of power: an allusion to God that does *not* invoke the divine name but *does* evoke Psalm 110:1, which, in

Mark, Jesus has earlier interpreted as evidence that David recognizes a lord higher than himself (12:36-37a). In later Christian reflection that Lord is identified as Jesus (Mark 16:19; Acts 2:34-36; 7:56; 1 Cor 15:25-27; Heb 1:13), as Mark probably intends here. Mark 14:62 crystallizes the point that has been percolating since 2:1–3:6: Who speaks for God? For the Evangelist and his readers, the answer is Jesus. Naturally, the high priest violently rejects that suggestion.

To rend one's garments was a familiar token of distress (Gen 37:29; Num 14:6; Jdt 14:16; Acts 14:14). Still, the high priest's response is drastic (Mark 14:63): he rips his tunic apart, a gesture that, while scripturally forbidden of one in his position (Lev 21:10), could persuade a court when performed by those of high rank (*J.W.* 2.316, 322). By foreclosing further testimony (Mark 14:63), the high priest removes from the table the bogus dispute over Jesus' threat to the temple (14:55b-59). The magistrate uses the defendant's self-incrimination as the evidence necessary to convict: "blasphemy" (14:64a). What constitutes blasphemy? Strictly speaking, it is either "cursing" (Heb. *qll*) or "expressly pronouncing" (*nqb*, "piercing" or "boring through") the divine name. Jesus has done neither; indeed, he employs a circumlocution ("the right hand of the Power") to avoid utterance of the Deity's name. The high priest's *interpretation* of the evidence mirrors that of his subordinates on the court: whereas *they* heard Jesus threaten the temple (14:58), *he* has heard Jesus blaspheme. Having ears to hear, they have not heard (4:12; 8:18). When the high priest misconstrues, whether by accident or intention, the mistake is fatal because no one will contradict him. Soliciting the court's assessment is pro forma (14:64b); the verdict handed down has been a foregone conclusion (14:55): "All of them condemned him as deserving death" (14:64c). The dissolution of the high court into a thugs' gallery (14:65) is reminiscent of more sufferings endured by Israel's servant (Isa 50:6; 53:3-5). Transmission of the text of 14:65 is mildly chaotic: "Prophesy to us," "Prophesy [now] to us, Christ," "Prophesy to us who just hit you," or "Prophesy" (Swanson 1995, 244). The simplest form appears in the best, most diverse range of ancient manuscripts.

The shortest taunt is the most pointedly ironic: any further prophecy of the blindfolded Jesus is superfluous in the light of what he has repeatedly predicted (9:31; 10:33-34a; 14:30) and what is now happening in the courtyard below (14:66-72).

◊ ◊ ◊ ◊

The theological issues raised by Mark 14:53, 55-65 are as complicated as the historical problems we have noted. Converging in this passage are four unlikely coordinates: the temple (v. 58), the Messiah (v. 61), the Son of Man (v. 62), and blasphemy (v. 64). Each has appeared previously in Mark; only here are they conjoined. The Evangelist does not logically connect them; the job of puzzling things out is left to the reader.

There is conceptual resonance between blasphemy and the temple in one obvious sense: a brazen curse of God would have been regarded as incurring a stain on the Jewish community. To make restitution at least two things were required: to hurl stones at the offender as he had hurled invective upon Israel's God (Lev 24:13-16; Douglas 1999, 206-7) and to offer up sacrificial blood as a societal purgation or "ritual detergent" to cleanse the nation of that sin (Milgrom 1991, 253-64).

In Mark the scribes have judged Jesus blasphemous (2:7), and Jesus warned his disciples away from blasphemies (7:22), particularly those against the Holy Spirit (3:28-29). Though he has upset the temple's proceedings (11:15-16, 27–13:2), Jesus has uttered neither of the things of which the Sanhedrin charges him: a promise to destroy the temple, then rebuild it; and blasphemy against God. On both accounts his auditors were wrong, or wrongheaded. Both cases, however, point up something that is correct but unacknowledged during this trial: Jesus radically *redefines* Israel's social and religious responsibilities—its understanding of blasphemy (3:28-29), cultic practice (11:15-19), forgiveness (2:6-10), Sabbath observance (3:1-6), and kosher laws (7:1-23). This Jesus *does* because of who Jesus *is*. Here enter the key titles as epitomes of his character in Mark. Jesus' extraordinary authority derives from his proper identification not as God's reviler but as God's beloved Son (1:11; 9:7; 12:6), the Christ (1:1; 8:29; 14:62), the Son of Man whose earthly authority (2:10, 28) must surrender to death by persecution (8:31; 9:31; 10:33-34), thereby redeeming many (10:45) before his glorification (13:24-27; 14:62b). It is critically important that only here in Mark does Jesus accept identification as the Messiah (14:62a), because only here, *by that acceptance*, does he guarantee his death in the manner divinely ordained.

The Sanhedrin's blundering attempts to pin blame on Jesus bring into focus what the reader has observed throughout Mark: the application of conventional, unreliable yardsticks to measure Jesus' identity and actions (2:1–3:6; 3:19b-35) when, by God's decree ("Listen to him!" [9:7]), Jesus himself is the most unconventional yet only dependable criterion of God's kingdom and will (1:14-15; 3:31-35; 10:1-31; see Donahue 1973). This has been neglected or denied not only by Jewish authorities but also by the pious (8:11-13), Jesus' family (3:21, 32), and his closest adherents (8:32-33; 9:32-34; 10:35-41). "By the measure you measure, you will be measured" (4:24b AT). By applying their own ruler to the Ruler, the Christ, Israel's authorities homicidally reject God's beloved Son just as they always have (12:1:1-12). Regarded from a cultic perspective, the irony is fierce: for Mark the stone over which they are stumbling (12:10-12) will stand as the cornerstone after the temple's stones lie as rubble (13:1-2). The high priest and his yes-men, who should be executing justice, deserve death for killing an innocent (Lev 24:17). For this blot on Israel's escutcheon the high priest will not pour out sacrificial blood. As Mark tells it, *Jesus already has done so,* for the sake of preserving Israel's covenant with God (14:24). Hence the reason for Jesus' passivity, from this point to the Gospel's end: except to speak truth (14:62) and hold fast to the path "as it has been written" (14:49), he has nothing more to do than to die. By responding to that death, others reveal themselves.

Mark sets the stage for 14:55-65 by (a) locating Jesus amid a multitude of interrogators (14:53), then instantly contrasting that tableau with (b) Peter's pursuit of his captive leader (14:54). The disciple's portrait is ambiguous. On the one hand, he follows Jesus "as far inside" (AT) as the high priest's courtyard. Simon has not vanished into the night like the naked young man (14:52). On the other, Peter follows "at a distance," then seats himself with the guards, warming himself by their fire. Peter's presence while his teacher is on trial does not show the makings of a profile in courage.

Peter's Trial (14:54, 66-72)

Mark then interposes Jesus' trial (vv. 55-65). As Jesus is being taunted as a prophet and "received with blows" (v. 65 AT), Peter is below in the courtyard, accosted by one of the high priest's maidservants (v. 66). The contrast could not be sharper: the teacher in the hands of scores of unhinged assailants; his disciple confronted by a single girl. Studying him hard, she observes, simply and accurately (cf. v. 56), "You also were with the Nazarene, Jesus" (v. 67 AT). Yes, he was. "Being with" Jesus has been requisite for discipleship since the Twelve's formation (3:14). Peter answers her, "I do not know or understand what you are talking about" (v. 68a). Having said that—no closer to Jesus than the courtyard downstairs—Peter distances himself from his teacher at even greater remove, to the gateway (*proaulion*, v. 68b, NRSV footnote). At this point many ancient manuscripts read, "And the cock crowed," probably to fulfill the punch line in 14:72 to the letter. Most of the oldest and finest manuscripts omit this detail in 14:68b; probably Mark did not write it. He is a subtler writer than some of the scribes who transcribed him: the Evangelist's concern at this point is not with a bird but with Peter's pulling even farther away from Jesus, toward the action's periphery. Another step outward and Peter would no longer be in the courtyard at all.

The maidservant persists. Still looking at him, she now points him out to bystanders: "This man is one of them," a member of the Twelve (v. 69). "But again he denied it" (v. 70a).

The bystanders pick up the girl's question, focusing it more sharply on Peter's identity as a Galilean himself (v. 70b). At this point Peter's composure collapses altogether: cursing himself, he swears ignorance of Jesus (v. 71). Now falls the hammer of judgment: a rooster, or a Roman signal (*alektōr*; cf. 13:35), sounds for a second time (v. 72a). Once before in Mark, Peter has remembered something Jesus has said (11:21). Here, for the second and last time (14:72b), he does so again: Jesus' prophecy of Peter's denial (v. 30). The last clause in verse 72c is difficult to translate with precision. Different versions try to capture its spirit: "And he broke down and wept" (RSV, NIV, NRSV); "And he threw himself down and wept" (Lattimore); "And he burst into tears" (Goodspeed, Moffatt, JB, NEB, GNT).

Mark's intercalation of Peter's denials (14:54, 66-72) into Jesus' self-identification (14:53, 55-65) again offsets the conduct of the teacher and his disciples in subtle yet pointed ways:

- Jesus is the central figure inside the high priest's chamber (v. 55); Peter lingers on the fringe outside (vv. 53-54, 66).
- Jesus is interrogated by Jerusalem's highest echelon, with murderous intent (vv. 53-55). Confronted by nobodies, Peter is never actually threatened (vv. 66, 69, 70b).
- The questions put to Jesus are false (vv. 56-58) and incoherent (vv. 56, 59). The statements addressed to Peter are crisp and accurate (vv. 67, 69, 70).
- Jesus holds his ground and truthfully acknowledges his identity (vv. 61a, 62); Peter retreats, lying about himself and Jesus (vv. 68, 70a, 71).
- Jesus is falsely charged with cursing God (v. 64a), while Peter curses and swears in prevarication (v. 71).
- After others pass sentence upon Jesus, they assail him (vv. 64b-65). After bringing down an oath (v. 71), Peter humiliates himself (v. 72).

Each scene mirrors its counterpart. It is hard to say which is darker.

Although the disciples do not at this point disappear from Mark (cf. 15:41–16:1), the story of Peter's denials sums up their characterization in this Gospel. From the beginning Jesus has called followers (1:16-20) to be with him (3:13-19a). Under his supervision, they have performed ministry like his own (6:7-12, 30, 39-44; 8:6-10). Exemplified by Peter, they have left everything to follow Jesus (10:28) and have shown a flash of insight about him (8:29), immediately quenching that flicker (8:32-33). Though Jesus has defended them from others (2:23-28) and has explained everything to them privately (4:34; 7:17-23), the Twelve in Mark, from start to finish, are never fully on Jesus' wavelength. They are cowardly and faithless (4:40), lack understanding (4:41; 8:17b, 18), demonstrate stunning misapprehension of his teaching (9:32-34; 10:13-14, 35-41), and prove incapable of watchfulness and prayer (9:29; 14:32-42). Jesus wonders whether their hearts have also been hardened (8:17b), as God has hardened others' hearts (4:11-12). Mark says that is so (6:52). They are not the villains of this story—Peter is remorseful (14:72)—but certainly they are no heroes. If God is the unseen agent in softening and hardening hearts, then perhaps neither "heroes" nor "villains" populate this Gospel. One thing is clear: the most complete expression of discipleship in Mark is Jesus himself.

Not only does Peter lie about his discipleship (14:70a); he does it in a way revealing the unintended truth about himself and all of the Twelve: "I neither know nor understand what you are saying" (v. 68 AT; see 4:13; 6:52; 8:17, 21; 9:32). (Similarly, the high priest has just declared that Jesus is "the Christ, the Son of the Blessed One" [14:61] without for a moment believing it.) The final denial is richly ironic: responding to an accurate identification of him (v. 70b), Peter replies, "I do not know this man you are talking about" (v. 71: the last words uttered by a disciple in Mark). Obviously Peter is lying about Jesus; in a deeper sense he is denying the truth about himself. By rejecting Jesus, desperately trying to save his own life, Peter has lost himself—again, just as Jesus has promised (8:35-37).

From Israel's Chief Priests to the Roman Governor (15:1-5)

Jesus' execution by decree of Pontius Pilate, fifth prefect (26–36 C.E.) of the Roman province of Judea, is recorded in non-Christian sources (*Ant.* 18.3.3; 20.9.1; *Ann.* 15.44; Minucius, *Octavius*) and memorialized in earliest versions of the Apostles' Creed (mid-second century). Also beyond reasonable doubt is Jesus' crucifixion as an enemy of the Roman order (the charge "King of the Jews" [Mark 15:26]). The portrait of Pilate in the writings of Philo (*Embassy* 38.301-2) and Josephus (*J.W.* 1.167-77; 2.175-77; *Ant.* 18.55-62) is that of an insensitive, arrogant governor who aggravated Jewish agitation. His depiction in the Gospels is different. At best, he comes off as a discerning judge of Jesus' character (Mark 15:14; Matt 27:19; Luke 23:4) and a buck-passing politician (Matt 27:24; Luke 23:13-25), outmaneuvered into condemning an innocent (John 18:12-16). At worst, Pilate seems a lackey of the Jewish priesthood, intimidated by mobs (Mark 15:15; Matt 27:24; Luke 23:20-24; John 18:29-31a; 19:7-8). Another question in Mark 15 attaches to the so-called Passover amnesty (vv. 6-15), by which a single prisoner was released on the Feast Day. In this, other Gospels follow Mark's lead (Matt 27:15-23; Luke 23:18-24; John 18:39-40; *Acts Pil.* 9.1-2). No extant extrabiblical source corroborates this custom, and its veracity is contested (cf. Bammel 1970; Winter 1974). Certainly the Barabbas account is theologically significant for Mark, and that is his primary interest.

◊ ◊ ◊ ◊

Jesus' arraignment continues with his transfer to Roman custody (15:1-5). Mark's specification of early morning (v. 1) is the first of five carefully measured, temporal indicators in this chapter (see also vv. 25, 33a, 33b, 42). Since Jesus' entrance to Jerusalem, the Evangelist has been clocking the last days (11:1, 12, 20; 14:1, 12). From here until his death Mark will decelerate time by tolling the last final hours. At dawn on the day of the Sanhedrin trial, chief priests, elders, and scribes (14:53) convene a second session to finalize Jesus' delivery to Pilate (15:1). In these negotiations the chief priests appear to be *primi inter pares*: the others are "with" (*meta*) them (see 14:55). Historically that makes sense. Jesus' earlier adversaries, the Pharisees, have faded from the picture entirely.

Pilate says to Jesus, "You're the King of the Jews" (15:2a AT). The sentence's construction in Greek is the same as in 14:61: an ironically accurate though faithless affirmation that may be punctuated as a question in context. This is the first of five occurrences of "King of the Jews" in Mark (vv. 9, 12, 18, 26; see Matera 1982). It recalls Mark's five references to Jesus as the Messiah (1:1; 8:29; 9:41; 12:35; 14:61): a valid attribution, even if some who make it, like Peter (8:29) or the high priest (14:61), cannot understand its implications. Roman overlords, Pilate (15:2a, 9, 12) and his cohort (15:18, 26), call Jesus "King of the Jews," in contrast to Jesus' coreligionists, who as insiders mock him as "Israel's king" (15:32). The charge of "blasphemy" (14:64) has evaporated. Pilate would not have cared about the Jews' religious sensibilities; his interest is in Jesus as a threat to the imperium (15:26). Jesus' ironic words to Pilate, "You say so" (15:2b), are his last until just before his death (v. 34).

Registering perplexity, Pilate emphatically questions the defendant: "Do you *not* have *nothing* to answer?" (a Greek double negative, for emphasis [v. 4]). With equal force "Jesus *no* longer answered *nothing*" (v. 5a). Pilate marvels (*thaumazein*, v. 5b), as have others in Mark (5:20; 6:6a; 12:17). Jesus' silence before the prefect can be differently interpreted. It may have been customary for Jews in Roman custody to say nothing to their accusers, lest their rebuttal incriminate fellow Jews. If that is the case here, then Jesus refuses to expose the chief priests (Bammel 1984, 421-22). Mark may also allude to Israel's Suffering Servant (Isa 53:7). Recalling the defendant's silence before the chief priest (14:61a), Mark juxtaposes Jesus' two trials before two magistrates—one Jewish, the other Roman—both unable to recognize the King they are judging.

A Criminal Son Escapes, an Innocent Son Is Hanged (15:6-32)

Mark 15:6-32 consists of three balanced, interlocking stories:

A.   Pilate's sentencing of Jesus (vv. 6-15)
        B. The soldiers' abuse of Jesus (vv. 16-20)
A.´ The soldiers' execution of Jesus (vv. 21-32)

Whether these segments form a final Markan intercalation (see table 2) is a good question. Usually the same characters and activities of the framing pericopae (A) are interrupted by interlaminated material (B). Substantively, 15:6-32 deviates from that pattern. Structurally, the component elements do mirror one another:

- The principal theme is ironic rejection of Israel's true yet hidden king.
- The central element (vv. 16-20) amplifies Jesus' abuse at the Sanhedrin trial (14:65): (a) the humiliation is rendered in greater detail; (b) its agents are Gentiles.
- The primary agents of Jesus' destruction are now Rome's prefect (15:8-10, 12, 14-15) and provincial military (vv. 21-28), provoked by Jewish officialdom (vv. 10, 11, 30) and Jerusalem's rabble (vv. 8, 11, 13, 15, 29).
- Pilate's mockery of Jesus as "the King of the Jews" (vv. 9, 12) mirrors comparable taunts at the crucifixion (vv. 26, 32).
- The release of a known, murderous bandit (vv. 7, 15) is answered in verses 27, 29b by the innocent Jesus' execution between a pair of revolutionary bandits.
- The faux regalia in which the cohort first clothe, then undress, Jesus (vv. 17, 20a) anticipate their callous disposition of his garments after crucifixion (v. 24).
- The viciousness of this tableau escalates from the demand for Jesus' crucifixion (vv. 13-14) to his physical abuse (v. 19) to the ultimate penalty, crucifixion itself (vv. 24a, 25).

The Release of Barabbas (15:6-15)

Jesus' trial before Pilate concludes with the release of Barabbas (15:6-15), which Mark describes as customary (vv. 6, 8). Earlier in this Gospel the crowd (*ochlos*) has been favorably disposed toward Jesus (2:12; 3:32; 4:1; 8:1; 12:37). Mark has also planted clues that they are not to be trusted: a hindrance (5:30-31; 10:46) that Jesus tried to overcome (1:35-37; 4:36; 6:35; 7:17, 33). Their danger to his safety (3:9, 20) culminated in armed assistance at his capture (14:43). The multitudes in Mark have turned on their leaders (11:18, 32; 12:12); in 15:11 they do the same against Jesus.

While our knowledge of provincial trial law in this era is spotty, by the first century C.E. Roman authorities may have reviewed some cases among their subjects to assure just sentences and to reverse egregious decisions (Bammel 1974, 35-40; cf. Mark 15:9-10). Although 15:7 does not identify a particular revolt, Luke (13:1; Acts 5:36-37) and Josephus (*J.W.* 2.167-77, 228-56; *Ant.* 18.55-62; 20.113-21, 208-10) refer to Jewish insurrections (*stasiasotōn*) against Rome in the early first century. Mark characterizes Barabbas as one among several who had committed murder during "the insurrection" (*stasei*, 15:7). The Evangelist repeats, without translating, this rebel's curious Aramaic name (vv. 7, 11, 15): "Son of the Father." By contrast, the name "Jesus" is mentioned only once, after judgment has been pronounced (15:15). Twice Pilate refers to Jesus as "the King of the Jews" in solicitous, highly ironic questions (15:9: in effect, "Why not grab your opportunity?"; 15:12: "Wouldn't you like to reconsider your decision?"). Insisting on Barabbas's release (v. 11), the crowd is even more determined that "the King of the Jews" be crucified (vv. 13, 14b), in spite of the fact that Rome's prefect judges him innocent (v. 14a). Pilate capitulates: releasing Barabbas, he has Jesus flogged, then "hands over" (*paredōken,* v. 15) the condemned to crucifixion.

◊ ◊ ◊ ◊

Mark 15:6-15 is a kind of ghost story, and Barabbas is Jesus' doppelgänger. Jesus says and does nothing; he is but vaguely present, talked about before being whipped. He and Barabbas are opposite subversives. Barabbas has opted for violent revolution (15:7). Jesus has proclaimed an alternative kingdom that depends on repentance and forgiveness (1:15; 11:25). The most obvious irony in 15:6-15 lies in the Evangelist's restrained contrast between one "Son of the Father," a convicted murderer, and another "Son" of a different "Father" (1:9; 9:7; 13:32; 14:36 [abba]) who, as his executioner concedes, has done no evil (15:14). "The Son of Man came not to be served but to serve and to give his life as release for others" (10:45 AT). In 15:6-15 this redemption is played out before the reader's eyes.

There are other ghosts in this story. Jesus' trial and sentencing by Pilate do not stand alone in this Gospel; it is, rather, the last of three trials narrated in rapid succession, accompanied by Jesus' threefold anguish in Gethsemane (14:35-36, 39, 41a), three attempts to awaken his disciples (vv. 37-38, 40, 41b-42), and Peter's trio of denials (vv. 68, 70a, 71). The first trial was of Jesus by the Sanhedrin (vv. 55-65); the second, that of Peter in the high priest's courtyard (vv. 66-72). Each of these proceedings has blended truth ("You are the Christ"; "[Peter,] you are one of them"; "You are the King of the Jews") with lies (false witness; denials of discipleship; the chief priests' enmity). Each has fitfully escalated to its conclusion. At first the Sanhedrin cannot pin anything on Jesus; Peter keeps retreating until he crumples; Pilate's amazement is trumped by Barabbas's release. Each trial ends furiously, with physical abuse (14:65b; 15:15) or emotional collapse (14:72). At every point justice is miscarried: the Son of Man goes as it is so written, but woe betide those who collude (14:21a).

Responsibility for Jesus' death lies finally with Pilate, who has his own spectral doppelgänger: Herod (6:14-29). Oddly, Mark opened that legend with the comment that, on hearing of Jesus, Herod believed him a revenant: John the Baptist, raised from the dead (vv. 14, 16). Ostensibly describing the death warrants of two "righteous and holy" men (6:20; 15:14), both 6:14-29 and 15:1-15 are actually stories about weak authorities who bungle their objectives while being outfoxed. The king no more wants to kill John (6:20) than the prefect wants to execute Jesus: it is *Pilate's* idea to release him (15:9). But the adversaries (6:19, 24; 15:3, 10, 11) possess malicious wit to turn custom against their political superiors: irrevocable oaths (6:26b), a Passover privilege (15:6). The manipulators get their way by using pawns who demand grisly death: Herodias's daughter for John's head (6:22-25); Jerusalem's crowds for Jesus' crucifixion (15:11, 14b). Neither politico gets what he wanted. Herod paints himself into the corner of beheading John (6:26-28); Pilate suckers himself into executing Jesus (15:15) by releasing a manifestly guilty felon back into Judea's social and political turmoil (v. 7).

After the Holocaust, Christian exegetes have the best of reasons to beware biblical interpretation that feeds anti-Jewish slander and hatred. Mark's Passion Narrative arguably contributes to healthier Jewish and Christian relations. Who misunderstands and betrays this Galilean Jesus? As this Evangelist tells it, *virtually everyone* does: his nearest and dearest (3:21b), his countrymen (6:1-6a), Judas (3:19a; 14:10-11, 43-46), Peter (8:32-33; 14:29-31, 66-72), the Twelve as a whole (9:32-34; 10:35-41; 14:27, 50-52), pious Pharisees (7:1-23; 8:11-13; 12:13-17), chief priests, scribes, and elders (8:31; 10:33; 11:27-32; 14:53, 55; 15:1), Jerusalem's crowds (15:11, 13-14), and Pilate and his regiment (15:15). Ultimately, the Son of Man is killed by delivery into *human* hands (*paradidotai eis cheiras anthrōpōn*, 9:31). His betrayers are friend and foe, disciple and adversary, the oppressed and their oppressors, Jew and Gentile. All are culpable. All will haunt others in the story to come.

◊ ◊ ◊ ◊

Jesus' Ridicule by Provincial Soldiers (15:16-20)

The account of Jesus' ridicule by provincial soldiers (15:16-20) has a historical basis: flogging is well documented as preparatory for Roman execution (*Ant. rom.* 5.51.3). Some victims did not survive preliminary scourging. Mark's mention (v. 16) of "an entire *speiran*" inside the palace *praetorium*, the prefect's headquarters and residence, may raise one's eyebrows: a Roman "cohort" (JB, NAB, NRSV) or "battalion" (Goodspeed, RSV, Lattimore) was a detachment of two hundred to six hundred soldiers. Attraction to Jesus has been hyperbolic in this Gospel (1:28, 45; 3:7-8; 6:44, 56; 8:9; 10:46); 15:16-20 reverses the polarity by spotlighting another horde's enmity. Unlike Mel Gibson's *The*

Passion of the Christ (2004), Mark does not exaggerate the soldiers' sadism and their victim's suffering, merely noted in a brief adverbial participle (v. 15). While there is physical insult (v. 19), the Evangelist's emphasis lies instead on the magnitude of Jesus' *humiliation*: dressing him in royal purple (1 Macc 8:14; 10:20), crowning him with plaited thorns (Mark 15:17), and using a reed as a faux scepter (v. 19) plus giving the ironic salute: "Hail, King of the Jews" (v. 18). The fourth time in eighteen verses that Jesus has been so addressed by a Gentile (see vv. 2, 9, 12), this may be a lampoon of the legionary salute, "Hail, Caesar, Conqueror, Emperor" (*Ave Caesar, victor, imperator; Claud.* 21.6). The sarcasm is compounded by their "bending their knees" (v. 19 AT). The scene is one of unbridled mockery (*enepaixan,* v. 20), a term used in this Gospel once previously, in the third prediction of the Son of Man's ridicule (*empaixousin*) by Gentiles (10:33c-34). Subliminally, the dark minor chord of Isaiah 50:6 and Micah 5:1 may also drone. In 15:16-39 Mark may be turning inside out the type-scene of a Roman triumphal procession, which included the victorious general's acclamation, his procession through a captured city with trophies of conquest, and a culminating offer of religious sacrifices (Dio Cassius, *Roman History* 6.23; 58.11; 64.20-21; cf. Mark 11:1-11; 2 Cor 2:14-15; Schmidt 1995). In effect, this pericope is also the photographic negative of Paul's Hymn to Christ (Phil 2:5-11), whose last stanza thunders Christ Jesus' exaltation (vv. 9-11), with every knee bowed and every tongue confessing (cf. Isa 45:23). Mark recasts such an image in a stridently minor key, with vacuous acclamation and farcical homage, underscoring the Messiah's descent in self-abasement to the nadir of crucifixion (Phil 2:7-8; Mark 15:20).

Golgotha (15:21-32)

Encapsulating circumstances just before and after Jesus' crucifixion, Golgotha (15:21-32) closes a narrative ring opened in 15:6, serving as the final scene in an act that began at the high priest's court in 14:53. In some respects Golgotha answers Gethsemane (14:32-42) as theological ground-clearing for the Son of Man's delivery into human hands (9:31). The violence attending Jesus' arrest—the swords, the clubs, the butchering of a slave's ear (14:47-48)—is now unleashed without restraint. As was written of Elijah the precursor, so it follows for his successor: both have come, and people did to them whatever they willed (9:12-13).

En Route (15:21)

A condemned prisoner like Jesus carried only the crossbeam; the stake or gibbet waited at the place of execution. Into the story flits another character who will vanish as fast as he appears: a passerby named Simon. Cyrene (Acts 6:9; 11:20; 13:1) was a city in what is now Libya. It is hard to determine significance in the detail of Simon's "coming in from the country" (or "field"), unless Mark is juxtaposing a single follower of Israel's soon-to-be-crucified king with those who cut "leaves from the fields" while welcoming the advent of "the kingdom of our ancestor David" (11:9-10). When Jesus entered Jerusalem, the cry was "Hosanna," "Lord, save" (11:9-10); he exits to a very different cry—"Crucify" (15:13-14)—and the one who most obviously needs saving is Jesus himself. Presumably, Mark's audience would have recognized Simon's sons (15:21, as Matthew's [27:32] and Luke's [23:26] readers would not; see table 16 #24). A certain "Rufus, chosen in the Lord," is among many at the church in Rome whom Paul greets (Rom 16:13); it is impossible to confirm that Mark refers to the same person. The Evangelist's introduction of another "Simon" at this point is intriguing. Mark mentions no motive for the soldiers' pressing him "to carry his cross" (15:21). In context "his cross" refers, of course, to Jesus'; still, after Simon Peter refused the Son of Man's ordained suffering and death (8:31-32), the teacher insisted that those coming after him "take up their cross and follow me" (8:34). Sheer coincidence? Perhaps—though it is strange that one Simon does as another Simon was instructed. Like Barabbas in 15:6-15, Cyrene's Simon is another "ghost," reminding the reader of a key disciple who lost himself in a frightened attempt to save himself (8:35a), with miserable consequences (14:70-72).

At "Skull-Place" (15:22-27)

Though it can no longer be certainly located, Golgotha (v. 22) at the time of Jesus may have been just outside Jerusalem's walls (John 19:20; Heb 13:12). Since the fourth century C.E., it has been associated with the site of the Anastasis Church, now known as the Basilica of the Holy Selpuchre. Mark translates its Aramaic name (*gulgalta*) as "Place of a Skull" (*kraniou topos*, which Jerome's Vulgate translated as *Calvariae locum* [Calvary]). In antiquity myrrh had several uses: a garment freshener (Ps 45:9), a cosmetic (Esth 2:12), and incense (Exod 30:23). Previously in Mark (14:3, 8) it was a fragrant perfume, which Jesus associated with his death. At his crucifixion it is offered to him mixed with wine (15:23b), probably as an analgesic (Prov 31:6). Jesus' refusal of this painkiller has been foreshadowed: he has chosen to drink from a different cup (10:38b), which precludes drinking of "the fruit of the vine" (14:25). Although Mark does not quote it, Psalm 69 lingers in the reader's imagination. The psalmist who laments his unjustified reproach—his shame, heightened by merciless witnesses (vv. 19-20)—cries that his enemies "gave me poison for food, / and for my thirst they gave me vinegar to drink" (v. 21).

Crucifixion (15:24a)

"And they crucify him"—stated in the historical present tense.

Crucifixion was the impaling of a victim onto a stake and crossbar. Cicero identifies this capital punishment as the supreme Roman penalty over burning, beheading, or using a simple noose (*Verr.* 2.5.168). For its alleged deterrent value, it was commonly used in executing cases of imperial sedition, violent crime, and slaves' revolts (*Decl.* 274; *Metam.* 3.9.1-2; *Sat.* 6.219-22). Convicted Roman citizens were generally protected from a penalty so obscene (*Rab. Perd.* 16; cf. Hengel 1977, 39-45). Marcus (2006) suggests that there may have been an element of grotesque parody in crucifixion: to hang transgressors who had elevated themselves beyond their station.

Unlike modern forms of capital punishment, crucifixion's raison d'être was protracted, mortifying torture. Josephus, who had witnessed men crucified during Titus's siege of Jerusalem (70 C.E.), called it "the most wretched of deaths" (*J. W.* 7.203). Seneca asked rhetorically (*Ep.* 101), "Can anyone be found willing to be fastened to the accursed tree, long debilitated, already deformed and swelling with ugly welts on the shoulders and chest, drawing the breath of life amid long-drawn out agony?" Elsewhere (*Dialogue* 6) Seneca answers his own question with a simple, gruesome report: "I see crosses there... made in many different ways: Some have their victims with head down to the ground; some impale their genitals; others stretch out their arms on the gibbet." The causes of death were multiple: excruciating pain, exposure to the elements, and asphyxiation when gravity's force prevented the victim's chest cavity from elevation. The *crucifragium,* or crushing of the victim's ankles (John 19:31b-32), was the coup de grâce. Even after the victim's death, the barbarism continued: "The vulture hurries from dead cattle and dogs and crosses to bring some of the carrion to her offspring" (*Sat.* 14.77-78).

◊ ◊ ◊ ◊

Mark's initial commentary on Jesus' crucifixion is drawn from Psalm 22, which becomes the soundtrack for the Evangelist's portrayal of Jesus' imminent death. Having alluded (15:23) to Psalm 69, Mark in 15:24 paraphrases Psalm 22:18: "They divide my clothes among themselves, / and for my clothing they cast lots." The Evangelist does not quote the psalm's preceding verses (16-17 AT), though some readers might be reminded of them:

> For many dogs encircle me,
> an assembly [*synagōgē*] of evildoers surround me.
> They ripped my hands and feet.
> I numbered all my bones,
> and they looked right through me and put me down.

The "wagging [of] their heads" (15:29a KJV) also paraphrases the Psalter (22:7; 109:25). There was no need to spell out the grisly details of Jesus' execution: ancient audiences were well aware of them. Mark is encouraging scripturally informed readers to tap the event's deeper resonances. It is now terribly lucid how the Son of Man must go "as it has been written about him" (9:12 AT; 14:21; A. Y. Collins 1997a).

In 15:25 Mark tolls the first of three hours in his deathwatch: the third, or nine o'clock in the morning, when Jesus was crucified (cf. 15:33-34). From crossing off the days (11:11-12; 14:1, 12, 17, 15:1), Mark decelerates the final hours. The *titulus*, or placard that the victim customarily wore, is a reminder of the political aspect of Jesus' death: he was executed for presumed sedition, as "the King of the Jews" (15:26; cf. 15:2, 9, 12, 18), which for Mark is socially preposterous (14:48) yet religiously valid (1:1; 6:34; 8:2, 29; 12:35-37). The Second Evangelist intimates what the Fourth asserts: Jesus' kingship is not of this world (John 18:36). With Jesus are crucified two actual bandits (*lēstas*), one on his right and one on his left (Mark 15:28). This is a pair of doppelgängers: phantom surrogates for the sons of Zebedee, who had requested seats "one at your right hand and one at your left" when their teacher came into glory (10:35-38). Jesus replied that his disciples did not know what they were asking (10:38a); now the reader can understand that answer's import. Confident that it spelled glory—perhaps prerogatives over their peers among the Twelve (cf. 10:41)—James and John were certain they could drink from Jesus' cup (10:39). At Golgotha, bereft of the Twelve, Jesus alone takes the cup (14:36), which contains a slave's submission to barbarous torture (cf. 10:42-44). In the KJV 15:28 reads, "And the scripture was fulfilled, which saith, And he was numbered with the transgressors." Omitted from the earliest Eastern and Western manuscripts, this verse is probably a later interpolation; had it originally appeared in Mark there is no good reason why so many scribes would have deleted it.

At Jesus' Cross (15:29-32)

In contrast with Luke (23:39-43) and John (19:25-27), *everyone* ridicules the crucified Jesus in Mark: random bystanders

(15:29), the chief priests (15:31), and even those crucified with him (15:32b). English versions adopt colorful expressions of the scornful conduct by "those walking about" (AT): they "railed on him" (KJV), "jeered" (Goodspeed, REB), "derided" (RSV, NRSV), "hurled insults" (JB, NIV), "poured abuse" (Cassirer), or "reviled" (NAB). Lattimore renders what the Greek text literally says: "They were *blaspheming* him." Since in subsequent verses (31, 32b) the Evangelist uses different synonyms ("ridiculing" [see 10:34; 15:20]; "disgraced" AT), we may assume that Mark has selected his words with care. In Jesus' first run-in with certain scribes (see 15:31), he was silently accused of blasphemy (2:7); in 14:64 the Sanhedrin convicted him of blasphemy. Convicted of divine offense, Jesus is blasphemed by others in his final hours.

The explicit jeers of the "walkabouts" (15:29) and the religious elite (15:31) are ironic, eerie reminders of earlier statements in Mark. (1) *Oua* (v. 29b) is practically untranslatable, though an exclamation expressive of amazement (BDAG 734a)—"Ah!" (KJV) or "Aha!" (Goodspeed)—is better than "Bravo" (REB, which sounds more suitable for Carnegie Hall). (2) "The destroyer of the temple and its rebuilder in three days" (v. 29b AT) recalls the bogus charge against Jesus before the Sanhedrin (14:57-59). (3) "Having come down from the cross, save yourself" (v. 30 AT) perverts Jesus' requirement that his disciple *take up the cross* and *lose one's life* for the gospel (8:34-35). (4) "He saved others; he cannot save himself" (v. 31) is an uncomprehending paraphrase of Jesus' interpretation of himself as Son of Man, who "came not to be served but to serve, and to give his life a ransom for many" (10:45). (5) "Let the Christ, the King of Israel [cf. 15:2, 9, 12, 18, 26], come down from the cross now, so that we may see and believe" (v. 32a): this challenge *reverses* the sequence of faith and mighty works in this Gospel. Already Jesus has refused a faithless demand for "a sign from heaven" (8:11-13); repeatedly (2:5; 5:34, 36; 6:5-6a; 9:19, 23-24; 11:22-24) faith has proved the *condition* of restoration, not its outcome. (6) The chief priests and scribes, who should know Jewish tradition better than anyone, articulate the *ungodly's* taunts against Israel's righteous (Wis 2:13, 17-18 AT):

He professes to have knowledge of God,
And calls himself a servant of the Lord....
Let us see if his words are true,
And let us test things in his way out:
For if the righteous one is God's son, [God] will come to his aid
And will rescue him from adversarial hands.

Scholars continue to debate the dominant biblical referents in Mark 15:21-32 (whether the Psalter's laments [Ahearne-Kroll 2007] or Deutero-Isaiah's Servant Songs [Marcus 1992]). Perhaps more important is recognizing Mark's determination that readers see all unfolding in accordance with God's will, scripturally disclosed, in Jesus' darkest hour. Ordering this scene's chaos is the Evangelist's faith that none of this narrative's protagonists and antagonists are in control of the proceedings in spite of their delusions to the contrary.

From Christianity's beginnings up to the present, Jesus is remembered as the one crucified. It is imperative for the modern reader to grasp the import of the way Jesus died. He was not accidentally run over by a chariot. He did not live tranquilly to a ripe old age. He was executed in the cruelest, most deliberately barbarous manner that his contemporaries could concoct. It was just this, yoked to a confession of Jesus as the Messiah, that Paul acknowledged as scandalous for Jews and moronic to Gentiles (1 Cor 1:23). In that context it is significant to note *how* Mark narrates the crucifixion. When the crowd twice announces to Pilate its will for Jesus—"Crucify him" (15:13, 14)—it comes, or should come, as a shock. Even if his countrymen wanted him punished, less hideous options were available. Even if they were bent on seeing him dead, there were faster, "cleaner" methods. They demanded the worst. In narrating its execution Mark uses the most understated, least pathetical means: "And they crucified him" (15:24a). Mark is no Cicero, plucking his listeners' heartstrings, milking the event for pity (*Rab. Perd.* 16). The Evangelist tells it plain, devoid of all the gruesome details of how harrowing a death crucifixion assured.

What Mark *does* emphasize in 15:21-32 is Jesus' utter aban-donment: without friends, lacking consolation of any kind. The story's characters have turned against him, sadistically enjoying the spectacle—even those crucified with him, who should know better than anyone what he is enduring. The terror of crucifixion was a given. To die in such manner completely derelict, altogether *alone,* is a vision of hell. The worst of this nightmare is still to come.

Death in the Afternoon (15:33-47)

With breathtaking concision 15:33-47 sums up almost every-thing of consequence that Mark has to say, and does so in this Evangelist's peculiar blend of stark, ironic understatement. The section has three components: (1) the death of Jesus (vv. 33-37); (2) its immediate aftermath (vv. 38-41); and (3) the confirmation of death and burial (vv. 42-47). The presence of the women in verses 40-41 links the surrounding events: they behold (*theōrou-sai,* v. 40) Jesus' death; they behold (*etheōroun,* v. 47) the place of his interment.

The Death of Jesus (15:33-37)

Mark began tolling the hour in 15:25, when Jesus was cruci-fied ("the third hour," nine in the morning). The next chime is at noon, "the sixth hour" (15:33), when normally the sun is at its summit. Instead, "darkness came over the whole land until three in the afternoon." Midday darkness enshrouding the earth is an apocalyptic image of divine judgment and human mourning (Amos 8:9-10). Jesus predicted the sun's darkening after terrible tribulation (13:24). What the reader is witnessing is not The End: no angels are dispatched to the ends of heaven and earth to gather the elect (13:27). Rather, the three-hour eclipse and ensu-ing events are a preview, a real-time harbinger of the end, even as Jesus' ministry has occurred on the threshold of God's kingdom (1:14-15) and his transfiguration has offered a glimpse of that dominion's coming with power (9:1-8).

At three in the afternoon (15:34) "Jesus cried out with a loud voice." The verb *eboēsen* has appeared once previously in Mark: in the quotation (1:3) of Isaiah 40:3 (LXX) to describe John the Baptist, Jesus' precursor (1:2-11; 6:6b-29; 9:9-13; 11:29-33). In classical and Hellenistic Greek *boaō* connotes the sea's howl (Homer, *Iliad* 14.394) or a lion's roar (*Acts Pil.* 2.6; see LSJ 319b-320a; BDAG 180a). Before their exorcisms (1:26; 5:7), demoniacs have howled "with a loud voice," as Jesus does here. Like them, Jesus has reached the nadir of distress. Mark hardly considers Jesus diabolically possessed, for his last articulate words are scriptural: the opening lament of Psalm 22:1, which Mark renders in Aramaic, then translates for his audience (cf. 5:41; 7:34). Mark adopts the Semitic text, which intensifies the psalmist's affiliation with God by repeating the first-person possessive pronoun: "*My* God, *my* God" (cf. Ps 21:2 LXX: *ho theos ho theos mou*, "God, my God"). Of all the Psalter's laments, Psalm 22 most passionately disclaims any sense of the petitioner's sin. In it the penitent prays not to be expelled from the divine presence. By contrast, in Mark 15:34, Jesus stares into God's veiled face and asks why the Almighty *enkatelipes*—"has forsaken" (RSV, NRSV, NAB), "abandoned" (GNT, Cassirer), "deserted" (JB), or "left him in the lurch" (AT). Jesus hurls back to an apparently absent God the intense, personal address that the heavenly voice (*phōnē*) has twice used in addressing the beloved Jesus: "You are *my* Son" (1:11); "This is *my* Son" (9:7). None other than the beloved Son, faithfully going as it is written of him (14:21), the dying Jesus prays to the God who, like everyone else, has evidently deserted him (14:27; 15:29-32).

"And when they heard, some of the bystanders said, 'Look—he's calling Elijah'" (15:35 AT). Earlier Jesus has warned listeners, "Watch what you hear" (4:24a). Usually they have failed to do so (4:12; 8:14-21). So it goes to the end: quoting Psalm 22, Jesus *cries, Eloi,* "My God"; what his audience *hears* is *Hēlias* (cf. Matt 27:46). Perhaps evolving from 2 Kings 2:9-12, some Jewish traditions envisioned Elijah as protector of the righteous in dismay (Evans 2001, 507-8). Someone fills a sponge with vinegar and puts it on a reed, offering it to Jesus on the chance that Elijah may remove him from the cross (15:36). The irony of this act is so multilayered that it can set the reader's head spinning. (1) Before crucifixion, Jesus refused refreshment (v. 23). Why would he accept this now? (2) The previous offering was probably a painkiller; this is vinegar (*oxos*), extended on a reed (*kalamos*) of the sort the soldiers used to club him (v. 19). (3) The runner fulfills Scripture by unwittingly mimicking another lament (Ps 69:21). (4) That Mark intends this action to be taken as torment, not an errand of mercy, is suggested by the context, coupled with 8:11-12: a faithless generation seeks a sign—even one so gruesome as the spectacular rescue of a tortured innocent. "Truly I tell you, no sign will be given to this generation" (8:12b). (5) The reader *knows* no sign is forthcoming, because in John the Baptist, Elijah already has returned "and they did to him whatever they pleased" (9:13): namely, decapitation (6:27-28). (6) During his ministry, few have understood Jesus; at his death others maintain that stupidity.

After releasing a second loud cry (cf. 15:34). Jesus "expired" (*exepneusen*). As the KJV memorably puts it, "[He] gave up the ghost."

The Immediate Aftermath (15:38-41)

Each of three reactions to Jesus' death is narrated in sequence; none is interconnected with the others. If the Gospel were unspooling as a motion picture, each of these would be "hard cuts": the viewer, the Gospel's reader, sees and hears things the story's characters cannot. Nevertheless—and this is of crucial importance—in no case does Mark offer the reader a definitive interpretation of what is witnessed.

"And the Curtain of the Temple Was Torn in Two, from Top to Bottom" (15:38)

Mark's conjugation of the main verb in the passive voice suggests divine agency of cultic destruction (cf. God as the unnamed agent of the heaven's tearing in 1:10). At 15:38, in response to Jesus' death, *God is present yet remains hidden*. A "sign from heaven" *has been* granted, which *no one has seen*—save the reader. But what is the significance of what the reader has seen? If one answers, "Why, that Jesus is truly God's Son," then consciously or not, one has smuggled into the Second Gospel the interpretation of the First: namely, that the centurion made his declaration having witnessed the curtain's rending and other extraordinary phenomena (Matt 27:51-54). Mark never makes Matthew's connection. In fact, the Second Evangelist expressly positions the centurion as "facing [Jesus]" (15:39).

Another exegetical conundrum: the temple had at least two curtains. An outer curtain (*to kalumma*) separated the temple's entrance from its forecourt; an inner curtain (*to katapetasma*) demarcated the temple's expansive interior from its most sacred precinct, the Holy of Holies. To which drapery does Mark refer? Complicating this question is the bothersome fact that the LXX and Josephus employ the term Mark uses, *to katapetasma,* for both the outer curtain (Exod 26:37; 38:18; Num 3:10, 26; *Ant.* 8.75; *J.W.* 5.212) and the inner curtain (Exod 26:31-37; Lev 21:23; 24:3; *Ant.* 8.75). Given such indiscrimination, one wonders whether Mark would have rigorously differentiated the two. If one must guess, probably the inner curtain is intended in 15:38 since, as far as we know, the outer curtain had no special religious significance. That may explain the NT's exclusive use of *to katapetasma* (Mark 15:38; Matt 27:51; Luke 23:45; Heb 6:19; 9:3; 10:20). However, if Mark knew details of the outer curtain that Josephus reports—that "its tapestry portrayed a panorama of the heavens" (*J.W.* 5.212-14)—then it is barely possible that 15:38, like 15:33, recalls Jesus' prediction of astral turbulence in 13:24-25.

A temple curtain was ripped, and God was its invisible ripper. This is a divine revelation. *What* is being revealed? For the first and only time Mark allows the reader a vision of something unseen by any figure in the story. Are adequate resources offered to infer its interpretation? A traditional exegesis is that "God's judgment has fallen on the temple" (Michel 1967, 885). Although there is truth in this, it essentially reiterates 13:1-2 while leaving unspecified the *reason* for judgment. A more specific suggestion takes its cues from 2 Kings 2:12b and Mark 14:63: the rending of a mantle in two parts is a mourning rite, reminiscent of the high priest, grieved by Jesus' alleged blasphemy, and Elisha's distress at Elijah's ascension (cf. Mark 15:36; Daube 1956, 20-26). Another option: the curtain's tearing epitomizes the temple's devastation, opening the prospect that the risen Jesus will replace it with "another temple not made with hands," unwittingly prophesied by Jesus' accusers in 14:58 (Juel 1977, 143-57). Still another possibility, developed in Hebrews (9:1-28; 10:19-20), is that Jesus' death creates unmediated access to God: through divine intervention, there is no longer any shield between the holy presence and the world outside it. Jesus' death spells the end of all human attempts to localize divinity—whether in a religious structure, like temple or tabernacle (see 9:5-6), or in the religious imagination that would fix God in the heavens, which, like the curtain in 15:38, have been decisively ripped asunder (*schizō*) by God (1:10). The expiration of the beloved Son thereby coincides with, and is ratified by, the apocalyptic release of God's living yet hidden, holy presence.

As Hercule Poirot ruefully mused in the Calais coach, "One cannot complain of having no clues in this case. There are clues here in abundance" (Christie 1933, 71). It is hard to escape the same impression while pondering Mark 15:38. The Evangelist describes but offers no conclusive interpretation, perhaps purposefully so. To pin down the significance of a manifestly divine action would attempt exposure of the God who remains hidden from everyone, even from Jesus (15:34).

"Now When the Centurion, Who Stood Facing Him, Saw That in This Way He Breathed His Last, He Said, 'Truly This Man Was God's Son!' " (15:39)

At first this verse appears as transparent as 15:38 is opaque. From this Gospel's beginning the reader has known beyond doubt's shadow that its Evangelist considers Jesus "the Son of God," if one accepts the longer reading attested in the manuscript tradition (1:1). With supernatural cognition the unclean spirits have so acknowledged their foe (3:11; 5:7). Jesus has referred to himself as "the Son" (12:6; 13:32) and has spoken of God as his Father (8:38; 11:25; 13:32; 14:36). Most telling, the heavenly voice has acclaimed Jesus as "my Son, the Beloved" (1:11; 9:7). At 15:39, for the first and only time in Mark, a mortal other than Jesus himself has made the correct identification. The centurion is a Gentile, and Gentiles have been receptive to Jesus (3:8; 5:20; 7:24-31; 11:17; 13:10), though ironically this Gentile has been one of Jesus' executioners. Heightening the irony, a Roman legionnaire would betray his imperial fealty by acclaiming anyone other than Caesar Augustus a *divi filius* (a divine son). At this point clear waters turn murky. Is this a sincere confession of faith (thus, Gundry 1993, 950-51)? Or (with Juel 1994, 74) is it every bit as faithless, sarcastic, and ironic as the high priest's *"You* are the Christ, the son of the blessed?" (14:61 AT), Pilate's "Shall I release for you the King of the Jews?" (15:9 AT), and the rabble's taunt of "the Christ, the King of Israel" (15:32 AT)? Without direction from the Evangelist of the kind that Matthew (27:51-54) and Luke (23:47-48) provide, it is impossible to judge with certainty. The reader who faithfully accepts the Son of Man's self-assessment (8:31; 10:45) is in proper position to judge the accuracy of the centurion's verdict and the basis on which it is reached: no miracle of any kind, only direct confrontation of one who has thus died (15:39a). Whether the centurion believes what he is saying is a different, irresolvable, and ultimately inconsequential question. As Davis has observed (1989, 15), "The issue, after all, is not what Mark's readers thought of the centurion and the quality of his faith; it is what they were to think of Jesus."

"There Were Also Women Looking on from a Distance" (15:40-41)

The camera pulls back, as it were, from the foot of the cross to a wider angle. The reader now learns that, contrary to appearances, Jesus has not been altogether deserted (cf. v. 38). Hanging on by a thread are Mary Magdalene, Mary the mother of Joses and James the younger (literally, Little James: *Iakōbou tou mikrou*), and Salome. The first and third of these women appear in this Gospel for the first time. What of the second? Is this Mary the same as the mother of James and Joses in 6:3? Possibly, but probably not: If so, why would not Mark have identified her as

Jesus' mother? Moreover, these are women who followed him while he was in Galilee (15:41). Mark has made no such claim for Jesus' mother and, indeed, has impugned her motives (3:21, 31). In any case these women perform important functions. For one, they remind the reader of those *absent* from the scene: the Twelve, who have long since defected (14:50-52). Mark 15:41 is pointed that "many other women" (*allai pollai*) had come up with Jesus to Jerusalem. Second, their presence clarifies the fact that, from the start, Jesus' entourage has included female followers (*ēkolouthoun*), disciples beyond the Twelve. The earliest so described was Simon's mother-in-law, who served (*diēkonei*) Jesus and four of the Twelve just as 15:42 describes these three women's ministry (*diēkonoun*). More subtly, the Evangelist's description of their distance is reminiscent of yet another of the Psalter's laments: "kinfolk who stand afar off" from a sufferer (Ps 38:11 AT; Mark 14:54). Is Mark planting doubt about the durability of *these* disciples' ministry?

In ancient context Mark 15:33-37 is stunning for its dearth of dignity (see A. Y. Collins 1998). Socrates thus concluded his address to the Athenians who had sentenced him to death:

> Wherefore, O judges, be of good cheer about death, and know this of a truth—that no evil can happen to a good man, either in life or after his death.... The hour of departure has arrived, and we go our ways—I to die, and you to live. Which is better, God only knows. (*Apology* 41, 42)

"Were you yourself, Phaedo, in the prison with Socrates on the day when he drank the poison?" asked Echecrates. Phaedo was, and reported how Socrates died:

> And now I will make answer to you, O my judges, and show that he who has lived as a true philosopher has reason to be of good cheer when he is about to die, and that after death he may hope to receive the greatest good in the other

world.... Then holding the cup to his lips, quite readily and cheerfully he drank off the poison. (*Phaedo* 57, 117)

Likewise, the Stoic emperor Marcus Aurelius Antoninus (161–80): "Depart then [this life] satisfied, for he also who releases thee is satisfied" (*Meditations* 12.36).

The contrast with Jesus' death, depicted by Mark, could not be more bitter. The cup Socrates calmly quaffed Jesus also accepted, though not without praying that it might pass from him (14:36). In this Gospel there is attached to Jesus' death neither good cheer nor equanimity nor satisfaction that either Jesus or God is pleased by this outcome. The whole earth is plunged into darkness. Jesus dies in abject shame, asking why his God has forsaken him. God responds with destruction in the temple where faithful Jews revere holy majesty.

Even by comparison with the other Gospels (see table 16 #26), Mark's account of Jesus' death stands out in its terror. It is not a question of judging any of the Gospels better or worse in their various presentations of Jesus' death: considered theologically, all are valid. The point is to perceive Mark's distinctive version more clearly.

If we let Mark be Mark, this episode deserves consideration in the light of his Gospel as a whole. Jesus' crucifixion and death might be considered the third panel of another narrative triptych, parallel with Jesus' baptism and his transfiguration:

Table 19: *Three Claims for "The Son of God" in Mark*		
Mark 1:5-11	*Mark 9:2-8*	*Mark 15:33-41*
It came to pass <u>in those days</u>	And <u>after six days</u>	When it came to be <u>the sixth hour</u> ... <u>until the ninth hour</u>
When <u>he came up</u> out of the water	<u>He led them up</u> to a high mountain	"<u>Let him come down</u> now from the cross..."

All of the Judean countryside	And his garments became dazzling, intensely white	Darkness came upon the whole land
And a voice came from the heavens	And a voice came from the cloud	He howled with a loud voice
John dressed as Elijah	Moses with Elijah	"He is calling for Elijah."
The Spirit came down into him		He let out the spirit (expired)
The heavens were ripped		The temple's curtain was ripped
"You are my Son,	"This is my Son,	"Truly this [person] was God's Son."
the Beloved; with you I am well pleased."	the Beloved; listen to him."	

Several of these elements have been shuffled or contrasted; some areas have no overlaps. Indisputably Mark has framed his Gospel—at beginning, middle, and end—with three different stories that are similarly patterned and at points identically worded ("voice" [phōnē], "Elijah," "[God's] Son" [huios]). A graceful theologian, the Evangelist has not merely *reiterated* the Son of Man's destiny (8:31; 9:31; 10:33-34); three times he has *shown* the reader how precisely Jesus' zenith corresponds to its nadir (see table 10; Black 2005a).

Some have suggested that Jesus' last words in Mark, which replicate the beginning of Psalm 22, direct one to that psalm's *concluding* verses, which describe the psalmist's vow of thanksgiving for healing (vv. 25-31; e.g., Blinzler 1959, 373-74; Evans 2001, 507). That suggestion seems tendentious. Had the Evangelist wished to place on the dying Jesus' lips "Those afflicted shall partake of the temple's thank-offerings, and shall be satisfied" (v. 26a AT), he could easily have done it. Are some interpreters discomfited by Mark's lacerating cry of dereliction? In this Gospel Jesus does not die by cursing God; he dies, himself accursed (Deut 21:22-23; Gal 3:13), praying to the God whose presence now eludes him. In effect Jesus enunciates the cry of the epileptic child's father: "I trust—help my lack of trust" (Mark 9:24 AT). Is there a prayer more faithful than that addressed to the God whose presence is no longer palpable?

On a cellar's walls in Cologne, where Jews hid from Nazis, these words were inscribed (Glatzer 1996, xxvii):

> I believe in the sun even when it is not shining.
> I believe in love even when feeling it not.
> I believe in God even when He is silent.

According to Mark, so also did Jesus believe at the moment of his death.

The Burial (15:42-47)

The deathwatch having ended, the Evangelist returns to the calendar for numbering days (cf. 14:1, 12; 15:1): "And by now it was early evening, the day of preparation, the day before the Sabbath" (15:42 AT). The reader is introduced to Joseph from Arimathea, a town perhaps twenty miles east of modern Jaffa. Its exact location is disputed: it could be the same town as either Ramathaim (1 Sam 1:1; *Ant.* 13.4.9) or Rathamin (1 Macc 11:34). One learns much about Joseph. The timing of his appearance is important: if Jesus' body was not to linger on the cross for days, then hasty preparations were required before Sabbath. "Early evening before the Sabbath" suggests only a few hours before sundown. Mark characterizes Joseph as a well-positioned councilor (*euschēmōn bouleutēs*, 15:43a). On which council he sat is unclear: there is nothing to suggest it was the Sanhedrin (*synedrion*, 14:55; 15:1) that condemned Jesus, though Luke (23:50-51) goes out of his way to exculpate Joseph from its decision. Implicitly, however, Joseph overrides the Sanhedrin's judgment by giving Jesus' body a proper burial: sinners were cursed by their bodies' lack of interment or by exhumation (Deut 28:25-26;

1 Kgs 14:10-11; Jer 16:4). As one also expectantly awaiting God's kingdom (Mark 15:43b), Joseph would have been a man after Jesus' own heart (1:15; 4:11; 9:1; 14:25). Joseph has "been so bold" (*tolmēsas*) to approach the prefect himself, requesting Jesus' remains (15:43c). As in life, so in death Jesus is a source of wonder to Pilate (15:5, 44), who is surprised that the victim has already died (cf. Seneca's description of crucifixion as "long-drawn out agony" [*Ep.* 101]). The detailed confirmation of Jesus' death "for some time" (Mark 15:44-45) may be an early refutation of Christian fraud, differently elaborated by Matthew (27:62-66). Mark's description of the treatment of the body and its interment (15:46) comports with archaeological findings for ancient Jewish burials: rock-hewn *loculi* (little places) with a rectangular blocking stone constituted a basic type of entombment in Jerusalem's ancient cemeteries (Finegan 1992, 292-318). Joseph is yet another ghost in Mark's Passion Narrative: by faithfully burying Jesus' remains, he does for the teacher what John's disciples did for theirs (6:29) but the Twelve do not. By observing where the body was laid (15:47), Mary Magdalene and Mary the mother of Joses are tacit witnesses against any subsequent charge that the women later visited the wrong tomb (cf. 15:40; 16:2).

THE FINAL DISCLOSURE:
A STORY WITH MANY ENDINGS—
AND NO ENDING AT ALL (16:1-20)

When the Sabbath Was Over (16:1-8)

As elsewhere in the Passion Narrative (14:1, 12, 17; 15:1, 25, 33, 42), the Evangelist sets the clock with precision. So, too, in 16:1: "when the sabbath was over," that is, after six o'clock on Saturday evening. Though infrequently mentioned in this Gospel, the Jewish Sabbath has been respectfully guarded as a time for religious instruction (1:21; 6:2). The visitors to the tomb have kept the Sabbath inviolate, in spite of the fact that the Son of Man has declared himself "lord even of the sabbath" (2:28; 3:2), defending his disciples for its soft violation (2:23-26). Though awkwardly worded in Greek, which Matthew 28:1 and Luke 24:1 smooth out, the Evangelist's repetitive description, "very early on the first day of the week [after Sabbath]"—presumably, Sunday—"when the sun had risen" (v. 2), suggests perhaps several things. First, it reinforces the women's respect for the Sabbath; it has passed, so now they have come. Second, the curious Greek construction *tē mia tōn sabbatōn*—roughly, "the day counting forward from the Sabbath"—may hint what Revelation 1:10 states: that "the Lord's day," Sunday, is coming to be regarded as a Christian Sabbath. Third, one wonders whether a conceptual (though not verbal) pun is in play: on this day one soon discovers that more than just the sun has arisen (*anateilantos tou hēliou*).

Visiting the tomb are Mary Magdalene, Mary the mother of James, and Salome (16:1): the same trio who beheld from afar Jesus' crucifixion and death (15:40), two of whom witnessed his burial (15:47). These are among many women who followed and ministered to Jesus while in Galilee before accompanying him to Jerusalem (15:41). Long after the Twelve fled the scene (14:50, 72), these female disciples hung on, now intending to anoint their teacher's remains with aromatic spices (16:1). Like Barabbas (15:7), Pilate (15:9-15) Simon (15:21), and Joseph (15:43-46), these women are narrative revenants, "ghosts" of another character in the story: the woman in Bethany who anointed Jesus beforehand for his burial (14:3-9). Though well intentioned, the three women's mission is superfluous and futile. Their teacher's body has already been anointed; soon it will be evident that the tomb contains no corpse.

Verses 3-4 pertain to the stone-stopper Joseph used to seal the tomb (15:46). Though it seems odd that the women would only now express concern over the door's removal (16:3), Mark applies the logic of storytelling. First, he tacitly rebuts any charge that the body could have been stolen (cf. Matt 28:11-15); second, he plants in the women's (and the reader's) minds doubt that they can make good on their purpose. Verse 4a lays to rest that worry: "And looking up, they behold [historical present

Table 20: The Events after the Resurrection in the Four Gospels

Episode	Matthew	Mark (oldest manuscripts end at 16:8)	Luke	John
1. Early on the First Day of the Week, Women Discover the Empty Tomb	Mary Magdalene and the other Mary	Mary Magdalene; Mary, the mother of James; Salome	Mary Magdalene; Mary, the mother of James; Joanna; the other women	Mary Magdalene
2. A Great Earthquake	An angel rolls away the stone			
3. Messenger at the Tomb	An angel whose appearance was like lightning	A young man in a white robe	Two men in dazzling apparel	[Two angels in white; 20:11-13]
4. The Message	"He has been raised; go tell his disciples that he is going ahead of you to Galilee; there you will see him."	"He has been raised; go tell his disciples and Peter that he is going ahead of you to Galilee; there you will see him."	"Why do you look for the living among the dead? Remember how he told you while he was still in Galilee . . ."	
5. Women's Response	They departed quickly with fear and joy, ran and told the disciples	They fled from the tomb and said nothing to anyone, "for they were afraid"	They remembered and, returning from the tomb, told this to the Eleven and to the rest	Mary flees from the empty tomb and tells Peter and the other disciple
6. Appearances of the Risen Christ Near the Tomb	He meets the women while they are en route	[Cf. Mark 16:9-10 with Matt 28:9-10; Luke 8:2; John 20:1-18]		Jesus meets Mary Magdalene in the garden

Episode	Matthew	Mark (oldest manuscripts end at 16:8)	Luke	John
7. *Jesus' Instructions*	"Go to Galilee...."			"Do not hold me."
8. *Response of the Eleven*	They worshiped him; some doubted	[Cf. Mark 16:11, 13 with Luke 24:11]	Disbelief [Variant reading: Peter runs to the tomb and sees the linen cloths]	Peter and the Beloved Disciple race to the tomb; the Beloved Disciple wins the race, but Peter is first in the tomb
9. *Response of the Chief Priests*	Bribery of the guard at the tomb to spread false rumor			
10. *Appearance of the Risen Christ outside Jerusalem*		[Cf. Mark 16:12 with Luke 24:13-35]	On the road to Emmaus	
11. *Appearance of the Risen Christ in Jerusalem to the Disciples*		[Cf. Mark 16:14 with Luke 24:36-43]	To the Eleven at table, opening their minds to understand the Scriptures	To the Ten (Thomas absent), breathing the Spirit upon them
12. *Another Appearance of the Risen Christ in Jerusalem*				Thomas present; "Blessed are those who have not seen and yet believe."
13. *Appearance of the Risen Christ to the Disciples in Galilee*	The Great Commission to baptize and teach	[Cf. Mark 16:15-18 with Matt 28:18-20]		

Episode	Matthew	Mark (oldest manuscripts end at 16:8)	Luke	John
14. *Another Appearance of the Risen Christ to the Disciples in Galilee*				By the sea of Tiberias; the miraculous catch of fish; "Simon. . . . feed my lambs."
15. *The Departure of the Risen Christ*		[Cf. Mark 16:19-20 with Luke 24:50-52; John 20:30-31; Acts 1:6-8]	The ascension	

tense] that the stone has been rolled away" (AT). The two verbs for visual perception are noteworthy. Elsewhere in Mark "looking up" (*anablepō*) carries a religious connotation: the same verb describes Jesus' regard of heaven before performing mighty works (6:41; 7:34) as well as return of sight after two blind men have encountered Jesus (8:24; 10:51-52). "Behold" (*theōrousin*) has been applied twice before to these women: they beheld events at Golgotha (15:40) and the place where Joseph buried Jesus' body (15:47). In Mark the verb *theōreō* connotes wondrous apprehension (3:11; 5:15, 38; 12:41). The stone's removal from the tomb's mouth is expressed with a verb conjugated in the passive mood (a divine passive): its unseen mover must have been God—"for this was a very big rock" (16:4b AT).

The stage is set for a revelation. "And going into the tomb they saw a young man [*neaniskon*], seated to the right, wrapped in a white robe [*stolēn leukēn*], and they were flabbergasted [*exethambēthēsan*]" (16:5 AT). Mark's description of the messenger is more reserved than that of Matthew, Luke, or John (see table 20 #3). In the Second Gospel the reporter is simply a young man: a doppelgänger for the story's only other *neaniskos*, the one who fled naked after Jesus' arrest (14:51). There is no more reason to suppose that these two youths are identical than to identify one of the tomb's female visitors as the woman in Bethany (14:3-9). Rather, each character mirrors the other, triggering a reader's imagination of how "the Son of Man has gone as it has been written of him" (14:21 AT)—both in accord with Scripture and in alignment with characters and episodes *within Mark itself*. The details of Mark's young man are simple but noteworthy: he is seated "at the right," which in antiquity is the favored place (Mark 10:37, 40), especially if one is seated at the right hand of power (1 Kgs 2:19; Pss 45:9; 110:1; Mark 12:36; 14:62; 16:19). Besides Jesus on the mount of transfiguration (9:3), this is the only character in Mark who wears white, the color of apocalyptic glorification (Dan 7:9; 12:3; Matt 13:43; Rev 7:9, 13). Maybe he is an angelic figure: Who else could report with authority the intelligence entrusted him? As he is wont, Mark abjures supernal pyrotechnics. Rendered with simplicity, this vision is enough to leave the women staggered.

The testimony is in four parts, beginning with reassurance: (1) "Don't be alarmed."

> You are looking for Jesus, the Nazarene, the one crucified. He has been raised. He is not here. Look at the place where they laid him. But go tell his disciples and Peter that he is going before you into Galilee. There you will see him, just as he said. (16:6-7 AT)

(2) The women are "looking for" (*zēteite*) Jesus. Throughout Mark, this verb has emitted a steady red beam. Those searching for Jesus have been up to no good (1:37; 3:32; 8:11-12; 11:18; 12:12; 14:1, 11, 55). The cognate *syzēteō* (to debate, argue) has carried an equally pejorative sense when Jesus or his disciples have occupied a controversy's center (8:11; 9:10, 14, 26; 12:28). What is wrong with what the women have done? If, throughout their travels with Jesus, they have been privy to his passion predictions (8:31; 9:31; 10:34), then by now they—certainly Mark's readers—should have learned that Jesus would not only be killed but would also rise after three days (or within three days, by modern measure of time). Like others (3:21, 32; 8:11-13), these women have mistaken what they found because of what they were looking for: a dead Jew rather than a living Messiah.

(3) "Jesus the Nazarene, the one crucified, has been raised": in a Gospel so murky, this identification could not be clearer. Repeatedly Jesus has been identified as "the Nazarene" (Mark 1:24; 10:47; 14:67). It is this Jesus—not John the Baptist, as Herod erroneously concluded (6:14, 16)—the one crucified, who has been raised (*ēgerthē*, another divine passive). Previously Jesus has "raised up" sufferers from various afflictions (1:31; 2:9, 11-12; 3:3; 5:41; 9:27; 10:49); now God has raised up his Son. The selection and tight juxtaposition of both verbs are theologically significant: the one who has been *crucified* is the one who has been *raised* (Hoskyns and Davey 1981). It is because of God's direct, eschatological intervention that Jesus is not there in the place where they laid him. This is one of the NT's most funda-

mental claims (John 5:21; Acts 4:10; Rom 4:24; 1 Cor 15:3-4; 2 Tim 2:8). Another now follows.

(4) The women are entrusted with a message for his disciples, among whom Peter is singled out (perhaps because his betrayals were recounted in such excruciating detail: 14:66-72). The risen Jesus has gone before them to Galilee, where he awaits them. This simple detail is quadruply significant. First, as throughout this Gospel (6:45; 10:32), Jesus is in the lead and others must catch up (Burdon 1990). Second, a return to Galilee indicates a fresh start, since it was there that Mark's narrative began (1:9, 14, 16, 28, 39; 3:7). Third, Jesus will appear to his disciples: alongside the resurrection itself, the other basic Easter confession (John 21:14; Acts 2:32; 1 Cor 9:1; 15:5-8). Fourth, this announcement is indeed "just as he said" to the Twelve at their last supper: "But after I am raised up, I will go before you to Galilee" (14:28). At the empty tomb two promises of fidelity were proved valid: God's vindication of Jesus, and Jesus' dedication to his disciples.

Everything runs true to Markan form—*including the women's response*: they flee the tomb, tremulous and bewildered (v. 8a). The final, ironic twist: even these women, who followed longer than all others, fall short from fear, just as Jesus' disciples have always done (4:40-41). And now, when at last the time has come to speak in faith (cf. 1:34; 3:12; 8:29-30; 9:9), "They said nothing to nobody [*sic*], for they were afraid, you see" (AT). The tag at the end of the preceding sentence's paraphrase of verse 16:8b is a feeble attempt to convey in English its last word in Greek, the particle *gar*. It is grammatically possible, albeit inelegant, to end a Greek sentence with *gar*, and many sentences in ancient texts do so (van der Horst 1972). Could Mark have concluded not merely a sentence, but the entire Gospel in this way?

The End of Mark

By accident or by design, Mark's Gospel withholds its greatest mystery until its end. The fundamental conundrum is text-critical; from that puzzle flow all others. In the ancient manuscript tradition, there are no fewer than four endings for Mark. Moving from the best to the most poorly attested alternatives, they are as follows:

1. The shortest ending, at 16:8, with the final words "and [the women] said nothing to anyone, for they were afraid," is preserved in Codex Sinaitic (‭א‬) and Codex Vaticanus (B), the two earliest (fourth-century) extant Greek parchment books, which represent the generally superior Alexandrian textual family. Third-century church fathers Clement of Alexandria, Origen, and Ammonius appear unaware of another ending of Mark.

2. The longer ending, with verses 9-20 continuing beyond verse 8, appears in the vast majority of ancient witnesses, most of which issue from a later date or a generally inferior textual family, or both: among others, Codex Alexandrinus (A, fifth-century Byzantine textual family), Codex Ephraemi (C, fifth-century Byzantine), and Codex Bezae (D, fifth-century Western). Some manuscripts preserve this ending with an asterisk or other editorial notation. While including it in the Latin Vulgate, Jerome wrote, "Almost all the Greek copies [that I know] do not have this concluding portion [of Mark]" (*Epist.* 120.3). It is well known from the KJV and the many English versions and lectionaries it has influenced.

3. By the fifth century (Codex Washingtonianus [W], also known as the Freer Codex), the previous ending also circulated in Egypt with an expansion inserted between verses 14 and 15. These verses are presented by the NRSV in a footnote: "And [the disciples] excused themselves, saying, 'This age of lawlessness and unbelief is under Satan....' "

4. Several Greek manuscripts of the seventh, eighth, and ninth centuries (among others, Codex Regius [L] and Codex Athous Laurae [Y]) preserve, in addition to verses 9-20, what is sometimes called "the intermediate ending." It stands by itself in the Old Latin Codex Bobbiensis ([*k*] fourth or fifth century): "But [the women] reported briefly to Peter and to those with him all that they had been told. And after these things Jesus himself sent out through them, from east to west, the sacred and imperishable proclamation of eternal salvation. Amen" (Metzger 1994, 103).

By accepted canons of NT textual criticism, this evidence is not as hard to adjudicate as it may appear. In every material respect the probabilities point to 16:1-8 as the earliest ascertainable conclusion. (1) This ending is attested in the earliest manuscripts of highest quality. The shortest ending is supported by a convergence of Alexandrian and Western witnesses; in general such a combination tends to afford readings superior to others. (2) After 16:1-8, alternative endings multiply like rabbits—not only within Mark's transmission (the second, third, and fourth options, above) but also among its earliest commentators: namely, Matthew (28:1-8a + 28:8b-20) and Luke (24:1-7 + 24:8-53). When the best attested text of Mark runs out and can no longer provide a control, the textual tradition ramifies in many different directions (see table 20 ##6-15). One can observe this having occurred in the third option, above: the insertion of material between verses 14 and 15 in W. (3) As one can see from table 20, the widely circulated 16:9-20 reads as a pastiche of elements drawn from the other Gospels, especially Matthew's Great Commission (28:16-20) and Luke's legend of the Emmaus Road (24:13-35). (4) The seam joining 16:9 and 16:8 is rough: verse 9 awkwardly restates Jesus' resurrection, its timing, and the identity of Mary Magdalene as though the reader had not just read all these things in 16:1a, 6b. (5) The Greek vocabulary and style of all the longer endings deviate from the rest of the Gospel. Words in these endings appear here and nowhere else in Mark: for instance, *apthartos* ("imperishable," in the intermediate ending); *apisteō* ("disbelieve" [vv. 11, 16]); and *theaomai* ("see" [v. 14] versus Mark's preferred synonym *theōreō* [3:11; 5:15, 38; 12:41; 15:40, 47; 16:4]). "The spiritual and imperishable glory of right-eousness in heaven" (W) is more like 1 Peter's liturgical language (1:4; cf. 2 Tim 4:8) than anything in the Second Gospel. (6) A basic principle of textual criticism, often tried, usually holds true: *lectio brevior et difficilior, lectio potior,* "the more probable reading is the shorter and more difficult." It is easy to understand why scribes, perplexed by Mark's ending at 16:8, would have appended other conclusions, peppered with elements consistent with other Gospels. Had Mark's earliest retrievable form extended beyond verse 8, why would any scribe have amputated it?

Though few things in biblical interpretation can be certain, the evidence favoring the shortest of all Markan endings is as solid and as coherent as one could expect. That, of course, does not solve the interpreter's problem; it merely sets the stage for its next phases. First, how does one account for a Gospel that ends at 16:8, with the women fleeing the empty tomb, terrified and mute? Second, what is the exegete's responsibility to the other endings of Mark that circulated during and after the Christian canon's formation? To answer the first, one must imagine circumstances, such as the Evangelist's incapacitation or his Gospel's mutilation, that are impossible to verify. An answer to the second depends on the interpreter's judgment, informed by considerations scholarly and religious.

Mark's longer endings are embedded, often in brackets, not only in the NRSV, but also in most English versions (KJV, Goodspeed, Moffatt, RSV, NEB, JB, NIV, NAB, REB, Cassirer, Lattimore). To ascribe them to the Evangelist is, for most scholars, indefensible and intellectually dishonest. To pretend they do not exist, however, is fatuous. The better path lies in treating the three endings beyond Mark 16:8 as some of the church's earliest *commentaries* on the Second Gospel. Their points of view should not be identified with the Evangelist's own, and Mark's theology should not be forced to fit theirs. Each ending may be considered for its own literary and theological interests, before returning to the foundation they share: Mark 16:1-8, the Gospel's earliest recoverable conclusion.

The Intermediate Ending

This, the fourth option 4 (above), is the simplest elaboration beyond 16:1-8. It consists of (a) the women's report to Peter and the rest of the Eleven about what they had been told (see table 20 #5); (b) Jesus' dispatch, through his disciples "from east to west" (#13), (c) of "the holy and imperishable proclamation of eternal salvation." How does this ending fare as an interpretation of Mark's intent?

The intermediate ending is more smoothly sutured to 16:8 than the longer ending's 16:9. In the first verse "they reported" (*exēngeilan*) to Peter and company "the things commanded" (*parēngelmena*) them to say. That wording follows the flow of 16:7-8, except for immediate contradiction of the women's silence in verse 8b. Universal proclamation following Jesus' resurrection picks up a thread in 13:10. Yet the *kerygma* (cf. Rom 16:25; 1 Cor 1:21; 2 Tim 4:17; Titus 1:3) is described in a non-Markan way: "the *holy* and *imperishable proclamation* of eternal *salvation*." None of the italicized words appears elsewhere in the Second Gospel. "Salvation" (*sōteria*) is a favorite Lukan and Pauline term (e.g., Luke 1:69, 71, 77; Acts 4:12; 13:26, 47; Rom 1:16; 2 Cor 1:6; Phil 1:19, 28; 1 Thess 5:8, 9). Receipt from God or Christ of that which is "imperishable" (*aphthartos*) is also a Pauline coinage (Rom 1:23; 1 Cor 9:25; 15:52) and is notably characteristic of 1 Peter (1:4, 23; 3:4). In Mark "amen" appears exclusively in Jesus' emphatic sayings, "Truly [*amēn*], I say to you" (3:28; 8:12; 9:1, 41; 10:15, 29; 11:23; 12:43; 13:30; 14:9, 18, 25, 30 RSV) but never, as here, in a closing benediction. The term *kerygma* (preaching) appears nowhere else in Mark and only once in all the Gospels: a Q saying about Nineveh's repentance because of Jonah's *kerygma* (Luke 11:32 = Matt 12:41).

To summarize: the intermediate ending rounds off Mark's shortest ending (16:1-8) by stressing (a) the delivery of news about Jesus' resurrection (16:6-7) and (b) that report's impetus for propagation of the gospel, described in an exalted tone that departs from Mark's style while conforming with that of other early Christian witnesses.

The Longer Ending (16:9-20)

The ending of Mark that became canonical in Roman Catholic, many Orthodox, and some Protestant traditions (option #2, above) may be divided into at least three sections:

• Perpetual disbelief of Jesus' resurrection (vv. 9-14);
• Jesus' commission of the Eleven, with a promise of confirmatory signs (vv. 15-18);

• The Lord's ascension, exaltation, and direction of the disciples' mission (vv. 19-20).

Uniting these segments is a common question: On what basis, and with what resources, may the church address lack of faith in the Christian gospel, within and outside the church?

Persistent Disbelief of Jesus' Resurrection (16:9-14)

The first six verses reiterate persistent disbelief of Jesus' resurrection (vv. 9-14). Those hearing Mary Magdalene's report that Jesus had appeared to her (cf. John 20:1-18) "were disbelieving" (Mark 16:11). The report of a pair to whom Jesus also appeared is similarly rebuffed (v. 13b). Climactically, the risen Jesus appears to the Eleven, "and he rebuked their disbelief and hardheartedness, because they had disbelieved those who had seen him who was raised" (v. 14 AT). The same motif recurs in this ending's other segments (vv. 15-20 AT): "The one who has believed . . . will be saved, but the one without belief will be condemned" (v. 16). "These signs will follow closely upon those who believe" (v. 17a).

Troubling the author(s) who crafted verses 9-20 as a conclusion to Mark was a disbelief in Jesus' resurrection that hobbled Christian preaching (v. 20). Verses 9-14 repeatedly stress disbelief among fellow disciples. The cause for their faithlessness is not stated but may be implied. The first impediment may have been grief (v. 10). In addition, Mary Magdalene was the sole reporter (see table 20 #6). Was her news disregarded because she was a woman? Mark 16:11 does not say this, even though Luke—on whom the author of 16:9-20 appears dependent elsewhere—characterizes the apostles' dismissal of many women's comparable testimony as "an idle tale" (24:10-11; table 20 #8).

Mark 16:12-13 alludes to Luke's richly detailed story of the risen Christ's appearance to two disciples en route to Emmaus (24:13-35; table 20 #10). Mark 16:12-13 replicates the pattern discernible in verses 9-11: (a) the risen Jesus takes the initiative in revealing himself (vv. 9a, 12a); (b) one (v. 9b) or two disciples (v. 12b) receive this revelation and then (c) report it to other disciples (vv. 10, 13a), who (d) disbelieve (vv. 11b, 13b). Three's a charm: in verse 14 the risen Jesus appears to the Eleven while they are reclining (*anakeimenois*), probably at supper (cf. 6:26; 14:18; Luke 24:30, 35, 36a; see table 20 #11). Again (a) the risen Jesus takes the initiative, (b) appearing to his disciples. The third item of the established pattern—(c) a report to others—is omitted, for it is now superfluous; the rest are present. The fourth element, (d) disbelief, recurs and is rebuked by Jesus (Mark 16:14bc).

Mark 16:9-14 exhibits narrative elegance. Beyond the four-step pattern replicated in its components (vv. 9-11, 12-13, 14), each marked by a change of scene, the progression moves to a climax: from a sole witness, to two witnesses, to the risen Jesus himself, whose witness is irrefutable. The disciples' struggle to accept the truth of his resurrection accomplishes two things. Implicitly, it serves an apologetic purpose: by resisting various testimonies, his followers were hardly gullible (cf. Matt 28:17; Luke 24:11, 13-24; John 20:24-29). Explicitly, the Eleven's response occasions the risen Jesus' reprimand of their faithlessness, which could apply also to those among the Gospel's readers who still doubted the truth of the Easter preaching. The struggle for faith, particularly among Jesus' heart-hardened followers, is an important area of overlap between 16:9-14 and the rest of Mark (4:40; 6:6a; 8:17-18; 9:42).

Jesus' Commission in Ministry and the Promise of Missionary Confirmation (16:15-18)

The upbraiding of distrustful disciples elides into Jesus' commission of them in ministry and the promise of their mission's confirmation (16:15-18). Like its predecessor (vv. 9-14), this segment consists of three parts:

- The commission itself (v. 15);
- Repeated stress on faith, coupled with another warning against disbelief (v. 16);
- Specific, dramatic signs that will accompany those who believe (vv. 17-18).

The risen Jesus' charge is brief yet comprehensive: "all the world" is the theater for his disciples' mission; "the whole creation," the recipients of the gospel's proclamation (v. 15). This recalls Jesus' mandate at the Mount of Olives (13:10), conflating what was assumed in his pronouncement in 14:9: an unnamed woman's beautiful gift for Jesus will be remembered as her memorial "wherever the good news is proclaimed in the whole world." The gospel's limitless reach is a recurrent theme throughout the NT (e.g., John 3:17; Acts 1:8; Col 1:5b-6; 1 Tim 1:15; 1 John 2:2; Rev 11:15), as is the belief that creation's destiny is bound up with the gospel's fulfillment (e.g., Rom 8:19-23; 2 Cor 5:17; Col 1:15, 23; Rev 3:14).

Faith and unbelief in Mark 16:9-14 are juxtaposed in 16:16, which serves as a hinge between verse 15 and verses 17-18: the gospel demands a faithful response; reassurance will accompany those who faithfully persist. For the only time in Mark, verse 16 cites baptism as confirmatory of Christian faith. The NT holds no uniform view of this matter: Paul expresses reserve (1 Cor 1:13b-17; cf. Rom 6:1-11); Luke seems insistent (Acts 2:37-42; 8:12; 9:18; 16:15, 33; 19:4-6); Peter, very confident (1 Pet 3:21). Elsewhere in Mark, baptism is favorably associated with John the Baptist (1:4-11). In 10:38-39 baptism, like the cup (14:36), serves as a metaphor for the suffering that Jesus and his followers must undergo.

The concomitants of faithful preaching are enumerated in 16:17-18: a series of remarkable, presumably representative "signs" (*sēmeia*) that believers will perform in Jesus' name (cf. 9:37). Previously in Mark "signs from heaven" have been regarded askance (8:11-12), as characteristic of false prophets who would deceive God's elect (13:22). By contrast, 16:9-20 values signs as positive evidence of faith's outworking. Their reliability is a matter of circumspection in the rest of the NT. When performed by God or God's accredited agents, signs are valid and dependable (Luke 2:12, 34; John 2:23; 4:54; Acts 2:19, 22, 43; Rom 15:19; 2 Cor 12:12; Heb 2:4). John of Patmos styles some of his visions as signs (Rev 12:1, 3; 15:1). Yet most of these authors consider signs as equivocal (John 6:26, 30; 1 Cor 14:22), sometimes as evidence of faithlessness (Luke 11:16, 29-30; John

2:18; 4:48; 1 Cor 1:22) or evil (Rev 13:13-14; 16:14; 19:20). No writer in the NT seems as convinced of signs' probative quality for faith as the author of Mark 16:17-18. The closest counterpart is Luke, who in Acts (4:16, 22, 30; 8:6) identifies apostolic healings as signs. "Cast[ing] out demons" (Mark 16:17b) and laying hands on the sick (v. 18c) have characterized the ministry of Jesus and the Twelve in Mark (6:5, 13b, 14a; cf. Jas 5:14-15). "Speaking in tongues"—only here in Mark—is a hallmark of the Spirit's power at Pentecost (Acts 2:1-13), though the "new tongues" mentioned in Mark 16:17b may be closer to what Paul calls "angelic speech," requiring translation for the church's benefit (1 Cor 13:1; 14:6-19). In Luke (10:19) Jesus says he has given his followers *exousia* (power or authority) to trample snakes and scorpions unharmed. Yet the Third Evangelist reins in the disciples' joy over this wondrous prerogative (10:20) and never promises safe ingestion of poisons (Mark 16:18b).

The closest correspondences between 16:15-18 and the rest of Mark are (1) the universal scope of the gospel's preaching (13:10; 14:9), (2) the importance of faith (1:15; 5:36; 9:23-24; 11:23-24), (3) the capacity for faithful works in Jesus' name (6:12; 9:38-39), and (4) the ability of disciples to heal (6:7c, 13). The rest of Mark 16:15-18 shows some correspondence with other NT witnesses, especially Matthew, John, and Luke-Acts (see Kelhoffer 2000).

Jesus' Ascension, Enthronement, and Ongoing Guidance (16:19-20)

The final portion of Mark 16:9-20 describes Jesus' ascension, enthronement, and continuing direction of his disciples (vv. 19-20). Verse 19 graphically depicts one of the NT's highest christological claims: Jesus' elevation to heaven, sitting at God's right hand. As in 16:9b, 11-13, 17b-18a, the notes remind one of the melody in Luke-Acts, which twice narrates the risen Jesus' departure from his disciples as an ascension (Luke 24:50-51; Acts 1:9-10a) and afterward describes Stephen's vision of "the Son of Man," "Lord Jesus," standing (not sitting) at God's right hand in heaven (Acts 7:55-56, 59). Apparently crafted from Psalm 110:1, the theological trope of Jesus' heavenly exaltation to God's right hand is common in the NT (Acts 2:33-34; 5:31; Rom 8:34; Eph 1:20; Col 3:1; Heb 1:3b, 13; 8:1; 1 Pet 3:22; Rev 5:7; see Juel 1988, 135-50). Earlier in Mark (12:35-37) Jesus mitigated David's authority by quoting Psalm 110:1 and predicted the high priest's vision of the Son of Man's coming while seated at the right hand of Power (14:62b). Neither there, however, nor anywhere else in the NT is Jesus' enthronement *narrated* as it is in Mark 16:19. Though applied to Jesus in the NT hundreds of times, "Lord" (vv. 19-20) is surprisingly rare as a title for Jesus in Mark (2:28; 7:28; 11:3). More often the term refers to God (11:9; 12:9, 11, 29-30; 13:20), though sometimes its antecedent is ambiguous (1:3; 5:19; 12:36-37; 13:35).

Mark 16:20 fittingly concludes the entire appendix of 16:9-20. (1) The gospel, incrementally released by Jesus' postmortem appearances (vv. 9a, 12a, 14a), is universally unleashed (vv. 15, 20a). (2) By accepting Jesus' commission (vv. 15, 17a), the Eleven are redeemed. The groundwork for their redemption has been laid by the faithful responses of Mary Magdalene (v. 10) and the two country travelers (v. 13a). (3) Because Jesus is "Lord" (vv. 19-20), he proves able to conquer not only death but also his followers' stubborn disbelief (vv. 9, 14). (4) They are not responsible for the signs that confirm their message (*logos*: Mark 1:45; 4:14-20, 33; 9:10); that is the doing of the Lord, who while in heaven continues to work with them (*synergountos,* 16:20). Initiative for the gospel's corroboration remains with the risen Jesus, who has seized that initiative throughout this appendix (vv. 9, 12, 14-18). Mark 16:9-20 is a christological blending of Luke-Acts with Matthew: Jesus is in heaven, *removed* from the worldly theater of the gospel's operation (Acts 1:10b-11), while at the same time forever *with* his disciples (Matt 1:23; 18:20; 28:20), directing and undergirding their endeavors.

How well does Mark 16:9-20 fare as an interpretation of the Gospel to which it was attached? It is faithful to some aspects of the Second Evangelist's theological view. Its presentation of Jesus as an assertive agent—appearing, commissioning, directing—is compatible with the figure who dominates the Gospel's first thirteen chapters (e.g., 1:14-20; 3:13-19a; 6:6b-13, 30-44; 8:1-10; 11:1-19; 13:1-37). That Jesus is "taken up" (*anelēmphthē*, conjugated in the passive voice) to sit at God's right hand in heaven (16:19) comports with his self-subordination to God throughout Mark (3:35; 4:10-12; 9:47; 10:9, 18-19; 12:17, 29-31; 14:36; 15:34). Jesus did not raise himself from the empty tomb: "he was raised [by God]" (*ēgerthē*, 16:6c). Concentration on "the good news" and its missionary expansion (16:15) is consistent with Mark (1:1, 14-15; 8:35; 10:29; 13:10; 14:9). The Eleven's ability to preach and heal under Jesus' direction (16:15-18, 20) was presaged in his earlier dispatch of the Twelve (6:12-13, 30). The difficulty of childlike trust, *pistis,* particularly among Jesus' followers (16:11, 13, 14), is one of Mark's most prominent themes (4:35-41; 6:52; 8:14-21; 9:35-37; 10:13-16, 35-45; 14:26-31). Mary Magdalene's return in 16:9-10 picks up yet another thread: Mark's presentation of a host of discerning, persistent, female ministers (1:31b; 5:25-34; 7:24-30; 12:41-44; 14:3-9; 15:40-41, 46; 16:1).

Once it entered the manuscript tradition, it is small wonder that 16:9-20 became the most widely dispersed conclusion to a bobtailed Gospel. Not only did it give readers of Mark a triumphant ending; it did so in a way close enough to the rest of the Gospel to have made sense of it. Theological elements in 16:9-20 also cohered well with those from other documents that were, like Mark, attaining canonical stature: Matthew (28:1-10, 16-20), Luke (24:1-53), and John (20:1-20, 30-31). The popularity of Mark 16:9-20 may have lain in its approximation of 1:1–16:8 and its précis of the Easter stories recounted in other Gospels. The longer ending's accent on baptism and its closing liturgical flourish ("Amen") were appropriate to Christian worship. The late fourth-century *Acts of Pilate* quotes Mark 16:15-18 in defense against anti-Christian propaganda.

And yet, by the time one reaches its last six verses, Mark 16:9-20 is ultimately false to the Second Gospel, in letter and in spirit. "The one who does not believe will be condemned" (16:16b) is a judgment unprecedented in Mark, even in 4:10-12. The Eleven's complete rehabilitation; their unbridled zeal in preaching the gospel; Jesus' stunning about-face on signs that verify faith—not just any signs, but those of the most fantastic sort; Jesus' final coronation, straining against a suffering messiahship: it all seems giddily over the top of Mark. It is as though someone had pasted the coda of *The Marriage of Figaro* onto the end of Mahler's *Ninth Symphony*. Some notes and figures may be the same, but their compositions and colors, timbre and tempo, do not match and cannot be made to do so.

The Longest Ending

Between Mark 16:14 (Jesus' blast of his disciples' stubbornness) and 16:15 (his clarion to preach the gospel universally), the Freer Codex inserts an eighty-nine-word exchange between the Eleven and the risen Jesus (option #3, above; see NRSV footnote for text).

The most obvious feature of this colloquy is its saturation in apocalyptic eschatology. The pressures of a lawless and unbelieving age, exerted by Satan and the unclean spirits, stand at the heart of the disciples' apology for their faithlessness and hardheartedness (cf. 16:14). By implication they further attribute their poor conduct to the influence of unclean spirits that cripple comprehension of the power that God exercised in raising Jesus from death (cf. 2 Cor 4:4; Gal 1:4). Their petition that Jesus disclose his righteousness "right now" (*ēdē*) is a formidable challenge, the equivalent of asking Christ to ring down history's curtain just this minute so that his triumphant justice may at last be revealed for all to see. That idea, with roots as old as Isaiah 5:16, is differently expressed, though with less urgency, in one of John's *paraclete* sayings (16:7-11): when the Holy Spirit comes, he will convict the world of the sin of having disbelieved Jesus; he will convince the world of the righteousness of the Son's return to his Father; he will execute judgment by judging "the ruler of this world."

Christ's reply is fourfold. (1) A boundary has been set to Satan's power in this world (cf. Luke 10:18). (2) Nevertheless, other terrors await even those for whom Christ died. (3) His death and resurrection do not signal the world's last night. By them, rather, (4) Christ intends to turn others away from sin, back to truth, and toward their intended, heavenly inheritance of the glory that is righteousness (cf. Acts 20:32; Eph 1:14, 18; Heb 9:15; 1 Pet 1:4; Rev 21:7). The theological arc of this reply roughly extends from Mark 13:8 and 13, which apply the brakes on end-time anxiety, to 2 Peter 3:9, which attributes the delay of the Day of the LORD to his forbearance that all should repent and none should perish. On this basis the manuscript then picks up Jesus' marching orders for evangelists in Mark 16:15.

It is fascinating that fifth-century Christians would still reckon persistent, internal problems of conduct in such vibrantly apocalyptic terms. It is one thing for workers of *anomia* (lawlessness) and *apistia* (faithlessness) to be eschatologically threatened some thirty to seventy years after Easter (Matt 13:41-42; 2 Cor 6:14-15; 2 Thess 2:1-12; Heb 3:12-19); the durability of that religious rhetoric across four centuries is something else. Equally striking is the persistence of apocalypticism's consolatory tenor, which we observed in Mark 13: reassurance of the faithful that evil's power is limited even though sufferings continue, and that Christ's intention is sin's defeat and sinners' redemption. The Freer Codex's expansion of 16:9-20 maintains the sympathetic, non-punitive tone of Mark 13:5-37.

Is this adornment to the more widely known longer ending a good exegesis of Mark overall? In addition to its links with Mark 13, the dialogue does draw on some typically Markan terms: *aiōn* (age), 3:29; 4:19; 10:30; 11:14; *apistia*, 6:6a; 9:24; *satan*, 1:13; 3:23, 26; 4:15; 8:33; *pneumata akarthata* (unclean spirits), 1:23, 26, 27, and elsewhere; and *paradidōmi* (hand over), 3:19a; 9:31; 14:41-44, among others. In other cases familiar words are used in a manner uncharacteristic of Mark. Thus, *doxa* (glory) appears in Mark (8:38; 10:37; 13:26) always in association with Jesus or the Son of Man, never as the content of believers' spiritual inheritance; *alētheia* (truth) occurs a few times in Mark (5:33; 12:14, 32) but never in the theological coinage "the truth of God." In Mark "Christ" is rarely used as Jesus' name (only 9:41); in this manuscript it appears customary. Some heavily freighted terms (AT)—"make excuses," "righteousness," "terrible afflictions"—never occur in Mark at all.

To continue the musical analogy, even when this passage's verbal "notes" occur elsewhere in the Second Gospel, the theological "chords" they form are different from Mark's. In the Freer Codex, Jesus' disciples are clever enough to defend their inadequacy with a theological argument: "The devil made us do it." In the rest of this Gospel, however, they are incapable of such creative thinking, typically reduced to terrified blather (9:6) or speechlessness (8:14-21). They never display the moxie to challenge their teacher to play an apocalyptic trump card (cf. 4:40; 10:32b). In Mark, Satan's kingdom is besieged and certain to fall (3:23-27); to claim "the measure of his years of power is filled up" is not quite the same. In 10:29-30 Jesus promises that disciples who have relinquished everything for him and for the gospel will receive in this life hundredfold recompense—with persecutions—and eternal life in the age to come. "[An inheritance of] the spiritual and imperishable glory of righteousness that is in heaven" is a beatific prospect—but it is not Mark's.

The intermediate, longer, and longest endings of Mark serve as important reminders that the challenge of biblical interpretation is as old as the Bible itself. Indeed, interpretation is *built into* the Bible. This is obviously true in cases like Mark 1:2-3, where the Evangelist employs Jewish Scripture to interpret John the Baptist and Jesus in a story that, in time, itself became scriptural for Christians: the NT's Second Gospel. Less obvious are the thousands of cases in which interpretations of Mark's intent, unclear to the scribes who copied it, were introduced into the Gospel's text (see 9:44, 46; 11:26; 15:28). Most of the textual variants, in Greek or other languages, have been disregarded in this commentary because they affect the text's meaning very little. Mark's conclusion is a different kettle of albacore: it makes a big difference for that Gospel's interpretation whether one judges it to have ended at 16:8 or somewhere else. And good judgment is requisite for sound biblical commentary.

The later endings of Mark, which crystallize early scribes' best attempts to make sense of one of the Gospel's most difficult problems of interpretation, stand as both consolation and caution for the modern exegete. These varied endings remind us that the task of biblical interpretation has never been easy. Even Jerome, an exceptionally able scholar who stood much closer in time to the Gospel's composition than we, puzzled over how Mark ended and the bearing of that decision on the complete book's understanding. As we have seen, the different endings appended to Mark's earliest recoverable text are in many ways theologically problematic: not so much because their points of view are offensive (save for those who erroneously construe 16:18 as a *mandate* for snake handling or imbibing toxins), but because those commentaries on the Gospel do not jibe with its comprehensive theological profile, as that emerges from the rest of the narrative not so textually disturbed. One may legitimately judge them inadequate, in varying degrees, as interpretations of Mark. In that process, however, the modern interpreter is herself escorted to the bar of judgment, challenged to render a more adequate account that does finer justice to the Gospel's probable intent. Wrestling with the Markan appendices should stimulate among the Gospel's modern readers a salubrious humility about their own exegetical endeavors.

Should the later endings of Mark, especially 16:9-20, constitute a basis for the modern church's teaching and preaching? This is a hard question, and a case can be made on both sides. On the one hand, one may carefully evaluate the manuscript evidence and conclude that, because the Evangelist almost certainly did not write 16:9-20, these verses should not be considered canonical, or regulative, for the church's instruction and edification. There is merit in that judgment. On the other hand, because those verses have become effectively canonized in most Bibles and are, therefore, a part of Mark for everyday readers, one could conclude that they should be drawn within the exegete's purview. That judgment also has merit. A roughly analogous problem, drawn from another Gospel, clarifies this alternative: few Johannine scholars regard 7:53–8:11 as part of John's original text. Like Mark 16:9-20, the pericope of Jesus and the adulterous woman is absent from most of the earliest and finest Greek manuscripts of the Fourth Gospel. On text-critical grounds John 7:53–8:11 may be safely disregarded in Johannine interpretation. Nevertheless, this is one of the best-known stories about Jesus, including one of his most memorable punch lines. Should the interpreter conclude that John 7:53–8:11 or Mark 16:9-20 is off-limits for interpretation?

This commentary suggests a third alternative, which aims to be fair both to Mark and to its readers. The interpreter has good reason to consider the Markan appendices as ancient commentaries on that Gospel, though not as representative of the Evangelist's own point of view. So regarded, the endings of Mark that extend beyond 16:8 offer one an opportunity to consider and to assess the church's reflections on its Scripture, especially when those interpretations came to be included within Scripture itself.

The Shortest Ending (16:1-8)

There are three ways in which one may construe the shortest and best attested of all Mark's endings (the first option, above). (1) The Evangelist himself continued beyond 16:8, but his original ending has been lost. (2) The Evangelist intended an ending beyond 16:8 but was precluded from writing it. (3) The Evangelist ended his Gospel at 16:8 with the intention of doing so. The second alternative is purely speculative: there is nothing in patristic tradition to verify it (see Black 2001a). The first is likelier, if one assumes unintended textual mutilation: the portions of manuscript scrolls most vulnerable to damage were their tops and bottoms. A strong case for this possibility has been mounted (Croy 2003); finally, however, it remains an argument from silence, much as are reasons suggested for the second alternative (the Evangelist's untimely death, for instance). There are such things as unfinished symphonies; by their own expansions Matthew and Luke manifestly reckoned Mark's ending incomplete. Unless, however, one has convinced oneself that 16:8 is no way to end a Gospel, is it exegetically inconceivable that Mark decided to do just that?

If the Gospel originally ended at 16:8, that surprising finale could mean many things. From the moment the Evangelist quit narrating, many have been the attempts to make sense of its conclusion. The most obvious expedient, as we have seen, has been the addition of clarifying material (Matthew; Luke; the various longer endings of Mark). Modern scholarship has anguished over the problem (Danove 1993). Suggested interpretations have ranged from Mark's intention to leave readers uncertain of the disciples' future (Rhoads and Michie 1982, 97-99) to purposeful undermining of Peter's authority (Crossan 1976, 135-52). At this Gospel's end the women have been looking for (*zēteite*) Jesus; the Gospel's readers have never stopped searching and arguing among themselves. Therein, perhaps, lies Mark's point.

The Second Gospel is not simply a tale well told about a wonder-working Jewish teacher who ended up on a Roman cross. It is a peculiar proclamation of the hidden explosion of God's kingdom into this world with Jesus, a strange messianic vanguard, and a befuddled band of followers who try riding that missile yet keep falling off (Black 2009). Jesus in Mark's Gospel does not merely tell parables; as God's crucified and risen Messiah, Jesus *is* a parable of the kingdom he preaches (Donahue 1979). To proclaim that proclaimer, Mark has tailored his Gospel into a parable itself: an announcement of good news that teases and offends, perplexes and provokes in the same way that Jesus does by action and deed (Black 1991). "What new teaching is this?" (Mark 1:27a AT). "Who then is this?" (4:41b NAB). Why does he teach to confuse (4:11-12)? By what authority does he do such things? Who gave him that authority (11:28)? What kind of kingdom is planted as the smallest seed and grows into the biggest broccoli (4:31-32)? What kind of disciple fails utterly to understand the teacher (6:52), nods off instead of staying awake (14:32-42), babbles when he should shut up and listen (8:32-33; 9:6-7), and goes mute when she ought to speak up (16:7-8)? What kind of Christ dies crucified (15:32, 39)? What kind of victor is vindicated from death, yet no one gets to see it?

Mark's Gospel ends with mysterious confirmation that God and Jesus have kept faith and have done just what they promised

(16:6-7; cf. 8:31; 9:31; 10:33-34; 14:28). For this Gospel to have ended on another's triumphant flourish—indeed, for it to have ended any way other than it does—would have undermined everything this Evangelist has said about God's kingdom, its Messiah, and his subjects. Mark is a book about God's shattering of human expectations; Mark *as* a book shatters everything its readers thought it understood—even the conventions of how a Gospel should end. Mark's conclusion is not clumsy (see Magness 1986, 107-25), though his interpreters may be and often are. "The good news must be preached to all nations" (13:10 AT): if Jesus commanded that, then that shall surely happen. When it does, however, it is likely to occur as much *in spite of* his disciples as because of them (Malbon 2000, 41-69). Reaching deep into Genesis 17–18, Paul articulates theologically what Mark's narrative suggests, from start to finish: a summons to "[trust] in God, who makes the dead live and calls things that are not into things that are" (Rom 4:17 AT): both life and speech.

Back to Galilee, back to the beginning, are sent the women and Peter and the disciples and the Evangelist's readers. When the latter return, they may notice with fresh eyes how this parabolic Gospel opened: *archē tou euangeliou*, "*a beginning* of the good news of Jesus Christ" (1:1, emphasis added). The reader starts afresh, reads through to the end, then repeats over and again an unending process by which disciples of God's kingdom are formed. Mark's last and greatest intercalation is the Second Gospel itself and as a whole: the interpreted interpolation of Jesus' summons to God's kingdom into the reader's life.

"Do not be afraid" (16:6a AT).

"Listen. Look" (4:3a AT).

"Do you not yet understand?" (8:21).

"Watch" (13:37 KJV).

SELECT BIBLIOGRAPHY

Commentaries on Mark

(Both Cited and Not Cited)

Achtemeier, Paul J. 1978. *Invitation to Mark*. Garden City, N.Y.: Doubleday. [Repr. 2002, in *Invitation to the Gospels*. New York and Mahwah, N.J.: Paulist.] An intelligent presentation for the common reader.

Anderson, Hugh. 1976. *The Gospel of Mark*. NCB. London and Grand Rapids: Marshall, Morgan & Scott/Eerdmans. A judicious historical and theological assessment.

Boring, M. Eugene. 2006. *Mark: A Commentary*. NTL. Louisville: Westminster John Knox. Balances historical, literary, and theological concerns in a winsome manner.

Byrne, Brendan, S.J. 2008. *A Costly Freedom: A Theological Reading of Mark's Gospel*. Collegeville, Minn.: Liturgical. For general readers, an approach intended to engage faith without being overtly devotional.

Collins, Adela Yarbro. 2007. *Mark*. Hermeneia. Minneapolis: Fortress. The Gospel viewed amid the history of religions, particularly Jewish and Greco-Roman culture.

Cranfield, C. E. B. 1959. *The Gospel according to St Mark*. CGNTC. Cambridge and London: Cambridge University Press. A still useful handbook to the Greek text.

Culpepper, R. Alan. 2007. *Mark*. SHBC. Macon, Ga.: Smyth & Helwys. Learned and level-headed, presented in an inviting format.

Donahue, John R., S.J., and Daniel J. Harrington, S.J. 2002. *The Gospel of Mark*. SP 2. Collegeville, Minn.: Liturgical. The Gospel in its final form, held in equipoise with its historical traditions.

Dowd, Sharyn. 2000. *Reading Mark: A Literary and Theological Commentary on the Second Gospel*. Macon, Ga.: Smyth & Helwys. Concise and readable, emphasizing Mark's Hellenistic background and literary construction.

Edwards, James R. 2002. *The Gospel according to Mark*. PNTC. Grand Rapids: Eerdmans. A perceptive evangelical approach.

Evans, Craig A. 2001. *Mark 8:27–16:20*. WBC 34B. Nashville: Thomas Nelson. An exhaustive commentary in the spirit of Guelich (see below), who died before completing his own.

France, R. T. 2002. *The Gospel of Mark: A Commentary on the Greek Text*. NICNT. Grand Rapids and Carlisle: Eerdmans/Paternoster. Uses Greek philology as an aid in theological understanding.

Guelich, Robert A. 1989. *Mark 1–8:26*. WBC 34A. Dallas: Word. Based on the Greek text, a moderately conservative commentary conversant with European scholarship. For its companion volume see above, Evans.

Gundry, Robert H. 1993. *Mark: A Commentary on His Apology for the Cross*. Grand Rapids: Eerdmans. A provocative analysis, arguing that the Gospel is an apology for Jesus' shameful death.

Hare, Douglas R. A. 1996. *Mark*. Louisville: Westminster John Knox. A reliable treatment for the church's laity.

Hooker, Morna D. 1991. *The Gospel according to Saint Mark*. BNTC. London and Peabody, Mass.: A & C Black/Hendrickson. Sound and cautious, a theologically sensitive reading.

Juel, Donald H. 1990. *Mark*. ACNT. Minneapolis: Augsburg. A fine, middle-level treatment, reflecting primary concerns in twentieth-century interpretation.

Marcus, Joel. 2000. *Mark 1–8: A New Translation with Introduction and Commentary*. AB 27. New York and London: Doubleday.

————. 2009. *Mark 9–16: A New Translation with Introduction and Commentary.* AB 27A. New Haven: Yale University Press. A standard commentary, creatively extending historical criticism of the Gospel.

Moloney, Francis J., S.D.B. 2002. *The Gospel of Mark: A Commentary.* Peabody, Mass.: Hendrickson. Insightful consideration of Mark's literary, historical, and theological dimensions.

Myers, Ched. 1988. *Binding the Strong Man: A Political Reading of Mark's Story of Jesus.* Maryknoll, N.Y.: Orbis. Brings liberation theology to bear on Markan interpretation, conversant with conventional scholarship.

Perkins, Pheme. 1995. "The Gospel of Mark: Introduction, Commentary, and Reflections." *NIB* 8:509-733. Incisive and alert to contemporary issues.

Schweizer, Eduard. 1970. *The Good News according to Mark.* Richmond, Va.: John Knox. A theologically penetrating application of redaction criticism to the Gospel.

Taylor, Vincent. 1981. *The Gospel according to St. Mark: The Greek Text with Introduction, Notes, and Indexes.* 2nd ed. Grand Rapids: Baker. First published in 1952, a classic form-critical commentary. Dated by its historical assumptions, yet still worth consulting for its care with Greek terms and syntax.

van Iersel, Bas M. F. 1998. *Mark: A Reader-Response Commentary.* JSNTSup 164. Sheffield: Sheffield Academic Press. An approach emphasizing the experience of reading of Mark.

Other Works Cited

Achtemeier, Paul J. 2008. *Jesus and the Miracle Tradition.* Eugene, Ore.: Cascade Books.

Ahearne-Kroll, Stephen P. 2007. *The Psalms of Lament in Mark's Passion: Jesus' Davidic Suffering.* SNTSMS 142. Cambridge: Cambridge University Press.

Ambrozic, Aloysius M. 1972. *The Hidden Kingdom: A Redaction-Critical Study of References to the Kingdom of God in Mark's Gospel.* CBQMS 2. Washington, D.C.: Catholic Biblical Association of America.

Anderson, Janice Capel, and Stephen D. Moore. 1992. *Mark and Method: New Approaches in Biblical Studies.* Minneapolis: Fortress.

Auerbach, Erich. 1953. *Mimesis: The Representation of Reality in Ancient Literature.* Princeton: Princeton University Press.

Balabanski, Vicky. 1997. *Eschatology in the Making: Mark, Matthew and the Didache.* SNTSMS 97. Cambridge: Cambridge University Press.

Bammel, Ernst, ed. 1970. *The Trial of Jesus: Cambridge Studies in Honour of C. F. D. Moule.* SBT 13. London and Naperville, Ill.: SCM/Alec R. Allenson.

———. 1974. "Die Blutgerichtsbarkeit in der römische Provinz Judäa vor dem ersten jüdischen Aufstand." *JJS* 25:35-49.

———. 1984. "The Trial before Pilate." In *Jesus and the Politics of His Day,* edited by Ernst Bammel and C. F. D. Moule, 415-51. Cambridge: Cambridge University Press.

Bammel, Ernst, and C. F. D. Moule, eds. 1984. *Jesus and the Politics of His Day.* Cambridge: Cambridge University Press.

Barrett, Charles Kingsley. 1975. "The House of Prayer and the Den of Thieves." In *Jesus und Paulus: Festscrhift für Werner Georg Kümmel zum 70. Geburtstag,* edited by E. Earle Ellis and Erich Gräßer, 13-20. Göttingen: Vandenhoeck & Ruprecht.

Barton, Stephen C. 1994. *Discipleship and Family Ties in Mark and Matthew.* SNTSMS 80. Cambridge: Cambridge University Press.

Bassler, Jouette M. 1986. "The Parable of the Loaves." *JR* 66:157-72.

Batey, Richard A. 1984. "Is Not This the Carpenter?" *NTS* 30:249-58.

Bauckham, Richard, ed. 1998. *The Gospel for All Christians: Rethinking the Gospel Audiences.* Grand Rapids: Eerdmans.

Beasley-Murray, George R. 1993. *Jesus and the Last Days: The Interpretation of the Olivet Discourse.* Peabody, Mass.: Hendrickson.

Beavis, Mary Ann. 1989. *Mark's Audience: The Literary and Social Setting of Mark 4.11-12.* JSNTSup 33. Sheffield: Sheffield Academic Press.

Best, Ernest. 1965. *The Temptation and the Passion: The Markan Soteriology.* SNTSMS 2. Cambridge: Cambridge University Press.

———. 1981. *Following Jesus: Discipleship in the Gospel of Mark.* JSNTSup 4. Sheffield: JSOT.

———. 1986. *Disciples and Discipleship: Studies in the Gospel according to Mark.* Edinburgh: T & T Clark.

Betz, Hans Dieter, ed. 1971. *Christology and a Modern Pilgrimage: A Discussion with Norman Perrin.* Claremont, Calif.: The New Testament Colloquium.

Bilezikian, Gilbert G. 1977. *The Liberated Gospel: A Comparison of the Gospel of Mark and Greek Tragedy.* Grand Rapids: Baker Book House.

Black, C. Clifton. 1989. *The Disciples according to Mark: Markan Redaction in Current Debate.* JSNTSup 27. Sheffield: Sheffield Academic Press.

———. 1991. "Ministry in Mystery: One Evangelist's Vision." *The Christian Ministry* 22:15-18.

———. 1993. "Was Mark a Roman Gospel?" *The Expository Times* 104:36-40.

———. 1996. "Christ Crucified in Paul and in Mark: Reflections on an Intracanonical Conversation." In *Theology and Ethics in Paul and His Interpreters: Essays in Honor of Victor Paul Furnish,* edited by Eugene H. Lovering Jr. and Jerry L. Sumney, 184-206. Nashville: Abingdon.

———. 1997. "The Evangelist Mark: Some Reflections Out of Season." *Theology* 99:35-42.

———. 2001a. *Mark: Images of an Apostolic Interpreter.* SPNT. Minneapolis and Edinburgh: Fortress/T & T Clark.

———. 2001b. *The Rhetoric of the Gospel: Theological Artistry in the Gospels and Acts.* St. Louis: Chalice Press.

————. 2005a. "The Face Is Familiar; I Just Can't Place It." In *The End of Mark and the Ends of God: Essays in Memory of Donald Harrisville Juel*, edited by Beverly Roberts Gaventa and Patrick D. Miller, 33-49. Louisville: Westminster John Knox.

————. 2005b. "Does Suffering Possess Educational Value in Mark's Gospel?" In *Character Ethics and the New Testament: Moral Dimensions of Scripture*, edited by Robert L. Brawley, 3-17. Louisville: Westminster John Knox.

————. 2008. "Windows, Gateways, and Mirrors: The Parables of Jesus." *Dialogue: A Journal of Religion and Philosophy* 31:37-46.

————. 2009. "Mark as Historian of God's Kingdom." *CBQ* 71:64-83.

————. 2010. "Trinity and Exegesis." *Pro Ecc* 19:151-80.

Black, Matthew. 1967. *An Aramaic Approach to the Gospels and Acts*. 3rd ed. Oxford: Clarendon.

Blinzler, Josef. 1959. *The Trial of Jesus: The Jewish and Roman Proceedings against Jesus Christ Described and Assessed from the Oldest Accounts*. Westminster, Md.: Newman Press.

Bolt, Peter G. 2004. *Jesus' Defeat of Death: Persuading Mark's Early Readers*. SNTSMS 125. New York: Cambridge University Press.

Booth, Roger P. 1986. *Jesus and the Laws of Purity: Tradition History and Legal History in Mark 7*. JSNTSup 13. Sheffield: JSOT.

Boring, M. Eugene. 1984. "The Christology of Mark: Hermeneutical Issues for Systematic Theology." *Semeia* 30:125-53.

————. 1990. "Mark 1:1-15 and the Beginning of the Gospel." *Semeia* 52:43-81.

————. 1999. "Markan Christology: God-Language for Jesus?" *NTS* 45:451-71.

Boring, M. Eugene, Klaus Berger, and Carlsten Colpe, eds. 1995. *Hellenistic Commentary to the New Testament*. Nashville: Abingdon.

Boucher, Madeleine. 1977. *The Mysterious Parable: A Literary Study*. CBQMS 6. Washington, D.C.: Catholic Biblical Association of America.

Broadhead, Edwin K. 1992. *Teaching with Authority: Miracles and Christology in the Gospel of Mark*. JSNTSup 74. Sheffield: JSOT.

Brown, Raymond E. 1971. "Jesus and Elisha." *Perspective* 12:85-104.

Bryan, Christopher. 1993. *A Preface to Mark: Notes on the Gospel in Its Literary and Cultural Settings*. New York and Oxford: Oxford University Press.

Bultmann, Rudolf. 1951. *Theology of the New Testament*. Vol. 1. New York: Charles Scribner's Sons.

———. 1963. *History of the Synoptic Tradition*. Rev. ed. New York: Harper & Row.

Burdon, Christopher. 1990. *Stumbling on God: Faith and Vision through Mark's Gospel*. London and Grand Rapids: SPCK/Eerdmans.

Burkett, Delbert. 1999. *The Son of Man Debate: A History and Evaluation*. SNTSMS 107. Cambridge: Cambridge University Press.

Burkill, T. Alec. 1963. *Mysterious Revelation: An Examination of the Philosophy of St. Mark's Gospel*. Ithaca, N.Y.: Cornell University Press.

Camery-Hoggatt, Jerry. 1992. *Irony in Mark's Gospel: Text and Subtext*. SNTSMS 72. Cambridge: Cambridge University Press.

Casey, Maurice. 2007. *The Solution to the "Son of Man" Problem*. LNTS 343. New York: T & T Clark.

Catchpole, David. 1984. "The 'Triumphal' Entry." In *Jesus and the Politics of His Day,* edited by Ernst Bammel and C. F. D. Moule, 319-34. Cambridge: Cambridge University Press.

Chilton, Bruce, ed. 1984. *The Kingdom of God in the Teaching of Jesus*. IRT 5. Philadelphia and London: Fortress, SPCK.

Chilton, Bruce, and Craig A. Evans, eds. 1999. *Authenticating the Activities of Jesus*. Leiden, Boston, and Köln: Brill.

Chilton, Bruce, Darrell Bock, Daniel M. Gurtner, Jacob Neusner,

Lawrence H. Shiffman, and Daniel Oden, eds. 2010. *A Comparative Handbook to the Gospel of Mark: Comparisons with Pseudepigrapha, the Qumran Scrolls, and Rabbinic Literature*. NTGJC 1. Leiden and London: Brill.

Christie, Agatha. 1933. *Murder on the Orient Express*. New York: Black Dog & Leventhal.

Collins, Adela Yarbro. 1997a. "The Appropriation of the Psalms of Individual Lament by Mark." In *The Scriptures in the Gospels,* edited by Christopher M. Tuckett, 223-41. BETL 131. Leuven: University Press.

———. 1997b. "The Significance of Mark 10:45 among Gentile Christians." *JR* 90:371-82.

———. 1998. "Finding Meaning in the Death of Jesus." *JR* 78:175-96.

———. 1999. "Mark and His Readers: The Son of God among Jews." *HTR* 92:393-408.

Collins, John J. 1995. *The Scepter and the Star: The Messiahs of the Dead Sea Scrolls and Other Ancient Literature*. ABRL. New York: Doubleday.

Collins, John N. 1990. *Diakonia: Re-interpreting the Ancient Sources*. New York and Oxford: Oxford University Press.

Cook, Michael J. 1978. *Mark's Treatment of the Jewish Leaders*. NovTSup 51. Leiden: Brill.

Crossan, John Dominic. 1976. "Empty Tomb and Absent Lord (Mark 16:1-8)." In *The Passion in Mark: Studies on Mark 14–16,* edited by Werner H. Kelber, 135-52. Philadelphia: Fortress.

Croy, N. Clayton. 2003. *The Mutilation of Mark's Gospel*. Nashville: Abingdon.

Dahl, Nils Alstrup. 1976. *Jesus in the Memory of the Early Church*. Minneapolis: Augsburg.

Danove, Paul L. 1993. *The End of Mark's Story: A Methodological Study*. BIS 3. Leiden, New York, and Köln: Brill.

Daube, David. 1956. *The New Testament and Rabbinic Judaism*. London: Athlone/University of London Press.

Davis, Philip G. 1989. "Mark's Christological Paradox." *JSNT* 35:3-18.

Dewey, Joanna. 1980. *Markan Public Debate: Literary Technique, Concentric Structure, and Theology in Mark 2:1–3:6.* SBLDS 48. Chico, Calif.: Scholars Press.

Dibelius, Martin. 1935. *From Tradition to Gospel.* New York: Charles Scribner's Sons.

von Dobschütz, Ernst. 1928. "Zur Erzälerkunst des Markus." *ZNW* 27:193-98.

Dodd, C. H. 1961. *The Parables of the Kingdom.* Rev. ed. New York: Charles Scribner's Sons.

Donahue, John R. 1971. "Tax Collectors and Sinners: An Attempt at Identification." *CBQ* 33:39-61.

———. 1973. *Are You the Christ? The Trial Narrative in the Gospel of Mark.* SBLDS 10. Missoula, Mont.: Society of Biblical Literature.

———. 1979. "Jesus as the Parable of God in the Gospel of Mark." *Int* 32:369-88.

———. 1982. "A Neglected Factor in Mark's Theology." *JBL* 101:563-94.

———. 1983. *The Theology and Setting of Discipleship in the Gospel of Mark.* Milwaukee, Wis.: Marquette University Press.

———. 1988. *The Gospel in Parable: Metaphor, Narrative, and Theology in the Synoptic Gospels.* Philadelphia: Fortress.

Doudna, John Charles. 1961. *The Greek of the Gospel of Mark.* JBLMS 12. Philadelphia: Society of Biblical Literature and Exegesis.

Douglas, Mary. 1966. *Purity and Danger: An Analysis of Concepts of Pollution and Taboo.* London, Boston, and Henley: Routledge & Kegan Paul.

———. 1999. *Leviticus as Literature.* Oxford: Oxford University Press.

Dowd, Sharyn Echols. 1988. *Prayer, Power, and the Problem of Suffering: Mark 11:22-25 in the Context of Markan Theology.* SBLDS 105. Atlanta: Scholars.

Drury, John. 1985. *The Parables in the Gospels: History and Allegory.* London: SPCK.

Duling, Dennis C. 1992. "Kingdom of God, Kingdom of Heaven." *ABD* 4:49-69.

Dwyer, Timothy. 1996. *The Motif of Wonder in the Gospel of Mark*. JSNTSup 128. Sheffield: Sheffield Academic Press.

Elliott, J. Keith. 1993. *The Language and Style of the Gospel of Mark: An Edition of C. H. Turner's "Notes on Markan Usage" Together with Other Comparable Studies*. NovTSup 71. Leiden, New York, and Köln: Brill.

Ellis, E. Earle, and Erich Gräßer, eds. 1975. *Jesus und Paulus: Festschrift für Werner Georg Kümmel zum 70. Geburtstag*. Göttingen: Vandenhoeck & Ruprecht.

Finegan, Jack. 1992. *The Archeology of the New Testament: The Life of Jesus and the Beginning of the Early Church*. Rev. ed. Princeton: Princeton University Press.

Fleddermann, Harry T. 1995. *Mark and Q: A Study of the Overlap Texts*. BETL 122. Leuven: Leuven University Press.

Freyne, Seán. 1980. *Galilee: From Alexander the Great to Hadrian, 323 BCE to 135 CE*. Edinburgh: T & T Clark.

———. 1988. *Galilee, Jesus, and the Gospels: Literary Approaches and Historical Investigations*. Philadelphia: Fortress.

Garrett, Susan R. 1998. *The Temptations of Jesus in Mark's Gospel*. Grand Rapids: Eerdmans.

Gaventa, Beverly Roberts and Patrick D. Miller, eds. 2005. *The End of Mark and the Ends of God: Essays in Memory of Donald Harrisville Juel*. Louisville: Westminster John Knox.

Geddert, Timothy J. 1989. *Watchwords: Mark 13 in Markan Eschatology*. JSNTSup 26. Sheffield: Sheffield Academic Press.

Geyer, Douglas W. 2002. *Fear, Anomaly, and Uncertainty in the Gospel of Mark*. ATLAMS 47. Lanham, Md., and London: Scarecrow.

Gibson, Jeffrey B. 1994. "Jesus' Wilderness Temptation according to Mark." *JSNT* 53:3-34.

Glatzer, Nathan N. 1996. *The Schocken Passover Haggadah*. New York: Schocken Books.

Gray, Timothy C. 2008. *The Temple in the Gospel of Mark*. WUNT 2nd series 242. Tübingen: Mohr Siebeck.

Hare, Douglas R. A. 1990. *The Son of Man Tradition*. Minneapolis: Fortress.

Hatina, Thomas R. 2002. *In Search of a Context: The Function of Scripture in Mark's Narrative*. JSNTSup 232. New York: Sheffield Academic Press.

Henderson, Suzanne Watts. 2006. *Christology and Discipleship in the Gospel of Mark*. SNTSMS 135. Cambridge: Cambridge University Press.

Hengel, Martin. 1976. *The Son of God: The Origin of Christology and the History of Jewish-Hellenistic Religion*. Philadelphia: Fortress.

———. 1977. *Crucifixion in the Ancient World and the Folly of the Message of the Cross*. London and Philadelphia: SCM/Fortress.

———. 1981. *The Charismatic Leader and His Followers*. Edinburgh and New York: T & T Clark/Crossroad.

———. 1985. *Studies in the Gospel of Mark*. Philadelphia: Fortress.

———. 1989. *The Zealots: Investigations into the Jewish Freedom Movement in the Period from Herod I until 40 A.D.* Edinburgh: T & T Clark.

———. 2000. *The Four Gospels and the One Gospel of Jesus Christ: An Investigation of the Collection and Origin of the Canonical Gospels*. Harrisburg, Pa.: Trinity Press International.

Higgins, A. J. B. 1964. *Jesus and the Son of Man*. Philadelphia: Fortress.

Hock, Ronald F. 1992. "Cynics." *ABD* 1:1221-26.

Hoehner, Harold W. 1972. *Herod Antipas: A Contemporary of Jesus Christ*. SNTSMS 17. Cambridge: Cambridge University Press.

Hooker, Morna D. 1959. *Jesus and the Servant*. London: SCM.

———. 1967. *The Son of Man in Mark: A Study of the Background of the Term "Son of Man" and Its Use in St. Mark's Gospel*. Montreal: McGill University Press.

Hoskyns, Edwyn Clement, and Francis Noel Davey. 1981. *Crucifixion–Resurrection: The Pattern of the Theology and Ethics of the New Testament*. London: SPCK.

Incigneri, Brian J. 2003. *The Gospel to the Romans: The Setting and Rhetoric of Mark's Gospel*. BIS 65. Leiden: Brill.

Iverson, Kelly R. 2007. *Gentiles in the Gospel of Mark:"Even the Dogs Under the Table Eat the Children's Crumbs."* JSNTSup 339. New York: T & T Clark.

Jensen, Morten Hørning. 2006. *Herod Antipas in Galilee.* WUNT 2.215. Tübingen: Mohr Siebeck.

Jeremias, Joachim. 1958. *Jesus' Promise to the Nations.* London: SCM.

———. 1966. *The Eucharistic Words of Jesus.* London and Philadelphia: SCM/Fortress.

———. 1971. *New Testament Theology: The Proclamation of Jesus.* London and New York: SCM/Charles Scribner's Sons.

———. 1972. *The Parables of Jesus.* 2nd rev. ed. New York: Charles Scribner's Sons.

Juel, Donald H. 1977. *Messiah and Temple: The Trial of Jesus in the Gospel of Mark.* SBLDS 31. Missoula, Mont.: Scholars.

———. 1988. *Messianic Exegesis: Christological Interpretation of the Old Testament in Early Christianity.* Philadelphia: Fortress.

———. 1994. *A Master of Surprise: Mark Interpreted.* Minneapolis: Fortress.

———. 1999. *The Gospel of Mark.* IBT. Nashville: Abingdon.

Jülicher, Adolf. 1899. *Die Gleichnisreden Jesu.* 2nd ed. 2 vols. Tübingen: J. C. B. Mohr [Paul Siebeck].

Kähler, Martin. 1964. *The So-Called Historical Jesus and the Historic Biblical Christ.* Philadelphia: Fortress.

Kaminouchi, Alberto de Mingo. 2003. *"But It Is Not So among You": Echoes of Power in Mark 10:32-45.* JSNTSup 249. London: T & T Clark International.

Käsemann, Ernst. 1969. *Jesus Means Freedom.* London: SCM.

Kazantzakis, Nikos. 1960. *The Last Temptation of Christ.* New York: Simon & Schuster.

Kealy, Seán P. 2007. *A History of the Interpretation of the Gospel of Mark.* Vol.1: *Through the Nineteenth Century.* Vol. 2, Books 1-2: *The Twentieth Century.* Lewistown, Queenstown, Lampeter: Edwin Mellen.

Keck, Leander E. 1966. "The Introduction to Mark's Gospel." *NTS* 12:352-70.

———. 1971. "The Spirit and the Dove." *NTS* 17:41-67.

————. 1986. "Toward the Renewal of New Testament Christology." *NTS* 32:362-77.

Kee, Howard Clark. 1977. *Community of the New Age: Studies in Mark's Gospel*. Philadelphia: Westminster.

————. 1983. *Miracle in the Early Christian World: A Study in Sociohistorical Method*. New Haven and London: Yale University Press.

————. 1986. *Medicine, Miracle and Magic in New Testament Times*. SNTSMS 55. Cambridge: Cambridge University Press.

Kelber, Werner H., ed. 1976. *The Passion in Mark: Studies on Mark 14–16*. Philadelphia: Fortress.

Kelhoffer, James A. 2000. *Miracle and Mission: The Authentication of Missionaries and Their Message in the Longer Ending of Mark*. WUNT 2nd series 112. Mohr Siebeck.

Kermode, Frank. 1979. *The Genesis of Secrecy: On the Interpretation of Narrative*. Cambridge, Mass., and London: Harvard University Press.

Kingsbury, Jack Dean. 1983. *The Christology of Mark's Gospel*. Philadelphia: Fortress.

Kinukawa, Hisako. 1994. *Women and Jesus in Mark: A Japanese Feminist Perspective*. Maryknoll, N.Y.: Orbis.

Kissinger, Warren S. 1979. *The Parables of Jesus: A History of Interpretation and Bibliography*. ATLAMS 4. Metuchen and London: Scarecrow/ATLA.

Klauck, Hans-Josef. 2000. *The Religious Context of Early Christianity: A Guide to Greco-Roman Religions*. SNTW. Edinburgh: T & T Clark.

Koester, Helmut. 1990. *Ancient Christian Gospels: Their History and Development*. Philadelphia and London: Trinity Press International/SCM.

Lachs, Samuel Tobias. 1987. *A Rabbinic Commentary on the New Testament: The Gospels of Matthew, Mark, and Luke*. Hoboken, N.J., and New York: KTAV.

Levine, Amy-Jill with Marianne Blickenstaff, eds. 2001. *A Feminist Companion to Mark*. Cleveland: Pilgrim.

Levine, Lee I. 2000. *The Ancient Synagogue: The First Thousand Years*. New Haven and London: Yale University Press.

Lindars, Barnabas. 1983. *Jesus, Son of Man: A Fresh Examination of the Son of Man Sayings in the Gospels*. London: SPCK.

McCowen, Alec. 1990. *St. Mark's Gospel: King James Version*. Produced by Arthur Cantor Films. New York: American Bible Society.

Madden, Patrick J. 1997. *Jesus' Walking on the Sea: An Investigation of the Origin of the Narrative Account*. BZNW 81. Berlin and New York: de Gruyter.

Magness, J. Lee. 1986. *Sense and Absence: Structure and Suspension in the Ending of Mark's Gospel*. SemeiaSt. Atlanta: Scholars.

Malbon, Elizabeth Struthers. 2000. *In the Company of Jesus: Characters in Mark's Gospel*. Louisville: Westminster John Knox.

―――. 2009. *Mark's Jesus: Characterization as Narrative Christology*. Waco, Tex.: Baylor University Press.

Malherbe, Abraham J. 1983. *Social Aspects of Early Christianity*. 2nd ed. Philadelphia: Fortress.

Mansfield, M. Robert. 1987. *"Spirit and Gospel" in Mark*. Peabody, Mass.: Hendrickson.

Manson, T. W. 1959. *The Teaching of Jesus: Studies of Its Form and Content*. 2nd ed. Cambridge: Cambridge University Press.

Marcus, Joel. 1984. "Mark 4:10-12 and Marcan Epistemology." *JBL* 103:557-74.

―――. 1986. *The Mystery of the Kingdom of God*. SBLDS 90. Atlanta: Scholars.

―――. 1992. *The Way of the Lord: Christological Exegesis of the Old Testament in the Gospel of Mark*. Louisville: Westminster/John Knox.

―――. 1997. "Scripture and Tradition in Mark 7." In *The Scriptures in the Gospels*, edited by Christopher M. Tuckett, 177-95. BETL 131. Leuven: University Press.

―――. 1999. "The Beelzebul Controversy and the Eschatologies

of Jesus." In *Authenticating the Activities of Jesus*, edited by Bruce Chilton and Craig A. Evans, 247-77. Leiden, Boston, and Köln: Brill.

——. 2006. "Crucifixion as Parodic Exaltation." *JBL* 125:73-87.

Marshall, Christopher D. 1989. *Faith as a Theme in Mark's Narrative*. SNTSMS 64. Cambridge and New York: Cambridge University Press.

Martin, Dale B. 1990. *Slavery as Salvation: The Metaphor of Slavery in Pauline Christianity*. New Haven and London: Yale University Press.

Marxsen, Willi. 1969. *Mark the Evangelist: Studies on the Redaction History of the Gospel*. Nashville and New York: Abingdon.

Matera, Frank J. 1982. *The Kingship of Jesus: Composition and Theology in Mark 15*. SBLDS 66. Chico, Calif.: Scholars.

Meier, John P. 1991. *A Marginal Jew: Rethinking the Historical Jesus*. Vol. 1: *The Roots of the Problem and the Person*. ABRL. New York: Doubleday.

——. 1992. "The Brothers and Sisters of Jesus in Ecumenical Perspective." *CBQ* 54:1-28.

——. 1994. *A Marginal Jew: Rethinking the Historical Jesus*. Vol. 2: *Mentor, Message, and Miracles*. ABRL. New York: Doubleday.

——. 2001. *A Marginal Jew: Rethinking the Historical Jesus*. Vol. 3: *Companions and Competitors*. ABRL. New York: Doubleday.

Merton, Thomas. 1960. *The Wisdom of the Desert: Sayings from the Desert Fathers of the Fourth Century*. New York: New Directions Books.

Metzger, Bruce M. 1994. *A Textual Commentary on the Greek New Testament*. 2nd ed. Stuttgart: Deutsche Bibelgesellschaft/United Bible Societies.

Michel, Otto. 1965. *"Kyon, kynarion." TDNT* 3:1101-4.

——. 1967. *"Naos." TDNT* 4:880-90.

——. 1972. *"Telōnēs." TDNT* 8:88-105.

Milgrom, Jacob. 1991. *Leviticus 1–16*. AB 3. New York and London: Doubleday.

————. 2000. *Leviticus 17–22*. AB 3A. New York and London: Doubleday.

Miller, Susan. 2004. *Women in Mark's Gospel*. JSNTSup 259. London and New York: T & T Clark.

Minor, Mitzi. 1996. *The Spirituality of Mark: Responding to God*. Louisville: Westminster John Knox.

Moeser, Marion C., O.S.F. 2002. *The Anecdote in Mark, the Classical World, and the Rabbis*. JSNTSup 227. London: Sheffield Academic Press.

Moore, George Foot. 1958. *Judaism in the First Centuries of the Christian Era: The Age of the Tannaim*. 2 vols. New York: Schocken Books.

Moule, C. F. D. 1959. *An Idiom Book of New Testament Greek*. 2nd ed. Cambridge: Cambridge University Press.

Neusner, Jacob. 1973. *The Idea of Purity in Ancient Judaism*. Leiden: Brill.

————. 1979. *From Politics to Piety: The Emergence of Pharisaic Judaism*. 2nd ed. New York: KTAV.

Neusner, Jacob, William Scott Green, and Ernest S. Frerichs, eds. 1987. *Judaisms and Their Messiahs at the Turn of the Christian Era*. Cambridge: Cambridge University Press.

Nickelsburg, George W. E. 1981. *Jewish Literature between the Talmud and the Mishnah: A Historical and Literary Introduction*. Philadelphia: Fortress.

————. 1992. "Son of Man." *ABD* 6:137-50.

Nickelsburg, George W. E., and Michael E. Stone. 1983. *Faith and Piety in Early Judaism: Texts and Documents*. Philadelphia: Fortress.

O'Connor, Flannery. 1969. "The Fiction Writer and His Country." In *Mystery and Manners: Occasional Prose*, edited by Sally and Robert Fitzgerald. New York: Farrar, Straus & Giroux.

Oepke, Albrecht. "*Pais, paidion*." 1967. TDNT 5:636-54.

Olekamma, Innocent Uhuegbu. 1999. *The Healing of Blind Bartimaeus (Mk 10, 46-52) in the Markan Context*. EUS 672. Frankfurt am Main: Peter Lang.

Ossom-Batsa, George. 2001. *The Institution of the Eucharist in the Gospel of Mark: A Study of the Function of Mark 14, 22-25 within the Gospel Narrative.* EUS 727. Bern and Berlin: Peter Lang.

Page, Sydney H. T. 1985. "The Suffering Servant between the Testaments." *NTS* 31:481-97.

Patten, Priscilla. 1983. "The Form and Function of Parable in Select Apocalyptic Literature and Their Significance for Parables in the Gospel of Mark." *NTS* 29:246-58.

Perrin, Norman. 1971. "Towards an Interpretation of the Gospel of Mark." In *Christology and a Modern Pilgrimage: A Discussion with Norman Perrin,* edited by Hans Dieter Betz, 1-78. Claremont, Calif.: The New Testament Colloquium.

————. 1995. "The Christology of Mark: A Study in Methodology." In *The Interpretation of Mark,* edited by William R. Telford, 125-40. 2nd ed. Studies in New Testament Interpretation. Edinburgh: T & T Clark.

Peters, F. E. 1985. *Jerusalem: The Holy City in the Eyes of Chroniclers, Visitors, Pilgrims, and Prophets from the Days of Abraham to the Beginnings of Modern Times.* Princeton: Princeton University Press.

Peterson, Dwight N. 2000. *The Origins of Mark: The Markan Community in Current Debate.* BIS 48. Leiden, Boston, and Köln: Brill.

Placher, William C. 1994. *Narratives of a Vulnerable God: Christ, Theology, and Scripture.* Louisville: Westminster John Knox.

Räisänen, Heikki. 1990. *The "Messianic Secret" in Mark's Gospel: Studies of the New Testament and Its World.* SNTW. Edinburgh: T & T Clark.

Rhoads, David, and Donald Michie. 1982. *Mark as Story: An Introduction to the Narrative of a Gospel.* Philadelphia: Fortress.

Richardson, Peter. 1996. *Herod: King of the Jews and Friend of the Romans.* SPNT. Columbia, S.C.: University of South Carolina Press.

Riches, John K. 2000. *Conflicting Mythologies: Identity*

Formation in the Gospels of Mark and Matthew. SNTW. Edinburgh: T & T Clark.

Ringe, Sharon H. 2001. "A Gentile Woman's Story, Revisited: Rereading Mark 7:24-31." In *A Feminist Companion to Mark,* edited by Amy-Jill Levine with Marianne Blickenstaff, 79-100. Cleveland: Pilgrim.

Robbins, Vernon K. 1984. *Jesus the Teacher: A Socio-Rhetorical Interpretation of Mark.* Philadelphia: Fortress.

Robinson, James M. 1982. *The Problem of History in Mark and Other Marcan Studies.* Philadelphia: Fortress.

Robinson, William C., Jr. 1973. "The Quest for Wrede's Secret Messiah." *Int* 27:10-30.

Roskam, Hendrika N. 2004. *The Purpose of the Gospel of Mark in Its Historical and Social Context.* NovTSup 114. Leiden: Brill.

Sabin, Marie Noonan. 2002. *Reopening the Word: Reading Mark as Theology in the Context of Early Judaism.* Oxford and New York: Oxford University Press.

Safrai, Shemuel. 1976. "The Temple." In *The Jewish People in the First Century: Historical Geography, Political History, Social, Cultural and Religious Life and Institutions,* vol. 2, edited by S. Safrai and M. Stern, with D. Flusser and W. C. van Unnik, 856-907. CRINT. Assen and Philadelphia: Van Gorcum/Fortress.

Safrai, S. and M. Stern, eds., with D. Flusser and W. C. van Unnik. 1974, 1976. *The Jewish People in the First Century: Historical Geography, Political History, Social, Cultural and Religious Life and Institutions.* 2 vols. CRINT. Assen and Philadelphia: Van Gorcum/Fortress.

Saldarini, Anthony J. 1988. *Pharisees, Scribes and Sadducees in Palestinian Society: A Sociological Approach.* Wilmington, Del.: Michael Glazier.

Sanders, E. P. 1977. *Paul and Palestinian Judaism: A Comparison of Patterns of Religion.* Philadelphia: Fortress.

——. 1985. *Jesus and Judaism.* Philadelphia: Fortress.

——. 1992. *Judaism, Practice and Belief: 63 BCE–66 CE.* London and Philadelphia: SCM/Trinity Press International.

Sanders, E. P., and Margaret Davies. 1989. *Studying the Synoptic Gospels*. London and Philadelphia: SCM/Trinity Press International.

Sawicki, Marianne. 2001. "Making Jesus." In *A Feminist Companion to Mark,* edited by Amy-Jill Levine with Marianne Blickenstaff, 136-70. Cleveland: Pilgrim.

Schildgen, Brenda Deen. 1999. *Power and Prejudice: The Reception of the Gospel of Mark*. Detroit: Wayne State University Press.

Schmidt, T. E. 1995. "Mark 15:16-32: The Crucifixion Narrative and the Roman Triumphal Procession." *NTS* 41:1-18.

Schürer, Emil. 1973, 1979, 1986, 1987. *The History of the Jewish People in the Age of Jesus Christ (175 B.C.–A.D. 135)*. New English version revised and edited by Géza Vermes, Fergus Millar, Pamela Vermes, and Matthew Black. 4 vols. Edinburgh: T & T Clark.

Shepherd, Tom. 1993. *Markan Sandwich Stories: Narration, Definition, and Function*. AUSS 18. Berrien Springs, Mich.: Andrews University Press.

Shiner, Whitney Taylor. 1995. *Follow Me! Disciples in Markan Rhetoric*. SBLDS 145. Atlanta: Scholars.

Smallwood, E. Mary. 1981. *The Jews Under Roman Rule from Pompey to Diocletian: A Study in Political Relations*. 2nd ed. Leiden: Brill.

Sontag, Susan. 1989. *Illness as Metaphor and AIDS and Its Metaphors*. New York: Farrar, Straus and Giroux.

Svartvik, Jesper. 2000. *Mark and Mission: Mk 7:1-23 in Its Narrative and Historical Contexts*. ConBNT 32. Stockholm: Almqvist & Wiksell International.

Swanson, Reuben, ed. 1995. *New Testament Greek Manuscripts: Mark*. Sheffield and Pasadena: Sheffield Academic Press/William Carey International University Press.

Tannehill, Robert C. 1975. *The Sword of His Mouth*. SemeiaSup 1. Philadelphia and Missoula, Mont.: Fortress/Scholars Press.

———. 1979. "The Gospel of Mark as Narrative Christology." *Semeia* 16:57-95.

————. 1995. "The Disciples in Mark: The Function of aNarrative Role." In *The Interpretation of Mark,* edited by William R. Telford, 169-95. 2nd ed. Studies in New Testament Interpretation. Edinburgh: T & T Clark.

Telford, William R. 1980. *The Barren Temple and the Withered Tree: A Redaction-Critical Analysis of the Cursing of the Fig-Tree Pericope in Mark's Gospel and Its Relation to the Cleansing of the Temple Tradition.* JSNTSup 1. Sheffield: JSOT.

————, ed. 1995. *The Interpretation of Mark.* 2nd ed. Studies in New Testament Interpretation. Edinburgh: T & T Clark.

————. 1999. *The Theology of the Gospel of Mark.* Cambridge: Cambridge University Press.

————. 2009. *Writing on the Gospel of Mark.* Guides to Advanced Biblical Research. Blanford Forum, UK: Deo Publishing.

Terrien, Samuel. 1985. *Till the Heart Sings: A Biblical Theology of Manhood and Womanhood.* Philadelphia: Fortress.

Theissen, Gerd. 1978. *Sociology of Early Palestinian Christianity.* Philadelphia: Fortress.

————. 1983. *The Miracle Stories of the Early Christian Tradition.* Edinburgh and Philadelphia: T & T Clark/ Fortress.

————. 1991. *The Gospels in Context: Social and Political History in the Synoptic Tradition.* Minneapolis: Fortress.

Theissen, Gerd, and Annette Merz. 1998. *The Historical Jesus: A Comprehensive Guide.* Minneapolis: Fortress.

Thompson, Henry O. 1992. "Jordan River." *ABD* 3:953-58.

Thrall, Margaret E. 1970. "Elijah and Moses in Mark's Account of the Transfiguration." *NTS* 16:305-17.

Tödt, Heinz Eduard. 1965. *The Son of Man in the Synoptic Tradition.* NTL. London: SCM.

Tolbert, Mary Ann. 1989. *Sowing the Gospel: Mark's World in Literary-Historical Perspective.* Minneapolis: Fortress.

Treggiari, Susan. 1991. *Roman Marriage: Iusti Coniuges from the Time of Cicero to the Time of Ulpian.* Oxford: Clarendon.

Trocmé, Etienne. 1975. *The Formation of the Gospel according to Mark*. London and Philadelphia: SPCK/Westminster.

Truffaut, François, with the collaboration of Helen G. Scott. 1984. *Hitchcock*. 2nd ed. New York and London: Simon & Schuster.

Tuckett, Christopher M., ed. 1997. *The Scriptures in the Gospels*. BETL 131. Leuven: University Press.

Turner, C. H. 1993. "Markan Usage: Notes, Critical and Exegetical on the Second Gospel." In *The Language and Style of the Gospel of Mark: An Edition of C. H. Turner's "Notes on Markan Usage" Together with Other Comparable Studies,* edited by J. Keith Elliott, 3-146. NovTSup 71. Leiden, New York, and Köln: Brill.

Turner, N. 1993. "The Style of Mark." In *The Language and Style of the Gospel of Mark: An Edition of C. H. Turner's "Notes on Markan Usage" Together with Other Comparable Studies,* edited by J. Keith Elliott, 213-37. NovTSup 71. Leiden, New York, and Köln: Brill.

Twelftree, Graham H. 2007. *In the Name of Jesus: Exorcism among Early Christians*. Grand Rapids: Baker Academic.

van der Horst, P. W. 1972. "Can a Book End with GAR? A Note on Mark xvi.8." *JTS* 23:121-24.

Vermes, Géza. 1973. *Jesus the Jew: A Historian's Reading of the Gospels*. Philadelphia: Fortress.

Via, Dan Otto, Jr. 1985. *The Ethics of Mark's Gospel: In the Middle of Time*. Philadelphia: Fortress.

Vines, Michael E. 2002. *The Problem of Markan Genre: The Gospel of Mark and the Jewish Novel*. SBLAB. Atlanta: Society of Biblical Literature.

Waetjen, Herman C. 1989. *A Reordering of Power: A Socio-Political Reading of Mark's Gospel*. Minneapolis: Fortress.

Watts, Rikki E. 1997. *Isaiah's New Exodus and Mark*. WUNT 88. Tübingen: Mohr/Siebeck.

Weeden, Theodore J., Sr. 1971. *Mark: Traditions in Conflict*. Philadelphia: Fortress.

Wefald, Eric K. 1995. "The Separate Gentile Mission in Mark: A Narrative Explanation of Markan Geography, the Two Feeding Accounts and Exorcisms." *JSNT* 60:3-26.

Whittaker, Molly. 1984. *Jews and Christians: Graeco-Roman Views*. Cambridge: Cambridge University Press.

Wilder, Amos N. 1964. *Early Christian Rhetoric: The Language of the Gospel*. London and Evanston, Ill.: SCM/Harper & Row.

Williams, Joel F. 1994. *Other Followers of Jesus: Minor Characters as Major Figures in Mark's Gospel*. JSNTSup 102. Sheffield: JSOT.

Wills, Lawrence M. 1997. *The Quest of the Historical Gospel: Mark, John, and the Origins of the Gospel Genre*. London and New York: Routledge.

Winn, Adam. 2008. *The Purpose of Mark's Gospel: An Early Christian Response to Imperial Propaganda*. WUNT 245. Tübingen: Mohr Siebeck.

Winter, Paul. 1974. *On the Trial of Jesus*. Berlin and New York: de Gruyter.

Wrede, William. 1971. *The Messianic Secret*. London and Cambridge: James Clarke.

Young, George W. 1999. *Subversive Symmetry: Exploring the Fantastic in Mark 6:45-56*. BIS 41. Leiden, Boston, and Köln: Brill.

SUBJECT INDEX

CPSIA information can be obtained at www.ICGtesting.com
Printed in the USA
LVOW060909150911

246320LV00001B/4/P